Pythagoras or Christ ?

Alberto A. Martínez

PYTHAGORAS

or

CHRIST?

Christians Against Pagans: from Pythagoras to Giordano Bruno

Saltshadow Castle

Alberto A. Martínez is a Professor
in the Department of History of the University of Texas at Austin.

Saltshadow Castle, Cambridge, Mass.

First printed in April 2022.

The back cover art includes a photograph of the statue of Giordano Bruno at the Campo de' Fiori, Rome, placed there in 1889. Other photographs show the Castel Sant'Angelo in Rome, and details of tapestry and wall artwork in Pisa and Rome. All original photographs are copyrighted by Alberto A. Martínez. In this work, the use of general descriptive names, trade names, trademarks, etc., even if they are not explicitly identified, should not to be misconstrued as a sign that such names, as understood by the Trade Marks and Merchandise Act, may be used freely by anyone.

Cataloging-in-Publication-Data:

Martinez, Alberto A.
Pythagoras or Christ? Christians against Pagans: from Pythagoras to Giordano Bruno / Alberto A. Martinez
    p.   cm.
Includes bibliographical references.
ISBN-10: 8-708-68133-1 (pbk.)
ISBN-13: 979-8-708-68133-1 (pbk.)
    1. Science—History. 2. Religion and Science—History. 3. Scientists—History.
    I. Title. II. Pythagoras, ca. 570-500 BC III. Bruno, Giordano, 1548-1600.

ISBN 8-708-68133-1

Printed in the United States of America

0 9 8 7 6 5 4 3 2 1

Maybe I too would believe the vulgar rumors that
Bruno was burned for Lutheranism, but I was
present at the Holy Office of the Inquisition
when the condemnation against him was voiced,
and therefore I know which heresy he professed.

Gaspar Schoppe, February 1600

Tables & Images

Contents

Introduction

For more than a thousand years, Christians denounced the Pythagoreans for heresies and blasphemies. They complained that Pythagoras had done "ten thousand kinds of sorcery." Allegedly he healed the ill, predicted future events, and calmed storms over rivers and seas so that his disciples might sail across them, like Jesus Christ. Some pagans said that Pythagoras was the son of the god Apollo and a human mother. Whereas Jesus had died and resurrected only once, Pythagoras had survived death multiple times as his soul was repeatedly reborn in other bodies. Saint Hippolytus of Rome criticized the "alliance between heresy and the Pythagorean philosophy," and he denounced the "enormous and endless heresies" of those "disciples not of Christ but of Pythagoras."

Whereas Jesus was dead for less than three days before his resurrection, Pythagoras allegedly spent two centuries in Hell, yet he returned to life. And Pythagoras taught that there was not just one God, but many. Moreover, similarly to the apostles of Jesus, some of the disciples of Pythagoras allegedly exorcised demons and resurrected the dead. But unlike the apostles, some of the Pythagoreans returned to life after death.

Early Church Fathers complained that all this was indecent madness, perverse falsehoods most deserving of ridicule, evil imitations of the miracles of Jesus. Saint John Chrysostom declared: "this is the snare of the Devil." Using magic and divination, the Pythagoreans seemed to control nature and get advice from demons. The Christians complained that the Pythagorean philosophers presumed to claim not just a likeness to God but equality with Him. One of the admiring biographers of Pythagoras, Porphyry, also authored a scathing attack on Christianity, *Fifteen Books Against the Christians*. These books were banned by two Christian Roman

Emperors. The Christians exerted extensive censorship, they seized and burned the most offensive Pythagorean works until only scattered quotations remained. Later, Saint Augustine said that Porphyry hated Christ and was the most bitter enemy of the Christians. And Augustine criticized Pythagoras as a necromancer who tried to divine the future by speaking with the dead, or demons pretending to be gods.

The Pythagorean cosmology troubled the Christians. The Pythagoreans said that that the infernal regions begin with the Milky Way and souls fall from it to Earth and that animals' souls come from the stars. They said that the Earth is a planet, and that stars and planets were other worlds. They said that souls live in those infinitely many worlds, and that there were demons living on the Moon. They said that Pythagoras came from Jupiter and had lived on the Moon as a demon.

For centuries, the Christians rejected these "poisonous doctrines," "devilish lies," and perverse blasphemies of the Pythagoreans. They declared: "Philosophers are the patriarchs of heretics."

Nevertheless, curious philosophers continued to seek the obscure secrets of Pythagoras. In the Renaissance, the renegade Catholic friar, Giordano Bruno praised the School of Pythagoras. Yet Catholics and Protestants excommunicated Bruno for heresies. The Venetian Inquisition captured and imprisoned him; he denied having said any blasphemies, but always he defended his identity as a philosopher. And there were some beliefs that he refused to renounce: his ideas about souls and the plurality of worlds, that "there are infinitely many individual worlds like our Earth. I regard it, like Pythagoras, as a star, and the Moon, the planets and the stars are similar to it, the latter being of endless number." The Roman Inquisition proclaimed that "all these propositions are heretical, and not now declared so for the first time, but by the most ancient Fathers of the Church and the Apostolic Chair." In 1600, Giordano Bruno was burned alive.

Prominent Christians criticized the wayward inquiries of philosophers as infected with speculations. Pythagoras appeared in books on astrology, divination, and demonology. And against this background, Galileo used a telescope to suggest that maybe Pythagoras was right: there were mountains and landscapes on the Moon, it was another world.

Although writers and historians sometimes discuss the Pythagoreans, there did not exist, until now, any account of how their religious beliefs led Christian writers to denounce them. The present book traces the development of ancient Pythagorean beliefs about religion, astronomy and their interconnections, explaining how early Church Fathers condemned such beliefs, and how that conflict reappeared in the Renaissance.

This book is a companion to my previous book, *Burned Alive: Giordano Bruno, Galileo, and the Inquisition* (Reaktion, 2018). While that book focused on Bruno, Galileo, and the Inquisition, this new book focuses on the religious conflicts between Christians and Pythagoreans.

Among the outstanding puzzles of Bruno's trial by the Inquisition, there is the question: what were the ancient "heretical propositions" that the Inquisitors said were not original in Bruno but which had been denounced by "the most ancient Fathers of the Church and the Apostolic Chair"? Likewise, in Galileo's trial by the Catholic Inquisition, there is the question of why some Church officials were so extremely upset by the "false Pythagorean doctrine" of the Earth's motion. Even Galileo's former ally Pope Urban VIII became bitterly enraged. The Pope complained that Galileo "dared entering where he should not have, and into the most severe and dangerous matters that could be stirred up at this time. …matters, which involve great harm to religion and more awful than were ever devised." The Pope denounced it as "the most perverse subject matter that one could ever handle."[1] Likewise, members of the Society of Jesus said that Galileo's vile book was "more harmful to the Holy Church than the writings of Luther and Calvin."[2] How could the "Pythagorean doctrine" of the Earth's motion involve the "most perverse subject" imaginable?

In my previous book, *Burned Alive*, I placed the Copernican Revolution in that neglected historical context: the beliefs of the cult of Pythagoras. I argued that Earth's motion was associated with religious *heresies*.

According to Copernicus and Bruno, the Earth moves because "it is a star," a heavenly body, yet to Catholic critics it meant that countless stars are worlds—and it was a *heresy* to believe in many worlds. According to Bruno and Kepler, the Earth moves because it's alive, animated by a divine soul—but it was a *heresy* to say that the soul of the world is the Holy Spirit.

Historians know that the Pythagoreans were a secretive religious group, yet there was no historical account of how early Christians criticized their

---

[1] Pope Urban VIII, quoted by Francesco Niccolini to Lord Balì Cioli, 11 September 1632, in Galileo Galilei, *Opere*, Vol. 14, pp. 383, 384, trans. Martínez. Translations of many documents are available in Maurice A. Finocchiaro, *The Galileo Affair: A Documentary History* (Berkeley: University of California Press, 1989), e.g., 229.
[2] As quoted by Galilei to Elia Diodati, 15 Jan. 1633, in Finocchiaro, *Galileo Affair*, 225.

evolving pagan beliefs and how such heresies resurfaced in the Copernican Revolution. How did the ancient Pythagorean religion relate to astronomy? How did it clash with Christianity? These questions require discussion of events across many centuries, so for clarity I will proceed chronologically. Otherwise, historical discussions about the Pythagoreans have been confused by lack of attention to historical sequence, projecting later notions into the ancient past, to concoct imaginary histories.

First, I will trace the evolution of ancient Pythagorean beliefs, to explain how early Church Fathers criticized them. I will analyze how key discoveries and theories in astronomy became attributed to Pythagoras. Then I will discuss why the early Christians criticized Pythagoras. I will compare the miracles of Jesus of Nazareth to those attributed to Pythagoras and his followers, which led Christians to suppress the pagan cults. Finally, I will trace certain Pythagorean beliefs in the Copernican Revolution. The ancient Pythagorean thread is remarkable because it explicitly shows up in the works of important figures in the Copernican Revolution: Copernicus, Zúñiga, Bruno, Bellarmino, Kepler, Galilei, Foscarini, Campanella, Inchofer, and others. Hence I will review well-known events, while setting them in the context of others that are relatively unknown.

Although historians usually refer to Pythagoras as a mathematician and precursor of Copernicus, both are actually mythical identities. There is no reliable evidence that he was an astronomer or even a mathematician. Instead, the most ancient sources portray him essentially as a wise man who taught a particular way of living, apparently including some unusual religious views. His followers developed and expanded upon his beliefs, sometimes creating opposite views. And some of his followers cultivated a secretive, mystical cosmology.

I will show how the cult of Pythagoras became notorious for anti-Christian beliefs: polytheism, the transmigration of souls, divination, the plurality and eternity of worlds, and denials of the uniqueness of Jesus.

In the study of classics, writers often use very different standards for assessing the credibility of sources than the standards used in the study of far more recent events. My first field of expertise is the history of Einstein's special theory of relativity, which he formulated in 1905. A hundred years later, writers from many professions—magazine writers, historians, physicists, educators, novelists, moviemakers, bloggers, etc.—wrote all kinds of things about Einstein, many of them false, many contradictory. They were often motivated by curiosity, attractive conjectures and an unwillingness to portray ambiguities in old sources. For example, instead of fairly writing: We do not know what happened to Einstein's daughter, they write: "she was given up for adoption," or "she probably died of scarlet fever." Yet one can doubt such guesswork, by showing that it isn't definitively warranted by the extant primary sources.

In contrast, when writing the history of antiquity, historians often attribute credibility, say, to accounts that date from a century or more after the facts in question, as if somehow the Greek or Roman writers of antiquity had higher standards of honesty, accuracy, or a better ability to verify past information than we do. But that was not the case. Nowadays, thanks to the proliferation of printed sources, photographs, and the abundant handwritten materials that are often preserved, the accuracy with which in 2022 we can ascertain what really happened in the year 1922, is many orders of magnitude greater than however well people in 400 BCE could possibly know what happened in 500 BCE.

Therefore I decided to investigate very old and ancient accounts with at least the same level of critical skepticism, and usually more, than is necessary when assessing the credibility of textual accounts from the 1900s. In doing so, the kind of picture that arises of the ancient past is very different from common accounts. For example, historians who write about Pythagoras have often readily accepted short claims by ancient poets, satirists, and playwrights as if such claims had historical substance. They often do so by not even mentioning that such claims appeared in fanciful love poems, fictional dialogues, etc., written in distant lands and times relative to the actual historical events that they supposedly describe. Historians often construe such claims in themselves as "fragments" which have been previously extracted and authenticated by classicists and philologists.

When I first started dealing with ancient history, I was puzzled by how often writers do not specify when anything was written. They presuppose, of course, that their readers are well versed in classical studies and will usually know when Ovid, Lucian, or others wrote. And certainly, some works can hardly be dated because they include modifications or interpolations that were added over centuries by writers or copyists. But instead, I wanted to place more emphasis on chronology. In antiquity, the farther an account dates relative to the events in question, the less likely am I to grant it as much credibility as earlier sources. A sentence about Pythagoras by the historian Herodotus from around 430 BCE has far more credibility in my account than many verses by the poet Ovid four hundred years later.

Therefore, when analyzing ambiguous sources, I tried to systematically abstain from using later sources to figure out what the earlier writers meant. Instead, I've consistently used earlier sources to analyze the later accounts. Consider an example. In 1900 Henri Poincaré analyzed the effects of motion on the synchronization of clocks. Later, in 1905, Einstein likewise similarly analyzed how motion would affect clock synchronization. It is fair to therefore ask whether Poincaré influenced Einstein. After all, Poincaré's argument had been published in 1900 in a book that Einstein had read by 1906. However, it seems ridiculous to ask whether the young Einstein influenced Poincaré, because Einstein had not published and because the famous Poincaré did not yet know about him.

This kind of interpretive principle, rather obvious for sources from the early 1900s, is not nearly as common in the study of ancient sources. For example, in writing about the Pythagoreans, some writers say that since Plato wrote about heavenly spheres that generated musical harmonies, he had been influenced by the Pythagoreans. But why? Because *later* records show that some Pythagoreans believed in that notion. To the contrary, since Plato wrote *before* any such records about Pythagoreans believing in any such thing, and since he did not attribute such beliefs to the Pythagoreans, then I do not claim that Plato wrote such things owing to their influence. Someone might of course *imagine* that there might have existed sources, now lost, that were indeed written by Pythagoras or his followers, which Plato in turn studied, and which led him to such notions. But instead, I have chosen to write in a way that avoids such speculations. Instead, if the beliefs of later Pythagoreans resemble those of Plato, then so be it. I will be glad to say the converse if only someone finds evidence that the Pythagoreans before Plato indeed invented or developed such notions.

I try to not write as if there exist probabilities or possibilities in the past. Strictly speaking, either events happened or they didn't. For example, it is not "probable" that yesterday you went to the library. Seriously, either you did or you did not. What we might well say, instead, is that we do not know what you did, and hence, we might say that it is *conceivable* that you did that, we might well *imagine* that you did. But such statements do not describe the past; properly, they're part of the realm of fiction. They can be very interesting, and useful, especially in developing directions for research, but I'm interested in the possibility of writing history without mixing it with many of those statements. Accordingly, in the present book you will find that, excepting quotations and accounts of what some writers have thought, I do not use any of the following expressions: *possibly*, *probably*, *very likely*, *everyone knew that*, and so forth. Also, I have abstained from using expressions such as *he may have*, *he must have*, and so forth. Such expressions facilitate much interpretive drift: if we say that someone *may have* known this, and that *he would have* done that, then multiply by *he must have*—then we can infer almost anything we want.

Finally, I have to beg, please believe me: *I am not implying anything*. I have no difficulty or insecurity in saying whatever I want to say, so if I do not literally specify something, in a particular and explicit sentence, then really, I am not trying to imply it. I might even disagree with such a claim, which might be why I did not state it. To be sure, readers can draw their own inferences, impressions, or questions, but I hope that you will appreciate that I've really tried to be explicit, to abstain from making generalizations or inferences that are unwarranted. Therefore, if it seems that I am implying something ridiculous, please try to find if I actually say it in any one sentence, and if I don't, then I guarantee you that such an apparently strange implication was not intentional. Books are like machines that generate meaning; the author is not in control of all the meaning that combinations of sentences can generate in the mind of each reader, which brings its own interests, definitions, contexts, and concerns. And it's certainly a valuable interaction; I hope that this book will trigger interesting thoughts and discussions. I just ask that my intended meanings be appreciated as what I've literally written. Even then, I'll be glad to hear any disagreements or suggestions. I recognize that this book, like others, is bound to have defects. To be sure, whether my approach is worth repeating depends on how useful it seems, and I'm not proposing that everyone should follow it. I've enjoyed and learned much from the works of many writers, even from their provocative conjectures. I just want readers to know why my approach differs from others, and the concerns that led me to it.

Acknowledgments

I warmly thank Hilary Gatti, William R. Shea, Richard J. Blackwell, John Heilbron, Jole Shackelford, Maurice Finocchiaro, Miriam Bodian, H. Darrel Rutkin, Alexander P. D. Mourelatos, Michael Shank, Miguel A. Granada, and Jane Wickersham for helpful suggestions and assistance. I thank Frances Y. Rivera Avilés for kindly helping me to gather information from sources in Rome, and for several suggestions. I thank the College of Liberal Arts of the University of Texas at Austin for funding my research trips to Rome. I've presented parts of this research at conferences and universities, including: the American Physical Society, the 12th Biennial Conference on the History of Astronomy at the University of Notre Dame, the History of Science Society, twice, the University of Colorado Boulder, Cornell University, and Caltech. I thank the participants for their feedback, especially Michael Crowe, Steven J. Dick, Mordechai Feingold, Owen Gingerich, and Stephen Case. I also value the assistance of Jorge Luis Pardo and Lillian Yvonne Martínez on the cover design.

I thank the following libraries, and their archivists, for enabling me to access their rare manuscripts and books: the Biblioteca Casanatense in Rome, the Archivio di Stato di Roma, the Archivio Storico Capitolino in Rome, the Archivum Romanum Societatis Iesu, the Biblioteca Vallicelliana in Rome, the Archivio Storico of the Academia Nazionale dei Lincei in Rome, the Galileo Museum in Florence, and the Biblioteca Nazionale Centrale di Roma. In particular, I thank Maria Temide Bergamaschi, Laura Giallombardo, Michele Di Sivo, Alessandra Marrone, Brian Mac Cuarta SJ and Elisabetta Caldelli. Plus, I also thank the librarians of the Perry-Castañeda Library of the University of Texas, the Harry Ransom Humanities Research Center, and the Library of the University of Notre Dame.

Chapter 3 includes a section based on an article I published previously: "Ten Censured Propositions in Giordano Bruno's Books," *Bruniana & Campanelliana* 22, No. 2 (Fall 2016), 27-42. Chapters 4 and 5 are based on four articles I had also published: "Why did the Catholic Church really condemn Giordano Bruno?" *Dialog: Theologie & Naturwissenschaften*, February 2019; "Giordano Bruno and the Heresy of Many Worlds," *Annals of Science* 73, No. 4 (October 2016), 345-74; "Giordano Bruno and the Spirit that Moves the Earth," *Not Even Past*, March 8, 2017; and "Melchior Inchofer, Giordano Bruno, and the Soul of the World," *Annals of Science* 76, No. 3-4 (October 2019), 267-302. Finally, there is some overlap between chapters 4 and 5 and parts of my book, *Burned Alive*, yet there is also much material that is not in that book.

1

Who was Pythagoras?

____

In schools, teachers told us that Pythagoras was an ancient mathematician. Alongside problems or exercises, science or math books often have a few sentences of text, a human interest sidebar, telling us a brief story about that man. For example, this is what a typical textbook states:

> The Pythagorean theorem is named for the Greek philosopher Pythagoras (c. 580-500 B.C.) because he was the first person known to have proved it deductively. However, the theorem was known to many ancient cultures and already had been used for at least a thousand years before the time of Pythagoras. These ancient cultures probably never bothered to prove it.[3]

Thousands of books say that Pythagoras was the first to prove the hypotenuse theorem: that the square on the hypotenuse of a right triangle equals the sum of the squares on its other two sides. But not a single one of those books states any evidence that Pythagoras ever really did this. There exists, however, much evidence that other ancient cultures were aware of the relations among the sides of right triangles: the Babylonians, the Hindus, the Chinese. We actually have ancient texts from those cultures: on stones, on clay tablets, or paper that show how they used this knowledge. But we have no copy of anything by Pythagoras showing that he even ever wrote about

____

[3] Jeffrey O. Bennett and William L. Briggs, *Using and Understanding Mathematics* (Addison Wesley, 1999), 46.

triangles or squares. Strangely, teachers and writers claim that Pythagoras "probably" proved it, while people in other cultures "probably" did not.

Likewise, teachers and writers posit probabilities about the history of astronomy. They say that Pythagoras probably was the first person to argue that the Earth is a sphere. They also say that he was probably the first person to argue that the Earth is not the center of the universe. Books on the history of astronomy often mention Pythagoras as a pioneer of the theory that the Earth moves. Even leading historians of science refer to him as a precursor of Copernicus. Consider some examples. Stillman Drake was an outstanding expert on Galileo Galilei's life and works, and in his classic book, *Discoveries and Inventions of Galileo*, Drake said: "Pythagoras was a mathematician and philosopher." Likewise, the distinguished Galileo scholar, Maurice Finocchiaro, referred to Pythagoras as one of the earliest thinkers to advance the idea that Earth circles Sun. And in a remarkable book on Galileo's troubles, Pietro Redondi described Pythagoras as a philosopher who worked on astronomy and physics.[4]

However, it is not well known that contrary to such claims there is actually no substantive ancient evidence that Pythagoras worked on mathematics or astronomy at all.[5] In addition to there being no texts by Pythagoras himself, the extant texts of early Greek writers on mathematics and astronomy, by Plato, Aristotle, Archimedes, Apollonius of Perga, and numerous others, make no claim whatsoever that Pythagoras worked on mathematics or astronomy.

There are no primary sources by Pythagoras, or even by anyone who knew him, so we cannot speak with certainty about his life or beliefs. It seems that he lived in the sixth century BCE, born in the island of Samos, and that he lived in Croton in Southern Italy. The popular legend that Pythagoras made mathematical discoveries seems to begin around 45 BCE, four and a half centuries after his death, when the Roman statesman Cicero briefly criticized a vague claim that Pythagoras immolated an ox "upon finding something new in geometry."[6] Subsequently, other writers made ever

---

[4] Stillman Drake, *Discoveries and Opinions of Galileo* (Doubleday: 1957). Finocchiaro, *The Galileo Affair*, pp. 7, 15. Pietro Redondi, *Galileo Heretic,* trans. Raymond Rosenthal (1983; Princeton: Princeton University Press, 1989).

[5] Alberto A. Martínez, *The Cult of Pythagoras: Math and Myths* (Pittsburgh: University of Pittsburgh Press, 2012). Walter Burkert, *Lore and Science in Ancient Pythagoreanism,* trans. Edwin Minar (Cambridge, MA: Harvard University Press, 1972).

[6] Marcus Tullius Cicero, *De Natura Deorum* (ca. 45 BCE), book 3, sec. 88.

more specific allegations. At around 15 BCE, the Roman architect Vitruvius commented that Pythagoras discovered the hypotenuse relation for a 3-4-5 triangle.[7] Later, roughly around the year 100 CE, other writers who also were not mathematicians vaguely said that Pythagoras sacrificed an ox for a diagram about "the hypotenuse power."[8] And a century later, other writers who also were not mathematicians said that he found that the power of the hypotenuse is equal to the powers of its sides.[9] Subsequently, people have usually construed those latter statements as meaning that this relation is valid for *any* right triangle, something those ancient writers just did not specify.

Consider a typical, confused example: historian Leonid Zhmud claims that Diogenes (ca. 225 CE) reported that a certain Apollodorus said that Pythagoras "proved" the theorem. Yet the actual source in Greek simply says that Pythagoras "found" (εὑρόντα) or "discovered" it:

Diogenes Laertius, ca. 225 AD :

φησὶ δ' Ἀπολλόδωρος ὁ λογιστικὸς ἑκατόμβην
θῦσαι αὐτόν, **εὑρόντα** ὅτι τοῦ ὀρθογωνίου τριγώνου
ἡ ὑποτείνουσα πλευρὰ ἴσον δύναται ταῖς περιεχούσαις.
καὶ ἔστιν ἐπίγραμμα οὕτως ἔχον:
    ἡνίκα Πυθαγόρης τὸ περικλεὲς **εὕρετο** γράμμα,
    κεῖν' ἐφ' ὅτῳ κλεινὴν ἤγαγε βουθυσίην.

Apollodorus the reasonable said that he [Pythagoras]
offered a hecatomb, having **found** that the hypotenuse side
of the right-angled triangle is equal to those enclosing it.
And thus there is an epigram that says:
    when Pythagoras **found** the famous inscription,
    for which he gave an acclaimed sacrifice of oxen. [10]

Likewise, Zhmud mistakenly claims that Vitruvius was "The first to report that the epigram [of Apollodorus] relates to the theorem that the sum of

---

[7] Vitruvius, *De Architectura Libri Decem* (ca. 15 BCE), ed. Valentin Rose (Lipsiae: B. G. Teubneri, 1909), book 9.

[8] Plutarch, "That It Is Not Possible to Live Pleasurably by the Doctrine of Epicurus," (ca. 100 CE), in Plutarque, *Oeuvres Morales,* vol. 5, ed. and trans. into French by Victor Bétolaud (Paris: Hachette, 1870), sec. 11.

[9] Athenaeus, *Deipnosophistai* (ca. 200 CE), in *The Deipnosophists,* ed. and trans. Charles Burton Gulick (Cambridge, MA: Harvard University Press, 1928), book 10, chap. 13.

[10] For analysis, see Martínez, *The Cult of Pythagoras.*

the squares on the sides of a right-angled triangle is equal to the square on the hypotenuse." But this too is an exaggeration. Because, Vitruvius did not write that Pythagoras affirmed this for any and all right-angled triangles, but only specified a 3-4-5 triangle. Zhmud believes, edits, and cultivates various stories about Pythagoras in mathematics; this is a consequence of multiplying conjectures: the pages of his book abound with expressions such as "probably," "most likely," "it is quite possible," "may have been," etc. My systematic avoidance of such speculative expressions leads to explanations that differ from his.[11]

And many centuries later, some writers further expanded such stories to infer that Pythagoras actually *proved* the hypotenuse theorem. One notable instance (the earliest I have found so far) is a work on Euclid's *Elements* published in 1557, in which the author, Jacques Peletier, commented about the hypotenuse theorem: that "Pythagoras proved a general demonstration of it."[12] In time, the ancient mystic became portrayed as a great mathematician, as high school students imagine him still today.

But who was Pythagoras, really?

The earliest account I know about Pythagoras of Samos dates from around 430 BCE, roughly seven decades after his death. It is an account by the Greek historian Herodotus: a story not about Pythagoras himself, but about a man who was said to be his slave. According to Herodotus, some people said that that man, after he was freed from slavery, taught some acquaintances that they would never die:

> I understand from the Greeks who live beside the Hellespont and Pontus, that this Salmoxis was a man who was once a slave in Samos, his master being Pythagoras son of Mnesarchus; then, after being freed and gaining great wealth, he returned to his own country. Now the Thracians were a poor and backward people, but this Salmoxis knew Ionian ways and a more advanced way of life than the Thracian; for he had consorted with Greeks, and moreover with one of the greatest Greek teachers, Pythagoras; therefore he made a hall, where he entertained and fed the leaders among his countrymen, and taught them that neither he nor his guests nor

[11] See Leonid Zhmud, *Pythagoras and the Early Pythagoreans* (Oxford: Oxford University Press, 2012), 59, 267. See Martínez, *The Cult of Pythagoras*, 5-6.
[12] Iacobi Peletarii, *In Euclidis Elementa Geometrica Demonstrationum Libri Sex* (Lvgdvni: Ioan Tornæsivm et Gvl Gazeivm, 1557), bk. 1, pp. 47-48, trans. Martínez.

any of their descendants would ever die, but that they would go to a place where they would live forever and have all good things. While he was doing as I have said and teaching this doctrine, he was meanwhile making an underground chamber. When this was finished, he vanished from the sight of the Thracians, and went down into the underground chamber, where he lived for three years, while the Thracians wished him back and mourned him for dead; then in the fourth year he appeared to the Thracians, and thus they came to believe what Salmoxis had told them. Such is the Greek story about him.[13]

Thus, Salmoxis reportedly pretended to die, he then hid underground for years, only to reappear in order to trick ignorant people into believing him. Herodotus remarked that he neither disbelieved nor entirely believed the story, but he said that he thought that Salmoxis actually lived many years before Pythagoras.

Herodotus told this story during his discussion of a Persian attack against Thracian tribes in 513 BCE, in what is today northern Bulgaria or Romania. These tribes were distinct from other Thracians because of their religion. According to Herodotus, they claimed to be immortal, and they believed that when they died they would go to their god, Salmoxis. And allegedly, these Thracians had a way of communicating with their god even before dying. They would choose someone as "messenger" to report their needs to Salmoxis. And in order to interact with the god, they would hurl this messenger onto three spears—and if he died, they would interpret this to mean that the god favored them. If he did not die, they blamed the messenger, and selected a new messenger to hurl onto the spears.[14]

The story about how Salmoxis was originally just a Thracian slave at the island of Samos, as Herodotus explained, was merely an explanation provided not by Thracians but by neighboring Greeks. Therefore, it seems merely to be fiction, concocted to belittle the beliefs of the poor Thracians and to ridicule their god. Still, the account by Herodotus provides us some information about Pythagoras. It places him on the island of Samos, mentions his father, says that he owned slaves, and it refers to him as "one of the greatest Greek teachers." But apparently not great enough to be

[13] Herodotus, *The Histories* (ca. 430 BCE), trans. A. D. Godley (Cambridge: Harvard University Press, 1920), bk. 4, chap. 95.
[14] Ibid., chap. 94.

mentioned again in Herodotus's *Histories*. Still, the fact that Greeks associated him with Salmoxis suggests that perhaps there was something appropriate in this connection: maybe Pythagoras had similar, unusual religious beliefs, maybe about life after death or immortality. But this is merely a conjecture, it is important to bear in mind that Herodotus specified no such claim about Pythagoras himself.

The brief allusions to Pythagoras, in the story about Salmoxis, were the only instances in which Herodotus referred to Pythagoras in his *Histories*. Still, in a previous section of the *Histories*, Herodotus briefly referred to what he called a "Pythagorean" custom. Herodotus had traveled to Egypt roughly around 455 BCE, and while discussing contrasts between Greek and Egyptian practices, he noted a few similarities, including a religious restriction: that the custom of not bringing wool into temples was "Egyptian and Pythagorean: for it is impious, too, for one partaking of these rites to be buried in woolen wrappings. There is a sacred legend about this."[15] Unfortunately, Herodotus did not state that legend, and specified nothing more about any Pythagorean customs in the *Histories*. But together with the story of Salmoxis, this passage suggests that the followers of Pythagoras carried out some unusual religious practices.

The religious connection is echoed or confirmed by a later writer, Isocrates. At around 375 BCE, this Greek rhetorician also briefly referred to Pythagoras. Isocrates discussed the piety of the Egyptians and noted that others had previously discussed the topic, "including Pythagoras of Samos." Isocrates claimed that Pythagoras visited Egypt, became a student of the religion of the Egyptians, "and was the first to bring to the Greeks all philosophy, and more conspicuously than others he seriously interested himself in sacrifices and in ceremonial purity, since he believed that even if he should gain thereby no greater reward from the gods, among men, at any rate, his reputation would be greatly enhanced."[16]

At first sight, Isocrates seems to confirm and illuminate the words of Herodotus. However, the similarities between aspects of their accounts suggests that perhaps Isocrates was merely paraphrasing Herodotus. Isocrates says merely a couple of sentences about Pythagoras but yet states several of the same points found in Herodotus's very brief lines: that

---

[15] Ibid., bk. 2, chap. 81.
[16] Isocrates, *Busiris* (ca. 375), in George Norlin, ed., *Isocrates with an English Translation* (Cambridge: Harvard University Press, 1980), sec. 28.

Pythagoras lived in Samos, that Pythagorean beliefs resembled some Egyptian beliefs, that the Egyptians showed great piety, plus, the parallelism between the story of the deception by Salmoxis, and Isocrates's disparaging claim that Pythagoras did not really expect rewards from gods but merely sought to enhance his reputation among men. Unlike Herodotus, Isocrates was not a historian, he was a rhetorician. His brief mention of Pythagoras shows up in a comic declamation, what Isocrates described as "the false tale" or "not serious" of the heroic Heracles and Busiris, an evil king of Egypt. That fictional Egyptian villain supposedly captured all visitors and sacrificed them to the gods, until one defiant captive, Heracles, managed to break his shackles and then killed Busiris.

The tale of Heracles was well known before Isocrates; it appears in imagery on ancient vases, and even Herodotus had briefly told it, disparagingly:

And the Greeks say many other ill-considered things, too; among them, this is a silly story which they tell about Heracles: that when he came to Egypt, the Egyptians crowned him and led him out in a procession to sacrifice him to Zeus; and for a while (they say) he followed quietly, but when they started in on him at the altar, he resisted and killed them all. Now it seems to me that by this story the Greeks show themselves altogether ignorant of the character and customs of the Egyptians; for how should they sacrifice men when they are forbidden to sacrifice even beasts, except swine and bulls and bull-calves, if they are unblemished, and geese?[17]

A recent commentator on Isocrates, Niall Livingstone, has argued that perhaps Herodotus's brief allusions to a particular Pythagorean burial custom originated the story that Pythagoras visited Egypt: "by taking the first two steps of the reasoning which leads to the idea of a visit (similar feature, therefore same feature; same feature, therefore borrowed feature)."[18] That is, since according to Herodotus, both the Pythagoreans and the Egyptians did not use wool in their burial practices, a reader might infer that these

[17] Herodotus, bk. 2, chap. 45.
[18] Niall Livingstone, *A Commentary on Isocrates' Busiris* (Leiden/Boston: Brill, 2001), 159. Leonid Zhmud agrees that the claim that Pythagoras acquired his philosophy from the Egyptian priests "is, of course, Isocrates' invention." Zhmud, *Pythagoras and the Early Pythagoreans*, 257.

were not just similar, but that the Pythagoreans had copied the Egyptians. Since the Pythagoreans followed Pythagoras, someone might further infer that Pythagoras himself taught that burials should not involve wool, and furthermore, that Pythagoras had learned this from Egyptians, and moreover, that he had traveled to Egypt. Such inferences are all unwarranted, the initial claim does not necessarily entail the latter claims, but they are the sort of thing that anyone might say when trying to recall something they only once read in Herodotus.

This kind of confusion happened often in ancient times, when few individuals even owned books, or checked the accuracy of every sentence they once read or heard. It even happens nowadays, even from authoritative writers. For example, in an otherwise excellent survey of ancient science, historian David C. Lindberg, a former president of the History of Science Society, noted that "Herodotus (fifth century B.C.) reported that Pythagoras traveled to Egypt, where he was introduced by priests to the mysteries of Egyptian mathematics." But as we've seen, Herodotus wrote no such thing, it's just an example of how we can misremember texts. Herodotus did not write that Pythagoras traveled to Egypt, and he did not say that Pythagoras studied mathematics. Such confusions are common in accounts about Pythagoras. I will later show that the story about Salmoxis rising from the dead became misrepresented later as a story about Pythagoras himself. A story that was denounced by the Christians.

So what can we trust about Isocrates's account of Pythagoras? He confirmed the claim that Pythagoras was well known, and added claims about him traveling to Egypt, being very interested in sacrifices and ceremonies, and "was the first to bring to the Greeks all philosophy." The latter claim sounds like an exaggeration, and Isocrates, at the start of his "false tale," admitted that exaggeration was part of his occupation as a rhetorician: "everyone knows that those who wish to praise a person must attribute to him a larger number of good qualities than he really possesses…"[19] And in fact, there were other philosophers in Greece before Pythagoras, so the claim is just false.

We can see that neither Herodotus nor Isocrates said that Pythagoras worked on mathematics or astronomy. Next, consider another example of an early characterization of Pythagoras. At around 380 BCE, in *The Republic*, the prolific and famous philosopher Plato made a single brief reference to

---

[19] Isocrates, *Busiris*, sec. 4.

Pythagoras. Plato described Socrates as discussing whether the great poet Homer had ever directly helped anyone in anything concerning medicine, education, government, law, politics, or military tactics; as opposed to merely writing about such things. Socrates also asked: "Or is there any invention of his, applicable to the arts or to human life, such as Thales the Milesian or Anacharsis the Scythian, and other ingenious men have conceived, which is attributed to him?" And to all such queries, Socrates's companion, Glaucon, replied in the negative. And right then, Socrates briefly mentioned Pythagoras: "But, if Homer never did any public service, was he privately a guide or teacher of any? Had he in his lifetime friends who loved to associate with him, and who handed down to posterity an Homeric way of life, such as was established by Pythagoras who was so greatly beloved for his wisdom, and whose followers are to this day quite celebrated for the order which was named after him?"[20] This passage establishes several points about Pythagoras. First, that unlike Homer, he established a way of life. Second that Pythagoras was a wise man who, unlike Homer, contributed something to knowledge or education. Third, that Pythagoras had organized followers or disciples who loved him and who transmitted their leader's way of life. Finally, that the followers of Pythagoras were successful at least inasmuch as they were still admired in the times of Socrates and Plato.

There are no primary sources about Pythagoras: no writings by Pythagoras himself, and no accounts of his teachings by anyone who knew him. There are also no secondary sources: for example, there are no accounts by acquaintances of his students. Therefore, the brief accounts by Herodotus, Isocrates, and Plato can best be described as third-hand sources. The earliest is the account by Herodotus, which was roughly from seven decades after Pythagoras had died.

But there are also several *indirect* third-hand accounts, namely, late quotations of passages that were reportedly written in the century after Pythagoras died. I have to distinguish these accounts from those of Herodotus, Isocrates, and Plato, because these three are found in complete treatises, not mere fragments, so it is easier to believe that they constitute words actually written by their authors, not words that were paraphrased, modified, or misquoted. By no means would I give as much credibility to the

---

[20] Plato, *The Republic*, bk. 10.

subsequent accounts as to those of Herodotus, Isocrates, and Plato. Nevertheless, consider a few examples of the earliest *indirect* third-hand accounts.

First, Xenophanes was a philosopher, theologian and poet who lived roughly around 570 to 475 BCE. So he was a contemporary of Pythagoras, though there is no evidence that they lived in the same cities, or ever knew one another. According to one account *written seven centuries later*, Xenophanes reportedly once said something about Pythagoras: "And they say that once, passing by a puppy being beaten, he took pity, and made the following statement: 'Stop, do not beat him, since this is the soul of a dear friend, which I recognized hearing him yelp!'"[21] The writer, Diogenes Laertius, said that Xenophanes here referred to Pythagoras, but the quotation itself does not say his name, and we only have that brief fragment. The alleged quotation suggests that Pythagoras believed in life after death, or at least the transmigration of human souls into the bodies of animals. However, Xenophanes was a poet, so there is no reason to believe that the anecdote was necessarily true, and moreover, it might sound as an expression meant to ridicule Pythagoras.

Next, Heraclitus of Ephesus lived from around 535 BCE to about 475 BCE. According to an account *seven centuries later*, again by Diogenes, Heraclitus once briefly noted that: "Pythagoras, son of Mnesarchus, practiced inquiry beyond all other men, and in this selection of his writings made himself a wisdom of his own, showing much learning but poor workmanship."[22] As in Plato's account, Heraclitus, who shows up in Plato's dialogues, apparently described Pythagoras as a wise man. But he also seems to have criticized Pythagoras, as did Isocrates. Likewise, in another passage, Heraclitus reportedly said: "Much learning does not teach one to have understanding, otherwise it would have taught Hesiod and Pythagoras, and again Xenophanes and Hecataeus."[23]

Later, Heraclides of Pontus was a Greek philosopher who lived roughly from 390 to 310 BCE. According to Diogenes, again, writing more than five centuries later, Heraclides wrote some comments about Pythagoras:

---

[21] Xenophanes, quoted in Diogenes, "Life of Pythagoras," sec. 38, trans. Martínez.

[22] Heraclitus, quoted in Diogenes, "Life of Pythagoras," sec. 6.

[23] Heraclitus, quoted in Diogenes, "Life of Heraclitus," sec. 1.

This is what Heraclides of Pontus tells us he [Pythagoras] used to say about himself: that he had once been Aethalides and was reportedly Hermes' son, and Hermes told him he might choose any gift he liked except immortality; so he asked to retain through life and through death a memory of his experiences. Hence in life he could recall everything, and when he died he still kept the same memories. Afterwards in course of time his soul entered into Euphorbus and he was wounded by Menelaus. Now Euphorbus used to say that he had once been Aethalides and obtained this gift from Hermes, and then he told of the wanderings of his soul, how it migrated hither and thither, into how many plants and animals it had come, and all that it underwent in Hades, and all that the other souls there have to endure. When Euphorbus died, his soul passed into Hermotimus, and he also, wishing to authenticate the story, went up to the temple of Apollo at Branchidae, where he identified the shield which Menelaus, on his voyage home from Troy, had dedicated to Apollo, so he said: the shield being now so rotten through and through that the ivory facing only was left. When Hermotimus died, he became Pyrrhus, a fisherman of Delos, and again he remembered everything, how he was first Aethalides, then Euphorbus, then Hermotimus, and then Pyrrhus. But when Pyrrhus died, he became Pythagoras, and still remembered all the facts mentioned.[24]

This passage is wonderful: it embodies and elaborates the apparent but faint implication of the claims by Herodotus and Xenophanes, in that it portrays Pythagoras as having believed in life after death. Moreover, it portrays him as a demigod, the son of the god Hermes. I will discuss the stories about the transmigrations of the soul of Pythagoras later, but for now, suffice to say that his fame as a religious leader developed greatly thanks to such stories and their allusions to the alleged proofs of his divinity. As told by Heraclides, if indeed these were his words, it is unclear whether this extraordinary story about multiple lives was intended merely as a kind of hearsay reporting or as a kind of ridicule.

Hence, it is important to point out that several of the ancient commentators referred to Pythagoras in somewhat disparaging ways, including Xenophanes, Isocrates, and Heraclitus. Likewise, Herodotus, Plato, Aristotle, and others spoke in critical ways at least about some of the followers of Pythagoras. Later writers echoed both positive and disparaging stories. For

[24] Heraclides, quoted in Diogenes, "Life of Pythagoras," sec. 4.

example, Plutarch quoted Timon the Philasian for writing that Pythagoras was an impostor who studied magic and divine arts to mock and deceive men.[25]

Yet we can leave the real Pythagoras in the background. He was somehow popular and influential, and after his death, some people, rightly or arbitrarily, called themselves Pythagoreans. Consider now the legends about the feats of Pythagoras in astronomy. Such stories seem to have begun long after his death, so we should trace how each of them developed.

Did he say the Earth orbits the Sun?

At around 340 BCE, Plato's extraordinary student, Aristotle, criticized a group of "so-called Pythagoreans" who made speculations about numbers and cosmology.[26] It is interesting that he referred to them, a few times, as if they did not necessarily deserve the designation of Pythagoreans. Unfortunately, there are no extant comments by Aristotle about Pythagoras himself in any of Aristotle's works, so we do not know what contrast Aristotle would have made between Pythagoras and his self-proclaimed admirers two hundred years later.

Aristotle complained about these "Italian philosophers" that: "they say that fire is at the center [of the universe] and that the Earth is one of the stars, and that moving in a circle about the center it produces night and day."[27] Historians know, from the details of Aristotle's account, that the "central fire" was not the Sun, because the Sun too was said to move quickly.[28] Yet nonetheless, this claim led to the common confusion, centuries later, that the Pythagoreans believed that the Earth orbits the Sun. It also led to the common arbitrary conjecture that since some of Pythagoreans discussed cosmology, then their inspirational leader, Pythagoras, centuries earlier, was an astronomer. This fiction is comparable to this one: since

---

[25] Plutarch, "Numa Pompilius" (ca. 75 CE), in Plutarchi Chaeronensis, *Summi et Philosophiet Historici Parallela, id est, Vitæ Illustrium Virorum Græcorum et Romanorum* (Frankfurt: Ioannis Saurii/Eliæ Willeri, 1600), 43.

[26] Aristotle, *Metaphysics* (ca. 350 BCE) bk. 1, secs. 5 and 9.

[27] Aristotle, *On the Heavens* (ca. 340? BCE), bk. 2, sec. 13.

[28] Ibid., bk. 2, sec. 9.

certain ancient astronomers were Christian, then Jesus of Nazareth was an astronomer who proposed new explanations of planetary motions. The latter claim sounds ridiculous, of course, but I'm just trying to convey the principle that we should not attribute to someone the occupations of his followers or admirers. At any rate, following Aristotle's remarks, a few writers later noted that the Pythagoreans claimed that stars are worlds in infinite space.

In addition to arguing that fire, instead of earth, "lies at the center of the sphere," the Pythagoreans, wrote Aristotle, "hold that the most important part of the world, which is the center, should be strictly guarded, and name it, or rather the fire that occupies that place, the 'Guardhouse of Zeus.'"[29] He added that "some of the Pythagoreans" believe that the heavens and all of nature are composed of numbers.[30]

An ancient author wrote a work about the views of many philosophers, which became known as the *Placita Philosophorum*. It was based on a work by Aetius, from about 50 BCE, but it was elaborated by other writers. The author or authors made various claims about Pythagoras and his followers. Among many thinkers, the book attributed some interesting opinions or theories to the philosopher Philolaus, who apparently lived from roughly around 470 to around 385 BCE. About him, the book notes: "Some insist that the Earth is immovable; but Philolaus the Pythagorean says that it moves circularly around the central fire, in an oblique circle like the Sun."[31] This claim confirms or echoes the account written by Aristotle.

A subsequent account is important because it attributes the doctrine of the Earth's motion not only to the Pythagoreans but also to Plato. At around 75 CE, the Greek historian and biographer Plutarch, who became a Roman citizen, wrote a biography of the legendary second kind of Rome, Numa Pompilius, in which Plutarch made several references to Pythagoras and his followers. Plutarch said that some people claimed that king Numa was a student and follower of Pythagoras, but Plutarch denied it and instead pointed out the similarities between them, as if sometimes Numa copied

---

[29] Aristotle, *On the Heavens*, bk. 2, sec. 13.
[30] Ibid., bk. 3, sec. 1. See also, *Metaphysics*, bk. 13, sec. 6; and bk. 14, sec. 3.
[31] [falsey attributed to Plutarch], *Placita Philosophorum* [actually by another writer, based on a work by Aetius, ca. 50 BCE, as noted by Theodoret], *Peri ton Areskonton Philosophois Physikon Dogmaton* [and falsely attributed to Qusta ibn Luqa by Ibn al-Nadim], in Hans Daiber, ed., *Aetius Arabus: Die Vorsokratiker in Arabischer Überlieferung* (Wiesbaden: Franz Steiner Verlag, 1980), bk. 3, chaps. 7.

Pythagorean practices. In this connection, Plutarch explained that Numa constructed a temple that embodied the cosmology of the Pythagoreans.

> Tradition also says, that Numa kept the perennial fire encircled by the temple of Vesta: which was built around it to represent not the Earth (as if it were Vesta) but the figure of the whole universe, in the center of which the Pythagoreans placed the fire, namely Vesta, and they called it unity. They held that the Earth is not immobile and is not located in the center of the circumference, but is carried in a circle around the fire, and is not the most excellent, nor is it one of the primal parts of the world. And they say that Plato, when he was of advanced age, thought the same thing about the Earth: that it was not placed in the center of the universe, but that the central and principal place should be for a more noble nature.[32]

Owing to this account, subsequent writers occasionally attributed the heliocentric universe to Pythagoras and Plato, as if the accounts by Plutarch and Aetius referred to the Sun's centrality.

Later, at around 225 CE, Diogenes Laertius wrote a very brief chapter about Philolaus, in his book *Lives of Eminent Philosophers*. Reportedly, Philolaus was a contemporary of Plato (Diogenes mentions him both in this chapter as well as in a chapter about Plato), and Diogenes said that "His doctrine is that all things are brought about by necessity and in harmonious inter-relation. He was the first to declare that the Earth moves in a circle, though some say that it was Hicetas of Syracuse."[33] Likewise, at around 400 CE, Joannes Stobaeus, a compiler of Greek texts, copied a similar account, this one with many details:

> Philolaus says that there is fire in the middle at the center; he calls it Hestia, of the All, the Guardpost of Zeus, the Mother of the Gods, the Altar, the Link, and the Measure of Nature. Besides, he locates a second fire, quite at the top, surrounding the world. The center, he says, is by its nature the first, around it, the ten different bodies carry out their choral dance. These are: the heaven, the planets, lower the Sun, and below it the Moon, lower the Earth, and beneath this, the counter-Earth, then beneath these bodies

---

[32] Plutarch, "Numa Pompilius" (ca. 75 CE), in Plutarchi, *Summi et Philosophiet Historici Parallela*, 45, trans. Martínez.

[33] Diogenes Laertius, *Lives of the Eminent Philosophers*, chap. 7.

the fire Hestia, in the center, where it maintains order. The highest part of the Covering, in which he asserts that the elements exist in a perfectly pure condition, is called Olympus; the space beneath the revolution-circle of Olympus, and where in order are disposed the five planets, the Sun and the Moon, forms the Cosmos; finally, beneath the latter is the sublunar region, which surrounds the Earth, where are the generative things, susceptible to change.[34]

This account integrates pagan theology and cosmology. As in Aristotle's account, the Earth orbits not the Sun, but a central fire. The sequence of heavenly bodies shows that the ordering of the planets around the central fire was hardly motivated by astronomical reasons or observations. For example, the Earth is treated as distinct from the planets: all orbit the central fire, but the Earth is neither called a planet nor grouped with them, it is instead placed in an orbit beneath the Sun and the Moon. And strangely, the Sun and the Moon seem to be comparable, bodies that circle the center, that is, no indication is given that one orbits the Earth and the other does not. Moreover, the strangest aspect of the scheme seems to be the so-called "counter-Earth," mysteriously closest to the center, but the passage gives no reason why. Therefore, aside from the concept of the Earth moving in circles, the scheme of Philolaus was thoroughly different from what Copernicus later proposed.

Apparently Philolaus is also the earliest Pythagorean, known by name, who emphasized the importance of numbers. According to Stobaeus, Philolaus said: "And indeed all things that are known have number. For it is not possible that anything whatsoever be understood or known without this."[35] Reportedly, Philolaus also valued the role of simple ratios of whole numbers in the musical harmonies. By the way, contrary to later stories, there's no evidence that Pythagoras himself really discovered (or even knew about) such numerical ratios in the lengths of harmonic strings.[36]

---

[34] Stobaeus, *Eclogarum Physicarum*, in August Meineke, ed., *Ioannis Stobaei Eclogarum Physicarum et Ethicarum*, ed. Vol. 1 (1860), translation modified from: David R. Fideler, ed., *The Pythagorean Sourcebook and Library: An Anthology of Ancient Writings*, trans. Kenneth Sylvan Guthrie (Grand Rapids, Michigan: Phanes Press, 1987), 170.

[35] Philolaus, quoted in Stobaeus (ca. 425 CE), Eclogae 1.21.7b, known as Fragment 4, trans. and authenticated in Carl A. Huffman, *Philolaus of Croton, Pythagorean and Presocratic* (Cambridge: Cambridge University Press, 1993), 172-177.

[36] For example, see Huffman, *Philolaus*, 147-148.

Did he say
the Earth is Round?

Many writers have said that Pythagoras believed that the Earth is spherical. For example, historian Thomas Heath wrote that "It seems certain that Pythagoras himself conceived the universe to be a sphere and attributed to it daily rotation about an axis; … [and] declared the Earth to be spherical."[37]

The story that Pythagoras was the first person to argue that the Earth is round is found in an account by Diogenes Laertius, book 8 of his *Lives of Eminent Philosophers*, written roughly around 225 CE. Diogenes remarked: "Furthermore, we are told that Pythagoras was the first to give the name 'cosmos' to the heavens, and the first who called the Earth round; though according to Theophrastus it was Parmenides, and according to Zeno it was Hesiod."[38] While Diogenes cited no source for such claims about Pythagoras, he does at least give sources for the competing claims about Parmenides and Hesiod, which perhaps insinuates that whomever made such claims about Pythagoras was not as worthy of being named, that is, was no big authority. Here, we can doubt Diogenes for making striking claims that, if true, should have been recorded by any of various writers who commented on the history of astronomy during the long period of time after Pythagoras died. But in another passage, Diogenes at least cited one source, he wrote:

> Alexander also says, in his *Successions of Philosophers*, that he found the following dogmas also set down in the "Commentaries of Pythagoras": That the monad was the beginning of everything. From the monad proceeds an indefinite duad, which is subordinate to the monad as to its cause. That from the monad and the indefinite duad proceed numbers. And from numbers signs. And from these last, lines of which plane figures consist. And from plane figures are derived solid bodies. And from solid bodies sensible bodies, of which last there are four elements; fire, water, earth, and air. And that the world, which is endued with life, and intellect, and which is of a spherical figure, having the Earth, which is also spherical, and inhabited all over in its center, results from a combination of these

[37] Ibid., xxix.
[38] Diogenes Laertius, bk. 8, 48 (?).

elements, and derives its motion from them; and also that there are antipodes, and that what is below, as respects us, is above in respect of
them.[39]

Apparently Diogenes was paraphrasing passages from a work, now lost,
Successions of Philosophers, by the prolific Greek scholar Lucius Cornelius Alexander. The author lived in the 1st century CE and he became known as
Alexander Polyhistor because he wrote many books on history, philosophy,
and geography. But his writings are lost, only fragments survive, such as
some passages in Diogenes Laertius's accounts of some philosophers.

It is not known whether Diogenes's two passages about the Earth being round came from one source, Alexander. One of Diogenes's passages
notes that there exists a claim that Pythagoras was the first to call the Earth
round, while the other passage, the one that cites Alexander, merely states
that the Earth is spherical, and that this dogma was set down in a work
titled "Commentaries of Pythagoras." Subsequently, Diogenes refers to
more "doctrines which Alexander asserts he discovered in the Pythagorean
treatises." The works of Alexander were relatively recent, less than a century
before Diogenes, so it is reasonable to assume that indeed Diogenes was at
least roughly echoing whatever Alexander wrote.

However, there is no evidence that whatever treatises Alexander used
when discussing Pythagoras were accurate, and not merely any of the many
forgeries and fictions that circulated since at least 300 BCE. Nonetheless,
some historians believed Diogenes's account of Alexander's indirect account, partly because the name of Aristotle appeared briefly in this connection. Diogenes wrote: "These are the doctrines which Alexander asserts that
he discovered in the Pythagorean treatises; and Aristotle gives a similar account of them." If we wish to gift credibility to whichever of Alexander's
claims we prefer, we might imagine that the reference to the authority of
Aristotle had a direct bearing on that particular claim. But there is no evidence for that. Diogenes did not specify which work by Aristotle he referred to, in this sentence, and worse, there are no known works in which
Aristotle spoke about Pythagoras.[40] Moreover, in his book *On the Heavens*,

---

[39] Diogenes Laertius, Sec. 19.
[40] A typical claim to the contrary is found in: Christiane L. Joost-Gaugier, *Measuring
Heaven: Pythagoras and His Influence on Thought and Art in Antiquity and the Middle Ages*

Aristotle did discuss the question of whether the Earth is spherical, and alluded to authors who had opinions about the subject, but he did not specify Pythagoras or his followers.

If, instead, we analyze Diogenes's account, we see that the "doctrines" that he was immediately discussing before his mention of Aristotle were mostly Pythagorean dietary restrictions and rules about food: about fish, bread, salt, etc. So it is apparent that the allusion to Aristotle referred not to astronomy or the shape of the Earth, but to food. Indeed, a few paragraphs above the vague phrase "Aristotle gives a similar account," Diogenes actually refers to the title of an alleged work by Aristotle:

"And Aristotle says, in his *Treatise on Beans*, that Pythagoras enjoined his disciples to abstain from beans, either because they resemble some part of the human body, or because they are like the gates of hell (for they are the only plants without parts); or because they dry up other plants, or because they are representatives of universal nature, or because they are used in elections in oligarchical governments. He also forbade his disciples to pick up what fell from the table, for the sake of accustoming them not to eat immoderately, or else because such things belong to the dead."

The claim that the Earth is round is not found between this passage and the next, so there is really no reason to think that Aristotle confirmed Alexander's account. Moreover, there exists no independent evidence at all that Aristotle really wrote a *Treatise on Beans*, none of the many other commentators on Aristotle, history, literature, philosophy, food, or agriculture wrote any such thing. Thus it seems that Diogenes was referring to a spurious work falsely attributed to Aristotle.

Summing up, the claim that Pythagoras claimed, or was the first to claim, that the Earth is spherical dates to the time of Alexander Polyhistor, the first century CE, but there is no evidence for it in previous centuries. Six hundred years had passed since the death of Pythagoras, too much time to explain why the various Greek writers who discussed topics such as

(Ithaca: Cornell University Press, 2006), 18. Joost-Gaugier claims that Aristotle praised Pythagoras as a mathematician interested in numbers; yet the purported evidence is only a phrase attributed to Apollonius (ca. 150 BCE), for which there is "no reason whatever to think that the statement derives from Aristotle," as explained by W. A. Heidel, "The Pythagoreans and Greek Mathematics," *The American Journal of Philology* 61, no. 1 (1940), 8.

philosophy, astronomy, geography, or history did not take the opportunity to even briefly mention that the famous Pythagoras somehow argued that the Earth was round. I therefore conclude that Alexander's claim is spurious.

In order to understand how mistakes propagate in the history of science, let me illustrate how, in hindsight, we can identify "red flags" when what we're reading lacks evidence. If even the best historians make mistakes, we should try to learn from such mistakes, so that we can learn to better write historical accounts. Consider an example, which shows how particular sentence constructions belie problems. In a history of Greek astronomy, first published in 1932, Thomas Heath wrote: "PYTHAGORAS, born at Samos about 572 B.C., was probably the first to hold that the Earth is spherical in shape."[41] We may well doubt where or when Pythagoras was born, and if we pursue this line of uncertainty we will soon find that accounts of his lifespan date from centuries after his death, so that they can well be doubted. But the more important red flag is the expression "was probably the first." If we demand the evidence for this claim we get only hearsay: Diogenes said that Alexander said that some unspecified author at some unspecified time said… Hence there is just no good evidence that Pythagoras ever even claimed that the Earth is spherical.

Alexander gained fame, during his lifetime, for his prolific works, but such works were apparently not precious enough or sufficiently valued to survive the passage of time. Nevertheless, thanks to Diogenes, Alexander's claims about Pythagoras and the Pythagoreans spread and became very influential. For example, seventeen centuries later, in one of the most popular science books ever, *Cosmos*, based on the popular television series of the same name, the engaging astronomer Carl Sagan duly noted that on the island of Samos local tradition says that their native son Pythagoras was "the first person in the history of the world to deduce that the Earth is a sphere."[42] Sagan likewise remarked that Pythagoras was the first person to give the name "cosmos" to the universe.

[41] Thomas L. Heath, *Greek Astronomy*, Vol. 10 of *The Library of Greek Thought* (London: J.M. Dent & Sons, 1932), xxix.
[42] Carl Sagan, *Cosmos* (New York: Random House, 1980), 183.

Did he hear
the Music of the Spheres?

One of the most popular ideas about Pythagoras is that he believed that the heavens or the movements of the planets emit some sort of musical harmonies, and that allegedly he could hear it. Yet again, this story does not begin with Pythagoras. Early writers apparently did not ascribe such notions to Pythagoras, but some of them did say that his followers or admirers somehow associated harmonies and the cosmos.

To start, at around 380 BCE, Plato discussed some "Pythagoreans" in his *Republic*. In this dialogue, Socrates and Glaucon discussed the sequence in which the State should educate its citizens. When they reached the topics of astronomy and harmonics, they briefly mentioned the Pythagoreans, as follows. Socrates remarked that in addition to the study of visible motion, there was another kind of motion that should be studied. So Glaucon asked:

> And what may that be? The second, I said, would seem relatively to the ears what the first is to the eyes; for I conceive that as the eyes are designed to look up at the stars, so are the ears to hear harmonious motions; and these are sister sciences—as the Pythagoreans say, and we, Glaucon, agree with them?

> Yes, he replied. But this, I said, is a laborious study, and therefore we had better go and learn of them; and they will tell us whether there are any other applications of these sciences. At the same time, we must not lose sight of our own higher object.

> What is that? There is a perfection which all knowledge ought to reach, and which our pupils ought also to attain, and not to fall short of, as I was saying that they did in astronomy. For in the science of harmony, as you probably know, the same thing happens. The teachers of harmony compare the sounds and consonances which are heard only, and their labor is in vain, like that of the astronomers.

> Yes, by heaven! he said; and it's as good as a play to hear them talking about their condensed notes, as they call them; they put their ears close alongside of the strings like persons catching a sound from their neighbor's wall—some of them declaring that they distinguish an intermediate note and have found the least interval which should be the unit of measurement; the others insisting that the two sounds have passed into the same—either party setting their ears before their understanding.

You mean, I said, those gentlemen who tease and torture the strings and rack them on the pegs of the instrument: might carry on the metaphor and speak after their manner of the blows which the plectrum gives, and make accusations against the strings, both of backwardness and forwardness to sound; but this would be tedious, and therefore I will only say that these are not the men, and that I am referring to the Pythagoreans, of whom I was just now proposing to enquire about harmony. For they too are in error, like the astronomers; they investigate the numbers of the harmonies which are heard, but they never attain to problems—that is to say, they never reach the natural harmonies of number, or reflect why some numbers are harmonious and others not.

That, he said, is a thing of more than mortal knowledge. A thing, I replied, which I would rather call useful; that is, if sought after with a view to the beautiful and good; but if pursued in any other spirit, useless. Very true, he said.[43]

In these passages, the Pythagoreans are mentioned twice, but briefly. First, they mention that the Pythagoreans said that astronomy and harmonics are sister sciences. Second, Socrates and Glaucon criticize them for how they investigated and taught harmonics. Allegedly, the Pythagoreans focused only on harmonies that are heard, studying them numerically but without ever focusing on the harmonies of numbers themselves. This "error" was analogous to that of astronomers who studied heavenly motions but did not study relations among number themselves. These passages jointly seem to suggest that the Pythagoreans did not necessarily work on astronomy (note the comparison between the Pythagoreans on the one hand, and astronomers on the other), though perhaps they at least spoke about astronomy; instead, apparently they worked on the study of sounds.

Nevertheless, Plato gave evidence of someone else, not a Pythagorean, who did discuss the idea that moving planets emit sounds: Socrates. In the last book of the *Republic*, toward the very end, Socrates discussed a tale about a man called Er who reportedly died and witnessed the afterlife. After seeing souls be judged on their way to heaven or hell, Er and other souls traveled to a place far, far above, from which he could see a steel spindle that connected all the parts of the universe, from the top of heaven down to the center of the Earth. The spindle held different whorls or spheres: one carried all the fixed stars, there was one for each of the five planets,

---

43 Plato, *Republic*, bk. 7.

plus one for the Sun, and another for the Moon, making a total of eight concentric spheres. On the upper surface of each revolving sphere there was

> a siren, who goes around with them, hymning a single tone or note. The eight together form one harmony; and round about, at equal intervals, there is another band, three in number, each sitting upon her throne: these are the Fates, daughters of Necessity, who are clothed in white robes and have chaplets upon their heads, Lachesis and Clotho and Atropos, who accompany with their voices the harmony of the sirens—Lachesis singing of the past, Clotho of the present, Atropos of the future...[44]

We can well refer to the joint songs of those eight sirens as a "music of the spheres." Yet Pythagoras and his followers were not mentioned. There is no need to imagine that Socrates or Plato were influenced by Pythagoras about these concepts, basically because there is no evidence that Pythagoras himself formulated or ever considered these concepts. One might just as arbitrarily imagine that some Pythagoreans borrowed such concepts from Plato. The only evidence we have is that such concepts appeared in Plato's account, before anyone associated them with the Pythagoreans.

Yet the association came, at the latest, just a few decades later. At roughly around 340 CE, Aristotle similarly discussed the topic at hand, in his *Metaphysics*. This is what he said about the Pythagoreans:

> They thought that the whole heaven is harmony and number; thus whatever admitted facts they were in a position to prove in the domain of numbers and harmonies, they put these together and adapted them to the properties and parts of the heaven and its whole arrangement. And if there was anything wanting anywhere, they left no stone unturned to make their whole system coherent. For example, regarding as they do the number ten as perfect and as embracing the whole nature of numbers, they say that the bodies moving in the heaven are also ten in number, and as those that we see are only nine, they make the counter-Earth the tenth."[45]

---

[44] Plato, *Republic*, bk. 10.
[45] Aristotle, *Metaphysics* A 5, 986 a 1.

Like Plato, in his passage about harmonics and its sister science, Aristotle was essentially criticizing the Pythagoreans. Since they presupposed that the number 10 is perfect, and they wanted astronomy to match their numerology, they expected that there should be 10 heavenly bodies. But there seemed to be only nine: Earth, the Moon, the Sun, Mercury, Venus, Mars, Jupiter, Saturn, and the sphere of the stars; therefore, some Pythagoreans reportedly imagined the existence of a tenth body, a "counter-Earth" that like the rest supposedly circled the fiery center of the universe.

In another book, *On the Heavens*, Aristotle elaborated the point about the heavenly harmony. He specified that "the Pythagoreans say that the motion of the stars produces a concord," some sort of harmony.[46] He explained that moving bodies produce noise and friction, and such sounds are caused when a moving body is enclosed or in contact with a non-moving body. He therefore argued that if the heavenly bodies were to move within a diffused mass of air and fire, as people then thought, "their motion would necessarily cause a noise of tremendous strength and such a noise would necessarily reach and shatter us."[47] He therefore concluded that the heavenly bodies do not move as constrained bodies, that is, as bodies on Earth. Thus, from the silence of the heavens, Aristotle denied that the planets, Sun and Moon experience enforced or frictional motions. Thus he also denied the existence of any Pythagorean heavenly sounds: "From all this it is clear that the theory that the movement of the stars produces a harmony, i.e. that the sounds they make are concordant, in spite of the grace and originality with which it has been stated, is nevertheless untrue."

Aristotle only briefly discussed the notion of harmony in relation to the heavens; for example, he did not describe the kinds of sounds that each planet allegedly made. The latter idea, however, was formulated at least as early as 51 BCE, when Cicero composed the sixth book of his work *On the Commonwealth*. That book described a fictional dialogue in which a wise old man, the Roman general Scipio Aemilianus, described the visions that he had in a dream.

The ancient Greeks and the Romans attributed importance to dreams as a means to divine the future. So supposedly Scipio dreamed that his dead grandfather visited him, and they looked down upon the Earth from a high, starry place. The grandfather asked him to look at the whole universe, not

[46] Aristotle, *On the Heavens*, bk. 2, sec. 9.
[47] Ibid.

just the Earth. The universe was a system of nine spheres: the outermost being the starry Heaven, which contains all others and was described as none other than the supreme deity. Within it were the other spheres, in this sequence: Saturn, Jupiter, Mars, the Sun ("the soul and principle of order in the world"), Venus, Mercury, the Moon, and lowest of all, the Earth, unmoving. Seeing all this, Scipio suddenly realized that he could hear a "sweet harmony." Then his dead grandfather explained:

> This music is produced by the friction and revolution of those very spheres. As the unequal intervals between them are arranged according to a fixed law of proportion, and as the high tones agreeably blend with the low, various sweet harmonies are bound to result therefrom. Such colossal revolutions cannot, of course, be swiftly executed in silence, and it is but natural that the extremes should elicit deep sounds at one end and high ones at the other. Accordingly, that highest starry orb of Heaven, whose revolution is comparatively swift, moves with a high and shrill sound, whereas this lowest lunar orb rotates with a deep sound. The Earth, of course, the ninth sphere, remains fixed and stationary, occupying as it does the center of the universe. These eight orbs, two of which have the same musical value, produce seven different sounds—a number, by the way, which is the key of almost everything. Inspired bards reproduce this celestial strain on stringed instruments and thus pave the way for their own return to this place; so do other men of brilliant parts who spend their life in the pursuit of things divine.
>
> Men's ears have become stunned by this music and, in consequence, are now deaf to it. Indeed, none of your senses is so blunt as hearing. ... As for this music of the spheres, it is so overpowering, by reason of the amazing speed with which the cosmos spins round, that no human ear can endure it, any more than you can look straight into the Sun, whose brightness would blunt the keenness of your sight.[48]

[48] Marcus Tullius Cicero, "Somnium Scipionis," in *De Re Publica*, bk. 6, sec. 7, reissued as: Cicero, *The Dream of Scipio*, trans. James A. Kleist (New York: Schwartz, Kirwin & Fauss, 1915), pp. 31-33.

Writers who do not quote this passage refer to it often as being very Pythagorean in character.[49] However, let's note first some ways in which it does not seem Pythagorean. It does not echo aspects of the account given by Aristotle: that the Pythagoreans thought the there is a counter-Earth, that the heavens involve the number ten, or that the Earth moves and orbits the fire at the center of the universe. This leaves a few points of similarity. Aristotle had said: "They thought that the whole heaven is harmony and number." Accordingly, Cicero's account of the dream of Scipio refers at least to a particular number, seven, as being important, "the key to almost everything," which matches Aristotle's claim that "they considered the principles of numbers to be the first principles of all things."[50] Also, both accounts discuss human beings' apparent inability to hear the heavenly sounds, both say that this would result from a kind of deafness (Aristotle used the example of coppersmiths accustomed to noises), both discuss friction, and both say that the sounds of the heavenly spheres should be painfully loud. In sum, the similarities between these accounts are so striking, that either Cicero had based his story on Aristotle's *On the Heavens*, taking many liberties, or he used a similar source.

By the Renaissance, ancient notions about the harmony of the spheres became advocated by astronomers such as Johannes Kepler. By then, writers regularly attributed such notions to the inspirational philosopher from Samos. When did such attributions begin? There seem to be no such attributions in the first several centuries after Pythagoras died.

By the 1st century CE, the concept or story of the harmony of the spheres was finally attributed to Pythagoras himself. At around 77 CE, in his *Natural History*, Pliny the Elder ridiculed Pythagoras for "occasionally" drawing on music theory to describe the distances between the Earth and the heavenly bodies, as tones and half-tones, producing "a universal harmony" of seven tones, "a refinement more entertaining than convincing."[51] This story seems to derive from the "Dream of Scipio" inasmuch as it refers to seven tones. Incidentally, by the ordering of the heavenly bodies, here Pliny seems to assume that Pythagoras envisioned the Earth at the center

---

[49] For example, see Christiane L. Joost-Gaugier, *Measuring Heaven: Pythagoras and His Influence on Thought and Art in Antiquity and the Middle Ages* (Ithaca: Cornell University Press, 2006), 28.

[50] Aristotle, *Metaphysics*, bk. 1, chap. 5.

[51] Pliny the elder, *Natural History* (ca. 77-79 CE), translated by H. Rackham (Cambridge: Harvard University Press, 1949-54), bk. 2, sec. 20.

of the heavens. This is significant, as it shows that the later claim that Pythagoras taught that Earth moves, as Galileo claimed, is not found in the most ancient sources.

Next, an important commentator on Aristotle also seems to have relied tacitly on Cicero. At roughly around 200 CE, the philosopher Alexander of Aphrodisias wrote a commentary on Aristotle's *Metaphysics*. Alexander repeated Aristotle's characterization of the Pythagoreans as believing that the universe was composed of harmony and numbers, that the distances of the heavenly bodies are in proportion to musical consonances. But Alexander also explicitly included something that Aristotle did not specify, but was stated in the "Dream of Scipio," that the "the sound made by the slower bodies in their movement is lower in pitch, and the faster higher."[52]

Consider a few more examples of writers who attributed the theory of the music of the spheres to Pythagoras himself. At some point, the date is unknown, a writer who pretended to be Plutarch wrote a treatise "On Music," which states: "Pythagoras, Archytas, Plato, and many other of the ancient philosophers, were of the opinion, that there could be no motion of the world or rolling of the spheres without the assistance of music, since the Supreme Deity created all things harmoniously."[53] Later, at around 225 CE, a theologian of the Church of Rome, Hippolytus, complained that: "Pythagoras claimed that the universe sings, and is constructed in accordance with a harmony; and he was the first to reduce the motion of the seven heavenly bodies to rhythm and song."[54] Accordingly, one of the later biographers of Pythagoras, Porphyry, made similar statements around 300 CE:

He himself could hear the harmony of the Universe, and understood the universal music of the spheres, and of the stars which move in concert with them, and which we cannot hear because of the limitations of our weak nature. ... Pythagoras affirmed that the nine Muses were constituted

---

[52] Alexander of Aphrodisias, quoted in W. K. C. Guthrie, *A History of Greek Philosophy*, Vol. 1: *The Earlier Presocratics and the Pythagoreans* (Cambridge: Cambridge University Press), 296.
[53] Plutarch, "Concerning Music," in *Plutarch's Complete Works: Essays and Miscellanies*, Vol. 2 (New York: Thomas Y. Crowell & Co., 1909), 597.
[54] Hippolytus [traditionally misattributed to Origen], *Κατα ποσων αιρεσεων ελεγχοσ* (ca. 225 CE); trans.: *Philosophumena: Refutatio Omnium Haeresium*, and *The Refutation of all Heresies*, trans. J. Macmahon, ed. by Alexander Roberts and James Donaldson (Edinburgh: T&T Clark, 1867), I, 2, 2.

by the sounds made by the seven planets, the sphere of the fixed stars, and that which is opposed to our earth, called "counter-Earth."[55]

In this passage, it is interesting to see that instead of there being *eight* sirens that sang eight musical tones, as in Plato's account, or *seven* tones as in the accounts of Cicero and Pliny, according to Porphyry there were *nine* sounds of nine heavenly bodies (Moon, Sun, five planets, sphere of stars, plus the counter-Earth), which were the cause of there being nine Muses.

Summing up, we can see that by tracing the chronology of statements, it seems that by the time of Aristotle some followers of Pythagoras believed that the motions of the planets and stars emitted harmonious sounds, and that by the time of Pliny some people thought that Pythagoras himself had developed such beliefs. But that was more than five hundred years after Pythagoras had died. Importantly, the earliest passages do not specify whether Pythagoras himself in any way studied harmonies, astronomy, or numbers. Yet later writers freely attributed any reported achievements of the Pythagoreans, true, exaggerated, or imaginary, to Pythagoras himself.

What did Pythagoras really do in Astronomy?

An early association of Pythagoras with some notion of geometry or cosmology appears briefly in an ancient verse by the poet Hermesianax of Colophon, who thrived around 300 BCE. At around 100 CE, Athenaeus quoted a section of a long poem in which Hermesianax listed historical and mythical instances showing the power of love. He wrote about, for example, how Homer suffered for his love of Penelope, how Philoxenus pursued Galatea, how Socrates escaped a plague but surrendered to Aspasia, and likewise, how Pythagoras was strung up by his wife Theano:

> rage, but the fearful reins of the charioteer
> such as Theano truly used to bind
> Pythagoras, winding refined geometry

---

[55] Porphyry, "Life of Pythagoras" (ca. 300 CE), secs. 30-31.

> found, and encompassed a circle as great as the aether,
> walked onto every side of the globe undone...[56]

Common expectations that Pythagoras was a pioneering geometer and astronomer have led some writers to interpret this passage in ways that enable them to confirm their assumptions. But the passage is just too brief and vague: Hermesianax was not a geometer or astronomer, so his vague, poetic words lack substance. In countless contexts, many people wrote about circles and the aether, the heavens, without necessarily meaning anything about mathematical or physical astronomy. Likewise, the single instance of the word geometry does not entail that it echoed anything definite in the actual history of mathematics, as opposed to anything analogous to mystical numerology, cosmogony, geography, or poetic notions of space.

Next, Pliny the Elder made several comments about Pythagoras in connection with astronomy. He wrote that "the penetrating genius of Pythagoras" had inferred that the distance from the Sun to the Zodiac stars is merely three times the distance between the Earth and the Moon.[57] If Pythagoras ever made such a claim, it was grossly incompatible with the allegedly Pythagorean claim that the Earth moves, because its motion would then cause apparent changes in the distances between the stars.

Furthermore, Pythagoras had allegedly discovered that the evening and morning stars near the Sun are the same: Venus.[58] Pliny claimed that Pythagoras made this discovery at around the 42nd Olympiad, which was impossible because that Olympiad began on 612 BCE, and Pythagoras was not even born until decades later. Nevertheless, thanks to Pliny's accounts, whatever his dubious sources, Pythagoras gained a reputation as an ancient astronomer, in addition to being a mystic sage. Eager to synthesize information from many sources, Pliny unscrupulously assigned to Pythagoras discoveries that were not clearly his.

Next, did Pythagoras invent the famous astronomical system of epicycles and eccentrics? Every night the stars and planets cross the sky in a seemingly circular path, westwards. But the planets lag slightly eastwards,

---

[56] Hermesianax, quoted in Athenaeus, *The Deipnosophists*, trans. Charles Burton Gulick (Cambridge: Harvard University Press, 1927), sec. 599a, p. 227, trans. Martínez.

[57] Ibid., Book 2, Section XIX. According to Pliny's Pythagoras, the Moon was 15,750 miles away from the Earth; the actual distance is more than 233,000 miles from the surface of the Earth to that of the Moon.

[58] Ibid., Book 2, Section VI.

week after week, and when we track the positions of a planet such as Mars against the background of stars, we find that sometimes, instead of moving uniformly eastwards in a circular path, Mars seems to slow down and pause, then go back. It loops backward and then again it continues eastwards. For example, every 780 days, Mars, as viewed from Earth, begins a retrograde loop that lasts almost 12 weeks. This is called retrograde motion, and the ancient astronomers wanted to explain it.

In the third century BCE, Apollonius of Perga argued that by analyzing the motion of a heavenly body, the Moon, for example—in terms not just of its main orbital circle around the Earth, but also another circle, an epicycle, moving on the orbit and carrying the Moon—one could better explain its path as actually observed. Subsequently, Hipparchus developed the system of epicycles and circles not centered on Earth, known as eccentrics. But regarding retrograde motions, apparently it was disturbing to think that heavenly things start and stop. In the first century BCE, the Greek writer Geminos commented:

> The Pythagoreans, who first approached such investigations, hypothesized that the movements of the Sun, Moon, and the 5 wandering stars are circular and uniform. For they did not accept, in things divine and eternal, such disorder as moving sometimes more quickly, sometimes more slowly, and sometimes standing still. . . . One would not accept such an anomaly of movement in the goings of an orderly and well-mannered man. This business of life is often the cause of slowness or of swiftness for men. But in the case of the incorruptible nature of the stars, it is not possible to adduce any cause of swiftness or slowness. For this reason, they put forward the question: how would the phenomena be accounted for by means of uniform and circular motions?[59]

Again, we encounter a claim about priority, that the Pythagoreans were the first to analyze the motions of the planets. But again, there is no prior evidence for such a claim; instead, numerous persons before them tried to analyze heavenly motions in terms of circles. In any case, astronomers such as Hipparchus and Ptolemy described the motions of the planets in terms

---

[59] Geminos, *Eisagōgē eis ta Phainomena* (ca. 1st c. BCE); James Evans and J. Lennart Berggren, *Geminos's Introduction to the Phenomena: A Translation and Study of a Hellenistic Survey of Astronomy* (Princeton: Princeton University Press, 2006), 117-119.

of epicycles. Ptolemy argued that a planet such as Mars is carried along not in one circular motion alone but by two. Imagine that there is a great sphere that rotates around the Earth, and it traces a path as large as the orbit of Mars. And on this sphere there is a wheel, centered on a point on the sphere's surface, and Mars is attached to this wheel, as the wheel spins slowly around its center. Thus Mars traces a small loop on the sky as it moves, carried by the sphere and wheel (epicycle).

But later, such analyses became misattributed to the Pythagoreans. At around 300 CE, the Assyrian philosopher Iamblichus claimed that Pythagoras had discovered the system of epicycles and eccentrics.[60] The historian Walter Burkert rightly remarked: "tradition boldly asserted that Pythagoras himself was the inventor of epicycles, or eccenters—one of the most horrendous examples of anachronism in the construction [misattribution] of a science for Pythagoras."[61]

Furthermore, throughout the centuries, writers increasingly attributed other great discoveries in astronomy to him. By 460 CE, the pagan theologian Proclus claimed that Pythagoras discovered "the structure of the cosmic figures," the five regular solids.[62] By 1615 Galileo mistakenly believed that Pythagoras knew that the Earth moves and the Sun does not.[63] In the 1690s Isaac Newton speculated that Pythagoras had secretly known the inverse square law of gravity.[64] By the 1830s, some reference works in English noted that Pythagoras said that planets orbit the Sun in elliptical paths.[65]

[60] Iamblichi, *De Vita Pythagorica* (ca. 300 CE), reissued as Iamblichus, *On the Pythagorean Way of Life*, ed. and trans. John Dillon and Jackson Hershbell (Atlanta: Scholars Press, 1991), chap. 6, pp. 55–57.

[61] Burkert, *Lore and Science in Ancient Pythagoreanism*, 325. While Zhmud believes and cultivates some of the stories about Pythagoras in mathematics and harmonics, he too admits that "an individual contribution to astronomy by Pythagoras or specific early Pythagoreans cannot be identified." Zhmud, *Pythagoras and the Early Pythagoreans*, 337.

[62] Proclus, *A Commentary on the First Book of Euclid's Elements* (ca. 460 CE), trans. Glenn R. Morrow (Princeton: Princeton University Press, 1970), 53.

[63] Galileo's Letter to the Grand Duchess Christina (1615), in Finocchiaro, *The Galileo Affair*, 97.

[64] Newton manuscript, early 1690s, quoted in J. McGuire and P. Rattansi, "Newton and the 'Pipes of Pan,'" *Notes and Records of the Royal Society of London*, 21 (1966), 108-143; see 116-117.

[65] *A Compendious Classical Dictionary*, in *The Treasury of Knowledge and Library Reference*, Fifth ed., Part III (New York: Conner & Cooke, 1834), 185. Also in *Harper's Book of Facts: A Classified History of the World, embracing Science, Literature and Art*, comp. Joseph H. Willsey, ed. Charlton Thomas Lewis (New York: Harper & Brothers, 1895), 742.

But again, the oldest sources do not refer to Pythagoras as a mathematician or astronomer at all. Various ancient writers mentioned him, including Heraclitus of Ephesus, Plato, Herodotus, Heraclides, and Isocrates. The sum of their various brief comments gives the impression that Pythagoras was a wise man, a popular religious leader who argued that the human soul is born repeatedly, even in animal bodies. Apparently he taught his followers to live in a disciplined way, including some dietary restrictions, such as not eating beans or animals, at least of certain kinds. In antiquity, the teachings of Pythagoras, whatever they were, became far more famous in religion than in any sciences. And religion structured society in ways that the sciences did not. Once the Roman Empire became Christian, the Pythagorean beliefs became construed as increasingly offensive, even dangerous. Myths made Pythagoras famous in the sciences, while legends made him infamous in Christianity.

2

Pythagoras or Christ?

There's nearly no evidence that Pythagoras contributed to mathematics or astronomy. Similarly, it's difficult to know with certainty anything about his religious beliefs. Historians make various conjectures, depending on which later sources they construe as echoing lost sources. But presently, such conjectures are inessential, because our focus is the evolving *legends* about Pythagoras. What matters is how pagan notions evolved and how Christians opposed them, including eventually the Roman Inquisition in the times of Giordano Bruno and Galileo. But first we must consider the Roman Empire, when paranoid Christians destroyed Pythagorean works.

Pythagorean religious beliefs evolved in complex ways. To start, our story might be simpler if we focus on one belief, such as the transmigration of souls. That belief appeared repeatedly in Bruno's trial. But other Pythagorean beliefs were also important: that the soul comes from the soul of the world, or the Sun, and that human souls are imprisoned in bodies, and upon death souls travel to other worlds, including the Moon or the planets; there are many gods, the universe was not created, the Earth is alive, therefore it moves, and hell is a prison at the center of the universe. Such beliefs affected the trials of Bruno and Galileo.

But first we need to discuss the early history of such beliefs, irrespective of later developments in the Renaissance. Too often discussions about Pythagorean notions have been distorted by interpreting the distant past in terms of recent notions. So let's proceed chronologically. But curiosity usually goes in the opposite direction: to rush to the end of the story. So I fear that readers strongly interested in the Copernicans might skip this important chapter about ancient pagan notions. I too began by studying puzzles about Galileo. It was an interesting process that led me to focus on so-called Pythagorean doctrines. And only after investigating them for years, in works from antiquity and the Renaissance, did I finally find them in Bruno's works and trials. Galileo led me to Pythagoras, which led to the so-called Pythagoreans, which eventually led me to Bruno, which led me back to Galileo. How does a chronological ordering match the winding and surprising process of research? I don't know, but as I started understanding how the stories about Pythagoras and his admirers actually developed, I became fascinated by how thin simple claims grew dramatically over time. We will connect ancient notions to events in the Copernican Revolution, but I now understand what classicists knew all along: that the stories about antiquity are fascinating and important in themselves, irrespective of how they were later interpreted.

In the 1590s and early 1600s, various officials of the Catholic Church became hostile to Pythagorean beliefs, just as they rejected Protestantism. In that period, cardinals and consultors of the Inquisition as well as some members of the Congregation of the Index of Forbidden Books examined and denounced various Pythagorean ideas. Such developments echoed an earlier conflict in which early Church Fathers, from roughly 150 CE to 430 CE, denounced Pythagorean notions as false or heretical.

To understand the developments in the Renaissance, it's necessary to first reconstruct and analyze the conflicts in early Christianity. Because, the ancient theologians, such as Hippolytus, Chrysostom, Jerome, and Augustine, formulated the core texts and judgments that were echoed much later by Catholic theologians. Moreover, for those of us who are most interested in the conflicts between such later theologians against Bruno and Galileo, bear in mind that the ancient notions that I will now reconstruct were not obsolete or forgotten. To the contrary, these were the classical texts that were read and discussed by educated men such as Copernicus, Bruno, and the Jesuits. The ancient theology is *directly relevant* to the later conflicts.

One of the earliest claims about Pythagorean beliefs about human souls is not found in a discussion about Pythagoras himself. As is often the case, it's found instead in a discussion about his self-denominated admirers. What we now have are mostly not accounts by the Pythagoreans themselves but by their highly influential critics.

In his book *On the Soul*, Aristotle briefly criticized religious beliefs of some Pythagoreans. He noted that some of them claimed that the soul consists of motes in the air, while others claimed that it consists of whatever moves such motes. He explained: "These motes were referred because they are seen always in movement, even in a complete calm."[66] Aristotle complained about "Pythagorean myths, that any soul could be clothed upon with any body—an absurd view, for each body seems to have a form and shape of its own. It is absurd as to say that the art of carpentry could embody itself in flutes; each art must use its tools, each soul its body."[67]

Aristotle's remarks are significant because they explicitly criticize the idea of transmigration that Diogenes later quoted. When Christian writers eventually appropriated the views of Aristotle, they readily agreed with his rejection of Pythagorean notions of soul. Also, Artistotle's claims about motes of air that always move are the earliest evidence I know about a so-called Pythagorean idea: that seemingly inanimate matter is alive and has a soul. It's a beautiful idea; remember it the next time you see particles of dust floating in a sunbeam. This view, as we will see, was later echoed in notions that the Earth has a breath of life, or more generally, the notion that the entire world has a soul.

Meanwhile, by the 3rd century BCE several forgers composed fake memoirs attributed to Pythagoras and his followers. Among such texts are "The Golden Verses" (ca. 325? BCE), allegedly by Pythagoras himself, and "Lysis's Letter to Hipparchus" (ca. 225? BCE). At the same time, his followers or admirers continued to interpret and modify the "Pythagorean" religion. For example, in 56 BCE the Roman statesman Cicero criticized another politician, Vatinius, for unjustly calling himself a Pythagorean while carrying out awful sacrifices: using the entrails of murdered boys "to evoke the spirits of the shades below, and to appease the spirits of the dead."[68]

At around 44 BCE Cicero mentioned Pythagoras in his book *On Divination*, mostly referring to him as a religious leader, commenting about him as a prognosticator: that Pythagoras "added a great weight of authority to

[66] Aristotle, *On the Soul* (ca. 350?), in W. D. Ross, ed., *The Works of Aristotle*, Vol. 3, trans. J. A. Smith (Oxford: Clarendon Press, 1928), bk. 1, pp. 3 verso.
[67] Ibid., bk. 1, p. 8 reverso.
[68] Marcus Tullius Cicero, *In Vatinium Testem* (56 BCE), in *The Speech of M. T. Cicero against Publius Vatinius: Called Also, the Examination of Publius Vatinius*, ed. C. D. Yonge (London: George Bell & Sons, 1891), sec. 14.

this belief—and indeed he himself wished to acquire the skill of an augur."[69] In his book, *On the Nature of the Gods*, Cicero made additional remarks about Pythagoras. Cicero said that Pythagoras "supposed that [God] is a soul that interpenetrated and pervaded all natural things, of which our souls are fragments." This particular claim will be very significant in our project to understand the connections between the Pythagoreans and the Copernicans, as we will see, because some of the advocates of Copernicus spoke about "the soul of the world." Yet Cicero himself disagreed with the claim that God is a soul that infuses everything. He argued that if Pythagoras were right, then God must be maimed or lacerated when each human soul is torn from Him. When human souls are ill then God too would be ill, which Cicero said is impossible. "How can the human soul ignore anything, if it is God? How can this be God, if it is nothing but soul, either implanted or infused in the world?"[70]

At around 50 BCE, Diodorus of Sicily also wrote about Pythagoras. He echoed claims that Pythagoras did not eat meat and that he believed in the transmigration of souls.[71] Diodorus also claimed that the Gauls believed in the Pythagorean doctrine of immortality and rebirth in other bodies.[72] Subsequently, other writers claimed that "foolish barbarians" shared the faith of Pythagoras, such that "it is said that they lend each other sums that are repayable in the next world."[73]

We should ask whether the early Pythagoreans really believed in immortality. Belief in the immortality of the soul was not uncommon among the ancient Greeks and Romans. In his dialogue *Phaedrus*, Plato had argued that whatever is eternal moves itself, and that the soul is self-moving, therefore it too is eternal. This is will be important in the trial of Bruno: since nothing seems to push the Earth, yet it moves, then Bruno inferred that it has a soul, and the world is an eternal being.

---

[69] Marcus Tullius Cicero, *On Divination* (ca. 44 BCE), translated by C. D. Yonge (1853), Book 1, Section 3.

[70] M. Tullii Ciceronis, *De Natura Deorum Libri Tres*, Vol. 1 (Cambridge: Cambridge University Press, 1880), bk. 1, pp. 10-11, trans. Martínez.

[71] Diodorus Siculus, *The Historical Library of Diodorus the Sicilian, in Fifteen Books,* trans. G. Booth (London: J. Davis, 1814), vol. 1, book 1, p. 97.

[72] Diodorus Siculus, *Histories*, V (ca. 50 BCE), 28, 6.

[73] Valerius Maximus, II, 6, 10 (early 1st c. CE). See also Clement of Alexandria, *Stromata*, I, xv, 70, 1 and 71, 3.

In the "Dream of Scipio," ca. 51 BCE, Cicero discussed immortality in a very similar way as Plato: Cicero echoed the same argument about the soul being self-moving and therefore eternal.[74] However, the earliest accounts about the Pythagoreans do not specify that they believed in immortality. Although Herodotus said that the Thracians believed in immortality, he doubted that their deity, Salmoxis, had really lived *after* Pythagoras, and therefore he doubted that Pythagoras was really his master. So any inference about the story of Salmoxis, as a means to ascribe beliefs in immortality to Pythagoras or his earliest followers, seems uncertain. Moreover, if we believe in the fragment that Diogenes quoted about what Heraclides of Pontus (ca. 360? BCE) said about Pythagoras, then it seems that Pythagoras did not believe in immortality because supposedly the god Hermes told Pythagoras that "he might choose any gift he liked *except* immortality."

Nevertheless, at the time when Cicero wrote, it seems that a few other writers thought that the Pythagoreans (perhaps of that time?) believed in the immortality of the soul. Diodorus and apparently Aetius mentioned that some Pythagoreans believed in immortality.[75] Subsequently, as we will see, the belief in immortality became a point of contention between late Pythagoreans and early Christians. While both developed some notions of immortality, the Christians complained that the Pythagoreans had distorted or misunderstood the true religious knowledge.

Just as the notion of immortality (not just rebirth) later became attributed to the Pythagoreans, other Greek religious notions became attributed to them. In particular, some later Pythagoreans, or at least some persons who wrote about them, came to believe that souls have the ability to communicate with dead people in dreams. And they allegedly believed that such dreams might give foresight about the future. These ideas became common among the beliefs attributed to the Pythagoreans, but we should note that just because they appeared in the "Dream of Scipio" they were not necessarily allusions to the Pythagoreans. Again, in that work, Cicero did not mention either Pythagoras or his followers.

The poet Ovid also attributed belief in immortality to Pythagoras, writing half a millennium after his death. Pythagoras was a principal character

---

[74] Cicero, "Dream of Scipio," pp. 41-43.
[75] Diodorus Siculus, *The Historical Library of Diodorus the Sicilian, in Fifteen Books,* trans. G. Booth (London: J. Davis, 1814), vol. 5, book 28(?). [Aetius?], *Placita Philosophorum,* bk. 1, chap. 3; bk. 4, chaps. 4 and 7.

in Ovid's poem, *Metamorphoses*, circa 8 CE. Strangely, Ovid did not refer to Pythagoras by name, but his identity is clear from his many statements from the start. Ovid's fictional account is extremely important because in the Renaissance it became very influential in portraying the Pythagorean religious beliefs. This will be especially significant when we analyze the works of Bruno, and his depositions to the Roman Inquisition. For those reasons, we have to quote Ovid at length. Speaking about the Italian city of Croton, Ovid discussed the life of an unusual man:

There was a man here, a Samian by birth, but he had fled forth from Samos and its rulers, and through hatred of tyranny was living in voluntary exile. He, though the gods were far away in the heavenly regions, still approached them with his thought, and what Nature denied to his mortal vision he feasted on with his mind's eye. And when he had surveyed all things by reason and wakeful diligence, he would give out to the public ear the things worthy of their learning and would teach the crowds, which listened in wondering silence to his words, the beginnings of the great universe, the causes of things and what nature is: what God is, whence come the snows, what is the origin of lightning, whether it is Jupiter or the winds that thunder from the riven clouds, what causes the earth to quake, by what law the stars perform their courses, and whatever else is hidden from men's knowledge. He was the first to decry the placing of animal food upon our tables. His lips, learned indeed but not believed in this, he was the first to open in such words as these:

"O mortals, do not pollute your bodies with a food so impious! You have the fruits of the earth, you have apples, bending down the branches with their weight, and grapes swelling to ripeness on the vines; you have delicious herbs and vegetables . . . . Oh how criminal it is for flesh to be stored away in flesh, for one greedy body to grow fat with food gained from another, for one live creature to go on living through the destruction of another living thing! . . . .

"Further impiety grew out of that, and it is thought that the sow was first condemned to death as a sacrificial victim . . . . Nor is it enough that we commit such infamy: they made the gods themselves partners of their crime and they affected to believe that the heavenly ones enjoyed the blood of the toiling ox.

"Now, since a god inspires my lips, I will dutifully follow the inspiring god; I'll open Delphi and the heavens and unlock the oracles of the sublime mind. Great matters, never traced out by the minds of former men, things that have long been hidden, I will sing. It is a delight to take one's way along the starry firmament and, leaving the Earth and its dull regions behind, to ride on the clouds, to take stand on stout Atlas' shoulders and see far below men wandering aimlessly, devoid of reason, anxious and in fear of the hereafter, thus to exhort them and unroll the book fate!

"O race of men, stunned with chilling fear of death, why do you dread the Styx, the shades and empty names, the stuff that poets manufacture, and their fabled sufferings of a world that never was? As for your bodies, whether the burning pyre or long lapse of time with its wasting power shall have consumed them, be sure they cannot suffer any ills. Our souls are deathless, and ever, when they have left their former seat, do they live in new abodes and dwell in the bodies that have received them. I myself (for I well remember it) at the time of the Trojan War was Euphorbus, son of Panthoüs, in whose breast once hung the heavy spear of Menelaüs. Recently, in Juno's temple in Argos, Abas' city, I recognized the shield that I once wore on my left arm! All things are changing; nothing dies. The spirit wanders, comes now here, now there, and occupies whatever frame it pleases. From beasts it passes into human bodies, and from our bodies into beasts, but never perishes. And, as the pliant wax is stamped with new designs, does not remain as it was before nor keep the same form long, but is still the selfsame wax, so do I teach that the soul is ever the same, though it passes into ever-changing bodies. Therefore, lest your piety be overcome by appetite, I warn you as a seer, do not drive out by impious slaughter what may be kindred souls, and let not life be fed on life.

"And since I embarked on the boundless sea and have spread my full sails to the winds, there is nothing in all the world that keeps its form. All things are in a state of flux, and everything is brought into being with a changing nature. Time itself flows on in constant motion, just like a river. For neither the river nor the swift hour can stop its course; but, as wave is pushed on by wave, and as each wave as it comes is both pressed on and itself presses the wave in front, so time both flees and follows and is ever new. For that which once existed is no more, and that which was not has come to be; and so the whole round of motion is gone through again.[76]

---

[76] Ovid, *Metamorphoses* (ca. 8 CE), with an English trans. Frank Justus Miller, Vol. 2 (London: William Heinemann, 1916), bk. 15, pp. 369-377.

Many centuries later, as we will see, two of the major themes in this passage emerged prominently in the protracted trial of Giordano Bruno: the transmigration of souls and the nature of change.

Ovid's Pythagoras spoke of the importance of not eating meat, and also about the "the moving soul," as he said, in another translation: "It may pass from beasts to human bodies, and again to those beasts. The soul will never die, in the long lapse of time."[77] Ovid portrayed Pythagoras as a master of transmutations, one who claimed that nothing in the world remains unchanged; he spoke of a stream of water that turned the drinker's entrails to stone, other streams that "will turn the hair to something like clear amber or bright gold," rotting horses generating hornets, dead humans' spine marrow mutating into snakes, and mud giving birth to green frogs.[78] He said that even the elements can change. Yet Ovid's poem was grossly ahistorical, as the character of Pythagoras described events that did not happen until centuries after his death.

Likewise, at around 77 CE, in his *Natural History*, Pliny the Elder claimed that Pythagoras studied magic.[79] This topic too will be relevant for our discussion of developments during the Renaissance, since magic and divination became concerns of the Inquisition. Pliny claimed that Pythagoras had written an entire book on the medicinal and magical properties of bulbs and herbs, knowledge gained from Apollo, the god. Pliny noted that some writers attributed that book instead to the physician Cleemporus. Pliny commented that an author should be glad to assign his worthy labor to the great Pythagoras, to enhance the book's authority.[80] According to Pliny, Pythagoras said that epileptic seizures cannot happen to one who holds anise in hand, and that squills hung on a doorway would keep out evil spirits.[81]

Writers portrayed Pythagoras as a man of great learning, but some ridiculed him. Even centuries later, Bruno and Kepler praised Pythagoras as a heroic and inspirational figure, while others portrayed him as a fraud, an

---

[77] Ovid, *Metamorphoses*, ed. Brookes More (Boston: Cornhill Publishing Co., 1922), bk. 15.

[78] Ibid.

[79] Pliny the elder, *Natural History* (ca. 77-79 CE), translated by H. Rackham (Cambridge: Harvard University Press, 1949-54), Books 24, 25, 30, Sections 99, 5, 2, respectively.

[80] Ibid., Book 19, Section 30.

[81] Ibid., Books 20, Sections 33, 73, 87, respectively.

anti-Christian deceiver. Such Christian critics built upon an ancient tradition that ridiculed Pythagoras as a pretentious imposter. For example, a
character in one of Plutarch's dialogues said that Socrates, "received philosophy from Pythagoras and Empedocles, full of dreams, fables, supersti-
tions and perfect raving," before Socrates tried to improve wisdom.[82] And
another character in the same dialogue replied: "Was it a mere juggle? Indeed, nothing that is told of Pythagoras regarding divination seems to me
so great and divine." Elsewhere, Plutarch also claimed that Pythagoras engaged in false divination and controlled his disciples' curiosity by restricting
them from speaking for five years, whereas, "they say, Pythagoras one time
ranted a friend of his so terribly before company, that the poor young man
went and hanged himself."[83] Nonetheless, in other writings Plutarch also
described Pythagoras in a less negative light, saying that Pythagoras taught
that souls are reborn, and that he discovered something in geometry.

Incidentally, Plutarch himself believed in the soul's immortality and in
transmigration. For instance, when Plutarch's daughter died at age two, he
wrote a letter to his wife, reassuring her: "since the soul cannot be destroyed, you can compare what happens to it to the behavior of a caged
bird: if it has made a physical body for its home for an extended period of
time, and has allowed a plethora of material events and a long familiarity to
domesticate it to this way of life, then it resumes its perch inside a body and
doesn't let go or stop its involvement, through rebirth after rebirth, with
worldly conditions and fortunes."[84]

Like Pythagoras, Plutarch also gained fame for works that he did not
write. At some point, the *Placita Philosophorum* became misattributed to Plutarch. This book summarized the views of famous philosophers. It became
very influential. In particular, it conveyed to Copernicus and others the alleged views of Pythagoras and his followers.

The *Placita* claimed that Pythagoras believed that the number four com-
poses the human soul, that the soul is immortal and is a number moving

[82] Plutarch, "A Discourse Concerning Socrates's Daemon," in *Plutarch's Miscellanies and
Essays. Comprising All His Works Under the Title of "Morals,"* revised by William W.
Goodwin, vol. 2, Sixth ed. (Boston: Little, Brown, and Company, 1898), sec. 9, p. 388.
[83] Plutarch, "How to Know a Flatterer from a Friend. To Antiochus Philopappus," in
Plutarch's Miscellanies and Essays, vol. 2, sec. 32, p. 148.
[84] Plutarch, "In Consolation to His Wife," in Plutarch, *Essays*, trans. Robin Waterfield
(London: Penguin, 1992), 373.

itself, and that when bodies die, souls join the soul of the world.[85] Also, in this work, Aristotle's claim about "the so-called Pythagoreans" became attributed to Pythagoras himself: that numbers are the principles of all things. Supposedly Pythagoras taught that unity is God, while the dyad or binary number is an evil daemon, and that daemons are essences endowed with souls.[86] Allegedly Pythagoras also taught that matter is convertible into all things, and that the world was formed of the five regular solid figures.[87] Oddly, the *Placita* also tried to prove that Pythagoras was really from Tuscany.[88]

The *Placita* also notes individuals who believed that the Earth moves, including Philolaus the Pythagorean, Heraclides of Pontus, and Ecphantus the Pythagorean.[89] It also says that Hicetas the Pythagorean believed that there exist two Earths.[90] Consequently, these ancient authorities were cited by Copernicus, Kepler, and Galileo when trying to give credibility to the idea of the Earth's motion.

Meanwhile, the mystical or religious reputation of Pythagoras grew even more thanks to one of his admirers, the Greek philosopher Apollonius (ca. 15-100 CE) from the town of Tyana, in the Roman province Cappadocia in Asia Minor. Little is known about him for certain, but he wrote a biography of Pythagoras, which is now lost. Reportedly, Apollonius there said that Pythagoras was the son of the god Apollo.[91] Likewise, in an ancient letter attributed to Apollonius, he claimed: "The most wise Pythagoras belonged to the class of daemones."[92] According to the Pythagoreans, *daemons* (or *daimones*) were beings intermediate between gods and men.[93] Also, an extant fragment by Apollonius, "On Sacrifices," shows some of his

---

85 [Aetius?], *Placita Philosophorum*, bk. 1, chap. 3; bk. 4, chaps. 4 and 7.
86 Ibid., bk. 1, chap. 7.
87 Ibid., bk. 1, chaps. 9 and 24; bk. 2, chap. 6.
88 Ibid., bk. 8, questions 7 and 8.
89 Ibid., bk. 3, chap. 13.
90 Ibid., bk. 3, chap. 9.
91 Apollonius, quoted in Porphyry, *Life of Pythagoras* (ca. 300? CE), in *The Pythagorean Sourcebook and Library,* trans. Kenneth Sylvan Guthrie (New York: Platonist Press, 1919), rev. ed. David R. Fideler (Grand Rapids: Phanes Press, 1987), sec. 2.
92 Apollonius to Euphrates (n.d.), in Robert J. Penella, ed., *The Letters of Apollonius of Tyana: A Critical Text with Prolegomena* (Leiden: E. J. Brill, 1974), letter 50, p. 61.
93 Marcel Detienne, *La Notion de Daimon dans le Pythagorisme Ancien* (Paris: Belles Lettres, 1963), 93-94, 132-36.

religious claims, in contradistinction with Christianity: that God cannot be influenced by prayers or sacrifices, and has no wish to be worshipped.

But before considering Apollonius himself, we should note that the legends about Pythagoras continued to grow in literature. The Assyrian writer, Lucian of Samosata (ca. 120-200 CE), wrote numerous treatises, dialogues, and satires, and in some of them he wrote about Pythagoras. In one satire, Pythagoras appeared as a wise rooster that spoke and remembered its many past lives. The rooster said that his soul first flew from the god Apollo down to the Earth. There, he lived first as Euphorbus, a soldier who fought and died in the Trojan war, then as a soul without a body for some time, then he was reborn as Pythagoras, "a great charlatan and a conjurer," who had a golden thigh that proved that he was divine; he traveled to Egypt to study, and later the Greeks in Italy admired him as a god. The rooster admitted that as Pythagoras he had invented arbitrary laws about being silent for five years and against eating meat and beans, to impress and deceive people. Later, he was reborn as Aspasia, the mistress of Pericles; next he became Crates, a cynic philosopher; and thereafter, "a King; then a beggar; then again a Persian satrap [a governor or official]; afterwards a horse, a jay, a frog, and a thousand other things," but that most frequently his soul had inhabited the body of a rooster, a servant of the god Mercury.[94]

In another dialogue by Lucian, Pythagoras was a wise philosopher, again a demigod with a golden thigh, who was sold by Mercury for his wisdom and apparent talents as an oracle.[95] In yet another story, Pythagoras spent time with the dead, lost his golden thigh, and learned to eat beans.[96] In one essay, Lucian described Pythagoras after seven transmigrations by noting that then "the entire right half of him was gold."[97] In another story a Pythagorean named Arignotus argued for the existence of supernatural things, describing in detail how he used Egyptian works and spells to exorcise a demon (which transformed into a dog or bull) from a haunted house, and later unearthed its bones. This Pythagorean exorcist said that if

---

[94] Lucian of Samosata, "The Dream of Micyllus, or the Cock" (ca. 170? CE), in William Tooke, ed., *Lucian of Samosata, from the Greek*, Vol. 1 (London: Longman, Hurst, Rees, Orme, and Brown, 1820), pp. 63-64, 73-77.

[95] Lucian, "The Sale of the Philosophical Sects" (ca. 170? CE), in Tooke, *Lucian*, Vol. 1, pp. 216-219.

[96] Lucian, "Conferences of the Dead" (ca. 170? CE), in Tooke, *Lucian*, pt. XX, p. 423.

[97] Lucian, "The True History" in *The Works of Lucian of Samosata*, trans. H. W. Fowler and F. G. Fowler, Vol. 2 (Oxford: Oxford University Press, 1905), bk. II.

someone suffers a violent death, being beheaded or crucified, then that person's spirit can walk the Earth.[98]

Lucian's allusions to exorcism and crucifixion are telling, we are approaching the juncture at which Pythagorean and Christian religions clashed, and each tried to appropriate appealing parts of one another. One of the abilities of Jesus Christ that most distinguished him from other reputed holy men was his ability to perform exorcisms. Exorcism is entirely absent in the early religious stories about Pythagoras, but it became a recurring element in stories about the Pythagoreans during the early Christian era. We will discuss how Christian notions became increasingly mixed with so-called Pythagorean beliefs. This will explain why Catholic clergymen became increasingly annoyed by the Pythagoreans.

Thus far I have traced the ancient origins of various beliefs that were attributed to the Pythagoreans: beliefs about magic (transformations), the soul's immortality and transmigrations, and about the Earth, Moon and the stars. Consider now how the early Christians reacted against these various Pythagorean beliefs. These were the precedents for later conflicts in the Renaissance, when the Protestant Reformation led Catholics to increasingly worry about all kinds of deviations from orthodoxy, even pagan beliefs.

Choosing a Savior in the 2nd Century

Scarcely any texts from the first century of the Common Era say anything about Christianity. Yet there are several extant texts from the following century. For example, one autobiographical account tells us how a young, pagan philosopher chose between Pythagoras, Plato, and Jesus.

Justinus (ca. 100 to 165 CE), later known as Justin the Martyr, was born in Palestine, the son of pagan parents. He received a Greek education, and became very interested in studying philosophy. He first studied with a Stoic philosopher but became disappointed because this teacher did not offer sufficient knowledge of God. Justin left this instructor and then began to

---

[98] Lucian, "The Liar; Philopseudes sive Incredulus," in *Works of Lucian of Samosata*, trans. Fowler, secs. 29-32.

study with a Peripatetic philosopher who, after a few days, asked for payment, and for this reason Justin abandoned him too. It was then that Justin approached a Pythagorean philosopher:

> But when my soul was eagerly desirous to hear the peculiar and choice philosophy, I came to a Pythagorean, very celebrated—a man who thought much of his own wisdom. And then, when I had an interview with him, willing to become his hearer and disciple, he said, "What then? Are you acquainted with music, astronomy, and geometry? Do you expect to perceive any of those things which conduce to a happy life, if you have not been first informed on those points which wean the soul from sensible objects, and render it fitted for objects which appertain to the mind, so that it can contemplate that which is honorable in its essence and that which is good in its essence?" Having commended many of these branches of learning, and telling me that they were necessary, he dismissed me when I confessed to him my ignorance. Accordingly I took it rather impatiently, as was to be expected when I failed in my hope, the more so because I deemed the man had some knowledge; but reflecting again on the space of time during which I would have to linger over those branches of learning, I was not able to endure longer procrastination.[99]

This anecdote illuminates the character of Pythagorean philosophy in the second century. Apparently it promised knowledge about immaterial things and God, what Justin Martyr sought, but as a prerequisite the Pythagorean philosopher required studies of certain sciences: music, astronomy, and geometry. It insinuates a distinctive trait that became a point of contention for the early Christians: the off-putting implication that the Pythagoreans were more educated, a sort of intellectual aristocracy.

Feeling impatient toward such prerequisites, Justin Martyr abandoned the Pythagorean path. Next, he turned to intense studies of Platonism, as it ultimately promised contemplation of God. But one day Justin unexpectedly met a man who challenged his belief in philosophy. They had a conversation in which the man inquired, among other things, what would

---

[99] Justin Martyr, "Dialogue of Justin, Philosopher and Martyr, with Trypho, a Jew," chap. 2, in Alexander Roberts and James Donaldson, eds., *Ante-Nicene Christian Library*, Vol. 2: *Justin Martyr and Athenagoras*, trans. G. Reith (Edinburgh: T. and T. Clark, 1870), 88.

happen to men who failed to contemplate God? To which Justin replied: "They are imprisoned in the bodies of certain wild beasts, and this is their punishment." The man then led Justin to recognize that this was not a fitting punishment because such souls did not know the sins or reasons why they had been reborn as animals: "Then these reap no advantage from their punishment, as it seems: moreover, I would say that they are not punished unless they are conscious of the punishment." Justin agreed, so the man continued: "Therefore souls neither see God nor transmigrate into other bodies; for they would know that so they are punished, and they would be afraid to commit even the most trivial sin afterwards. But that they can perceive that God exists, and that righteousness and piety are honorable, I also quite agree with you."[100] Again, Justin agreed. So the man concluded, convincingly, that such philosophers know nothing because they do not know what souls are, and they mistakenly think that souls are immortal, unbegotten. He explained, instead, that the souls of the pious go to a good place, while the souls of the unjust and wicked must go to a worse place, where they must await judgment and punishment. The man further argued that the opinions of Plato or Pythagoras were irrelevant to the truths about the soul. He explained that instead of learning from philosophers, Justin should trust the ancient prophets, the ones who actually spoke by the Divine Spirit and who foretold future events. He further explained:

For they [the prophets] did not use demonstration in their treatises, seeing that they were witnesses to the truth above all demonstration, and worthy of belief; and those events which have happened, and those which are happening, compel you to assent to the utterances made by them, although, indeed, they were entitled to credit on account of the miracles which they performed, since they both glorified the Creator, the God and Father of all things, and proclaimed His Son, the Christ [sent] by Him: which, indeed, the false prophets, who are filled with the lying unclean spirit, neither have done nor do, but venture to work certain wonderful deeds for the purpose of astonishing men, and glorify the spirits and demons of error.[101]

Immediately after this conversation, Justin Martyr recalled that it kindled in his soul a love for the prophets, the friends of Christ, and hence the Savior

---

[100] Ibid., chap. 4, p. 93.
[101] Ibid., chap. 7, p. 96.

Himself. Thus Justin's account is remarkable because it describes how, in the second century, a son of pagan parents came to reject Greek philosophies in favor of converting to Christianity.

Justin still considered himself a philosopher, but a Christian philosopher. In a separate work, Justin rejected the Greek notion of the immortality of the soul:

> [Since] the Savior in the whole Gospel shows that there is salvation for the flesh, why do we any longer endure those unbelieving and dangerous arguments, and fail to see that we are retrograding when we listen to such an argument as this: that the soul is immortal, but the body mortal, and incapable of being revived? For this we used to hear from Pythagoras and Plato, even before we learned the truth. If then the Savior said this, and proclaimed salvation to the soul alone, what new thing, beyond what we heard from Pythagoras and Plato and all their band, did He bring us? But now He has come proclaiming the glad tidings of a new and strange hope to men. For indeed it was a strange and new thing for God to promise that He would not keep incorruption in incorruption, but would make corruption incorruption. But because the prince of wickedness could in no other way corrupt the truth, he sent forth his apostles (evil men who introduced pestilent doctrines), choosing them from among those who crucified our Savior...[102]

Thus Jesus Christ went beyond the offerings of Pythagoras in that he promised not only life for the soul after death, but life also for the body itself again.

It is very significant, in the passage above, that Justin discussed both Pythagoras and Plato. It's important to realize that although we nowadays imagine them to have been essentially philosophers (what we would call a philosopher), the ancient perceptions about such men were quite different. For centuries now, philosophy has become an independent field of knowledge, reified by journals, buildings and departments in universities, as a sort of intellectual island quite separate from a science department or from a church. But in antiquity, philosophers were often admired as religious figures. The figures of Pythagoras and Plato offered not merely wisdom but

---

[102] Justinus Martyr, "Extant Fragments of the Lost Work of Justin on the Resurrection," chap. 10, trans. M. Dods, in *Ante-Nicene Fathers*, Vol. 1, p. 353.

knowledge about gods and the soul. Hence we shall see that when the Christians scorned the ancient philosophers it was not merely because of conceptual or philosophical views. They rejected Pythagoras and Plato as fake demigods, false saviors.

Another example of Justin's disapproval of the path offered by the philosophers in general, and Pythagoras in particular, appears in a separate work, titled "First Apology" (ca. 147 to 161 CE). In that work, Justin pleaded to the Roman Emperor and his sons on behalf of the Christians. He defended Jesus Christ's promise of the resurrection of the body after death, against the pagan authorities:

> For let even necromancy, and the divinations you practice by immaculate children, and the evoking of departed human souls, and those who are called among the magi, Dream-senders and Assistant-spirits (Familiars), and all that is done by those who are skilled in such matters—let these persuade you that even after death souls are in a state of sensation; and those who are seized and cast about by the spirits of the dead, whom all call dæmoniacs or madmen; and what you repute as oracles, both of Amphilochus, Dodona, Pytho, and as many other such as exist; and the opinions of your authors, Empedocles and Pythagoras, Plato and Socrates, and the pit of Homer, and the descent of Ulysses to inspect these things, and all that has been uttered of a like kind. Such favor as you grant to them, grant also to us, who not less but more firmly than they believe in God; since we expect to receive again our own bodies, though they be dead and cast into the earth, for we maintain that with God nothing is impossible.[103]

Thus Justin associated the name of Pythagoras with awful subjects: necromancy. The allusion to "immaculate children" referred to innocent children and even fetuses removed from the womb who were killed and their entrails inspected to divine the future; the mention of Ulysses refers to an event in the *Odyssey* in which he dug a trench with his sword, poured libations, and collected the souls of the dead.[104]

By the year 150 CE, Justin was preaching in Rome. A decade later, he presented a second Apology to the Emperor, complaining about the

---

[103] Justinus Martyr, "The First Apology of Justin," chap. 18, trans. M Dods, in *Ante-Nicene Christian Library*, Vol. 1, pp. 22-23.
[104] Homer, *Odyssey*, bk. 9, line 25.

arbitrary executions of fellow Christians. A recent Roman law required that nobody could refuse to participate in sacrifices to the gods, or refuse to swear by the name of the Emperor, which was considered a religious act. These requirements were difficult for Christians, so the law served to criminalize them.[105] Justin and many companions were denounced, and by 165 CE Justin was executed, beheaded; hence he became known as Justin the Martyr.

Consider now the example of someone who was unconvinced by the Christians, one who believed that Jesus was merely comparable to Pythagoras, not superior. At around 177 CE, the Greek philosopher Celsus wrote *The True Word*, in which he systematically criticized Jesus Christ by comparison to ancient philosophers and eminent individuals. Celsus had observed the Christian movement with skepticism, and he had read Christian works, including some by Justin Martyr. Celsus realized that Christians had split from Judaism, and that they worshipped God as if He were not subject to the laws of reason and nature. Celsus disbelieved the story of the resurrection of Jesus, which to him seemed to be based only on hearsay: the unverifiable gospels.

In *The True Word*, Celsus included Pythagoras and Plato as admirable learned men, while disregarding Moses. Celsus noted that by contrast to Christianity, Pythagoras and other philosophers argued that human souls are born into new bodies in accord with their actions in previous lives.[106] He argued that just as Jesus allegedly had been resurrected, so too the slave of Pythagoras, Salmoxis, had deceived people with a comparable story (according to Herodotus), and Celsus mentioned that Pythagoras himself had done this too (as claimed by Hermippus, as shown below).[107] If the miracles of Jesus were true, then he had done them by magic, and Celsus argued that one might well practice magic or sorcery rather than Christianity, and believe in an unlimited number of daemons rather than just one God. Celsus

---

[105] Edward Burton, *History of the Christian Church, from the Ascension of Jesus Christ, to the Conversion of Constantine* (New York: Wiley & Putnam, 1839), p. 213.

[106] Celsus's *The True Word* is not extant, but some of its contents are described in Origen's *Contra Celsum*, discussed below.

[107] Celsus, *True Word*, quoted in Origen, *Contra Celsum*, bk. 2, sec. 55, p. 109.

said: "Christians get the power which they seem to possess by pronouncing the names of certain daemons and incantations."[108]

Celsus had written a book in which he criticized magicians and discussed many kinds of fraud. Owing to his interest in magic and deception, Celsus apparently wrote to Lucian of Samosata, inquiring about a man who was notorious for contriving false miracles. Lucian's reply is a detailed narrative about the life of that false prophet, or "oracle-monger," Alexander of Abonoteichos, who became a bitter enemy of the Christians.

Alexander reportedly compared himself to Pythagoras, and he was the apprentice of a disciple of Apollonius of Tyana.[109] Lucian said that Alexander's mentor was a charlatan, addicted to deception, magic and the conjuration of spirits. Likewise, Alexander became a lewd and terrible impostor; he faked miracles about predictions and the public birth of the god Æsculapius (son of Apollo), who healed the sick, and "resuscitated some that were perfectly dead."[110] Alexander became wealthy and had many followers, and when skeptics rose against him he asked the populace to stone those atheists and Christians. He built a temple to his new god, and on its inaugural day, he expelled the Christians from it.

In some of his ceremonies, Alexander contrived, as if by accident, to let his clothing partly expose his leg, so that people could see that his thigh was golden (that is, deceptively covered by a shiny and very thin gilded leather).[111] This trick led people to debate whether Alexander actually embodied the soul of Pythagoras. They asked Alexander, and received a reply in the form of an oracle: that although the soul of Pythagoras often grows and ends, the soul of the prophet (Alexander) came from Jupiter and never ends. Furthermore, Alexander and his newborn god, an impersonator, taught the transmigration of souls after death, into the bodies of humans and animals.[112]

Against the pagan religions and philosophies, Christian apologists began to formulate systematic attacks. Irenaeus was Bishop of Lugdunum in Gaul (now Lyon), part of the Roman Empire. Although Irenaeus does not

---

[108] Celsus, quoted in Origen, *Contra Celsum* (248 CE), ed. Henry Chadwick, rev. ed. (Cambridge: Cambridge University Press, 1965), bk. 1, sec. 7.
[109] Lucian of Samosata, "Alexander sive Pseudomantis" (ca. 180 CE), or "Alexander; or the False Prophet," in Tooke, ed., *Lucian of Samosata*, Vol. 1, pp. 632-633.
[110] Ibid., 644.
[111] Ibid., 652.
[112] Ibid., 649, 654.

explicitly refer to Celsus in his work *Against Heresies*, around 180 CE, Irenaeus seems to have studied Celsus and to copy his critiques against a group known as the Marcionites. In *Against Heresies*, Irenaeus attacked various heresies that he deemed to be rooted in pagan beliefs, especially the beliefs of the Gnostics and Valentinus in particular.[113] The Gnostics were a group of Christians who claimed that they knew sacred, secret knowledge that was not written down by the apostles.

Irenaeus complained that some of the Gnostics dared to compare themselves to Jesus Christ himself and his apostles. "So unbridled is their madness," he argued, that they believed in the transmigration of souls from body to body, thus experiencing "every kind of life."[114] Allegedly they said that there are angels in the world and that the Devil is one of them, responsible partly for helping to transfer souls, so that another angel "may shut them up in other bodies; for they declare that the body is 'the prison.'"[115] After having lived in many bodies, eventually "all souls are saved." He said that they practiced magical arts and incantations, having recourse to "familiar spirits, dream-sending demons, and other abominations."[116] But Irenaeus said that these men actually "were sent forth by Satan to bring dishonor upon the Church," and deserved to be condemned by God.[117] They pretended to own copies of an actual portrait of Christ himself, supposedly commissioned by Pontius Pilate, and they would set it next to portraits of Pythagoras, Plato, and other philosophers.[118]

Irenaeus did not explicitly characterize the Gnostics as Pythagoreans. But they had committed a typical error of heretics: they had assumed that they could modify Christian beliefs by adding notions that were foreign to Christianity. This sort of syncretism worked sometimes, but not when the pagan beliefs in question seemed contrary to core Christian beliefs. The transmigration of souls, a way of returning from death, seemed to undermine the uniqueness of the resurrection of Jesus. Hence that pagan belief was intolerable to Irenaeus.

---

[113] Irenaeus, "A Refutation and Subversion of Knowledge Falsely So Called," also known as "Against Heresies" (ca. 180 CE).
[114] bk. 1, chap. 25: "Doctrines of Carpocrates," sec. 4, pp. 94-95.
[115] bk. 1, chap. 25, sec. 4, p. 95.
[116] bk. 1, chap. 25, sec. 3, p. 94.
[117] bk. 1, chap. 25, sec. 3, p. 94.
[118] bk. 1, chap. 25, sec. 6, p. 96.

Irenaeus said that Plato was the first person to introduce the doctrine of transmigration of souls.[119] But Irenaeus insisted that this doctrine must be false, mainly because people have no memories of past lives. To overcome this problem, he said, Plato had argued that a particular demon required that souls, before being reborn, had to drink from "the cup of oblivion," to forget all their memories. Irenaeus further objected: but how could Plato know of the cup of oblivion, if his soul too had to drink from it? Since souls really remembered nothing about past lives, then they did not really live in any previous bodies. Instead, Irenaeus explained the creation of souls: "as each one of us receives his body through the skillful working of God, so does he also possess his soul," and only some of these would eventually be resurrected, in their own individual bodies.[120]

Next, in keeping with the focus on how the early Christians repudiated Pythagorean beliefs, I should well mention another belief, which Irenaeus briefly rejected although he did not ascribe it to Pythagoras. Specifically, he ridiculed those who "introduced abstinence from animal food, thus proving themselves ungrateful to God, who formed all things."[121] Likewise Irenaeus criticized the idea that there exists "an intelligent, unbegotten, and invisible being," called the "Monad."[122] He criticized mystical heretics who "refer everything to numbers, maintaining that the universe has been formed out of a Monad and a Dyad. And then, reckoning from unity on to four, they thus generate the Decad."[123]

Again, these unnamed heretics voiced several beliefs that later became famously attributed to the Pythagoreans. Fourteen centuries later, their claims about monads, the transmigration of souls, the idea that all souls are saved, and that the body is the soul's prison, all reappeared in the trial of Giordano Bruno.

---

[119] bk. 2, chap. 33: "Absurdity of the Doctrine of the Transmigration of Souls," sec. 2, p. 248.

[120] bk. 2, chap. 33, sec. 5, p. 250.

[121] bk. 1, chap. 28: "Doctrines of Tatian, the Encratites, and others," sec. 1, p. 100.

[122] bk. 1, chap. 11: "The Opinions of Valentinus, with those of his Disciples and others," sec. 3, p. 47.

[123] bk. 1, chap. 16: "Absurd Interpretations of the Marcosians," sec. 1, p. 69.

Plato, Son of a God

Like Pythagoras, Plato too was sometimes considered divine. Plato matters because writers sometimes arbitrarily claimed that he was a follower of Pythagoras. Moreover, Plutarch had claimed that old Plato too had believed that the Earth moves. So, Plato was often mentioned alongside Pythagoras. In the Renaissance, as we'll see, Kepler praised them as his "true masters." Just as we expose the un-Christian aspects of stories about Pythagoras, so too we need to consider similar religious stories about Plato.

Roughly around 100 CE, Plutarch wrote a dialogue that discussed the divinity of Plato. Plutarch described a conversation that he apparently had a year before, on May 7th, allegedly Plato's birthday. In this dialogue, one of Plutarch's companions, Florus, said: "those who make Apollo Plato's father do not, in my opinion, dishonor the god." Then Florus "mentioned that vision and voice which forbade Aristo, Plato's father, to come near or lie with his wife for ten months."[124] It seems that this "vision and voice" was a divine being or manifestation. Then another discussant, Tyndares, replied: "It is very fit that we should apply to Plato [the saying]: He seemed not sprung from mortal man, but God." Consequently the companions discussed whether a god could really "fill a mortal creature by some certain divine conception."[125] This question applied not just to Plato, but to Pythagoras and Jesus.

Plutarch's account is especially interesting, not only because of its early date, but because he served for years as one of the priests at the temple of Apollo at Delphi. It was one of his main duties to interpret the statements of the Pythia, the Oracle of Delphi. Therefore, he was a widely respected authority in the Roman empire. Since Plutarch discussed the opinion of Plato's allegedly divine birth favorably, various subsequent writers supported the idea.

At around 160 CE, the Latin writer Apuleius composed an account of Plato's philosophy in which he too briefly described Plato's origins. Apuleius was born in a Roman colony in North Africa, but he had studied

---

124 Plutarch, "Symposiacs," bk. 8, Question 1, sec. 2., in A. H. Clough and William W. Goodwin, *Plutarch's Essays and Miscellanies*, Vol. 3 (Boston: Little, Brown and Company, 1909), p. 401.
125 Ibid., 402.

Platonist philosophy in Athens, and became a priest of the god Æsculapius, son of Apollo. In his "Dogma of Plato," he said that Plato was descended from illustrious families and noble parents: Ariston and his wife, Perictione. And Apuleius added that "There are also those who relate that Plato was descended from a more august conception, since a certain specter of Apollo had an affiliation with Perictione."[126] Apparently the god had sent a being or manifestation to make a child with her. Hence Plato was born, according to Apuleius, on the same day as the god Apollo had been born in the island of Delos. Moreover, allegedly Socrates recognized young Plato's divinity on the first day he saw him.

A second reading might suggest that Apuleius merely reported hearsay and did not actually believe that Plato was divine. But actually, he also stated that Plato "not only surpassed the virtues of heroes, but also possessed powers that resembled those of the gods." He explained that Plato was a genius since childhood; he learned the doctrines of Heraclitus, Socrates, Pythagoras, and others; and he demonstrated special knowledge about the gods and the immortality of the soul.

At around 225 CE, Diogenes too told a similar story. He wrote "it was said at Athens that Perictione was very beautiful, and that Ariston tried to violate her but did not succeed. And after he had desisted from his violence, he saw a vision of Apollo in a dream, and therefore he abstained from approaching his wife until her confinement had ended." According to Diogenes, this account was told by Speusippus in his book *Funeral Banquet of Plato*, and by Clearchus in his "Panegyric of Plato," and by Anaxilides in his second book on the *History of Philosophers*.[127] Diogenes also noted that the people of Delos said Plato was born on the very same day as Apollo.[128]

Next, Olympiodorus the Younger was a philosopher, astrologer and teacher who lived at around 495 to 570 CE, in the early years of the

---

[126] Apuleius, "De Dogmate Platonis," bk. 1, "On the Habitude of the Doctrines of the Philosophy of Plato," bk. 1, in Thomas Taylor, ed., *Metamorphosis of the Golden Ass of Apuleius*, 319, translation modified.

[127] Diogenes, "Life of Plato," *Lives and Opinions of Eminent Philosophers*, sec. 1.

[128] One of the sources mentioned by Diogenes was a nephew of Plato: Speusippus. Historians have argued that it seems unlikely that Speusippus tried to deify Plato, because he would have known that Plato was not the oldest son of Ariston and Perictione, as Plato mentioned in his *Apology*. But historians infer instead that Speusippus was relaying a story that was common in Athens. For discussion, see Leonardo Tarán, *Speusippus of Athens: A Critical Study With a Collection of the Related Texts and Commentary* (Leiden: E. J. Brill, 1981), pp. 228-235.

Byzantine Empire. In 529 CE, Emperor Justinian's Decree ordered that Plato's Academy in Athens should be shut down, along with other pagan schools. Olympiodorus was a pagan who continued to support the Platonist traditions. Among his works, he wrote a "Life of Plato," in which he argued that Plato was divine: "He came into the world by his mother Perictione, who was descended from Neleus, the son of Codrus. For they say that Apollo in a vision had an intercourse with his mother Perictione, and, appearing in the night to Ariston, ordered him to have no connection with Perictione until the time when she gave birth. And so he acted."[129] After Plato's birth, his parents took him to Mount Hymettus, "intending to make a sacrifice" to the deities: Pan, the Nymphs, and Apollo, but suddenly bees came and filled his mouth with honey, a sign of good things to come. After Plato died, the Athenians buried him and inscribed these words on his tomb:

> These two, Æsculapius and Plato, did Apollo beget;
> One, that he might save the soul; the other, the body.

The alleged divinity of Plato and Pythagoras was used as a rhetorical weapon against the Christians, but it was sometimes also used in defense of Christianity. In 248 CE, the Christian theologian Origen Adamantius tried to echo the claims about their divine births. Origen argued:

> "with regard to Plato, it is Aristander, I think, who has related that he was not the son of Ariston, but of a phantom, which approached Amphictione in the guise of Apollo. And there are several other of the followers of Plato, who, in their biographies of their master have made the same statement. What are we to say, moreover, about Pythagoras, who relates the greatest possible amount of wonders…"[130]

Origen complained that some critical persons committed slander against both the Greek philosophers and against Jesus, when they doubted

---

[129] Olympiodorus, "The Life of Plato," in George Burges, trans., *The Works of Plato: a New and Literal Version*, Vol. 4 (London: Henry G. Bohn, 1865), pp. 232-240, translation modified.
[130] Origen, *Contra Celsum*, bk. 6, chap. 8, in Alexander Roberts and James Donaldson, eds., *Ante-Nicene Christian Library*, Vol. 23 (Edinburgh: T. & T. Clark, 1872), 344.

miraculous stories. Since Celsus had used Plato's writings as arguments against the Christians, because Plato did not command his listeners to believe in a particular kind of god, Origen used claims about Plato's supernatural birth, Pythagoras, and the demon of Socrates, to defend the wonders of Christ.

However, Origen was in the minority in using pagan beliefs to validate Christianity. Two centuries after his death, the Fifth Ecumenical Council of 553 CE issued fifteen "Anathemas Against Origen," thus declaring him to be a heretic, along with anyone else who held such erroneous beliefs.[131] The very first statement reads:

If anyone says, or thinks, that there were human souls previously, preexisting as intellectual minds, or natural & holy powers, but that satiated with the contemplation of God, they had lapsed to detriment, & in this way the love for God in them had cooled down, and therefore they had become known as somewhat cold souls, & had been condemned to punishment by being sent down into bodies, let that person be anathema.[132]

The idea that souls preexist bodies was declared a heresy. Henceforth, to be a Pythagorean in the Christian world was to be a heretic.

Apollonius:
Magician and Exorcist

We may now return to the famous admirer of Pythagoras, Apollonius of Tyana. Historians of astronomy often mention "the Pythagoreans" in relation to Copernicus, yet they only mention the noteworthy astronomers who

---

[131] There has been some debate as to whether the "Anathemas Against Origen" were really discussed and issued at the Synod of 553, because they do not appear in the extant minutes of meetings. Some scholars conjectured that these anathemas were adopted instead at the "Home Synod" at Constantinople of 543 CE, yet there is insufficient evidence to conclude this. For discussion, see Henry R. Percival, *The Seven Ecumenical Councils of the Undivided Church*, in *A Select Library of Nicene and Post-Nicene Fathers, Second Series*, Vol. 14 (Oxford: James Parker, 1900), pp. 316-317.

[132] Nicephori Callisti, *Ecclesiasticæ Historiæ Libri Decem & Octo* (Basel: Ioannis Oporini, 1553), 892-893; trans. Martínez

in one way or another believed in the Earth's motion, such as Philolaus, Hicetas, and Heraclides of Pontus. But since my goal is to set the Copernican revolution in the context of Pythagorean heresies, we should well discuss the one Pythagorean who was most infamous among Catholics and famous among mystics and seekers of the occult. For many pagans, Apollonius was an alternative to Jesus of Nazareth. And for centuries, Apollonius drew the attention of eccentric writers, magicians, and heretics, including the fugitive friar Giordano Bruno.

As we saw, Lucian referred to Apollonius briefly in a disparaging way, yet most of what is known about Apollonius, including many mythical stories, dates from more than a century after his death, when at around 225 CE the sophist Philostratus wrote *Life of Apollonius of Tyana*, a long, novelistic biography. In that book the author explained that he had been commissioned to write this work at the request of Empress Julia, wife of the Emperor Septimus Severus Augustus. While some Roman Emperors had not supported philosophy, Julia was its patron. According to Philostratus she asked him to edit manuscript commentaries written by a disciple of Apollonius, a man called Damis. We do not know when Julia commissioned the book; Emperor Severus reigned from 193 to 211 CE when he died, whereupon Julia influenced their young sons, the new Emperors, but one of them soon killed the other, and finally she died, allegedly by suicide, in 217 CE. It seems that Philostratus completed the long biography of Apollonius several years after Julia died.

Philostratus claimed to use accounts by Damis, Maximus the Aegean, Meragenes, and texts by Apollonius himself, though it is conceivable that he invented some of those sources. However, not all such sources were fictional; for example, there indeed existed a work by Meragenes on Apollonius; since the theologian Origen likewise read it and remarked: "what has been written by Moiragenes regarding the memoirs of the magician and philosopher Apollonius of Tyana, in which this individual, who is not a Christian, but a philosopher, asserts that some philosophers of no mean note were won over by the magic possessed by Apollonius, and resorted to him as a sorcerer; and among these, I think, he especially mentioned Euphrates and a certain Epicurean."[133] Again, notice the apparent dichotomy between being either a Christian or a philosopher. As we will see later,

---

[133] Origen, *Contra Celsum*, bk. 6, chap. 41, in Alexander Roberts and James Donaldson, eds., *Ante-Nicene Christian Library*, Vol. 23 (Edinburgh: T. & T. Clark, 1872), 380.

individuals such as Bruno, Kepler, and Galileo thought that they had every right to be both.

The book by Philostratus described the allegedly extraordinary life of Apollonius, and it also made statements about other Pythagoreans. Philostratus made some claims about Pythagoras himself: that he didn't eat meat; that the god Apollo visited him; that he talked to gods; that silence enabled him to hear divine things; that his disciples observed his teachings as laws, and revered him as a man who came from Jupiter; that he conversed with the Magi of Babylon; and that one day he was in two cities at once.[134] Again, note that Pythagoras was remembered not merely a philosopher but as a divine man. Still, Philostratus scarcely discussed Pythagoras, he focused on the disciple. His story deserves close attention because it is an outstanding example of how someone who was revered as a heroic holy man by the pagans became simultaneously viewed as a devilish imposter by the Christians. Later, in the Renaissance, the rediscovery of neglected or lost works in Latin and Greek would propel such pagan heroes into prominence, as if they promised alternative kinds of occult wisdom that had not been conveyed by most Christian theologians. It was not clear that a devout or pious Christian could rightfully admire the alleged feats of such pagan heroes.

Regarding Apollonius, his story is the following. In the Greek town of Tyana, a woman had become pregnant by her husband, but then during her pregnancy a divine being appeared to her. She asked what she would give birth to, and the divinity replied: "Thou shalt bring forth me."[135] She asked him his identity and he replied that he was the Egyptian god Proteus. According to Homer, Proteus could take many shapes, and Philostratus added that this god also had the power of foreknowledge. Later, when the woman was about to give birth, she was told in a dream to go to a meadow to gather flowers. She went there with her maidens, but soon fell asleep on the grass, and then a flock of swans gathered around her and formed a chorus around her, which awakened her, and at that moment she delivered a son. Philostratus then added: "The natives of the place affirm, that at the instant of her delivery, a thunderbolt which seemed ready to fall on the ground, rose aloft, and suddenly disappeared. By this the gods prefigured, I think, the

---

[134] Philostratus, *The Life of Apollonius of Tyana*, trans. Edward Berwick (London: T. Payne, 1809), bk. 1, chap. 1, p. 2; bk. 1, chap. 2, p. 4; bk. 4, chap. 10, p. 196.
[135] Ibid., bk. 1, chap. 4, p. 8.

splendor of the child, his superiority over earthly beings, his intercourse with them, and what he was to do when arrived to manhood."[136]

Apollonius became an enthusiastic disciple of Pythagoras, living by his doctrines, observing five years of silence and some dietary restrictions; he obeyed the *ipse dixit*, the "*He said it*," of Pythagoras.[137] Unlike the early Christians, Apollonius was a polytheist, having learned to worship the gods by following the Pythagorean ways. And mainly, Apollonius worshipped the Sun, he prayed to it, swore by it.[138] He also decided that he should never marry, and that he should never have intercourse with women, in order to control his passions to gain temperance and virtue.[139]

Philostratus described Apollonius as a wandering teacher of philosophy and a miracle worker, active mostly in Greece and Asia Minor but who allegedly also traveled to Italy, Spain, North Africa, Mesopotamia, India, and Ethiopia. Centuries later, these extensive travels of Apollonius would be celebrated by Giordano Bruno but decried by Cardinal Roberto Bellarmino. In India, Apollonius allegedly met an old wise man who told him many things, including that the Earth is an animal and that it has a soul.[140] Philostratus also claimed that Apollonius had written four books on astrology and one treatise on sacrifices. Moreover, like Pythagoras, the soul of Apollonius had allegedly inhabited another body, previously, a captain of a ship.[141] Again, these very notions arose centuries later in Bruno's trial by the Roman Inquisition.

Like other writers, Philostratus characterized the soul as being imprisoned in the human body. In Cicero's the "Dream of Scipio," Scipio had commented: "you have to keep that spirit in the prison of your body."[142] Plutarch too had referred to the soul as a "caged bird." Likewise, Philostratus put similar words in the character of Apollonius: "Whilst we live, we are all men in prison. Our soul, attached to this mortal body, suffers much, and is subject to all the vicissitudes of mortality."[143]

---

[136] Ibid., bk. 1, chap. 5, p. 10.
[137] Ibid., bk. 3, chap. 12, p. 136.
[138] Ibid., bk. 1, chap. 31, p. 52; bk. 2, chap. 38, p. 118; bk. 6, chap. 10, p. 313, chap. 32, p. 354; bk. 7, chap. 10, p. 378, chap. 31, p. 410; bk. 13, chap. 13, p. 470.
[139] Philostratus, bk. 1, chap. 13, p. 22.
[140] Ibid., bk. 3, chap. 21, p. 166.
[141] Ibid., bk. 6, chap. 21, p. 340.
[142] Cicero, "Dream of Scipio," 27.
[143] Philostratus, *Life of Apollonius*, chap. 26, p. 405.

Apollonius acquired a reputation that he was either under the influence of a demon, or that he was divine, led by "wisdom and my demon."[144] (I use the words *demon* and *daemon* indiscriminately, following the translations quoted; frequently, what were helpful and familiar *daemons* to the pagans seemed instead to be deceptive and evil demons to the Christians.) He allegedly performed some miracles: he instantly appeared in a distant city, and predicted a plague. To stop another plague, in the Roman city of Ephesus in Asia Minor, Apollonius allegedly ordered the Ephesians to kill an old man with demon eyes, to stone him, so they did, and they buried him in stones. When they removed the stones, they uncovered instead a huge, fierce dog vomiting foam.[145]

Thus, like Arignotus the Pythagorean (in one of Lucian's stories), Apollonius too seemed to be an exorcist. Philostratus told another account of how Apollonius exorcised a demon, in this case from the body of an effeminate, rude and hysterical young man. Confronting the demon, it became angry and it twisted the youth's face into horrid expressions of torture, yet Apollonius expelled him, which made a statue tumble and shatter. Once exorcised, the young man changed his ways, and adopted the "plain garb of a philosopher, and lived after the rules of Apollonius."[146] In the Bible, the exorcisms by Jesus and the apostles converted witnesses to Christianity, but in the pagan book by Philostratus, exorcism led to the life of philosophy.

Furthermore, Apollonius allegedly brought a buried man back to life, the legendary Greek warrior Achilles, in accord with wisdom that he had supposedly learned from Pythagoras.[147] Philostratus also described another incident that resembled a resurrection. He said that once Apollonius was in Rome when a young woman was about to be married, but suddenly she seemingly died. She belonged to an important family, so "all Rome condoled," and Apollonius joined the funeral procession; but when people thought that he would deliver a funeral oration, he touched the woman, uttered some words, and she awoke from her apparent death. Philostratus

---

[144] Ibid., bk. 1, chap. 18, p. 31; see also bk. 1, p. 5; bk. 6, chap. 3, p. 304; bk. 7, chap. 9, p. 377.
[145] Ibid., bk. 4, chap. 10, p. 196.
[146] Ibid., bk. 4, chap. 20, p. 212.
[147] Ibid., bk. 4, chap. 16, p. 202-206.

commented that it was difficult to ascertain whether she had still been faintly alive, or whether Apollonius really brought her soul back to life.[148]

Apollonius used magic, and became known as the "Lord of Talismans." For the wise he was a philosopher, to the vulgar a magician. Reportedly, Apollonius defied emperor Nero's ban on philosophers, and he defied emperor Domitian. Therefore, Domitian chained Apollonius as a magician, accused of conspiring against him, performing human sacrifice, and predicting a plague by magic. Then in 96 CE, Domitian was murdered, and supposedly Apollonius instantly knew it.

Reincarnations of Pythagoras

The early Church Fathers vigorously criticized Pythagorean philosophy as heresy and lies. Christianity required that only Jesus and his apostles could perform miracles, so they rejected all miracles by Pythagoras, Apollonius and others. The Christian apologist Quintus Tertullian wrote a vigorous attack against prominent pagan heretics, titled "A Treatise on the Soul," at around 210 or 220 CE. Tertullian had warned about false prophets, so he now argued that the famous Pythagoras relied on shameful and dangerous lies in advocating the idea of the transmigration of souls.

Tertullian explained that to spread this lie, Pythagoras faked his own death and then hid underground for seven years, in tortured hunger, idleness, and darkness, "and when he thought that he had succeeded in reducing the frame of his body to the horrid appearance of a dead old man, he comes forth from the place of his concealment and deceit, and pretends to have returned from the dead."[149] Thus, Herodotus's ancient story about Pythagoras's deceitful slave, Salmoxis, became a story about Pythagoras himself, seven centuries later. Tertullian denied claims that previously Pythagoras, the reckless deceiver, had lived as Aethalides, Euphorbus, Pyrrhus, and Hermotimus. Tertullian said that perhaps a demon had been in the body of Euphorbus, and that Pythagoras had a master who had been a

[148] Ibid., bk. 4, chap. 45, p. 243.
[149] Quintus Septimus Florens Tertullian, *De Anima* (ca. 210 or 220 CE), in Alexander Roberts and James Donaldson, eds., *Ante-Nicene Christian Library*, Vol. XV: *The Writings of Tertullian*, Vol. 2 (Edinburgh: T. & T. Clark, 1870), chap. 28, pp. 477-478.

raving magician. Tertullain said that there were contradictions in the story of transmigration of souls. For how could the soul of Euphorbus and Pythagoras be the same, when the former was a warrior and the latter a peaceful recluse? How could Pyrrhus the fisherman become Pythagoras, who would never catch or eat fish? How could Aethalides and Hermotimus become Pythagoras if they used to eat beans, but Pythagoras did not?

Thus Tertullian attacked the "Pythagorean doctrine," as he called it, "that living men are formed from dead ones."[150] That's the key phrase; we'll see that Catholic theologians in Renaissance Italy continued to criticize what they too called "Pythagorean doctrines." Also, Tertullian criticized a story about Hermotimus: that whenever he slept, his soul left his body, as if to wander at night, but when his wife revealed this secret, his enemies attacked his sleeping body, burned it, before the soul could return.[151] With many arguments, Tertullian tried to refute the Pythagorean theory that living people come from the dead, for example, by noting that it failed to explain population growth.[152] He asked why the soul of the impostor of Samos, alone, had the privilege to be reborn.[153] He further censured the heresy that human souls can be reborn in animal bodies. He especially ridiculed Empedocles as insane, for having asserted transmigration into beasts, and for having said that he was a god and had lived as a fish. Tertullian also argued that the Pythagorean belief in transmigration of souls had caused "profane corruptions of Christianity," and he argued that "magicians and fornicators" had adopted these Pythagorean dogmas, denouncing two such sinners by name.[154]

In another work, *Against Marcion*, Tertullian pinpointed the key problem that, in his estimation, Greek philosophers embodied against Christianity. He criticized "those very professors of wisdom, from whose genius every heresy derives its spirit."[155] Here again, Christians did not appreciate wisdom as much as they valued absolute submission to the will of God, which was not bound by reason or by any laws of nature. Tertullian

[150] Ibid., chap. 29, p. 479.
[151] Ibid., chap. 44, p. 511-512.
[152] Ibid., chap. 29, pp. 479-480.
[153] Ibid., chap. 30, p. 484.
[154] Ibid., chap. 34, p. 492; chap. 35, p. 494.
[155] Tertillian, *The Five Books of Quintus Sept. Flor. Tertullianus Against Marcion*, bk. 1, chap. 13, trans. Peter Holmes, in Alexander Roberts and James Donaldson, eds., *Ante-Nicene Christian Library*, Vol. 7 (Edinburgh: T. & T. Clark, 1868), p. 23.

explained: "We are taught God by the prophets and by Christ, not by the philosophers."[156] And he quoted New Testament scriptures to argue that "God has chosen the foolish things of the world to confound the wise," and that God would "destroy the wisdom of the wise," as Jesus said.[157] Again, in his treatise *Against Hermogenes*, Tertullian condemned "the philosophers—those patriarchs of all heresy."[158] And again in a treatise on the soul: "We should then be never required to try our strength in contests about the soul with philosophers, those patriarchs of heretics, as they may fairly be called."[159] He rejected the philosophical ideas: that the world is eternal and was not created by God, that the soul is not corporeal, that it is divisible, that demons guide men, that God is not to be feared, and so forth, and he insistently linked philosophers and heretics.

Aside from Tertullian, other early Church Fathers also criticized the Pythagorean philosophy, in which "the Creator of all alleged existence is the Great Geometrician and Calculator a Sun; and that this one has been fixed in the whole world." They denounced various heretics as "disciples not of Christ but of Pythagoras."[160] These were the complaints of Hippolytus (formerly misattributed to Origen of Alexandria), a prominent theologian at the Church of Rome. Hippolytus made these claims in his influential *Philosophumena*, that is, *The Refutation of all Heresies*, at around 225 CE. Hippolytus copied extensively from the work of Irenaeus, *Against Heresies* (ca. 180 BCE), which we have reviewed, but he expanded greatly upon it by detailing the doctrines of many Greek philosophers, and arguing how such doctrines led to the false beliefs of Christian heretics.

In the second chapter of his *Refutation*, Hippolytus discussed the alleged beliefs of Pythagoras. He said that Pythagoras combined astronomy, geometry and music; he studied the nature of number, and proclaimed that "God

[156] Ibid., bk. 2, chap. 16, p. 90.

[157] Ibid., bk. 5, chap. 19, p. 472; 1 Corinthians 1:27, and 1 Corinthians 1:19.

[158] Tertullian, *The Treatise of Quintus Septimus Florens Tertullianus Against Hermogenes*, chap. 8, trans. Peter Holmes, in Alexander Roberts and James Donaldson, eds., *Ante-Nicene Christian Library*, Vol. 15: *The Writings of Tertulian*, Vol. 2 (Edinburgh: T. & T. Clark, 1868), 67.

[159] Tertullian, "A Tratise on the Soul," chap. 3, in ibid., p. 416.

[160] Hippolytus [traditionally misattributed to Origen], *Κατα ποσων αιρεσεων ελεγχοσ* (ca. 225 CE); trans.: *Philosophumena: Refutatio Omnium Haeresium*, and *The Refutation of All Heresies*, in Alexander Roberts and James Donaldson, eds. *Ante Nicene Christian Library*, Vol. VI: *Hippolytus, Bishop of Rome, Vol. 1* (Edinburgh: T. & T. Clark, 1868), bk. VI, chaps. 47, p. 259; see also chaps. 23-24.

is a monad."[161] He required that his disciples should be silent for three or five years in order to be purified. Pythagoras allegedly dealt also with magic. And he taught that "the soul is immortal and that it subsists in successive bodies. Wherefore he asserted that before the Trojan era he was Aethalides, and during the Trojan epoch Euphorbus, and afterward Hermotimus of Samos, and after him Pyrrhus of Delos; fifth Pythagoras."[162]

Hippolytus complained that Pythagoras said that the world is eternal, originated from the un-begotten monad.[163] Allegedly Pythagoras also said that the stars are fragments of the Sun, and that from the stars come the souls of animals, which are then buried into bodies, until later death separates them from bodies, whence their souls become immortal.[164] Human souls could pass between animals and plants, and souls who philosophized would eventually ascend to a kindred star. But if a soul did not escape the passions it could become mortal.[165] Those were some of the repulsive Pythagorean beliefs that the early Christians criticized, and interestingly, they mixed religion with elements of astronomy. A similar mixture developed later during the Copernican Revolution.

According to Hippolytus, one of the disciples of Pythagoras was Empedocles. Like Pythagoras, he taught that "the monad is the Deity," and that souls transmigrate from body to body. Hippolytus quoted Empedocles:

> "For surely I was both youth and maid,
> And shrub, and bird, and fish, from ocean strayed."[166]

Allegedly Empedocles taught that all souls transmigrate into any kinds of animals. Hippolytus further said that Empedocles posited many claims about demons: that they spend much time managing worldly concerns.

Furthermore, Hippolytus said that after Pythagoras died in the fire at Croton, his servant Salmoxis traveled to Celtic lands and had taught the

---

[161] Hippolytus, bk. 1, chap. 2, p. 31.

[162] Ibid., 33.

[163] On Pythagoras and the monad, see Hippolytus, *Refutation of all Heresies*, book 4, chap. 15, book 6, chap. 18; anonymous "Commentaries of Pythagoras," quoted by Alexander Polyhistor in Diogenes Laertius, "Life of Pythagoras," sec. 19.

[164] Hippolytus, *Philosophumena*, bk. 6, chap. 20, p. 220.

[165] Ibid., 221.

[166] Ibid., bk. 1, chap. 3, p. 36.

Pythagorean philosophy to the Druids, who learned to practice magic.[167] And hence Hippolytus argued: "the Celts esteem these [Druids] as prophets and seers, because they can foretell certain events from calculations and numbers by the Pythagorean art; on the methods of which very art also we shall not keep silence, since also from these some have presumed to introduce heresies; but the Druids result to magical rites likewise."[168]

Hippolytus denounced the "alliance between heresy and the Pythagorean philosophy," he criticized the "enormous and endless heresies" of those such as Colarbasus who attempted to explain religion by measures and numbers, and who deceived unsophisticated individuals with vain prophecies and calculation.[169] He convicted Valentinus of plagiarizing arithmetical philosophy, that he "may therefore justly be reckoned a Pythagorean and Platonist, not a Christian."[170] He said that Valentinus "collected the heresy" from opinions of Pythagoras and Plato. He complained that Marcus too and his followers practiced "portions of astrological discovery, and the arithmetical art of the Pythagoreans" and therefore were not disciples of Christ.[171] Marcus was allegedly a sorcerer, who deceived many Christians "partly by sleight of hand and partly by demons," for example, by secretly mixing an expansive and color-inducing drug into the wine cup of the Eucharist, to perform a false miracle of seemingly augmenting the blood of Christ.[172]

Hippolytus also dismissed Monoïmus as having too copied Pythagoras.[173] Furthermore, Hippolytus denounced the heretical system of Elchasai as being derived from Pythagoras, and he rejected especially the claim that Christ had been born a common man, and like all others had been born previously, and would be born repeatedly as "his soul transferred from body to body."[174] He denounced the followers of Elchasai for their incantations and for pretending "to be endued with a power of foretelling futurity, using as a starting-point, obviously, the measures and numbers of the

---

167 Ibid., bk. 1, chap. 3, p. 35.
168 Ibid., bk. 1, chap. 22, p. 61.
169 Ibid., bk. IV, chap. 13.
170 Ibid., bk. 6, chap. 24, pp. 224-225.
171 Ibid., bk. 6, chap. 47, p. 259.
172 Ibid., bk. 6, chap. 34, pp. 243-245
173 Ibid., bk. 8, chap. 8, p. 321.
174 Ibid., bk. 9, chap. 9: "Elchasai derived his System from Pythagoras—practiced Incantations," p. 347.

aforesaid Pythagorean art. These also devote themselves to the tenets of mathematicians, and astrologers, and magicians, as if they were true. And they resort to these, so as to confuse silly people, thus led to suppose that the heretics participate in a doctrine of power."[175]

By contrast, one Christian sect, from the start, was closely linked to the Pythagoreans, namely the Manichaeans. Around 250 CE, Mani (or Manes) was a Persian prophet who developed a kind of Gnostic religion, purporting to surpass Christianity. As a child slave, Mani had been purchased and adopted by a woman who gave him freedom along with the property and books of a mystic man who allegedly had been killed by a daemon. Mani adopted his doctrines, thus inheriting also the beliefs of that dead man's teacher, Scythianos, who had "introduced the doctrine of Empedocles and Pythagoras into Christianity."[176] Accordingly, the Manichaeans believed in the transmigration of souls. They also believed that the soul is imprisoned in the body.[177] Therefore, they also did not eat meat. Among the Christians, they were especially infamous for their dualistic view of good and evil: that the good power of God was opposed by an evil divine power. At around 278 CE, in Mesopotamia, Bishop Archelaus composed a "Disputation against Manes," in which the Bishop remarked that Manes's intellectual mentor, Scythianos, "was indebted to Pythagoras, as also all other followers of this dogma have been, who all uphold the notion of dualism, and turn aside from the direct course of Scripture."[178]

As we can see, there were growing rifts and tensions between Christianity and the Pythagoreans. While Christians believed that Jesus and only Jesus had resurrected, supposedly Pythagoras had been reborn several times. And Pythagoras taught that other human souls are also reborn repeatedly, even in animals. And the Bible told believers to eat meat and during the ceremony of the Eucharist, Christians ate the body of Christ. Yet Pythagoras allegedly taught the contrary: that we should not eat flesh. To

---

[175] Ibid.

[176] Socrates of Constantinople, *H. E.* (ca. 440), bk. 1, chap. 22, quoted in Nathaniel Larder, *The Credibility of the Gospel History, Part II* (London: A. Millar, 1745), 22.

[177] Samuel N. C. Lieu, *Manichaeism in the Later Roman Empire and Medieval China*, 2nd ed. (Tübingen: Mohr, 1992), pp. 161-162.

[178] Bishop Archelaus, "The Disputation with Manes" (ca. 277-278), in Alexander Roberts and James Donaldson, *Ante-Nicene Christian Library*, Vol. 20: *The Writings of Gregory Thaumaturgus, Dionysius of Alexandria, and Archelaus* (Edinburgh: T. & T. Clark, 1871), 405.

the Christians, Jesus and Pythagoras could not both be correct. This was a distinctive exclusivity of the Christian religion: it was not enough to assert and accept all the miracles of Jesus; the Christian faith required that all other claims about the supernatural powers and revelations of pagan holy men should be rejected as lies, trickery, or the work of demons. The holy men of the Pythagoreans became demonized by Christian theologians.

the Gospels of Pythagoras?

Just as the story of Jesus was gradually consolidated in the four gospels, so too the Pythagoreans gradually condensed the story and teachings of Pythagoras in several inspirational accounts. Alongside the *Life of Apollonius*, several biographies of Pythagoras circulated, including multiple points of agreement as well as numerous contradictions, confusions, and fictions.

One biography was written by Diogenes Laertius, a biographer of Greek philosophers who composed *Life of Pythagoras* at around 225 CE, based partly on older sources. He argued that Pythagoras worshipped only at the altar of Apollo, the Sun god, and that Pythagoras theorized that: "the Sun, and the Moon, and the stars were all Gods." He echoed claims that Pythagoras was actually the god Apollo, and that he had spent 207 years in the underworld, had there seen all the men who ever died: "he saw the soul of Hesiod bound to a brazen pillar, and gnashing its teeth; and that of Homer suspended from a tree, and snakes around it, as a punishment…" Diogenes added that Pluto, god of the dead, ate only with the Pythagoreans. According to Heraclides Pontus, as relayed by Diogenes, the soul of Pythagoras was originally born as Aethalides, the son of the god Mercury, who had granted him the gifts of "the perpetual transmigration of his soul, so that it was constantly transmigrating and passing into whatever plants or animals it pleased; and he had also received the gift of knowing and recollecting all that his soul had suffered in hell, and what sufferings too are endured by the rest of the souls."[179]

---

[179] Heraclides Ponticus (ca. 387 to 312 BCE) as paraphrased by Diogenes Laertius, *The Lives and Opinions of Eminent Philosophers* (ca. 225 CE), trans. C. D. Yonge, bk. 8: "Life of Pythagoras" (London: Henry G. Bohn, 1853), sec. IV.

According to Diogenes, Heraclides said that after living as the demigod Aethalides, the soul of Pythagoras was reborn as Euphorbus, a warrior in the Trojan War, and subsequently reborn as Hermotimus, and next, as Pyrrhus, a fisherman of Delos. And fifth, the soul was reborn as Pythagoras of Samos. (By contrast to Lucian's story, Diogenes did not claim that Pythagoras was once a mistress, a beggar, a horse, or a frog, etc., and instead of the chatty rooster who was the servant of Mercury, he appears more seriously as Mercury's son). Thus, Pythagoras seemed to be a master of the occult, because he had successfully requested of Mercury, "that whether living or dead, he might preserve the memory of what had happened to him."

Diogenes also noted some stories that cast doubt on the credibility of Pythagoras. He said that Hermippus had told this story: that while in Italy, Pythagoras made an underground dwelling, and he hid there while his mother sent down notes of all that happened above, for a long time, until Pythagoras reemerged, thin like a skeleton, and at a public assembly he spoke about having returned from the shades below, told them about all that had transpired during his absence, and then they wept and believed that he was a divine being, so that they even entrusted their wives to him.[180] This story echoes the one by Herodotus, by attributing to Pythagoras what Herodotus had said about his slave, Salmoxis.[181] Diogenes wrote many other claims and stories about Pythagoras, but again, I mention only some that are significant because of their clash with Christian beliefs.

Similarities between stories about Jesus and Pythagoras were growing. The biographers of Pythagoras nudged his stories a bit to resemble those about Jesus, which were becoming immensely popular. While writers such as Celsus had tried to place both Jesus and Pythagoras on a similar footing, others vigorously opposed such comparisons. In 248 CE, in Alexandria, the Christian theologian Origen Adamantius vigorously replied to the critiques against Christ voiced by Celsus. Regarding Pythagoras, Origen rejected the claim that souls are reborn according to their actions in previous lives. He noted that some of the followers of Pythagoras were content with his *ipse dixit*, and that Christians were no more secretive than the Pythagoreans. Origen rejected the "fantastic tales" of Pythagoras: about his thigh, about

---

[180] Hermippus, paraphrased by Diogenes Laertius in "Life of Pythagoras," chap. 21.
[181] Diogenes briefly noted that Herodotus had recorded that Pythagoras had a slave, but he did not compare the story by Herodotus to that by Hermippus.

Euphorbus, about being in two cities at once.[182] Also, he rejected "the myth of transmigration, that the soul falls from the vaults of heaven and descends as far as irrational animals, not merely the tame but even those which are very wild."[183] He complained also that Celsus agreed with Plato in their opinion that "souls can make their way to and from the Earth through the planets."[184] Regarding the story about how the soul of Hermotimus traveled while his body slept, Origen said that "probably certain demons had arranged for this story to be written," in order to attack people's belief in Jesus.[185] Origen criticized claims about Egyptian magicians and sorcerers, and he noted that some philosophers had been captivated by the alleged magic of Apollonius.[186] And of course, Origen denied Celsus's claims about Jesus being merely a deceptive magician, and he denied that Christian exorcists used spells or incantations to command demons (or *daemons*).

Regardless, prominent advocates continued to defend Pythagorean beliefs. In Rome, the philosopher Porphyry became known for his admiration for Pythagoras. Porphyry became famous and infamous for, on the one hand, praising Pythagoras while on the other hand he attacked the Christians. Porphyry's writings embody the height of the ancient conflict between Christians and Pythagoreans. According to Saint Augustine, Porphyry was "the most bitter enemy" of Christianity. His extremely inimical role for Christians is evident at a key moment of the Protestant Reformation. In 1520 Pope Leo X issued his Papal Bull against Martin Luther. The Pope condemned the heretical writings of Luther as "blinded in mind by the father of lies" the Devil. The Pope denounced Luther by declaring: "'a new Porphyry has arisen.'

Hence in fifteen centuries of Christianity, Porphyry stood out as one of the greatest enemies of the Church.

---

[182] Origen, *Contra Celsum* (248 CE), ed. Henry Chadwick, rev. ed. (Cambridge: Cambridge University Press, 1965), bk. 6 sec. 9, p. 322.
[183] Ibid., bk. 1, sec. 20, p. 21.
[184] Ibid., bk. 6, chap. 21.
[185] Ibid., bk. 3, sec. 33, pp. 148-149.
[186] Ibid., bk. 6, sec. 41; Origen referred to a book (now lost) by Merangenes on Apollonius.

At around 290 CE, Porphyry published *Against the Christians*, a set of fifteen books that denounced the early Christians.[187] Porphyry expressed some appreciation for the historical Jesus, for the most part, but he denounced contradictions in the Gospels. He complained: "The Gods have proclaimed Christ to have been most pious, but the Christians are a confused and vicious sect." Porphyry also criticized some alleged deeds and sayings of Jesus. He denied that Jesus was God incarnate, he denied the resurrection of Jesus and of select humans on Judgment Day, he denied the Christian doctrine that the world has a beginning and an end, and he denied that Jesus is the sole path to salvation. Porphyry criticized Christianity for its emphasis on faith, unreason, and its appeal to the gullible poor and uneducated, rather than the educated, philosophers. He gave some credit to the teachings and miracles of Jesus, but compared him to Apollonius, favoring the latter.

Soon thereafter, at around 300 CE, Porphyry published his account of the ideal moral leader, his *Life of Pythagoras*. Porphyry said that Pythagoras wrote no books, such that when he and his disciples died, most of their knowledge was lost, because of their secrecy, "except for a few obscure things which were commonly repeated by those who did not understand them."[188] Reportedly, a couple of his scattered disciples, including Lysis and Archippus, managed to preserve some obscure parts of his philosophy. The Pythagoreans became dispersed and isolated, but they wrote recollections, abstracts, and commentaries, which were allegedly preserved by their families for a long time.

According to Porphyry, when Pythagoras departed from his native island of Samos and arrived in the Italian city of Croton, he was promptly recognized as a great speaker, so that hordes of men, boys and women flocked to hear him speak, even magnates and kings of barbarians. Porphyry wrote:

"What he told his audiences cannot be said with certainty, for he enjoined silence upon his hearers. But the following is a matter of general

---

[187] Amos Berry Hulen, *Porphyry's Work Against the Christians* (1933); R. Joseph Hoffman, *Porphyry's Against the Christians: The Literary Remains* (Amherst, New York: Prometheus Books: 1994); Jeffrey W. Hargis, *Against the Christians: The Rise of Early Anti-Christian Polemic* (New York: Peter Lang, 1999).
[188] Porphyry, sec. 57.

information. He taught that the soul was immortal and that after death it transmigrated into other animated bodies. After certain specified periods, the same events occur again; that nothing was entirely new; that all animated beings were kin, and should be considered as belonging to one great family. Pythagoras was the first one to introduce these teachings into Greece."[189]

People received his teachings as divine ordinances, and ranked him among the divinities. And allegedly he founded various cities, and restored freedom in others. He allegedly rooted out dissension in all cities in Italy and Sicily.

Porphyry celebrated Pythagoras as being more than merely human, he claimed that Pythagoras had a golden thigh, evidence that he was divine, related to the Sun god Apollo. Porphyry said that Pythagoras predicted earthquakes, stopped violent winds, hail, and storms, and shot an arrow that carried his priest Abaris to practically walk on air. He wrote: "Of Pythagoras many other more wonderful and divine things are persistently and unanimously related, so that we have no hesitation in saying never was more attributed to any man, nor was any more eminent."[190]

Porphyry even rehabilitated the infamous deceptive slave: Salmoxis. According to him, Salmoxis was a beloved disciple of Pythagoras: "Pythagoras had another youthful disciple from Thrace. Salmoxis was he named because he was born wrapped in a bear's skin, in Thracian called Zalmus. Pythagoras loved him, and instructed him in sublime speculations concerning sacred rites, and the nature of the Gods."[191] He added that the barbarians worshipped him as Hercules, the legendary hero. Porphyry did not mention Herodotus, but he mentioned that Dionsysiphanes said that he was a servant of Pythagoras, who was captured by thieves, and they branded his forehead. But he returned to Pythagoras. By this explanation, Salmoxis now seemed to be not the slave of Pythagoras, as claimed in the story that Herodotus described and rejected, but a dutiful disciple and willing servant who was temporarily enslaved by thieves. Moreover, Porphyry insinuated that Salmoxis was special by saying that he was born wrapped in bear's skin.

---

[189] Porphyry, "Life of Pythagoras," sec. 19.
[190] Porphyry, *Life of Pythagoras* (ca. 300? CE), in *The Pythagorean Sourcebook and Library,* trans. Kenneth Sylvan Guthrie (New York: Platonist Press, 1919), rev. ed. David R. Fideler (Grand Rapids: Phanes Press, 1987), sec. 28, p. 128.
[191] Porphyry, "Life of Pythagoras," sec. 14.

Like other Pythagoreans, Porphyry believed in the existence of many gods and *daemons*, he asserted the eternity of the universe, with no Creation, again contrary to the beliefs of the Christians. He also argued that human souls transmigrate into various bodies as they travel for 9,000 years, descending from the Moon, to then spend time on each planet, and finally go to the Sun. In his work, "On the Cave of the Nymphs," Porphyry remarked: "According to Pythagoras, also, the people of dreams, are the souls which are said to be collected in the Milky Way, this circle being so called from the milk with which souls are nourished when they fall into generation."[192] Porphyry also noted that, "according to topologists, the Sun and the Moon are the gates of souls, which ascend through the Sun, and descend through the Moon."[193]

Porphyry's claims thus constitute a remarkable assault on Christianity. He denounced the Christians' irrational and uneducated notions while belittling Jesus as just another wise man. In contradistinction he heaped praise upon the divine Pythagoras and sketched the mysterious cosmology whereby immortal souls come from the Milky Way and travel to multiple heavenly bodies, to live multiple lives. Hence many Christians were deeply offended and agitated by Porphyry's pagan views.

But not all Christians criticized Pythagoras. To some he was merely another Greek philosopher, and some even tried to use stories about him as indirect evidence in favor of the plausibility of the miracles of Christ. For example, at around 176 CE, Athenagoras of Athens referred to Pythagoras and Plato, to use their opinions in support of the Christian idea of bodily resurrection, by saying that they argued that after the dissolution of bodies it is yet possible that such bodies may be reconstructed from the very elements that had constituted them.[194] Likewise, another author tried to use Pythagorean sayings as evidence in favor of monotheism. In that work, *The Hortatory Address to the Greeks*, the author apparently summarized several philosophies. Traditionally, this work had been attributed to Justin Martyr, but later research generated much debate about its author. Some claimed

---

[192] Porphyry, "De Antro Nympharum," in *Select Works of Porphyry*, trans. Thomas Taylor (London: T. Rodd and J. Moyes, 1823), "On the Cave of the Nymphs," 193.
[193] Ibid., 196.
[194] Athenagoras the Athenian, "A Plea for the Christians" (ca. 176 CE), chap. 36; in Alexander Roberts and James Donaldson, eds., *Ante-Nicene Christian* Library, Vol. 2: *Justin Martyr and Athenagoras*, trans. B. P. Pratten (Edinburgh: T. &. T. Clark, 1870), 420-421.

that this work dates from the time of Justin, ca. 180 CE, while others argue that it dates from as late as shortly after 362.[195] In any case, the writer explained: "Pythagoras the Samian, son of Mnesarchus, calls numbers, with their proportions and harmonies, and the elements composed of both, the first principles; and he includes also unity and the indefinite binary."[196] These words echo the account in "Plutarch's" *Placita Philosophorum*, just as its other characterizations of various Greek philosophies also match that work. The author discussed particular and prominent philosophies in order to warn his Greek audience that they should beware of the errors of their ancestors, or suffer the consequent dangers. However, his attitude toward Pythagoras was not entirely negative, because he argued that having visited Egypt, Pythagoras and others had benefitted from the history of Moses, and thereafter published doctrines about the gods that deviated from their previous pagan teachings.[197] The author listed Greek writers who had argued, in any way and to his satisfaction, in favor of monotheism: Orpheus, Sibyl, Homer, Sophocles, Plato. Thus he commented that Pythagoras too "seems to have entertained thoughts about the unity of God. For when he says that unity is the first principle of all things, and that it is the cause of all good, he teaches by an allegory that God is one, and alone."[198]

Nevertheless, the fact that some authors found some similarities between Christian beliefs and some of the reputed sayings of the ancient philosophers did not exempt the latter from embodying "false" and "dangerous" doctrines.

The Assyrian philosopher, Iamblichus, was a student of Porphyry, and like his teacher, he wrote a work *On the Pythagorean Way of Life*, at around 300 CE. Iamblichus gave the most expansive biography of Pythagoras.

According to Iamblichus, the parents of Pythagoras were Mnesarchus and Parthenis. For commerce, they once traveled to Delphi, a town famous for being the site of the Delphic oracle, the most important oracle in Greece. According to tradition, the god Apollo, as a boy, had shot an arrow that killed the serpent Python, or Pythia. Hence there was a temple or

---

[195] For a brief discussion, see Otto Bardenhewer, *Patrology: The Lives and Works of the Fathers of the Church*, trans. Thomas J. Shahan (St. Louis, Missouri: B. Herder, 1908), 54
[196] Justinus Martyr [apocryphal?], *Cohort ad Græcos* (ca. 150 CE), chap. 4; trans. by M. Dods, "Justin's Hortatory Address to the Greeks," in *Ante-Nicene Christian Library*, p. 305. Note: here the "chapters," are not book chapters, they are article chapters.
[197] Ibid., chap. 14, p. 301.
[198] Ibid., chap. 19, p. 305.

sanctuary dedicated to Apollo, and there, the god himself allegedly spoke through his Pythian oracle. At Delphi, Mnesarchus took the opportunity to approach the Pythian oracle to ask about a forthcoming journey. But surprisingly, the oracle then told him "that his wife was now pregnant, and would bring forth a son surpassing in beauty and wisdom all that ever lived, and who would be of the greatest advantage to the human race in every thing pertaining to the life of man."[199] When Mnesarchus realized that the god Apollo had given them a divine gift, he immediately renamed his wife Pythais, and decided to call their son Pythagoras, to signify that his birth had been predicted by the Pythian Apollo.

There is one obvious but striking implication about Iamblichus's story about the birth of Pythagoras: that it copies the birth of Jesus Christ. By the time Iamblichus wrote, there were many Christian texts; the early life of Jesus was a popular subject of discussion. The gospels of Mark and John do not describe the birth of Jesus, but the gospels of Matthew and Luke give accounts with many specific details. In particular, the Gospel of Matthew states that Joseph was supposed to marry a woman who was already pregnant, and as he thought about this: "an angel of the Lord appeared unto him in a dream, saying, Joseph, thou son of David, fear not to take unto thee Mary thy wife: for that which is conceived in her is of the Holy Spirit. And she shall bring forth a son; and thou shalt call his name JESUS; for it is he that shall save his people from their sins.[200] In the story described by Iamblichus, the Pythian oracle plays the role of the angel.

Yet nowhere in his narrative did Iamblichus refer specifically to Jesus or the Christian texts, he made no explicit comparisons. Still, the implication was that Pythagoras was a son of the god Apollo, as told by a poet of Samos, quoted by Iamblichus:

Pythagoras, whom Pythais bore for Apollo,
dear to Zeus, she who was the loveliest of the Samians.[201]

Iamblichus said that this impression had become prevalent, a plausible claim that can hardly be verified: several ancient sources do refer to Pythagoras as being related to Apollo, but Iamblichus was also crafting a rhetorical

[199] Iamblichis, chap. 2, p. 3.
[200] Matthew 1:20-21.
[201] Ancient poem quoted in Iamblichus, *Pythagorean Life* (ca. 300 CE), Chapter 2, p. 35.

argument, it was to his advantage to increase any impression of his subject's importance. At the same time, however, Iamblichus himself did not stress that Pythagoras was in fact the son of Apollo, just that he was certainly divine. Nevertheless, Iamblichus proclaimed: "no one can doubt that the soul of Pythagoras was sent to mankind from the empire of Apollo, either being an attendant on the God, or co-arranged with him in some other more familiar way: for this may be inferred both from his birth, and the all-various wisdom of his soul."[202]

In any case, Iamblichus told heroic and mystical stories: he claimed that Pythagoras invented political education, overthrew despotic regimes, freed cities from slavery, and abolished all discord and differences of opinion in and among all cities in Italy and Sicily, for many generations. He claimed that Pythagoras once spoke to a bull and convinced it not to eat beans, and that to divine the future he used numbers, instead of animal entrails. Iamblichus also claimed that Pythagoras spoke to the river Nessus, and the river replied, "Hail, Pythagoras!"[203] Above all, Pythagoras was "the most handsome and god-like of those ever recorded in history," a superhuman miracle-worker, sent from the domain of Apollo to enlighten humans to live properly.[204]

According to Iamblichus, there existed a treatise "Concerning the Gods," also known as the "Sacred Discourse," which was either written by Pythagoras himself or by his son on the basis of his father's written commentaries. It explained how Pythagoras was instructed about the gods and the principle of the universe: "that Pythagoras the son of Mnesarchus was instructed in what pertains to the Gods, when he celebrated orgies in the Thracian Libethra, being initiated in them by Aglaophemus; and that Orpheus the son of Calliope, having learnt wisdom from his mother in the mountain Pangceus, said, that the eternal essence of number is the most providential principle of the universe, of heaven and earth, and the intermediate nature; and farther still, that it is the root of the permanency of divine natures, of Gods and *daemons*."

[202] Iamblichus, chap. 2, p. 4.
[203] Iamblichi, *De Vita Pythagorica* (ca. 300 CE), reissued as Iamblichus, *On the Pythagorean Way of Life*, ed. and trans. John Dillon and Jackson Hershbell (Atlanta: Scholars Press, 1991), chap. 28, p. 154. See also p. 155, where the editors note that Porphyry stated that the river was the Caucasus, while Aelian stated that the river was the Casas, near Metapontium.
[204] Iamblichus, *On the Pythagorean Way*, chap. 2, p. 37.

Iamblichus also echoed the ancient story of the slave of Pythagoras, but in a modified form: "Salmoxis being a Thracian, and the slave of Pythagoras, after he had heard the discourses of Pythagoras, having obtained his liberty, and returned to the Getae, gave laws to them, as we have before observed in the beginning of this work, and exhorted the citizens to fortitude, having persuaded them that the soul is immortal."[205] And having instructed the Getae Thracians, and written laws for them, they considered him the greatest of the gods. Iamblichus's rendition of the tale resembles that of Herodotus, but it omits the ancient, critical point: that Salmoxis *deceived* the Thracians. It also adds a the claim that Salmoxis had heard Pythagoras lecturing, presumably about the soul or the afterlife, as if Iamblichus meant to imply that Salmoxis copied his master—yet none of this is in Herodotus.

Iamblichus claimed to explain an old, enigmatic assertion: "man, bird, and another third thing, are bipeds." He said that the "third thing" was Pythagoras, not merely a man, but a superior being.[206] In antiquity, the Greeks argued that certain men were really of a superior order, "terrestrial heroes." By various accounts, for example, Heracles, Theseus, Pythagoras, and Plato were souls of this kind, who became mortal to benefit mankind, and by being inferior to the gods their souls were obligated to occasionally descend.[207] Heracles, known by the Romans as "Hercules," was especially famous for his feats of strength and for defeating man-eating monsters such as the Hydra, and Cerberus, the three-headed hellhound that guarded the gates of the underworld. Theseus was the Athenian hero who slayed the Minotaur that killed children in the labyrinth of Daedalus.

the Miracles of
Jesus, Pythagoras, Apollonious

Thus far I have described the religious beliefs of the Pythagoreans, tracing aspects of theories that can roughly be characterized as a world-view. It was

---

[205] Iamblichus, chap. 30, p. 92. It another chapter (chap. 34, p. 124), Iamblichus mentioned the narrations of Herodotus, which suggests that he read his *Histories*.
[206] Iamblichus, chap. 28, p. 76.
[207] Ibid.

a minor religion, one of the various pagan cults that proliferated throughout the Greek realm in antiquity. But during the rise of Christianity, it became used by some of the Romans as a means to defend polytheism and classical values. At the same time, Christian writers criticized the Pythagorean teachings as heresies and lies. In order to discuss which aspects of the stories of Pythagoras and his followers most offended the early Christians, we should first compare some aspects of these belief systems in themselves.

We have already looked at a series of moves and countermoves by the advocates of either side. But beyond that sequence of events, we can further analyze the various conflicts by comparing canonical texts in these competing traditions. Similar and parallel claims serve to show just how rival sets of beliefs challenged each other. My main goal is to highlight a series of conflicts that have become nearly invisible ever since the ancient reputation of Pythagoras as a divine figure and moral teacher became eclipsed by his spurious canonization as a great pioneer of mathematics and astronomy. In order to understand the apparent threat and challenge that Pythagorean notions constituted for the early Christians we need to explicitly enumerate parallelisms and conflicts between such belief systems. Otherwise, recent writers tend to fall into the habit of imagining Pythagoras in the way that other recent writers have portrayed him. Instead, since his biographers said very little about Pythagoras in relation to the sciences, we should consider what they actually did say abundantly about his life as a moral teacher and a worker of miracles.

Miracles are also important because the later confrontation between the Catholics and Copernicans essentially involved a contentious disagreement over a miracle. Most Catholics said that in the Joshua miracle the Sun had literally stopped moving, whereas the Copernicans said that it had not stopped moving because, really, it had not been moving at all. Galileo and company offered a Pythagorean interpretation of the Biblical miracle: they said that it was really the Earth that had stopped moving. Debates over miracles are at the crux of questions about the authority of religion over science. The requirement that Christians should believe Biblical miracles, irrespective of any scientific arguments to the contrary, has constituted for centuries a point of contention between science and religion.

Aside from its moral teachings, Christianity distinguished itself by the particular kinds of evidence that it proffered. Someone can readily doubt or disbelieve an individual account of any single alleged miracle. It's an interesting question in the psychology of belief: individuals who hear about one alleged miracle are readily skeptical, yet if they hear many such claims then somehow they more easily tend to believe them. Some ensembles of improbable claims somehow seem more credible rather than less probable. Christianity promptly offered multiple accounts of scores of miracles and wonders that jointly seemed compelling, at least to some people. Stories about the miracles of Jesus and the apostles were widely accepted as *evidence*, say, that Jesus was really the son of God, and in some sense God himself, and that therefore, his way of life should be followed, not others. For example, according to the Gospel of John, Jesus said: "But if I do it, even though you do not believe me, believe the miracles, that you may know and understand that the Father is in me, and I in the Father."[208]

Historians occasionally note that the alleged divinity of Pythagoras, along with his various legendary miracles, embodied an alternative theology that challenged the popular accounts about Jesus and his miracles. Yet there exists no systematic account of how the feats and miracles of Pythagoras compared to those of Jesus. How similar were they? How did stories about Pythagoras change during the rise of Christianity? Did Christian accounts lead to new Pythagorean myths?

To answer some of these questions, let's first enumerate outstanding aspects of these belief systems: the miraculous claims that were often proffered as evidence. First I will list the miracles of Jesus and his apostles, then the miracles of Pythagoras and his disciples, especially Apollonius of Tyana. Biblical scholars define miracles variously; for example, some do not count the feats of Jesus after the Resurrection, or they do not count events that happened to Jesus when he was alone, or they do not count predictions as miracles. However, I will construe *miracle* broadly, to include both private and public events, and any supernatural feats. Consider first the Christian miracles, as described mainly in the gospels of Matthew, Mark, Luke and John, but with some references to other New Testament texts. By comparing accounts of miracles, we'll grasp the extent to which Pythagorean stories in late antiquity constituted a challenge against the growing appeal of Jesus Christ as the most worthy religious leader.

[208] John 10:38

Miracles of Jesus of Nazareth

1. An angel told Mary that she would conceive a child by the Holy Spirit, and, Joseph had a dream in which an angel told him that despite Mary's pregnancy he should marry her because the child was conceived by the Holy Spirit, and that Jesus would save people from their sins.[209]
2. Jesus turned water into wine[210], made fishermen fill their nets and boats with fish[211], and, using a few loaves, some of barley, and only several fish, Jesus fed thousands of people, on two occasions.[212]
3. Jesus calmed a storm, its winds and the waves, so that the boat that carried him and his disciples could peacefully cross a lake.[213]
4. On a lake, Jesus walked on water to meet a boat.[214]
5. Jesus cursed a fig tree for being barren, and it promptly withered.[215]
6. Jesus cured eleven lepers[216]; he also cured two paralytic men[217], a crippled woman[218], a woman with a fever[219], a woman who had bled for twelve years[220], a man with dropsy (edema)[221], another with a withered hand[222], and many other people.[223]
7. Jesus enabled several blind men[224], and a deaf mute[225], to gain sight and voice.

[209] Matthew, 1:18-25, Luke 1:26-56, Luke 2:4-21
[210] John 2:6-10
[211] Luke 5:1-9
[212] Matthew 14:13-21, Matthew 15:32-39, Mark 6:31-44, Mark 8:1-9, Luke 9:10-17, John 6:5-15
[213] Matthew 8:23-27, Mark 4:35-41, Luke 8:23-27
[214] Matthew 14:22-23, Mark 45-52, John 6:16-21
[215] Matthew 21:18-22, Mark 11:12-25
[216] Matthew 8:1-4, Mark 1:40-45, Luke 5:12-16, Luke 17:11-19
[217] Matthew 9:1-8, Mark 2:1-12, Luke 5:17-26, John 5:1-18
[218] Luke 13:10-17
[219] Matthew 8:14-15, Mark 1:29-34, Luke 4:38-39,
[220] Matthew 9:18-26, Mark 5:21-43, Luke 8:40-56
[221] Luke 14:1-6
[222] Matthew 12:10, Mark 3:1-3, Luke 6:6-8
[223] Matthew 8:5-13, Matthew 14:34-36, Mark 6:53-56, Luke 7:1-10, John 4:46-54
[224] Matthew 9:27-31, Matthew 20:29-34, Mark 8:22-26, Mark 10:46-52, Luke 18:35-43, John 9:1-12
[225] Mark 7:31-37

8. Jesus exorcised many people[226], including: Mary Magdalene (he expelled seven devils from her)[227], a man in a synagogue[228], a mute[229], plus a blind and mute man[230], a man who lived in tombs (Jesus expelled a legion of demons from him and put them into swine, which then drowned in a lake)[231], a little girl[232], a boy (who foamed at the mouth, gnashed his teeth, became rigid and fell into water and fire).[233]

9. Transfiguration: standing on a mountain, Jesus radiated light, then the prophets Moses and Elijah appeared next to him, and in the sky God's voice called him "Son."[234]

10. Jesus resurrected the dead: a twelve-year-old girl who seemed dead was made to wake and walk by Jesus.[235] A man's body was going to be buried, but Jesus told him to rise, and he did.[236] Also, Lazarus had been dead for four days, but Jesus revived him.[237]

11. Jesus predicted events: he predicted his death, by crucifixion, during Passover, and that it would be in Jerusalem.[238] He foresaw that Judas would betray him.[239] He predicted that once betrayed, his disciples would flee.[240] He predicted that Peter would deny him three times.[241] He predicted his resurrection on the third day.[242] He predicted the destruction of Jerusalem and its temple.[243]

12. Jesus himself resurrected from death.[244]

[226] Matthew 8:16-17, Mark 1:32-34, Luke 4:40-41, Luke 13:31-32

[227] Mark 16:9, Luke 8:2

[228] Mark 1:21-28, Luke 4:33-37

[229] Matthew 9:32-36

[230] Matthew 12:22-32, Mark 3:20-30, Luke 11:14-23

[231] Matthew 8:28-34, Mark 5:1-20, Luke 8:26-39

[232] Matthew 15:21-28, Mark 7:25-30

[233] Matthew 17:14-21, Mark 9:14-29, Luke 9:37-49

[234] Matthew 17:1-9, Mark 9:2-8, Luke 9:28-36, Peter 1:16-18

[235] Matthew 9:18-26, Mark 5:21-43, Luke 8:41-56

[236] Luke 7:12-17

[237] John 11:1-44

[238] Matthew 16:11-13, Matthew 16:21, Matthew 20:17-19, Matthew 26:1-2, Mark 8:31-33, Mark 9:31, Mark 10:32-34, Mark 15:40-41, Luke 9:22-27, Luke 18:31-34

[239] Matthew 26:21-25. John 6:64, John 13:27-28.

[240] Matthew 26:31-32, Matthew 26, 56.

[241] Matthew, 26:33-34, Matthew 26:74-75

[242] Matthew 16:21, Matthew 27:62-63, John 2:18-22

[243] Matthew 24:1-2, Matthew 24:34, Luke 19:43-44, Luke 21:20, Luke 21:24

[244] Matthew 28:1-9, Mark 16:5-15, Luke 24:1-47, John 20:1-31, 1 Corinthians 15:3-22, Acts 2:29-31, Revelation 1:17-18

13. Jesus vanished: after his resurrection, Jesus sat with the disciples, broke the bread, and suddenly "vanished out of their sight."[245]

14. Jesus enabled his apostles to experience miracles, wonders and signs.[246] They cured the sick, crippled, or paralyzed.[247] They witnessed sounds from heaven, an earthquake, "tongues of fire," they spoke in tongues, heard voices.[248] Cornelius saw an angel.[249] When apostles were jailed, an angel twice let them escape by releasing chains, opening doors and gates.[250] Later, Paul and Silas were jailed but an earthquake broke all chains and opened all prison doors.[251] On a rooftop, Peter saw heaven and God told him to kill and eat animals.[252] God spoke to Saul, who then became blind until Ananias cured him.[253] Paul blinded a man.[254] Paul expelled evil spirits.[255] Philip too expelled spirits.[256] Peter raised Dorcas from death.[257] Paul raised Eutychus from death.[258]

If we compare the gospels of Matthew, Mark, Luke, and John to accounts about Pythagoras, then the principal four such accounts about Pythagoras are those by Apollonius, Diogenes, Porphyry, and Iamblichus. However, the account by Apollonius is unfortunately lost, though there exist a few quoted fragments in other sources. In any case, unlike the gospels, these four accounts do not purport to be written by peers who actually knew Pythagoras. They also lack the unity of purpose of the gospels. They include many more contradictions than the gospels.

Still, at least three of them—Apollonius, Porphyry and Iamblichus—do share an aim similar to that of the gospels, namely, to give evidence of the *divinity* of a remarkable moral and religious leader, mainly biographically.

[245] Luke 24:13-25

[246] Acts 5:12, Acts 6:8, Acts 8:13, Acts 14:3, Acts 19:11

[247] Acts 3:7-11, Acts 5:12-16, Acts 9:33-34, Acts 14:8-18, Acts 19:12, Acts 28:8-9.

[248] Acts 2:2-12, Acts 4:31, Acts 19:6

[249] Acts 10:4.

[250] Acts 5:19, Acts 12:7-11

[251] Acts 16:24-27

[252] Acts 10:9-17.

[253] Acts 9:3-18

[254] Acts 13:11

[255] Acts 16-18, Acts 19:12

[256] Acts 8:6-7

[257] Acts 9:39-42

[258] Acts 20:9-12

The account by Diogenes includes fewer examples of such evidence, and most are instances in which Diogenes merely quoted what others said about the divinity of Pythagoras, rather than asserting it himself. Nevertheless, these four sources yield the following synthesis of the alleged miracles or supernatural feats of Pythagoras.

Miracles of Pythagoras of Samos

1. Pythagoras was born from a beautiful woman and the god Apollo.[259]

2. Pythagoras remembered the previous lives of his soul, its former identities, including the hero Euphorbus, and he gave evidence about this.[260]

3. Pythagoras knew the previous lives of some individuals, and reminded them by clear evidence.[261] In the voice of a dog, he recognized the soul of a dear friend.[262]

4. Pythagoras showed evidence that he was divine: he showed his golden thigh to Abaris, priest of the Hyperboreans, and to others, who therefore regarded Pythagoras as Apollo.[263]

5. Pythagoras cured the ill. He ended a plague.[264] He prepared and sang songs that cured bodily diseases.[265] With songs he also cured sorrow, rage, and lust.[266]

6. Pythagoras foretold future events: He correctly predicted the number of fish in many nets, and all the fish stayed alive though being out of water.[267] He correctly predicted that a ship arriving at a harbor carried a

---

[259] Apollonius, quoted in Porphyry, sec. 28. Porphyry also quoted a poet who claimed that Pythagoras was the son of Jupiter (Zeus). Iamblichus, chap. 2, p. 2.

[260] Diogenes, secs. 5 and 23. Porphyry, secs. 26 and 45. Iamblichus, chap. 14, pp. 30-31. Apollonius in Philostratus, bk. 3, chap. 19, p. 146; chap. 7, p. 440.

[261] Porphyry, secs. 26 and 45. Iamblichus, chap. 14, p. 30.

[262] Xenophanes, quoted in Diogenes, sec. 20.

[263] Diogenes, sec. 9. Porphyry, sec. 28. Iamblichus, chap. 28, p. 75.

[264] Porphyry, sec. 29. Iamblichus, chap. 19, p. 49; chap. 28, p. 72.

[265] Porphyry, sec. 33. Iamblichus, chap 15, p. 32; chap. 29, p. 88.

[266] Porphyry, sec. 33. Iamblichus, chap. 15, p. 32; chap. 25, p. 60.

[267] Porphyry, "Life of Pythagoras," sec. 25. Iamblichus, *Pythagorean Life*, chap. 8.

corpse.[268] He infallibly predicted earthquakes.[269] In Cauconia, he predicated the death of a white bear.[270] Pythagoras practiced divination.[271]

7. Pythagoras commanded animals: In Sybaris and in Tyrrhenia, he captured deadly, poisonous serpents and released them.[272] In Daunia, an aggressive bear terrorized a neighborhood, but Pythagoras subdued it with kindness and made it swear to never attack again.[273] He also spoke to an ox and convinced it not to eat beans.[274] At the Olympic games, a white eagle flew down to Pythagoras and let him stroke it; this happened again at Croton.[275]

8. Pythagoras was at two very distant cities on the same day, conversing with people in both places: Metapontum in Italy, and Tauromenium in Sicily.[276]

9. Pythagoras "walked on air," carried by an arrow of Apollo.[277]

10. Pythagoras calmed storms over rivers and seas, and the waters themselves, "in order that his disciples might easily pass over them."[278] He also suppressed violent winds and hail.[279]

11. One time, while crossing a river with his associates, he spoke to the river and it clearly replied "Hail Pythagoras!"[280]

12. Pythagoras enabled his disciples to effect similar miracles: Empedocles affected the winds, Abaris walked on air, carried by an arrow.[281]

---

[268] Porphyry, sec. 28. Iamblichus, chap. 28, p. 75.

[269] Porphyry, sec. 29. Iamblichus, chap. 28, p. 72.

[270] Iamblichus, chap. 28, p. 75.

[271] Diogenes, sec. 18. Porphyry, sec. 25. Iamblichus, chap 19, p. 50; chap. 32, p. 111; chap. 40, p. 26.

[272] Iamblichus, chap. 28, p. 75.

[273] Porphyry, sec. 23. Iamblichus, chap. 13, p. 29.

[274] Porphyry, sec. 24. Iamblichus, chap. 13, pp. 29-30.

[275] Porphyry, sec. 25. Iamblichus, chap. 13, p. 30. OR? Iamblichus, chap. 28, p. 74.

[276] Porphyry, sec. 27, and sec. 29. Iamblichus, chap. 28, p. 72-73. Philostratus, bk. 4, chap. 10, p. 195.

[277] Porphyry, sec. 29. Iamblichus, chap. 19, p. 49; chap. 28, p. 72, 75.

[278] Porphyry, sec. 29. Iamblichus, chap. 28, p. 72. Furthermore, Iamblichus chap. 3, p. 8, describes a similar event but without specifying any storm, that is, Egyptian sailors allowed Pythagoras on their ship, and he there sat unmoving for three days, while "contrary to their expectations, their voyage had been continued and uninterrupted, as if some deity had been present."

[279] Porphyry, sec. 29. Iamblichus, chap. 19, p. 49; chap. 28, p. 72.

[280] Diogenes, sec. 9, claimed that this happened at the river Nessus. Iamblichus too, chap. 28, p. 72, said that this happened at the river Nessus. But Porphyry, sec. 27, claimed that this happened at the Caucasus river.

[281] Porphyry, sec. 29. Iamblichus, chap. 28, pp. 72, 75.

13. Pythagoras visited hell, he spent 207 years there, and he remembered the suffering endured by souls there.[282]
14. Pythagoras said that one can speak with the dead: a man seemed to have spoken with his dead father, and Pythagoras said that it really did happen.[283]
15. Pythagoras' soul was reborn multiple times, as Aethalides, Euphorbus, Hermotimus, Pyrrhus, and fifth, as Pythagoras.

According to the biographers of Pythagoras, his miracles were mainly indications of his piety toward the gods. By comparison, the miracles of Jesus were mainly acts of compassion and mercy that simultaneously demonstrated his divinity. Thus, miracles about healing the ill and the disabled feature far more abundantly in the gospels, along with exorcisms for the mentally ill. The Christian writers emphasized distinct themes that are by no means as apparent in the biographies of Pythagoras. The gospels emphasized a central theme of loving God and loving your neighbor as yourself, including the importance of caring for the poor and forgiving people who "trespass against us." The biographies of Pythagoras emphasized the importance of philosophy in order to lead a good life, in harmony with nature and the gods.

Comparing the miracles of Pythagoras to those of Jesus, we find many similarities. Both were born from human women and gods, and their human fathers were both told that this would happen. Both promised life after death. Both gave evidence that they were divine, especially by carrying out miracles: Jesus walked on water, Pythagoras walked on air. Both calmed storms while on boats with their disciples, both stilled the waters and the winds. Both knew things that ordinary humans did not, including knowledge of future events. According to both Christians and the Pythagoreans, some extraordinary and true knowledge came from dreams. Both Pythagoras and Jesus cured the ill, and ended plagues. Both came back to

---

[282] Heraclides of Pontus, as paraphrased by Diogenes, sec. 5. Hieronymus, paraphrased in Diogenes, sec. 19. Austophon, quoted in Diogenes, sec. 20. Furthermore, Diogenes, sec. 15 claimed that Pythagoras "himself says in his writings, that he had come among men after having spent two hundred and seven years in the shades below."
[283] Iamblichus, chap. 28, pp. 74, 79.

life after their deaths. Both empowered their disciples to perform similar miracles.

But there were also various important differences. Pythagoras knew about past lives, while Jesus knew about the afterlife. Jesus exorcised many demons or evil spirits from people. Meanwhile, only in the stories about Arignotus and Apollonius did exorcisms appear in connection with the Pythagoreans, but not in accounts about Pythagoras himself. Also, Jesus cared for the poor and disadvantaged by using miracles to feed thousands. And another major difference: Jesus resurrected the dead.

In the biographies about Pythagoras, the earlier texts have less miracles than the later texts. Diogenes preceded Porphyry and Iamblichus, and his account lacks at least nineteen miracles that they later described. Still, Diogenes does include two extraordinary events that apparently were not mentioned by Porphyry and Iamblichus: that Pythagoras spent time in hell, and that he recognized a friend's voice in a dog. Diogenes gave ancient literary sources for both. Porphyry added roughly seventeen kinds of miracles into his short biography of Pythagoras. And finally, Iamblichus seems to have added only two distinct miracles that are not present in Porphyry's account: that Pythagoras predicted the death of a white bear, and that he explained that one can speak to the dead in dreams, if we count that as a miracle. Iamblichus did not cite any ancient sources for these new feats, nor did he specify sources for most others in his account. By counting only the different categories of miracles, Iamblichus lists only slightly more than Porphyry before him. However, Iamblichus also added several elaborations, reiterations, or slight variations of the miracles that Porphyry described.

Just as the earlier Pythagorean texts involved less miracles, so too the earlier gospels bear less miracles than the later gospels. The Gospel of John, in some early form, seems to have been quoted by Justin Martyr, so scholars judge that it was composed before 160 CE; plus, the seemingly oldest fragment of one page of that gospel, the Rylands Library Papyrus P52, has been dated roughly between 100 and 150 CE. In the Gospel of John, there appear only ten distinct miracles (that is, at least in the way in which I roughly count them in my list, in the footnotes), whereas in the gospels of Mark and Matthew, I count at least 22 and 23 distinct kinds of miracles, respectively, and roughly 26 distinct kinds of miracles in Luke. To make any such count, one must stipulate arbitrary counting conventions, so I do not attach any significance to my individual numbers, I use them only to illustrate a rough proportion of references to miracles in the gospels. Accordingly, scholars have shown that nearly all that is included in the Gospel of Mark is found in Matthew, but not vice versa, and both seem to share some of the content of John. The Gospel of Mark is much shorter than that of Matthew, and there is not much in Mark that is not found in Matthew. For example, Mark tells an anecdote about the family or kinsmen of Jesus saying that Jesus was "out of his mind," and also, it has a long description of how Jesus used his own saliva to cure a man.[284] It seems unlikely that the author or authors of the Gospel of Mark copied closely much of Matthew, but then added such unusual anecdotes. For those reasons and others, most scholars of the New Testament agree that Mark was composed before Matthew. Finally, Luke has more distinct content that is absent in the others, including events such as, after the resurrection, Jesus vanishing in front of his apostles. Therefore, most scholars think that the gospels were composed in this sequence: Mark, Matthew, Luke, which fairly matches the impression that later writers added miracles over time. If this trend were to hold for all four gospels then the earliest written one would be the Gospel of John. However, most scholars argue that it was actually the last one to be composed, and that it was written in stages mainly around 90 to 110 CE. I do not mean to thus insinuate that the gospels or the later miracles are therefore false; the Bible is not the focus of my analysis, and anyone can well imagine that sometimes as more accounts are collected, more anecdotes and hearsay are reported. I am just using the gospels as texts for analysis because such were the texts that pagans and Christians compared and discussed.

At around 185 CE, in his work *Against Heresies*, which we have discussed, Irenaeus criticized Christians who used only one gospel. Irenaeus advocated instead that four gospels should be used, and he selected these specific texts which henceforth became canonical. He insisted that only these four gospels included the truth, exclusively, and that it had to be four.

Many Christian texts were not included in the New Testament. For example, the so-called "Infancy Gospel of Thomas," which scholars have estimated to date sometime from the second century, describes several miracles that Jesus allegedly performed as a child; that was its purpose, as it begins: "I Thomas, an Israelite, write you this account, that all the brethren from among the heathen may know the miracles of our Lord Jesus Christ in His infancy, which He did after His birth in our country." It says, among

---

[284] Mark 3:21, and Mark 8:22-26, respectively.

other things, that Jesus made twelve birds of clay and brought them to life, that he stretched a wooden board that was too short for carpentry, that he healed a woodcutter's foot, and a snake bite, that he harvested a hundred bushels of wheat from a single seed, that a boy died after running into Jesus's shoulder, that Jesus then blinded the boy's parents, that he killed one of his teachers but later resurrected him, and that he resurrected three other people: a dead playmate, another dead child, and a dead man. This ancient text is fascinating but had nearly no influence on the early Christian writers that commented about scriptures and who argued against pagan writers. Accordingly, we can sense the importance that the authors of such texts allocated to the miracles of Jesus, especially the divine power of resurrection, but we need not categorize such accounts with the others that were more widely discussed.

According to Christian tradition, the most important miracle performed by Jesus was his Resurrection. We should compare it to the alleged rebirths of Pythagoras. The gospels specify that the Romans executed Jesus by crucifixion on a Friday. His body was then wrapped in a linen cloth and laid in a new tomb. What happened next has been a subject of much debate. A passage in one letter in the New Testament, namely 1 Peter 3:18-20, refers to Christ "being put to death in the flesh but made alive in the spirit, in which he went and proclaimed to the spirits in prison, because they formerly did not obey…" According to the interpretation formalized at around 390 CE, known as "The Apostles' Creed," the statement about proclaiming or preaching to "the spirits in prison" meant that after Jesus was dead and buried, he temporarily descended into Hades, the underworld. A separate passage, Acts 2:31, states, "he foresaw and spoke about the resurrection of the Christ, that he was not abandoned to Hades, nor did his flesh see corruption." This was construed as confirming the interpretation that indeed Jesus Christ visited hell or the underworld after dying. The Gospel of Luke refers to Hades as a place of torment (Luke 16:23), but in other parts of the New Testament, the term *Hades* is used in a more ambiguous way, for example, to refer to a place where the dead awaited the resurrection of Jesus, not necessarily a place of torment and punishment. In ancient Greek religions, Hades was the abode of the dead, which earned its name from the god of the underworld. In Christianity, the term *hell* is more similar to the Greek concept of Tartarus, a deep, gloomy part of Hades that served as a dungeon for the torment and suffering of souls.

Jesus's alleged descent into hell resembles the old stories about Pythagoras. Diogenes quoted what Austophon wrote about Pythagoras:

> He said that when he did descend below
> Among the shades in Hell [or Hades], he there beheld
> All men who ever had died; and there he saw,
> That the Pythagoreans differed much
> From all the rest; for that with them alone
> Did Pluto deign to eat, much honoring
> Their pious habits.[285]

Pluto was the god of the dead. I do not know when or where this Austophon lived, but according to Diogenes, the passage comes from a play. He cited another passage in the same work, which seems to ridicule the Pythagoreans, because although they only ate herbs and vegetables, and drank pure water, their clothes were filthy and had an unbearable smell. Diogenes also cited another source: "And Hieronymus says, that when he [Pythagoras] descended to the shades below [Hades], he saw the soul of Hesiod bound to a brazen pillar, and gnashing its teeth; and that of Homer suspended from a tree, and snakes around it, as a punishment for the things that they had said of the Gods. And that those people also were punished who refrained from commerce with their wives; and that on account of this he was greatly honored by the people of Croton."[286] Here, Diogenes referred to Hieronymus of Rhodes (frequently mentioned by Cicero), a peripatetic philosopher from around 290 to roughly 230 BCE, from whom we only have extant fragments. If we do not construe Jesus as having ever descended into hell, then there is no parallelism to such old stories about Pythagoras.

Still, as other Christians did not construe Jesus as descending into hell, perhaps prior to the Apostles' Creed (ca. 390 CE), then likewise Iamblichus denied that Pythagoras had descended into hell. Iamblichus said that Pythagoras had a school in which he taught that souls eventually return to the supernatural realms, but then someone (an ambassador from Sybaris) ridiculed Pythagoras by asking that the next time he descended to Hades he should take a letter to the man's father, and bring back a reply from the father. Iamblichus noted: "Pythagoras replied, that he was not about to

---

[285] Diogenes, sec. 20.
[286] Diogenes, sec. 19.

descend into the abode of the impious, where he clearly knew that murderers were punished." Here and in another passage Iamblichus referred to Hades as a place of punishment and where souls are judged.[287] Likewise, some Christians denied that Jesus visited hell.

In any case, whether Jesus descended into hell or not, soon women approached his tomb, and according to the Gospel of Matthew, an angel then appeared, removed the great stone that sealed the tomb, and told the women that Jesus had risen from death. The gospels of Luke and John also mention an intervention by angels, but the Gospel of Mark mentions no angel and says only that Mary Magdalene found that the stone that sealed the tomb of Jesus had been removed, and that the tomb itself was empty. Then Jesus appeared to her, resurrected, so she promptly told the mourning apostles, but they did not believe her. Then Jesus appeared to them, in some initially unrecognizable form, according to Mark, Luke, and John. Finally they recognized him, partly because he proved his identity, and he spoke to them about preaching the gospel, baptism, salvation, casting out demons, and more, and then he ascended into heaven.

We can compare now the accounts of the resurrection of Jesus to the accounts of the death and transmigrations of Pythagoras. According to Heraclides of Pontus (ca. 390-310 BCE), as relayed by Diogenes, Pythagoras retained the memory of his experiences through life and death. He remembered the wanderings of his soul, and even "all that it underwent in Hades, and all that the other souls there have to endure." Jesus offered his disciples proof of his identity. Likewise, at the temple of Juno, Pythagoras identified at the temple of Juno the decayed shield of Euphorbus, which Menelaus had dedicated to Apollo, proof that Pythagoras had been Euphorbus.

About the purported immortality of Pythagoras, Diogenes at least quoted an alleged sequence of lives: Aethalides, Euphorbus, Hermotimus, Pyrrhus, and Pythagoras. Similarly, Porphyry described a nearly identical sequence: "He referred his origin to those of past ages, affirming that he was first Euphorbus, then Aethalides, then Hermotimus, then Pyrrhus, and last, Pythagoras. He showed to his disciples that the soul is immortal, and to those who were rightly purified he brought back the memory of the acts of their former lives."[288] However, Iamblichus seemed less enthusiastic

---

[287] Iamblichus, chap. 28, p. 83; chap. 30, p. 94.
[288] Porphyry, sec. 45.

about the stories of Pythagoras's many lives. The only previous life that he specified was that of Euphorbus. Why? Given the satires of Lucian of Samosata, it is easy to imagine that the topic lent itself to ridicule. It suggests that Iamblichus was crafting a story to seem more credible than some fantastic myths. To that end, he succinctly specified plenty of miracles but immersed within an expansive, credible narrative that seemed historical.

Next, Jesus and Pythagoras were entombed, both for some time. As denied by Hermippus and relayed by Diogenes, Pythagoras hid underground for some time and later he emerged, looking deathly, and spoke about having been in Hades, which made his admirers weep and believe that he was divine.[289] Apparently neither Hermippus nor Diogenes believed the story, which just echoes the story about Salmoxis that Herodotus doubted. Nonetheless, according to Diogenes, Pythagoras "himself says in his writings, that he had come among men after having spent two hundred and seven years in the shades below," that is, in Hades.[290]

So allegedly, Pythagoras seemed to have been dead longer than Jesus. According to Hermippus (ca. 420? BCE), as told by Diogenes, Pythagoras pretended to be dead long enough to emerge looking like a skeleton. According to Tertullian (ca. 215 CE), Pythagoras pretended to have been dead for seven years, while he hid in a dark cave in tortured hunger. Diogenes (ca. 225 CE) further claimed that Pythagoras said that he spent 207 years in the shades below. In contradistinction, according to the gospels, Jesus was dead for less than three days: from Friday until Sunday.

Whenever the soul of Pythagoras was reborn, he seemed unrecognizable, so he had to prove his identity in various ways: by identifying a shield, by demonstrating his extensive knowledge, by performing miracles, or by describing what he saw during death. His most famous prior life was that of Euphorbus, hero of the Trojan War, and accordingly, the most famous proof of his former existence was that at the temple of Apollo or Juno; Pythagoras identified the worn shield that had belonged to Euphorbus. Diogenes quoted two accounts of that story, without expressly endorsing it as true. But strangely, Porphyry and Iamblichus both dismissed the story "as being of too popular a nature."[291] (They did not specify the dubious sources for the story, but at least it had been voiced by Ovid, and apparently much

---

[289] Hermippus, as paraphrased by Diogenes, sec. 21.
[290] Diogenes, sec. 15.
[291] Porphyry, sec. 27. Iamblichus, chap. 14, p. 31.

earlier by Heraclides.) They did not overtly deny it, but they did not deem it worthwhile to repeat, instead, they alluded to various other proofs of how Pythagoras convinced people of his identity: "by irrefutable arguments," which Porphyry and Iamblichus did not specify.

Similarly, when Jesus came back to life, his closest friends did not recognize him. According to the Gospel of John, Mary Magdalene was weeping at his tomb, and Jesus then spoke to her but she did not recognize his voice; she thought he was a gardener. Likewise, several of his disciples were later fishing, and Jesus, standing on the shore, spoke with them, but they did not recognize him. To convince his disciples, Jesus showed them his wounded hands and side, and "many other signs" as proofs that it really was him. According to Mark 16:12, Jesus "was manifested in another form unto two of them, as they walked, on their way into the country." And according to Luke 24:16-27, two disciples walked toward a village when Jesus joined them, "But their eyes were holden that they should not know him," so they did not recognize him, even though they conversed at length, not even when "beginning from Moses and from all the prophets, he interpreted to them in all the scriptures the things concerning himself." Only when he sat among them to eat meat, and then blessed the bread, broke it, and gave it to them, did they suddenly realize that it was Jesus—and right then he vanished.

Thus, there is an interesting parallelism between the resurrection of Jesus and the rebirths of Pythagoras, namely, that both entailed some sort of physical transformation that made them seem initially unrecognizable and therefore entailed a need for them to prove their identity. Also, Jesus seems to have confronted more skepticism: his apostles required more evidence than the followers of Pythagoras. While writers such as Porphyry and Iamblichus seemed eager to convey the impression that people quickly believed that Pythagoras was divine on the basis of any single impressive trait or event, the gospels show that even the closest disciples of Jesus were repeatedly skeptical or doubtful and therefore required many impressive demonstrations of divinity. The resulting Biblical accounts therefore have a more compelling narrative, inasmuch as they incorporate some of the natural doubts that readers would reasonably have.

Jesus resurrected the dead four times—that is, three individuals plus himself. However, we might note that this results only from taking the four gospels together; for example, in addition to the resurrection of Jesus himself, the Gospel of John mentions only the resurrection of Lazarus. Still, by

177 CE the story about the resurrection of Salmoxis had become, in the hands of Celsus, evidence of how stories about resurrection were actually fake. Hermippus and Celsus said that also about Pythagoras returning from death, when he had merely hidden underground. Thus, such Pythagorean tales were used as evidence against the veracity of the resurrection of Jesus.

In any case, the idea of resurrection was not new, and it was not distinctly Christian. For example, according to ancient Greek religion, Asclepius was the son of the god Apollo and a human woman. Asclepius developed abilities to cure many people, and one day, he somehow raised Hippolytus from the dead. This angered Zeus, who then killed Asclepius. As written by the Greek poet Pindar at around 474 BCE, Asclepius "was hired to retrieve from death a man already forfeit; [therefore, Zeus] the son of Kronos hurled and drove the breath, smoking from both their chests—savior and saved alike, speared by the lightning flash."[292] Similar accounts, some with more details, were written by Hesiod, Stesichorus, Philodemus, Aeschylus, Plato, and others, all several centuries before the gospels were written. Consequently, Asclepius became worshiped as a god himself.

Likewise, according to Herodotus, in the seventh century BCE the noble Aristeas of Proconnesus was found to have died one day, but later his body disappeared from a locked building. The story is noteworthy because in addition to predating the story of Jesus, it includes a few of the same elements: someone witnessed the death of Aristeas, news of his death spread, yet he somehow resurrected and escaped a locked enclosure, and subsequently he was witnessed alive, and later suddenly vanished from sight, as proof of his divinity. The story also includes elements that later became common in accounts of Pythagorean beliefs: the worship of Apollo and the belief in the transmigration of souls, even into animals. Aristeas lived not only as two men, but as a crow. Here is the full account by Herodotus:

> Aristeas, who was as well-born as any of his townsfolk, went into a fuller's shop at Proconnesus and there died; the owner shut his shop and went away to tell the dead man's relatives, and the report of Aristeas' death being spread about in the city was disputed by a man of Cyzicus, who had come from the town of Artace, and said that he had met Aristeas going toward

[292] Pindar, "Pythian Ode Three" (ca. 474 BCE), in *Pindar's Victory Odes*, trans. Frank J. Nisetich (Baltimore: Johns Hopkins University Press, 1980), p. 171.

Cyzicus and spoken with him. While he argued vehemently, the relatives of the dead man came to the fuller's shop with all that was necessary for burial; but when the place was opened, there was no Aristeas there, dead or alive. But in the seventh year after that, Aristeas appeared at Proconnesus and made that poem which the Greeks now call the "Arimaspea," after which he vanished once again.

Such is the tale told in these two towns. But this, I know, happened to the Metapontines in Italy, two hundred and forty years after the second disappearance of Aristeas, as reckoning made at Proconnesus and Metapontum shows me: Aristeas, so the Metapontines say, appeared in their country and told them to set up an altar to Apollo, and set beside it a statue bearing the name of Aristeas the Proconnesian; for, he said, Apollo had come to their country alone of all Italian lands, and he—the man who was now Aristeas, but then when he followed the god had been a crow—had come with him. After saying this, he vanished. The Metapontines, so they say, sent to Delphi and asked the god what the vision of the man could mean; and the Pythian priestess told them to obey the vision, saying that their fortune would be better. They did as instructed. And now there stands beside the image of Apollo a statue bearing the name of Aristeas; a grove of bay-trees surrounds it; the image is set in the marketplace.[293]

Other legendary men who allegedly also resurrected and became immortal include Achilles, Alcmene, Castor, Heracles, and Melicertes.

One more example is worth mentioning. In the last book of Plato's *Republic* (ca. 380 BCE), Socrates told Glaucon a story about a man called Er, the Son of Armenios.[294] According to Socrates or Plato, this hero died as follows:

[293] Herodotus, *Histories*, in *Herodotus*, trans. A. D. Godley (Cambridge: Harvard University Press. 1920), bk. 4, chap. 14.

[294] Although Plato notes that Er was "a Pamphylian by birth," the similarity of his story to that of another mythical hero, Ara, as led some historians to infer that maybe this was actually an Armenian (or Phrygian) myth, which perhaps reached Greece through a Pamphylian source, a conjecture further substantiated by the coincidence that the name of Er's father was supposedly Armenios. For discussion, see: Agop J. Hacikyan, Gabriel Basmajian, Edward S. Franchuk, Nourhan Ouzounian, eds., *The Heritage of Armenian Literature*, Vol. 1: *From the Oral Tradition to the Golden Age* (Detroit, Michigan: Wayne State University Press, 2000), pp. 41-42.

He was killed in battle, and ten days later, when the bodies of the dead were already in a state of decomposition, his body was found unaffected by decay, and carried away home to be buried. And on the twelfth day, as he was lying on the funeral pyre, he returned to life and told them what he had seen in the other world.[295]

Allegedly, Er said that his soul left his body and traveled with many others until they reached a place where there were two pairs of entrances, some into the earth, and others into heaven. There were also some seated judges, who judged the souls and then ordered them as follows: the just were told to go up to heaven, on the right, while the unjust were told to descend to the underworld, on the left entrance. The other two openings were for souls who were arriving, either from beneath or from above. The ones who returned from the heavens spoke of beautiful sights and delights, whereas the sinners who came from the underworld wept for all that they had suffered. For each wrong they had done during their lives, they had to pay ten times in punishment and tortures in hell. And strangely, Er witnessed a process whereby some human souls chose the bodies in which they would soon live again: bodies of animals. For example, Orpheus chose to be reborn as a swan, Agamemnon chose to become an eagle, and so forth. In closing, Socrates told Glaucon that because the tale of Er had been saved, their own souls would be saved if only they obeyed the spoken word, and thus their souls would safely pass over the river of Forgetfulness, and their immortal souls would eventually receive their rewards.

Plato's account was criticized by Epicurean critics who complained that instead of really trying to prove the soul's immortality, Plato had recurred to fiction. In Greek religions, immortality was traditionally construed as involving not just the soul but also the body. However, the Pythagorean beliefs promised immortality of the soul and only a chance of rebirth into a different human body or even into the body of an animal. The idea of continuing to exist as a disembodied soul held some appeal, but not nearly as much as the common desire to continue to exist as oneself. Yet some ancient Greek philosophers regarded it as preposterous that everyone who dies might return to life; death seemed much more final.

Hence, just as the Platonic or Pythagorean idea of transmigration did not sway most Greeks, it likewise stood at a disadvantage against Christians

---

[295] Plato, *Republic*, bk. 10.

who offered the eventual resurrection of the body. Against the hope of living as oneself, the Pythagoreans offered something that seemed strangely disquieting: that one might be reborn as someone else, without memories, somewhere else, or even as a dog. Certainly an interesting topic for speculation and discussion, but not very attractive to compel belief.

Along with the Resurrection, another important aspect of the gospels was the communion that Jesus established with his disciples. This communion was embodied by the ritual of breaking bread. By contrast, according to Diogenes, Pythagoras forbade the breaking of bread:

> Another of the precepts of Pythagoras was, that men ought not to break bread; because in ancient times friends used to assemble around one loaf, as they even now do among the barbarians. Nor would he allow men to divide bread which unites them. Some think that he laid down this rule in reference to the judgment which takes place in hell; some because this practice engenders timidity in war. According to others, what is alluded to is the Union, which presides over the government of the universe.[296]

Likewise, Iamblichus discussed the rule that "bread is not to be broken, because it contributes to the judgment in Hades."[297] Iamblichus briefly described but dismissed other justifications for this precept which he said had been contrived by other philosophers: that it is not proper to dissolve what congregates, or that it is improper to begin an undertaking by breaking or diminishing.

In ancient times, breaking bread was a way of sharing food in a thankful and modest way. But to the Christians, it also represented the communion between Jesus and his disciples on the Last Supper, shortly before his death:

> And as they were eating, Jesus took bread, blessed and broke it, and gave it to the disciples and said, "Take, eat; this is My body." Then He took the cup, and gave thanks, and gave it to them, saying, "Drink from it, all of you. For this is My blood of the new covenant, which is shed for many for the remission of sins. But I say to you, I will not drink of this fruit of the vine from now on until that day when I drink it new with you in My Father's kingdom." (Matthew 26:26-29)

[296] Diogenes, "Life of Pythagoras," sec. 19.
[297] Iamblichus, chap. 18, p. 46.

According to 1 Corinthians 11:23-24, "the Lord Jesus on the same night in which He was betrayed took bread; and when He had given thanks, He broke it and said, 'Take, eat; this is My body which is broken for you; do this in remembrance of Me.'" Henceforth, the disciples and followers of Jesus construed breaking bread as the communion of the body of Christ. According to Acts 2:46, the early Christians had the practice of daily "breaking bread from house to house."

By the time of Iamblichus, the Christians had suffered almost three centuries of persecution by the Roman Empire. In that context, to deny the breaking of bread was not merely about how to share meals. Furthermore, there is a similar contrast regarding the drinking of wine. While Jesus shared wine as a way to represent a communion of his blood, Diogenes mentioned a simpler restriction by Pythagoras, that he "never drank wine in the daytime."[298]

Another conflict between the teachings of Pythagoras and the miracles of Jesus is embodied in the strange story of the fig tree. The gospels of Matthew and Mark say that one day Jesus was hungry so he approached a fig tree, to eat some figs, and it had leaves, but no figs, because it was not the season for them. Then, according to the Gospel of Mark, Jesus cursed the tree: "he saith unto it, Let there be no fruit from thee henceforward for ever. And immediately the fig tree withered away. And when the disciples saw it, they marveled, saying, How did the fig tree immediately wither away?"[299] For centuries, theologians have tried to make sense of this passage, in various ways. Jesus insisted to his disciples that with faith they too would be able to do such things, not just to a fig tree, but even speak to a mountain to cast it into the sea.

In contradistinction, the legendary vegetarian Pythagoras would not curse a tree. A brief passage by Porphyry, gives the opposite impression; he said that Pythagoras taught that "A cultivated and fruit-bearing plant, harmless to man and beast, should be neither injured nor destroyed."[300] It was a fitting quotation for the author of the *Fifteen Books Against the Christians*.

There are other contrasts that warrant discussion. Pythagoras communicated with animals and seemed to control them. Jesus seems not to have

[298] Diogenes, sec. 18.
[299] Mark 21:19-20.
[300] Porphyry, sec. 39.

done such things, although previously, in the Hebrew Bible, the book of Job stated: "If you want to learn, then go and ask the wild animals and the birds, the flowers and the fish. Any of them can tell you what the LORD has done. Every living creature is in the hands of God."[301] Jesus was born in a stable, slept in a feeding trough, and was later called "the Lamb of God."[302] He retreated into the wilderness and spent time with wild animals, but he contrasted the lives of animals to his own itinerant life: "The foxes have holes, and the birds of the heaven have nests; but the Son of man hath not where to lay his head."[303] In contradistinction to the most popular portrayals of Pythagoras, Jesus ate meat and the Biblical God wanted humans to eat animals. The gospels are unclear about the status of animal sacrifices. At least in the Gospel of Matthew, reportedly during the Sabbath, Jesus said: "I desire mercy, and not sacrifice," without mentioning animals, yet Paul's letter to the Hebrews explained that sacrifices and burned offerings would no longer compensate for sins, that Jesus and God did not want sacrifices, against tradition.[304] Hence in the history of religion, the denials of animal sacrifices were instituted among the Pythagoreans, and later among the Christians, though further evidence would be needed to show whether these pagan traditions influenced the early Christians in this regard.

The Gospel of Luke, 5:1-8, describes a miracle in which fishermen on a lake had failed to capture any fish at all with their nets, but then Jesus instructed Simon to take his boat and nets to the deep, and surprisingly, the nets now captured many fish, enough to fill two boats. According to Luke, his miracle happened early in the ministry of Jesus. The Gospel of John does not describe any such event early on, but John 21:3-12 describes a similar event that happened soon after Jesus had resurrected: Jesus enabled his disciples to catch one hundred and fifty-three fish.

In contrast, Porphyry and Iamblichus described a somewhat opposite miracle: Pythagoras encountered fishermen who were drawing their nets full of fish; Pythagoras told them that he knew exactly how many fish were in the nets, he told them the number, and he was correct, so the fishermen

---

[301] Job 12:7-10.
[302] Luke 2:7, John 1:29.
[303] Mark 1:13, Luke 9:58.
[304] Matthew, 12:7, Matthew 9:13, Epistle to the Hebrews, 10:8-15.

agreed to return the fish to the water, all of which had strangely survived; and Pythagoras kindly paid them the price of the fish.[305]

Interestingly, an earlier version of the story does not attribute any miracle to how Pythagoras handled the fish. At roughly around 100 CE, Plutarch remarked: "And they say that Pythagoras bought a draught of fishes, and presently commanded the fishermen to let them all out of the net; and this shows that he did not hate or mind the fishes, as things of another kind destructive to man, but that they were dearly beloved creatures, since he paid a ransom for their freedom."[306] Plutarch described no miracle here, instead he said that this anecdote illustrated the tenderness and humanity of some philosophers. Plutarch said that the Pythagoreans, out of a broad sense of justice, believed that it was wrong to kill or eat fish because they do not harm humans, and because they are practically encompassed by another world, separate from ours.

Briefly consider another issue about animals: the New Testament was not sufficiently clear to compel all Christians to practice the same dietary restrictions. Against the advice of Pythagoras, most Christians continued to eat meat. Yet a few interpreted Jesus's words to mean that we should not; thus, in particular, the Roman theologian Jerome (ca. 393) argued that "The eating of animal flesh was unknown before the great flood. But since the great flood we have had the fibers and the stinking fluids of animal flesh stuffed into our mouths. . . . the Christ, who appeared when the time was fulfilled, again joined the end to the beginning, so that now we are no longer allowed to eat animal flesh."[307] This remained a minority view, but it shows how Christianity had the flexibility to absorb doctrines that at least to some people seemed Pythagorean.

Consider now *The Life of Apollonius of Tyana.* In view of the abundant miracles that Diogenes, Porphyry, and Iamblichus attributed to Pythagoras,

[305] Porphyry, "Life of Pythagoras," sec. 25. Iamblichus, *Pythagorean Life*, chap. 8.
[306] Plutarch, "Symposiacs," bk. 8, Question 8, sec. 3., in A. H. Clough and William W. Goodwin, *Plutarch's Essays and Miscellanies*, Vol. 3 (Boston: Little, Brown and Company, 1909), 421. In another work, Plutarch commented: "If then Pythagoras, accustoming his disciples to abstain from all cruelty and inhumanity to the brute creation, did right to discountenance bird-fouling, and to buy up draughts of fishes and bid them be thrown into the water again, and to forbid killing any but wild animals," in "Advantage and Profit from Enemies," in *Plutarch's Complete Works: Essays and Miscellanies*, Vol. 2 (New York: Thomas Y. Crowell & Co., 1909), 207.
[307] Hieronymus, *Against Jovinianus*, 1:30.

it is surprising that Philostratus stated very few miracles about Pythagoras: that he had been Euphorbus returned from death; that he was revered as the man who came from Jove (Jupiter); that he conversed with gods, including Apollo, Pallas (Athena), and the Muses; that he spoke as a man inspired; and that once he was in two cities at the same time.[308]

Philostratus wrote that the followers of Pythagoras claimed that his disciple Empedocles of Acargas too had become immortal, because he had written this line: "Rejoice ye, for I am unto you an immortal God, and no more mortal."[309] Philostratus also noted that "Empedocles marched boldly through the most frequented places of Greece with his hair tied up in fine purple fillets, reciting hymns in which he announced his change from a man to a God."[310] But these were merely passing allusions to a famous disciple of Pythagoras; the focus of Philostratus's narrative was instead the famous exorcist from Tyana.

Philostratus claimed to have collected most of the letters by Apollonius, and he cited the account of Apollonius's constant companion and disciple, Damis, as if such a document existed.[311] Like Pythagoras and Empedocles, allegedly some people viewed Apollonius as a demigod. Philostratus claimed that "All the people of the country [Tyana] say that Apollonius was the son of Jupiter, but he constantly called himself the son of Apollonius."[312] By denying that Jupiter (Zeus) was his father, Apollonius might seem modest, but the claim about being his own son insinuates immortality, and thus it could insinuate equality with the gods. This implication appears other times in the purported biography. When the sage Iarchas saw that Apollonius loved the art of divination, he esteemed him as "equal to the Delphic God."[313]

Thus like Jesus, Apollonius was identified as both equal and unequal to a god. But in the narrative of Philostratus, such points were hardly emphasized. The claims quoted above were only briefly stated and are submerged within hundreds of chapters. It seems that Philostratus wanted to challenge

---

[308] Philostratus, *The Life of Apollonius of Tyana*, trans. Edward Berwick (London: T. Payne, 1809), bk. 1, chap. 1, p. 1; chap. 2, p. 4; bk. 4, chap. 10, p. 195.
[309] Empedocles fragment, translation from: Philostratus, *The Life of Apollonius of Tyana*, Vol. 1, trans. F. C. Conybeare (London: William Heinemann, 19012), p. 5.
[310] Philostratus, (1809), bk. 7, chap. 6, p. 443.
[311] Philostratus, bk. 7, chap. 28, p. 407; chap. 35, p. 416.
[312] Philostratus, bk. 1, chap 6, p. 11.
[313] Philostratus, bk. 3, chap. 42, pp. 173-174.

Christianity, but in subtle ways. He did not refer to Christ or his followers, but occasionally he seems to insinuate that the ways of Apollonius were preferable.

For example, whereas Jesus and his disciples shared meat and wine, the followers of Apollonius offered him meat and wine but he refused. Damis offered him a cup of wine: "While they were eating their frugal meal by a fountain of clear water, Damis poured out part of the wine he got from the Indians, and said, I pledge you, Apollonius, in this cup, in honor of [the god] Jupiter Salvator, of which I think you may drink…"[314] But Apollonius did not drink from the cup; he argued that it was much better to drink water instead of wine. He gave four reasons: that those who drink water sleep better than those who drink wine, even in moderation; that complete abstinence enabled him to be a better philosopher; that he was able to foretell the future (in dreams) only by being very sober; and that only those who drink water are "fit vehicles for the reception of the God."[315] Apollonius allowed his followers to drink wine and eat meat; he did not forbid it, but the message was clear: there was a higher road of purity that led to enlightenment. Philostratus said that by following the example of Apollonius, men learned to become philosophers.

Such were some of the ways in which Apollonius diverged from the Christians, but overall, however, the text shows that Philostratus had fashioned this Pythagorean role model to increasingly *resemble* Jesus Christ. To illustrate this, consider his alleged feats.

Miracles of Apollonius of Tyana

1. Apollonius was divine by birth: his pregnant mother was told by a manifestation of the god Proteus that she would give birth to this god.[316]
2. Apollonius predicted a plague at Ephesus.[317]
3. Apollonius had a daemon that guided him.[318]

[314] Philostratus, bk. 2, chap. 7, p. 74.
[315] Philostratus, bk. 2, chap. 7, p. 74-75; bk. 1, chaps. 35-37, pp. 113-117.
[316] Ibid., bk. 1, chap. 4, p. 8.
[317] Philostratus, bk. 4, chap. 4, pp. 190-191; bk. 8, chap. 7, pp. 449, 452.
[318] Ibid., bk. 1, chap. 2, p. 5; bk. 1, chap. 18, p. 31;

4. Apollonius knew men's thoughts, and their languages without studying them.[319]

5. Apollonius instantly appeared in a distant city, Ephesus.[320] He later somehow traveled from Rome to Puteoli in hours instead of three days, and said "ascribe it to God."[321]

6. Apollonius witnessed cures by the god Æsculapius; and by the Indian sage Iarchas, who cured the following: a lame man, a man with a withered hand, a blind man, a woman who had seven difficult labors, and also, by writing a letter to exorcise a boy possessed by an evil demon, the ghost of a dead warrior.[322]

7. Apollonius cured people: he cured a young man of dropsy (edema),[323] he cured a boy who behaved like a mad dog,[324] he cured the people of Ephesus from a plague,[325] and he cured many other diseases.[326]

8. Apollonius influenced wild creatures. He made a mad dog obedient by stroking it.[327] Fierce guard dogs at Crete did not bark at him but gave him fawning attention.[328] Also, he subdued a satyr that hurt women, by getting it drunk, and he tamed another satyr.[329]

9. Apollonius exorcised demons. He ordered the Ephesians to kill a man that was possessed by a demon, to stone it to death, but it then became a huge, fierce dog, vomiting foam.[330] He exorcised a demon from an effeminate and belligerent young man, which made a statue shatter.[331] At a prenuptial banquet Apollonius unmasked the bride as a bloodthirsty Lamia specter and then all her gold, silver and ornaments vanished.[332]

---

[319] Ibid., bk. 1, chap. 19, p. 32.
[320] Philostratus, bk. 4, chap. 10, p. 195.
[321] Philostratus, bk. 8, chaps. 10-12, p. 466-468.
[322] Philostratus, bk. 3, chap. 39, pp. 170-171.
[323] Philostratus, bk. 1, chap. 9, pp. 14-16.
[324] Philostratus, bk. 6, chap. 43, pp. 365-366.
[325] Philostratus, bk. 4, chaps. 10-11, pp. 195-197
[326] Philostratus, bk. 4, chaps. 11, p. 197
[327] Philostratus, bk. 6, chap. 43, p. 365.
[328] Philostratus, bk. 8, chap. 30, p. 488.
[329] Philostratus, bk. 6, chap. 27, pp. 348-350.
[330] Philostratus, bk. 4, chap. 10, p. 196.
[331] Philostratus, bk. 4, chap. 20, p. 211-212.
[332] Philostratus, bk. 4, chap. 25, pp. 217-220. The references to a satyr, according to Greek mythology, a man with some of the body parts of a goat, might seem to

10. Apollonius resurrected people. He resurrected the buried body of the legendary warrior Achilles by summoning his soul.[333] At a funeral, Apollonius revived a young woman by saying a few words.[334]

11. At a temple, a tame lion approached Apollonius and he then identified him as the soul of the Egyptian King Amasis, and then the lion roared and cried.[335]

12. Transmigration and immortality. The soul of Apollonius had previously lived as captain of a ship, and he had memories of that life.[336]

13. Apollonius vanished. At the end of his public trial by Emperor Domitian, Apollonius said that they could not take his soul or his body, quoting Homer "not even deadly spear can slay me, because I am not mortal," at which moment he vanished from the tribunal.[337]

14. Apollonius knew things at a distance. One day at Ephesus, at around noon, he walked with people outdoors and suddenly yelled "Strike the tyrant!" And he announced that at that very moment, in distant Rome, Emperor Domitian had been killed, and he had seen it. His followers doubted him, but they learned he was right.[338]

15. After he died, a skeptical young man publicly denied the doctrine of immortality, but one day Apollonius spoke to him in a dream and convinced him of immortality.[339]

Among the alleged miracles of Apollonius, it is noteworthy that there are several kinds that had *not* been attributed to Pythagoras by his main

constitute a properly pagan notion in the stories about Apollonius. However, we might note that the Bible also has instances of mythical creatures, for example, Isaiah 13:21 mentions satyrs: "But wild beasts of the desert shall lie there; and their houses shall be full of doleful creatures; and owls shall dwell there, and satyrs shall dance there." Likewise, other Biblical texts include other unusual creatures, including: many references to dragons (e.g., Malachi 1:3), unicorns (Isaiah 34:7), cockatrices (Jeremiah 8:17), and fiery serpents (Numbers 21:6).

[333] Philostratus, bk. 4, chap. 16, pp. 202-206.

[334] Philostratus, bk. 4, chap. 45, pp. 242-243.

[335] Philostratus, bk. 5, chap. 62, p. 297-298.

[336] Philostratus, bk. 6, chap. 21, p. 340.

[337] Philostratus, bk. 8, chap. 5, p. p. 431. Strangely, chapter 8 of the same book refers to the same incident merely as "Apollonius departed from the tribunal," instead of (literally) vanished.

[338] Philostratus, bk. 8, chap. 26, p. 484.

[339] Philostratus, bk. 8, chap. 31, p. 490.

biographers but that were attributed to Jesus in the gospels. Specifically, that Apollonius exorcised demons, cured a man with dropsy, resurrected the dead, and once vanished. Likewise, Philostratus referred to miracles by the sage Iarchas which echoed miracles allegedly done by Jesus: curing a man with a withered hand, healing a blind man, and perhaps another miracle—curing a woman who had seven difficult labors, which might seem somewhat similar to Jesus curing a woman who had bled for twelve years.

Consider now some of the similarities more closely. The miracle in which Apollonius resurrected a young woman whom everyone regarded as having suddenly died resembles the miracle in which Jesus raised a twelve-year-old girl who suddenly died.[340] Philostratus remarked that it was unclear whether the young woman was faintly alive or whether Apollonius retrieved her soul, though a whole funeral crowd surrounded them, and similarly, contrary to a crowd's impression, Jesus remarked, "Why make ye a tumult, and weep? The child is not dead, but sleepeth."[341] Then, Jesus held the girl's hand and said, "Damsel, I say unto thee, arise," and she did; and likewise with Apollonius: "all he did was, to touch the maid, uttering a few words over her in a low tone of voice, he wakened her from that death with which she seemed to be overcome." In both cases, the damsel was instantly well.

Perhaps the most important similarity between the narratives about Jesus and Apollonius is their confrontation with Roman rulers and the subsequent demonstrations of the immortality of Jesus and Apollonius. The gospels say that the Roman authorities and priests at Judaea charged Jesus with blasphemy, a capital crime under Biblical law, they also accused him of claiming to be King of the Jews; then, the Roman Prefect, Pontius Pilate, reluctantly consented to executing Jesus. As for Apollonius, Philostratus portrayed him as being put on trial before the Roman Emperor Domitian for being accused of performing divination and magic, especially for bloody sacrificing a boy in a field, and for planning insurrection against the Emperor, and for pretending to be a God.[342] After being imprisoned and chained for some time, a disciple asked Apollonius how he should expect

---

[340] Ibid., bk. 4, chap. 45, p. 243.
[341] Mark 5:21-43
[342] Philostratus, bk. 7, chapter 20, pp. 395-396, chap. 21, p. 397; bk. 8, chap. 5, pp. 429-430.

to see him after his trial, and Apollonius replied: "alive, in my opinion, but in yours, raised from the dead."[343]

Along with the topics at hand, there is a significant issue of refusing to perform miracles on command. Jesus sometimes refused to perform miracles, especially for some persons who disbelieved in him, and also to save himself from crucifixion. When some skeptical people came up to Jesus and asked that he give them some sign of his divinity, Jesus refused.[344] When he was crucified, some passersby, the Roman soldiers, and the other crucified men challenged him to free himself if he was really the Christ or the King of the Jews, but he did not.[345] Likewise, when Apollonius was bound in chains, Emperor Domitian allegedly demanded: "I will not let you go until you first become either water, or a wild beast, or a tree." And then Apollonius insinuated his powers while abstaining to use them: "Though I was capable of becoming what you say, I will not do it, lest I should betray those men who run the risk of being unjustly put to death."[346]

The Emperor asked who would defend Apollonius, and he replied "Time, and the spirit of the Gods, and the love of philosophy, to which I have been addicted."[347] At his trial, Jesus had been asked if he was the Son of God, but he did not directly reply; he said that they had said so, and that they would not believe his answer, which still sounded like a blasphemy to the priests.[348] Whereas the main accuser of Apollonius asked him, "Why do men call you a God?" And he replied, "Because every man that is good is entitled to that appellation."[349]

At length, Apollonius argued that he had not done the things for which he was accused, but instead, that on the night when the boy was sacrificed, he had been outside the walls of Rome, caring for a dying friend, with witnesses. In the end, Apollonius defended himself so well that the Emperor acquitted him of all charges, but required that Apollonius remain in order to engage in private conversation. But Apollonius rejected the Emperor's request (rightly, said Philostratus, who explained that the Emperor was not sincere). He criticized the Emperor for ruining the cities, the continent, and

---

[343] Philostratus, bk. 7, chap. 41 p. 423.
[344] Matthew 12:38-40, Matthew 16:1-4, Mark 8:11-12, Luke 11:29
[345] Matthew 27:39-45, Mark 15:29-32, Luke 23:39.
[346] Philostratus, bk. 7, chap. 34, p. 415.
[347] Philostratus, bk. 7, chap. 34, p. 415.
[348] Matthew 26:63-67, Luke 22:69-71, John 19:7-11
[349] Philostratus, bk. 8, chap. 5, p. 429.

more. Philostratus claimed to quote directly from the written speech of Apollonius, who finally challenged the Emperor, asking him to "send persons to take my body for it is impossible to take my soul: and I will add, not even my body, for as Homer says, 'not even thy deadly spear can slay me, because I am not mortal.'"[350] Then suddenly Apollonius vanished from the imperial tribunal. Immediately afterward, the Emperor behaved strangely; stunned, he became confused and incoherent. A few hours later, Apollonius appeared in the distant city of Puteoli, a seemingly impossible feat, since it was a three-days journey away.

Comparisons to the narrative of Jesus are irresistible. Jesus was imprisoned and interrogated, but whereas a crowd chose to have him crucified, and then he soon died on the cross, the philosopher Apollonius instead defended himself so well that he was acquitted. Both then vanished: Apollonius at the end of his trial, and Jesus after his resurrection, in the company of his apostles, having revealed his identity to them. So what really happened to Apollonius? Philostratus said that after he had been imprisoned by the Emperor, nobody expected him to escape. Accordingly, Philostratus admitted that there were various accounts of what happened next, at least at the time of the trial: "Various rumors were spread concerning him; one was that he was burnt alive, another was that he was alive, but had his back stuck full of little hooks; some people said he was cast into a deep pit, and others that he drowned in a well. But as soon as his arrival was fully ascertained, all Greece flocked to see him with more eagerness than they ever did to the Olympic Games."[351] Allegedly, Apollonius himself did not explain how he escaped Domitian, yet people found out about his dramatic and miraculous escape, and they worshipped him as divine.

But Philostratus was not in Rome when Apollonius allegedly vanished, and he was not in Puteoli when Apollonius allegedly reappeared. So even if the sources that Philostratus mentions actually existed (letters and works by Apollonius and his disciples), Philostratus himself had few reasons to believe the miraculous parts of such accounts. So why did Philostratus choose to consecrate his hero as triumphant? An interesting analogy can be sensed in a similar dilemma that the writer ascribed to his subject. After all, an

---

[350] Philostratus, bk. 8, chap. 5, p. p. 431. Strangely, chapter 8 of the same book refers to the same incident merely as "Apollonius departed from the tribunal," instead of (literally) vanished.
[351] Philostratus, bk. 8, chap. 15, p. 472.

immortal being as powerful as Jesus or Apollonius could well choose to escape all harm. Philostratus explained Apollonius's choice as follows: "he judged that it would make his peculiar character better known to the world, and at the same time show that there would be no possibility of taking him against his will; and lastly, that it would free him from any fears he might have of injuring the men in question."[352] Would the hero really become more famous than the martyr? If Philostratus had the same opinion, then he was thoroughly mistaken. The image of Apollonius triumphant became as small as a single footnote by comparison to the story of Jesus crucified. Indeed, in some books that is what it is. The promise of life after death seemed more plausible when proffered by a martyr who had been wrongfully executed than when advocated by a philosopher who had avoided execution by speechifying.

Christians believe the narratives of the gospels as accurate historical accounts, while at the same time they dismiss Philostratus's account as mere fiction. Indeed, the novelistic structure of *Life of Apollonius* suggests that it was not a work that confronted the ambiguities of historical sources and the pervasive gaps in extant documentary evidence of whatever happened, how, and why. Still, it is interesting that as Christianity emerged, early Roman historians did not record any of its key events that later became so famous. We might expect that early historians likewise would not notice another religious man, the pagan philosopher from Tyana who merely became the subject of legends. But interestingly, that was not the case.

On 96 CE, Emperor Domitian was murdered. Later, the Roman consul and historian Cassius Dio wrote his extensive *Roman History*, during the years 200-222 CE. Philostratus's *Life of Apollonius* was published around 220 CE, so apparently Dio composed his account before that of Philostratus.[353] Among many topics, Dio discussed the death of Emperor Domitian, and he there briefly included a description of an apparently miraculous display of knowledge by Apollonius. Here is Dio's intriguing account of the death of Domitian, who was assailed by a conspiracy:

I have one more astonishing fact to record, which I shall touch on after I have given the account of Domitian's end. As soon as he rose to leave the

---

[352] Philostratus, bk. 8, chap. 5, p. 431.
[353] For discussion, see Maria Dzielska, *Apollonius of Tyana in Legend and History,* trans. Piotr Pienkowski (Rome: L'Erma di Bretschneider, 1986), pp. 30-32.

courthouse and was ready to take his afternoon nap, as was his custom, first Parthenius took the blade out of the sword, which always lay under his pillow, so that he should not have the use of that. Next he sent in Stephanus, who was stronger than the rest. The latter smote Domitian, and though it was not an opportune blow the emperor was knocked to the ground, where he lay. Then, fearing an escape, Parthenius leaped in, or, as some believe, he sent Maximus, a freedman. Thus both Domitian was murdered, and Stephanus perished likewise in a rush that those who had not shared in the conspiracy made upon him.

The matter of which I spoke, saying that it surprises me more than anything else, is this. A certain Apollonius of Tyana on the very day and at that very hour when Domitian was being murdered (this was later confirmed by other events that happened in both places) climbed a lofty stone at Ephesus (or possibly some other town) and having gathered the populace, uttered these words: "Bravo, Stephanus! Good, Stephanus! Smite the wretch! You have struck, you have wounded, you have killed him!!" This is what really took place, though there should be ten thousand doubters. Domitian had lived forty-four years, then months, and twenty six days. His reign had lasted fifteen years and five days. His body was stolen away and buried by his nurse, Phyllis.[354]

Against our natural urge to simply disbelieve Dio's account, we should at least articulate some textual reasons that justify our skepticism. First, it is bizarre to read someone so emphatically asserting that an incredible event in fact did happen, giving alleged quotations and alluding to many witnesses, yet at the same time expressing doubt about where the event happened: "Ephesus (or possibly some other town)." Also, Dio explicitly said that he believed that all events of such great magnitude have previous indications. Apollonius's apparently instant knowledge of the distant murder was not the only prediction—Dio specified three others. First, in a dream, Domitian had seen a man approaching him with a sword. Second, a man in Germany had publicly foretold that the emperor would die—even allegedly the specific day—correctly. Before that day, that man was brought to Rome, before Domitian, yet he declared again that this would happen, and

---

[354] Cassius Dio Cocceianus, *Dio's Annals of Rome*, Vol. 5 (A.D. 54-211), trans. Herbert Baldwin Foster (Troy, New York: Pafraets Book Company, 1906), chap. 67, sec. 17-18, pp. 174-175.

was detained. Third, Dio said that someone else had also predicted that the emperor would be killed, but by dogs. That man was then ordered to be burned alive, but rain extinguished his funeral pyre, and afterward, ironically, dogs found him, tied there, and killed him.

Thus it is clear that Dio collected not just historical accounts but any remarkable hearsay. Still, we do not have to dismiss Dio's account about Apollonius merely as fiction; a second reading will clarify that what Dio reported was not necessarily impossible. He did not say that Apollonius was divine, nor even that he had the power to see things at a distance; instead, he merely quoted something that Apollonius allegedly said. We might wonder or imagine whether Apollonius was part of a conspiracy, or whether he merely had heard of the date in which someone said that Domitian would be murdered. Still, it is striking to see a historian actually mention the man who otherwise seems fictitious in the narrative of Philostratus. It reminds us that apparently there really did live a person called Apollonius of Tyana. Notably, Dio reported the story about Apollonius, but said nothing at all about a Jesus of Nazareth.

Deaths of Pythagoras

Let's return now to Pythagoras. Just as the stories of Plato's birth sought to prove his divinity, so too with the stories about the death of Pythagoras, by showing his noble character and martyrdom. Apollonius said that Pythagoras was the son of the god Apollo. He also said that Pythagoras was a *daemon*. Owing to the antiquity of the many sources used by Diogenes, Porphyry and Iamblichus, there were many ambiguities about the religious identity of Pythagoras. Some persons said that he was the son of another god, Hermes. Even Iamblichus, who tried to craft a definite narrative, admitted that there were different opinions about Pythagoras. Some people said that Pythagoras was Apollo himself.[355] There was a temple of Apollo at Delphi, where its patron god was known as the "Pythian Apollo." But there were also reputed to be other worshippers of Apollo, in a distant land far north of Thrace, and since the Greeks thought that the North Wind,

---

355 Iamblichus, chap. 5, p. 14.

"Boreas," lived in Thrace, they referred to the people beyond Thrace as the Hyperboreans. Hence there was a distinct manifestation of the god, known as the "Hyperborean Apollo." So Iamblichus noted that some people viewed Pythagoras as the Pythian Apollo, and others as the Hyperborean Apollo. Iamblichus also said that "others celebrated him as one of the Olympian Gods, who, in order to benefit and correct the mortal life, appeared to the men of those times in a human form, in order that he might extend to them the salutary light of felicity and philosophy. And indeed a greater good never came, nor ever will come to mankind, than that which was imparted by the Gods through this Pythagoras."[356] Not that the Christians would agree.

My point is that the stories about Pythagoras did not converge, which undermined their clarity or credibility. There were certainly contradictions in the gospels too; for example, according to the Gospel of John, the cross of Jesus was carried by his disciple Simon, but in the other gospels Jesus himself carried it. Also, in John the Last Supper happened on Passover eve, while in the other gospels it happened on the previous night. Still, the gospels converged much more than the accounts about Pythagoras. To underscore this point, consider the question of how Pythagoras died.

There were many conflicting accounts about the death of Pythagoras. Diogenes wrote *six* different accounts, Porphyry wrote three, whereas Iamblichus gave one, plus, he quoted one variation from factors described by Apollonius. Among the stories relayed by Diogenes and Porphyry, two are from Hermippus and one from Dicaearchus. I also include brief but independent accounts by Athenagoras and Hippolytus.

At around 176 CE, Athenagoras, an Athenian Christian, commented: "from of old it has been the custom, and not in our time only, for vice to make war on virtue. Thus Pythagoras, with three hundred others, was burned to death."[357] This account might seem to differ only slightly from the following, but because it involves three hundred people instead of forty, it seems sufficiently distinct to be listed separately. Similarly, Hippolytus mentioned that Pythagoras was "burned along with his disciples in

---

356 Ibid.
357 Athenagoras the Athenian, "A Plea for the Christians" (ca. 176 CE), chap. 31; in Alexander Roberts and James Donaldson, eds., *Ante-Nicene Christian* Library, Vol. 2: *Justin Martyr and Athenagoras*, trans. B. Pratten (Edinburgh: T. &. T. Clark, 1870), 415.

Croton."[358] And according to Diogenes, he died in this way: "When he was sitting with some of his companions in Milo's house, some one of those whom he did not think worthy of admission into it, was excited by envy to set fire to it."[359] Porphyry seems to have agreed with Diogenes, and gave a more detailed account: at Croton, a wealthy but violent man, Cylon, wanted to join the Pythagorean brotherhood, but Pythagoras rejected him. Cylon was offended and became furious, so he and his friends raised accusations against Pythagoras and conspired against his disciples. Thus, when these disciples gathered at Milo's house, Cylon's followers set it on fire, thus burning or stoning to death all except two who managed to escape: Archippus and Lysis.[360] But according to Porphyry, Pythagoras was not then there, he had just traveled to Delos. Iamblichus told an even longer version, explaining that the Pythagoreans were involved in issues of government, but thereafter they withdrew from politics.[361] He noted that the account by Apollonius included additional factors regarding the political background for why some of the people of Croton disliked the Pythagoreans.

According to Porphyry, some writers claimed that when the meeting-house was set on fire, Pythagoras was in it, but some of his disciples "threw themselves into the flames, to make a bridge of safety for him, whereby he escaped." But then he died of grief.[362] Diogenes too reported an account in which Pythagoras did not die at the fire: "Dicaearchus, however, says that Pythagoras died a fugitive in the temple of the Muses at Metapontum after forty days' starvation." It is unclear who was this Dicaearchus, if he was a geographer from Messana then he lived at around 300 BCE. Similarly, Porphyry gave a more expansive account, that "Dicaearchus and other more accurate historians" said instead that Cylon's men attacked and killed forty of the Pythagoreans who were gathered in a house, and afterward they gradually killed others. Pythagoras fled to three cities, but in each of them he was accosted by mobs. So he went to the temple of the Muses, in Metapontum, stayed there for forty days, until he died of starvation.[363]

---

[358] Hippolytus, *The Refutation of All Heresies*, in Alexander Roberts and James Donaldson, eds. *Ante Nicene Christian Library*, Vol. VI: *Hippolytus, Bishop of Rome, Vol. 1* (Edinburgh: T. & T. Clark, 1868), bk. 1, chap. 2, p. 35.

[359] Diogenes, sec. 21.

[360] Porphyry, sec. 55.

[361] Iamblichus, chap 35, pp. 127-128.

[362] Porphyry, sec. 57.

[363] Porphyry, secs. 56-57.

And Diogenes relayed yet another version of the story: the people of Croton feared that Pythagoras would aspire to establish a tyranny, so they set a house on fire while he and his followers were there. Most were killed, but Pythagoras quickly escaped and reached a field full of beans, but suddenly "he stopped there, saying that it was better to be caught than to trample on the beans, and better to be slain than to speak; and so he was murdered by those who were pursuing him." Still, Archippus and Lysis managed to escape. Next, Diogenes quoted also: "Heraclides, in his *Epitome of the Lives of Satyrus,* says that, after burying Pherecydes at Delos, he returned to Italy and, when he found Cylon of Croton giving a luxurious banquet to all and sundry, retired to Metapontum to end his days there by starvation, having no wish to live longer."[364]

Furthermore, Diogenes reported a version in which Pythagoras died in a war: "But Hermippus says, that when there was war between the people of Agrigentum and the Syracusans, Pythagoras went out with his usual companions, and took the part of the Agrigentines; and as they were put to flight, he ran all round a field of beans, instead of crossing it, and so was slain by the Syracusans; and that the rest, being about thirty-five in number, were burnt at Tarentum, when they were trying to excite a sedition in the state against the principal magistrates."[365]

And Diogenes cited yet another story!

Hermippus gives another anecdote. Pythagoras, on coming to Italy, made a subterranean dwelling and enjoined on his mother to mark and record all that passed, and at what hour, and to send her notes down to him until he should ascend. She did so. Pythagoras some time afterwards came up withered and looking like a skeleton, then went into the assembly and declared he had been down to Hades, and even read out his experiences to them. They were so affected that they wept and wailed and looked upon him as divine, going so far as to send their wives to him in hopes that they would learn some of his doctrines; and so they were called Pythagorean women.[366]

<hr>

364 Diogenes, sec. 21.
365 Diogenes, sec. 21.
366 Ibid.

The Athenian Hermippus lived around 420 BCE, and he was a playwright who wrote satires, so it seems fitting that his account echoes but distorts the story about Salmoxis that Herodotus doubted.

As these stories show, there was much disagreement about basic aspects of the life of Pythagoras. Some claimed that he died in a fire, others that he died of starvation, still others that he died of grief, or was murdered by a mob in a field, or that he was killed at war with the Syracusans, or, that he just pretended to die and travel to the underworld and back. At least six different ways of dying, in eight or more distinct accounts.

In contradistinction, the gospels of the disciples of Jesus of Nazareth all converged on the same account: Jesus was crucified, yet he rose from the dead. We thus find a textual reason for why the Christian accounts of miracles convinced far many more people than the Pythagorean accounts, namely that the Christian gospels seemed to involve more certainty: they converged on one story, or at least, did not involve as many ambiguities and contradictions as the biographies of Pythagoras. Whereas Diogenes and Porphyry frankly acknowledged the ambiguities of ancient history, Iamblichus tried to remedy this. He willfully selected the anecdotes and stories that seemed preferable to him, and then he expanded and embellished them. In his biography, we clearly sense the work of someone manipulating history for desired ends. Likewise, in his *Life of Apollonius*, Philostratus omitted conflicting accounts about Pythagoras or about Apollonius, to present a clear narrative. We may wonder whether he intended it to be compelling, to educate people about how to lead a good and moral non-Christian life.

We have traced how Pythagorean views came to oppose Christianity and vice versa. Several famous philosophers, including Empedocles, Plato, Alexander of Abonoteichos, Apollonius of Tyana, and Porphyry, either associated themselves with the Pythagorean notions of became associated with them by various writers. And since their philosophies involved not just wisdom but also pagan beliefs about gods and the afterlife, such philosophers increasingly became construed as threats to the advocates of Jesus.

Some early Christians had to choose: either Pythagoras or Christ. The attractive answer: "both," became unacceptable. This deep religious dichotomy, crystal clear in antiquity, became obscured centuries later, when people disregarded the alleged divinity of Pythagoras and Plato. But we will see that even in the Renaissance there were Catholic clergymen who respected

the ancient sources so much that they were annoyed when Copernicus,
Bruno, Kepler or Galileo claimed to prove the views of Pythagoras.

3

Christians
Against the Pythagoreans

As Christianity grew in the Roman Empire, some Roman authorities used stories about the famous Apollonius to fight the Christian movement. The governor of Roman Bythinia, Hierocles, wrote a tract arguing that Apollonius the Pythagorean exceeded Jesus Christ as a wonder-worker, but was not worshipped as a god.[367] Hierocles argued that Apollonius's cultured biographers were more trustable than the uneducated apostles of Jesus. Hierocles said that Jesus was a hoodlum with a band of 900 robbers.[368] The Christians were irrational fools, the apostles Peter and Paul were charlatans, and the New Testament was full of contradictions. Jesus was not unique, because Apollonius, more recently, had accomplished similar and greater feats—not by magical arts, but by a divine secret wisdom. Soon after publishing his anti-Christian tract, Hierocles instigated the Great Persecution of Christians in 303.

Roman pagan attempts to portray Apollonius as a hero of the anti-Christian movement provoked sharp replies from Bishop Eusebius of Caesarea and from Lucius Lactantius. In his extant reply to Hierocles's pamphlet, Eusebius argued that Philostratus was a fabulist, and that Apollonius was a sorcerer in league with demons. He complained that some people pretended to perform magical incantations by invoking Apollonius.

---

[367] Hierocles, *The Word of the Lover of Truth* (ca. 303), a lost work.
[368] Hierocles, *Word of the Lover of Truth*, as conveyed by Lactantius in *Divine Institutes*, Vol. 5, chap. 3.

Thus started a long debate on the relative merits of Jesus and Apollonius. Also, Eusebius criticized Porphyry's beliefs and he referred to "Pythagoras of Rhodes" as a polytheist who argued that not all gods enjoy sacrifices, and who spoke of the sufferings of daemons superior to men.[369] Eusebius also wrote a work titled *Against Porphyry*, in twenty-five books, which do not survive. Meanwhile, Hierocles admired Pythagoras and wrote a *Commentary on the Golden Verses* of Pythagoras.

Christians versus
Pagan Philosophers

At some point between the years 303 and 313, Lactantius, a Christian professor of rhetoric in the Eastern Roman Empire, wrote his *Divine Institutes*, systematically criticizing pagan beliefs. Apparently Lactantius knew Hierocles and Porphyry while lecturing in Bithynia, but he converted to Christianity.

In his *Divine Institutes*, Lactantius ridiculed Pythagoras for having believed that souls are reborn in animals, and that the soul of Pythagoras himself, "the foolish man," had previously lived as Euphorbus in the Trojan War, and later as animals.[370] Lactantius complained that some learned men inherited that folly. He claimed that since the Pythagoreans and the Stoics had misunderstood the immortality of the soul, some of them had recklessly committed suicide, "and nothing can be more wicked than this."[371] He complained that Pythagoras, "invented fables as it were for credulous infants. ... claimed to himself the liberty of uttering such perverse falsehoods. But the folly of this most trifling man is deserving of ridicule."[372]

---

[369] Eusebii Pamphili, *Paeparatio Evangelica* (ca. 320? CE), new ed. (Coloniae: Mavritii Georgii Weidmanni, 1688), chaps. 5, 7, 8; on his critique of Porphyry, see chap. 10.
[370] Lactantius, *Epitome of the Divine Institutes*, chap. 36, in *Anti-Nicene Christian Library*, ed. Alexander Roberts and James Donaldson, Vol. XXII, *The Works of Lactantius* (Edinburgh: T. & T. Clark, 1871), pp. 119-120.
[371] Lactantius, *The Divine Institutes*, bk. III, chap. 18, in *Anti-Nicene Christian Library*, Vol. XXI, p. 182-183. Among the alleged Pythagoreans or Stoics who in one way or another embraced it, Lactantius listed Cleanthes, Chrysippus, Zeno, Empedocles, Cato, Democritus.
[372] Ibid., 185.

Lactantius argued that Pythagoras and Plato had sought knowledge from the Egyptians, the Magi, and Persians, instead of the Jews, because God did not yet permit them to know the true religion.[373] As for Apollonius, Lactantius rejected his reputed magic as fraud and tricks, false imitations of the divine powers of Jesus Christ.[374] Lactantius denounced Hierocles for folly, vanity, and error: being a polytheist and falsely portraying Apollonius as more worthy of being admired as divine than Jesus, while supposing that Jesus too was a magician. He said that Hierocles deceptively tried to destroy the truth with absurd, ignorant ravings. Finally, Lactantius did not refer to Porphyry by name, but historians infer that he did denounce him overtly: he criticized a senseless "high priest of philosophy" who "vomited three books against the Christian religion," who taught men to worship gods, but whose works were finally censured and blamed.[375]

The conflict became dire against the religious minority, the Pythagoreans, with the rise of the Christian Roman Emperors. Lactantius became an advisor to the Roman Emperor Constantine (306-337), to advise him on religious policies. Consequently, Constantine banned Porphyry's *Fifteen Books Against the Christians*. And in 325 CE, Emperor Constantine sent a letter to the Christian churches telling them that since Porphyry was "the enemy of the fear of God," and had written evil and unlawful things against Christianity, his writings were righteously destroyed, and that the followers of Arius the heretic should all be called Porphyrians, owing to Porphyry's evil (and hence, that the writings of Arius too has to be destroyed by fire).

Around 375 CE, Epiphanius, the Bishop of Salamis (also known as Constantia), in Cyprus, published his *Panarion*, or "medicine chest," a list of antidotes to cure those poisoned by the serpent of heresy (centuries later, this work became known as "Against Heresies"). In it, Epiphanius criticized Pythagoras for proclaiming "the wicked, extremely impious doctrine of the immortalizations and transmigrations of souls and the dissolution of bodies." He noted that his sect practiced five years of silence, and he complained that Pythagoras "says that God is a body, meaning heaven, and that the Sun and the Moon, and other stars, and the planets of heaven are God's

373 Ibid., bk. IV, chap. 2, pp. 213-214.
374 Ibid., bk. V, chap. 3, pp. 297-300.
375 Ibid., pp. 294-296.

eyes and his other features, as in man."[376] Likewise, Epiphanius denounced the Manichaeans as heretics. He complained that Mani taught that soul is dispersed in all things, and that the human soul is a fragment of God, imprisoned in the body.[377]

Epiphanius instigated a persecution of non-Christians in Cyprus. In 380, Emperor Theodosius made Christianity the official religion of the Eastern Roman Empire, and he later outlawed paganism in the entire Empire. He too also banned Porphyry's *Fifteen Books*, hence the Christians destroyed nearly all copies, burned them, so most of the text was lost, now only fragments remain. And the Christians destroyed works by Apollonius, Philostratus, and Hierocles.

At around 385 CE, the Roman historian Ammianus Marcelinus noted that certain famous men, including Pythagoras, Hermes Trismegistus, Apollonius of Tyana, and Plotinus (Porphyry's teacher), had manged to become eminent thanks to familiar "Genii" (or *daemones*) that had helped and protected them.[378] And somewhat resembling earlier claims by Hippolytus, Marcellinus wrote about the far-reaching influence of Pythagoras, he said that the Druids were bound in close brotherhoods "as decreed by the authority of Pythagoras," such that they sought occult things, and with contempt professed the immortality of the soul.[379]

Next, the Roman theologian Eusebius Sophronius Hieronymus (later St. Jerome) also commented on the teachings of the Pythagoreans. Like others, Jerome criticized Pythagoras for the doctrine of the transmigration of souls.[380] Like other writers, Jerome gave his version of the sequence of lives, but more importantly, he summed up the alleged teachings of Pythagoras, especially that the soul is immortal:

---

[376] Epiphanius, *Panarion* (ca. 374-377), in Saint Epiphanius, *The Panarion of Epiphanius of Salamis: Book I: Sects 1-46*, Second ed., trans. Frank Williams (Leiden: Brill, 2009), Sect. 7, p. 24.

[377] Epiphanius, *The Panarion of Epiphanius of Salamis: De Fide. Books II and III,* trans. Frank Williams (Leiden: Brill, 2012), 236.

[378] Ammianvs Marcellinvs, [*Res Gestae*, ca. 380? CE] *A Mariangelo Accvrsio mendis quinque millibus purgatus* (Augsburg: Silvani Otmar, 1533), bk. 21, pp. 130-131.

[379] Ibid., bk. 15, p. 34, trans. Martínez.

[380] St. Jerome to Avitus (409 or 410 CE), Letter 124, in *St. Jerome: Letters and Select Works*, sec. 4, p. 240, 241. Also, Jerome, *Against Jovinianus*, bk. 2, sec. 6, in *St. Jerome: Letters and Select Works*, 392.

Pythagoras taught, accordingly, that he had himself been originally Euphorbus, and then Callides, thirdly Hermotimus, fourthly Pyrrhus, and lastly Pythagoras; and that those things which had existed, after certain revolutions of time, came into being again; so that nothing in the world should be thought of as new. He said that true philosophy was a meditation on death; that its daily struggle was to draw forth the soul from the prison of the body into liberty: that our learning was recollection.[381]

Jerome claimed that Plato had developed the teachings of Pythagoras, after having learned (supposedly) that his own philosophy was defective on many points. He also said that Origen, in turn, echoed these doctrines. But Jerome distinguished such ideas from those of the Apostles. He said that he had previosuly confused them: "in my youth I had imputed to the Apostles ideas which I had found in Pythagoras, Plato and Empedocles."[382]

Jerome's objections against transmigration were directed not only at Pythagoras, but against heretics who made similar claims. For example, Jerome criticized the heretic Basilides as the master of sins and "after a lapse of so many years, and like a second Euphorbus, was changed by transmigration into Jovinian, so that the Latin tongue might have a heresy of its own."[383] Jovinian was a monk who argued that all sins are equal, and that in the afterlife there is only one degree of punishment and one kind of reward. Jerome authored an entire treatise, *Against Jovinian*, on 393 CE, and the allusion to Euphorbus was a passing insult. Likewise, when attacking another critic of Christianity, Jerome complained that the world had given birth to many monsters, including now Vigilantius, who had arisen "animated by an unclean spirit, to fight against the Spirit of Christ,… And as Euphorbus is said to have been born again in the person of Pythagoras, so in this fellow the corrupt mind of Jovinian has arisen; so that in him, no less than in his predecessor, we are bound to meet the snares of the Devil."[384] Jovinian had also made controversial comments about abstinence from food, and Jerome wished to criticize that too: "I will meet philosophic argument with argument, and will prove that we are not followers of

---

[381] St. Jerome, *Jerome's Apology for Himself Against the Books of Rufinus*, addressed to Pammachius and Marcella from Bethlehem, (402 CE), bk. 3, sec. 40.
[382] Ibid.
[383] Jerome, *Against Jovinianus*, bk. 2, sec. 37, in *St. Jerome: Letters and Select Works*, 415.
[384] Jerome, "Against Vigilantius" (ca. 406 CE), sec. 1, in *St. Jerome: Letters and Select Works*, 417.

Empedocles and Pythagoras, who on account of their doctrine of the transmigration of souls think nothing that lives and moves should be eaten, and look upon him who fells a fir-tree or an oak as equally guilty with the parricide or the poisoner; but that we worship our Creator who made all things for the use of man."[385]

Like other apologists, Jerome compared the feats of the philosophers to those of Christ. For example, he referred to the old claim that Plato too was the son of a god, but instead of portraying the story as a divine union, he claimed that the story said that Plato's mother had been raped by the pagan god Apollo. And, Jerome made explicit an inference about virginity which was only insinuated in the original tales:

> Seusippus also, Plato's nephew, and Clearchus in his eulogy of Plato, and Anaxelides in the second book of his philosophy, relates that Perictione, the mother of Plato, was violated by an apparition of Apollo, and they agree in thinking that the prince of wisdom was born of a virgin. ... And mighty Rome cannot taunt us as though we had invented the story of the birth of our Lord and Savior from a virgin; for the Romans believe that the founders of their city and race were the offspring of the virgin Ilia and of Mars.[386]

Although here Jerome drew a parallelism between Jesus and Plato, and he sometimes praised Plato, Jerome elsewhere criticized him. For example, he wrote that when the Lord God finally judges the world, then "Once mighty kings shall tremble in their nakedness. Venus shall be exposed, and her son too. Jupiter with his fiery bolts will be brought to trial; and Plato, with his disciples will be but a fool."[387]

What greatly bothered Jerome about philosophers was that they sought knowledge from many sources, in many directions, rather than having faith

[385] Jerome, *Against Jovinianus*, bk. 2, sec. 6, in *St. Jerome: Letters and Select Works*, 392.
[386] St. Jerome (Eusebius Sophronius Hieronymus), *Against Jovinianus* (393 CE), bk. 1, in Philip Schaff and Henry Wace, eds., *A Select Library of Nicene and Post-Nicene Fathers*, Second Series, Vol. 6: *St. Jerome: Letters and Select Works* (New York: The Christian Literature Company, 1893), pp. 380-381.
[387] St. Jerome to the monk Heliodorus (373 or 374 CE), Letter 14 in *St. Jerome: Letters and Select Works*, 18. See also: Jerome to Paulinus, Letter 53, in *St. Jerome: Letters and Select Works*, sec. 4, p. 98: "This truth Plato with all his learning did not know, of this Demosthenes with all his eloquence was ignorant. It is written: 'I will destroy the wisdom of the wise, and will bring to nothing the understanding of the prudent.'"

in the word of God. Philosophers discoursed as if there existed unknown sources of power over nature and over oneself, which seemed to depart from the specific path set by Christ. This potential knowledge also deviated from the humility expected from the pious. Hence Jerome criticized Pythagoras: "Can there be greater presumption than to claim not likeness to God but equality with Him, and so to compress into a few words the poisonous doctrines of all the heretics which in their turn flow from the statements of the philosophers, particularly Pythagoras and Zeno the founder of the Stoic school?"[388] Because, Pythagoras and Zeno had apparently taught that passions such as vexation, hope, fear and all the vices can be removed from the mind by practiced meditation. This was a secret doctrine of "sinlessness," as if humans could purify their souls with philosophy alone, without sufficient help from Christ. Jerome quoted Tertullian's maxim: "the philosophers are the patriarchs of the heretics," and added "It is they who have stained with their perverse doctrine the spotlessness of the Church," by not recognizing human weaknesses.[389]

At around 394, Jerome wrote a letter to Paulinus, Bishop of Nola, in which he argued that old tales tell of men who traveled great distances to see people they had only read about in books. Jerome wrote:

Thus Pythagoras visited the prophets of Memphis; and Plato, besides visiting Egypt and Archytas of Tarentum, most carefully explored that part of the coast of Italy which was formerly called Great Greece. In this way the influential Athenian master with whose lessons the schools of the Academy resounded became at once a pilgrim and a pupil choosing modestly to learn what others had to teach rather than over confidently to propound views of his own. Indeed his pursuit of learning—which seemed to fly before him all the world over—finally led to his capture by pirates who sold him into slavery to a cruel tyrant. Thus he became a prisoner, a bondman, and a slave; yet, as he was always a philosopher, he was greater still than the man who purchased him. … Livius … Apollonius too was a traveler—I mean the one who is called the sorcerer by ordinary people and the philosopher by such as follow Pythagoras. He entered Persia, traversed the Caucasus and made his way through the Albanians, the Scythians, the

---

[388] St. Jerome to Ctesiphon (415 CE), Letter 133 in *St. Jerome: Letters and Select Works*, sec. 1, p. 272.
[389] Ibid. pp. 272-273.

Massagetae, and the richest districts of India. At last, after crossing that wide river the Pison, he came to the Brahmans. There he saw Hiarcas sitting upon his golden throne and drinking from his Tantalus-fountain, and heard him instructing a few disciples upon the nature, motions, and orbits of the heavenly bodies. After this he travelled among the Elamites, the Babylonians, the Chaldeans, the Medes, the Assyrians, the Parthians, the Syrians, the Phoenicians, the Arabians, and the Philistines. Then returning to Alexandria he made his way to Ethiopia to see the gymnosophists and the famous table of the Sun spread in the sands of the desert. Everywhere he found something to learn, and he was always going to new places, he became constantly wiser and better. Philostratus has written the story of his life at length in eight books.[390]

Here Jerome spoke in a positive way about the merits of gaining knowledge by traveling to distant lands. He said that zeal and eagerness to learn were worthy of praise. Incidentally, the soaring, long list of places that Apollonius allegedly visited serves to neatly emphasize something that he supposedly said, according to Philostratus: "the whole Earth is mine, and I have leave to go wherever I please through it."[391]

More critiques against Pythagoras were voiced by Ioannes Chrysostom, a priest from Antioch, known as the greatest preacher of the early Church, and who became Archbishop of Constantinople in 397 CE. In popular homilies, Chrysostom preached against the ancient Greek philosophers, whom he belittled as excessively and shamefully ridiculous, and evil. He denounced Pythagoras, Plato, and other lesser philosophers whom he deemed not even worthy of being named. He said that their doctrines were ridiculous and chaotic. He complained: "As for doctrines on the soul, there is nothing excessively shameful that they have left unsaid; asserting that the souls of men become flies, and gnats, and bushes, and that God himself is a soul; with some other similar indecencies."

Chrysostom said that Pythagoras "practiced ten thousand kinds of sorcery," such as conversing with oxen, eagles, and other animals. "By magic tricks he deceived the foolish," taught silence, and allegedly his soul had been a bush, a girl, and a fish. Chrysostom preached that if the doctrines of

---

[390] St. Jerome to Paulinus, bishop of Nola (394 CE), Letter 53, in *St. Jerome: Letters and Select Works*, sec. 1, p. 96-97.
[391] Philostratus, *Life of Apollonius*, bk. 1, chap. 21, p. 36.

the philosopher are stripped of their flowery diction, their full abomination becomes visible as fallacious indecencies, especially on matters of the soul, and that "this is the snare of the Devil." In contrast, Chrysostom praised John the Apostle for not inventing "fables defining the universe to consist of numbers," and for "casting away all this devilish trash and mischief."[392]

Chrysostom criticized Greek philosophy in general as a main root of heresies. He complained that some people still did not believe in the Resurrection because they suffered "the disease of Grecian foolishness. For indeed all these things were the progeny of the madness which belongs to Heathen Philosophy, and she was the mother of all mischief."[393] He said that philosophers all contradicted their various opinions, by each being bent on making new discoveries all because of having erroneously trusted their own reasoning. They disparaged faith because they insisted on trying to figure things out by themselves and therefore found nothing.[394] Chrysostom said that philosophers agreed only about one thing: mockingly denying the Resurrection.[395] In another homily, Chrysostom argued that Gentile wisdom could not serve to ascertain "the things above us." Rejecting the popular idea that some philosophers or wise men had acquired divine insights, Chrysostom declared that "it is not possible that a natural man should know divine things." He said that instead we should follow the divine mind: *"But we have the mind of Christ.* That is, spiritual, divine, that which hath nothing human. For it is not of Plato, nor of Pythagoras, but it is Christ himself, putting His own things in our mind."[396]

In yet another popular homily, Chrysostom argued that Jesus Christ chose to influence the Apostle Peter instead of Plato or Pythagoras because the latter were less philosophical and in truth suffered of vainglory. Therefore, he said, "they suffered bitter calamities, exceeding all others in

[392] Ioannes Chrystostomos, Homily II (ca. 395 CE), in *The Homilies of S. John Chrystostom, Archbishop of Constantinople, on the Gospel of St. John*, Part 1: Hom. I – XLI, trans. G.T. Stupart (Oxford: John Henry Parker, 1848), pp. 11-14. See also: Chrysostom, Homily I, on 1 Tim. i. 1, 2, in *The Homilies of S. John Chrysostom, Archbishop of Constantinople, on the Epistles of St. Paul the Apostle to Timothy, Titus, and Philemon*, trans. James Tweed (Oxford: John Henry Parker, 1843), pp. 8-9.

[393] Chrysostom, *Homilies of St. John Chrysostom, Archbishop of Constantinople, on the First Epistle of S. Paul the Apostle to the Corinthians* (Oxford: John Henry Parker, 1845), Argument [Introduction], sec. 2, p. 3; see also p. 92.

[394] In ibid.: Homily 5 (on 1 Corinthians i 26, 27), sec. 2, p. 53.

[395] In ibid.: Homily 39 (on 1 Corinthians xv 11), sec. 8, p. 557-558.

[396] In ibid., Homily 8 (on 1 Corinthians ii 6, 7), sec. 11, pp. 89-90; see also p. 100.

misery," including burning cities and "manifold frantic horrors."[397] Repeatedly he complained that Pythagoras "said the soul becomes a bush, or a fish, or a dog," and against his followers, or those who used the wisdom of the Gentiles, he said "their throat is an open sepulcher, having all things full of impurity and corruption, and all their doctrines full of worms."[398]

Despite such censorship, and partly because of it, tales about the Pythagoreans continued to spread. Hermias the philosopher, a Christian satirist, ridiculed an alleged claim by Pythagoras: that souls are made of "number in motion."[399] Hermias mocked the ancient philosophers for their "folly, or madness, or rebellion," full of contradictions. He ridiculed the idea that humans can become animals, as well as the Pythagorean idea that unity is the principle of all things, that it generates numbers and elements. He said that Pythagoras allegedly measured the world (fire, air, water, earth, aether) with triangles and polyhedrons, using cubits and numbers, mocking: "and placing the world in a balance, I can easily learn its weight," to thus rule over all things. Hermias then attributed to Epicurus the notion that "there are many and endless worlds," and that one can travel between them. Hermias complained that such things "are the darkness of ignorance to me, and black error, and endless wandering, and unprofitable fancy," because such endless inquiry is useless and unconfirmed by facts.[400]

Likewise, at roughly around 260 CE, Pope Dionysius of Alexandria composed a work against the Epicureans, mainly to criticize their theory that all things are composed of atoms that came together without divine Providence. In it, Dionysius briefly dismissed one of the corollaries of the atomistic theory: that the atoms in the void casually clash and combine by chance "and thus gradually form this world and all objects in it; and more,

[397] Ioannes Chrysostomos, Homily IV, on Acts ii. 1, 2, in *The Homilies of S. John Chrysostom, Archbishop of Constantinople, on the Acts of the Apostles*, Part 1: Hom. I – XXVIII, trans. J. Walker, J. Sheppard, and H. Browne (Oxford: John Henry Parker, 1851), 63.
[398] Ioannes Chrysostomos, Homily LXVI, on John xii. 8, in *The Homilies of S. John Chrysostom, Archbishop of Constantinople, on the Gospel of St. John*, Part 2: Hom. XLII – LXXXVIII (Oxford: John Henry Parker: 1852), 590.
[399] Hermias the Philosopher, *Irrisio Gentilium Philosophorum* (ca. 250-550? CE), in ed. Rev. Dr. Giles, *The Writings of the Early Christians of the Second Century* (London: John Russell Smith, 1857), 193.
[400] Ibid., 199.

that they construct infinite worlds."[401] Pope Dionysius attributed this theory to Epicurus and Democritus, while he credited Pythagoras and Plato with the wiser view that the universe is one coherent whole.

Other prominent Christians continued the critiques against the pagan philosophers. Augustine of Hippo denied the claim that Pythagoras could remember events from his previous lives.[402] In his *City of God Against the Pagans* (ca. 412-427 CE), Augustine criticized Pythagoras for being a necromancer, one who tried to divine the future by talking with inhabitants of the netherworld: the dead, or demons pretending to be gods.[403] Augustine echoed Cicero who had cited Marcus Terentius Varro (ca. 40 BCE) as having made such claims about Pythagoras.[404] Augustine further complained that proud Porphyry hated Christ, and that he foolishly taught a convoluted theory of the transmigration of souls.[405] Augustine described Porphyry as "the most learned of the philosophers, though the bitterest enemy of the Christians."[406]

the Pagan Belief in Many Worlds

Aristotle complained about the so-called Pythagoreans, the "Italian philosophers," because: "they say that fire is at the center [of the universe] and that the Earth is one of the stars, and that moving in a circle about the center it produces night and day."[407] Around fifty years before Christ, the *Placita Philosophorum* claimed that the Pythagoreans said the stars are *worlds*.

---

[401] Dionysius of Alexandria, "Against the Epicureans," in Alexander Roberts and James Donaldson, *Ante-Nicene Christian Library*, Vol. 20: *The Writings of Gregory Thaumaturgus, Dionysius of Alexandria, and Archelaus* (Edinburgh: T. & T. Clark, 1871), 171.
[402] Augustine of Hippo, *De Trinitate, Libri XV*, in *Nicene and Post-Nicene Fathers*, First Series, Vol. 3, trans. Rev. Arthur West Haddan (1887), bk. 7, chap. 15, p. 164.
[403] Augustine of Hippo, *De Civitate Dei Contra Paganos* (ca. 412-427 CE); *City of God Against the Pagans*, Book 7 (ca. 417 CE), Chapter 35.
[404] Marcus Tullius Cicero, *On Divination* (ca. 44 BCE), translated by C. D. Yonge (1853), Book 1, Section 3.
[405] Augustine, *De Civitate Dei*, bk 10, chaps. 24, 29-30; bk. 13, chap. 19; bk. 22, chaps. 12, 26-28.
[406] Ibid., bk 19, chap. 22.
[407] Aristotle, *On the Heavens* (ca. 340? BCE), bk. 2, sec. 13.

According to the *Placita*, the Pythagoreans also said that the Moon is earth-like and inhabited, even with animals and plants.[408]

The relevant passages are noteworthy, since these were echoed later by astronomers and philosophers such as Copernicus, Giordano Bruno, and Johannes Kepler. The author, "Plutarch," discussed the alleged beliefs of various philosophers about the stars: reportedly Thales believed that they were burning globes of earth; Plato thought the stars were mostly fire but held together by another element; Xenophanes that the stars are clouds that are set on fire at night, etc. Then "Plutarch" mentions the reputed beliefs of "Heraclides and the Pythagoreans, that every star is a world in an infinite ether, and each encompasses air, earth and ether; this opinion is current among the followers of Orpheus, for they suppose that each of the stars is a world. Epicurus rejects none of these opinions, because he embraces anything that is possible."[409] The *Placita* also states that Hicetas the Pythagorean believed that there exist two Earths.[410]

In another brief chapter, on why the Moon seems Earth-like, "Plutarch" wrote: "The Pythagoreans say that to us the Moon seems terraneous, because it is inhabited just as our Earth, and in it there are animals that are larger in size and plants that have a rarer beauty than those found on our globe; that the animals there are fifteen times more virtuous and vigorous than ours; that they exude no excrements; and that there the days are fifteen times longer."[411] Such notions were echoed later by Johannes Kepler.

Epicurus lived much later than Orpheus and Pythagoras, around 300 BCE. Centuries later, Diogenes copied a letter in which Epicurus reportedly had argued:

worlds also are infinite, whether they resemble this one of ours or whether they are different from it. For, as the atoms are, as to their number, infinite, as I have proved above, they necessarily move about at immense distances; for besides, this infinite multitude of atoms, of which the world is formed,

---

[408] [Falsely attributed to Plutarch], *Placita Philosophorum* [actually by another writer, based on a work by Aetius, ca. 50 BCE, as noted by Theodoret], *Peri ton Areskonton Philosophois Physikon Dogmaton* [and falsely attributed to Qusta ibn Luqa by Ibn al-Nadim], in *Aetius Arabus: Die Vorsokratiker in Arabischer Überlieferung*, edited by Hans Daiber (Wiesbaden: Franz Steiner Verlag, 1980), bk. 2, chap. 30.
[409] *Placita*, bk. 2, chap. 13, trans. Martínez.
[410] Ibid., bk. 3, chap. 9.
[411] [Aetius?], *Placita Philosophorum*, bk. 2, chap. 30, trans. Martínez.

or by which it is produced, could not be entirely absorbed by one single world, nor even by any worlds, the number of which was limited, whether we suppose them like this world of ours, or different from it. There is, therefore, no fact inconsistent with an infinity of worlds.[412]

Epicurus reportedly also noted that such worlds might well be inhabited by plants and living creatures. The account quoted by Diogenes agrees with the brief account given by Aetius or "Plutarch."

Aristotle had said that the Pythagoreans claimed that the Earth is one of the stars. Apparently Aetius or "Plutarch" said the converse: that the Pythagoreans believed that stars are worlds. Later writers expanded that, on the basis of other classical sources that did not focus on Pythagoras. Namely, they read fictional accounts by Plutarch and Lucian, stories about voyages to the Moon. By a gradual syncretism, such stories became closely associated with the Pythagoreans. Since such stories are seldom read, we should summarize them.

First, Plutarch had written a dialogue titled: "On the Apparent Face in the Orb of the Moon." He explained that many people said that they could discern a lunar image of a face, something much too clear to be accidental or an optical illusion. In the dialogue, one character argued that the Moon acts like a mirror, reflecting the image of an ocean and lands from the Earth. Incidentally, the story does not specify this, but the *Placita* of "Plutarch" claimed that Pythagoras believed that the body of the Moon was like a mirror.[413] Plutarch's dialogue briefly mentioned an "Aristagoras the Stoic" who tried to explain visible phenomena by supposing that the sky remains fixed while Earth moves in a circle and turns on its axis. (Plutarch did not mean Aristarchus of Samos, because Aristarchus appeared by name in the dialogue.) But one of the main topics of discussion was whether the Moon was another Earth, a world. They discussed whether the inhabitants of the Moon might fall off as it orbits overhead, and whether they might suffer or be roasted by the heat of the Sun. (Centuries later, Kepler echoed this question about solar heat on the Moon's inhabitants.) They argued that just as there are plants that grow in deserts on Earth, there might likewise exist plants and woods on the Moon that do not require rain, but only some sort

[412] Epicurus, "Letter to Herodotus," quoted in Diogenes Laertius, *Lives and Opinions of Eminent Philosophers*, trans. C. D. Yonge (London: George Bell and Sons, 1901), 440.
[413] "Plutarch," *Placita*, bk. 2, chap. 25, p. 145.

of periodic dew. They pondered whether the Moon's inhabitants wondered about whether there is life on Earth or whether it only holds hell and Tartarus.

One of the characters in the dialogue, Sylla, explained that after humans die, their souls depart from the body, and are ordained to wander the region between the Earth and the Moon. During that variable time, the wicked souls pay penalties for their sins while the virtuous souls become further purified. Then the virtuous ones rise to the Moon, trying to hear "the harmony of the heavens," and they then see "the ghosts of people there turned upside down."[414] Meanwhile, the wicked souls scream and are horrified by the apparent face on the moon, composed of gulfs and deep crevices, including the largest called "Hecate's dungeon," in which souls suffer punishment after they have been converted into genii. Then the genii soon descend back to Earth, to possess oracles and to influence people. But if they did anything wrong, in such duties, they would be punished for it, by being forcefully attached again onto human bodies.

However, the souls who had separated from their bodies on Earth, once purified, eventually reach the Moon. At the Moon, those souls die a *second* death, which separates the mind from the soul. Then, that soul was left behind on the Moon, retaining an imprint and likeness of its former mind and body: a specter. Just as buried human bodies become part of the Earth, human souls would become part of the Moon's substance. Evil and passionate souls, mindless and irrational, could in some cases possess human bodies and even hinder oracles on Earth, even the oracle at Delphi, but eventually they too would return to the Moon and be absorbed by it. Meanwhile, the minds that departed from their souls might approach and reach the attractive Sun, revolve around it, and finally come into contact with him. As minds reach the Sun they would become impregnated with vitality that would produce new souls, for which the Earth would furnish new bodies. Thus, according to Plutarch, the character named Sylla argued that humans consist not of two parts but of three: body, soul, and mind. And, that while bodies are created on Earth, souls originate on the Moon, and minds are engendered in the Sun.

[414] Plutarch, "On the Apparent Face in the Orb of the Moon," in Plutarch, *Plutarch's Morals. Theosophical Essays*, trans. C. W. King (London: George Bell and Sons, 1898), sec. 28, p. 252.

The Assyrian writer, Lucian of Samosata (ca. 120-200 CE) also wrote a fictional account titled "A True Story." Consider the passage in which the travelers first arrive on the Moon:

We then took our casks, filled some of them with water, and some with wine from the river, slept one night on shore, and the next morning set sail, the wind being very moderate. About noon, the island being now out of sight, on a sudden a most violent whirlwind arose, and carried the ship above three thousand stadia, lifting it up above the water, from whence it did not let us down again into the seas but kept us suspended in mid air, in this manner we hung for seven days and nights, and on the eight, beheld a large tract of land [the Moon], like an island, round, shining, and remarkably full of light; we got on shore, and found on examination that is was cultivated, and full of inhabitants, though we could not then see any of them, as night came on. Other islands appeared, some large, others small, and of a fiery color; there was also below these another land with seas, woods, mountains, and cities in it, and this we took to be our native country: as we were advancing forward, we were seized on a sudden by the Hippogypi, for so it seems they were called by the inhabitants; these Hippogypi are men carried upon vultures, which they ride as we do horses: these vultures have each three heads, and are immensely large: you may judge of their size, when I tell you that one of their feathers is bigger than the mast of a ship. The Hippogypi have orders, it seems, to fly round the kingdom, and if they find any stranger, to bring him to the king: they took us, therefore, and carried us before him: as soon as he saw us, he guessed by our garb what we were, he said: "You are Greeks, are you not?" We told him we were, so he added: "And how did you get here through the air?" We told him all that had happened to us, and he then told us his own history, and told us that he too was a man, that his name was Endymion, that he had been captured from Earth while sleeping, and brought to this place where he reigned as king.[415]

According to ancient legends, Endymion was a king, or at least a shepherd, of the kingdom Elis, in southern Greece. Endymion was so very handsome

---

[415] Lucian of Samosata, "The True History," in Thomas Francklin, ed. and trans., *The Works of Lucian: From the Greek*, Vol. 1 (London: T. Cadell, 1780), bk. 1, pp. 416-417, translations modified by Martínez.

that one night as he slept on mount Latmos, the Moon saw him and fell in
love with him. Lucian's account did not specify this legend, but he continued to describe how king Endymion spoke to the travelers from Earth, as
they looked at the sky:

> "That spot," he told us, which now looked like a moon to us, "is the
> Earth." He wanted us to not be uncomfortable, because we would soon
> have everything we sought. He said: "If I win the war that I am now
> fighting against the inhabitants of the Sun, then you will be happy here."
> So then we asked him what enemies he had, and what was the quarrel
> about? He replied: "The king of the Sun, Phaeton (for the Sun is inhabited
> just like the Moon), has been at war with us for some time, because of this:
> I had previously wanted to send some of my poorest subjects to establish
> a colony in Lucifer [Mercury], which was uninhabited, but Phaeton, out of
> envy, put a stop to it, by opposing me midway with his Hippomyrmices
> [Horse-ants]. We were overcome and desisted, because at that time our
> forces were unequal to theirs. But now I resolved to renew the war, to
> establish my colony, and if you will, you should accompany us in that jour-
> ney; I will give each of you a royal vulture, and other equipment, we shall
> set out tomorrow.[416]

Lucian said that the travelers joined the unimaginably numerous armies of
the Moon, and he described the thousands of soldiers and strange, gigantic
creatures that constituted that army: horse-vultures, staggeringly huge spi-
ders, and many more. Meanwhile, the Sun king commanded an army of
gigantic flying ants, gnats, crows, men with heads of dogs ("Cynobalani,"
the inhabitants of the star Sirius), winged centaurs, and many more. Soldiers
from the Milky Way did not arrive, so the king of the Sun became so enraged that he set their city on fire. There was so much bloodshed that the
clouds became tinged with blood. In the end, the king of the Moon was
pushed back to his city, and three of the travelers from Earth were captured
by the army of the Sun. After the conquering armies left, peace was eventually negotiated, and the hostages were released. The protagonist of the
story, a traveler from Earth, returned to the Moon, and king Endymion
begged him to stay, "promising to give me his son in marriage, for they

---

[416] Ibid., pp. 417-418.

have no women there," but the traveler rejected the offer. He departed with
the other Earthlings, on their ship.

Lucian discussed many other adventures of those traveling humans
who sailed to the Moon, Mercury, and other "islands in the air." And they
met many famous men, including even Pythagoras: "I also met Pythagoras
the Samian, who arrived in these regions after his soul had gone round in
the bodies of several animals; having been changed seven times. All his right
side was of gold, and there was some dispute whether he should be called
Pythagoras or Euphorbus."[417]

As Lucian explained in his Preface, the "True Story" was a collection
of clever lies alluding to the works of ancient poets, historians, and philosophers, and ridiculing them for the sake of amusement. He explained: "as
I could not relate anything true (for I know nothing at present worthy to
be recorded), I turned my thoughts toward falsehood, a species of it, however, much more excusable than that of others, as I shall at least say one
thing true, when I tell you that I lie, and shall hope to escape the general
censure, by acknowledging that I mean to speak not a word of truth
throughout."[418] He warned his readers to please not believe him.

Apparently, the belief in multiple worlds was endorsed by Democritus
of Abdera, who died ca. 370 BCE, and by Epicurus, who also lived much
later than Orpheus and Pythagoras, around 300 BCE. Centuries later, Diogenes Laertius copied a letter in which Epicurus reportedly had argued:

> But worlds also are infinite, whether similar to ours or dissimilar. Since the
> atoms are infinite in number, as demonstrated, they must move across im-
> mense distances. Also, such atoms, which constitute the world, from
> which it came, could not be entirely used up by a single world, nor by any
> limited number of worlds, whether we suppose them similar to our world,
> or different. Hence, not one fact is contrary to an infinity of worlds.[419]

Epicurus reportedly also said that such worlds might be inhabited by plants
and living creatures. His account agrees with the brief account in the *Placita*.

---

[417] Ibid., Bk. 2, p. 438.

[418] Ibid., Preface, p. 414.

[419] Epicurus, ʽΕπίκουρος Ἡροδότῳ χαίρειν’, quoted by Diogenes Laertius, in *Βίοι καὶ
Γνώμαι τον εν Φιλοσοφίαι* (ca. 225 CE), reissued in *Lives of Eminent Philosophers*, ed.
Tiziano Dorandi (Cambridge: Cambridge University Press, 2013), bk. 10, p. 765,
trans. Martínez.

Around 45 BCE, Cicero criticized the Roman writer Marcus Terentius Varro for many things, including the claim that there exist many worlds like Earth:

> Then you [Varro] take refuge in those physicists who are most ridiculed in the Academy, but whom you do not abstain from quoting. And you say that Democritus said that there are innumerable worlds, and that among them there are some that are not only similar, but perfectly and absolutely equal in every part, that there is no difference between them and that they are innumerable; as well as men.[420]

Cicero complained that Varro said that since there is no difference between some worlds, then individual men on Earth are not unique and there exist innumerable others who are identical. This was an alleged consequence of Democritus's atomism. But Cicero rejected such theories by arguing that the best natural philosophers had explained that each and every thing has its own separate property. Even so-called identical twins are actually distinct. So Cicero rejected Varro's reasoning as false and absurd. In another work, Cicero had also attributed the belief in 'innumerable worlds' to Anaximander, but without explaining this in any detail.[421]

Around 30 CE, the Latin writer and collector of anecdotes, Valerius Maximus, commented that Democritus taught that, "innumerable worlds exist."[422] Around 77 CE, Pliny the Elder said that it is "madness" to assert that there exist "innumerable worlds," many suns, many moons, and "innumerable stars."[423] Later writers wrote stories about voyages to the Moon. These stories are significant for showing how pagan religious notions deviated from Christian ones.

First, around 100 CE, Plutarch wrote a dialogue titled: "On the Apparent Face in the Orb of the Moon." In it, the characters discussed whether

---

[420] M. Tullii Ciceronis, *Academicarum Quaestionum Liber Primus, ad M. Terentium Varronem* (ca. 45 BCE), in *M. Tullii Ciceronis Philosophica*, Vol. 4 (Paris: Roberti Stephani, 1538) bk. 4, p. 19, trans. Martínez.

[421] M. Tullii Ciceronis, *De Natura Deorum, ad M. Brutum* (ca. 45 BCE), in *Opera Ciceronis Philosophica* (n. p.: Ioanni Parvo & Iodico Badio, 1538), bk. 1, p. 127 reverso.

[422] Valerii Maximi, *Dictorum Factorumque Memorabilium Libri IX* (L. Elzevirii, 1650), p. 283.

[423] Caii Plinii Secundi, *Naturalis Historia Libri XXXVII* (Paris: Franciscum Muguet, 1685), bk. 2, chap. 1, pp. 30-31.

the Moon is another Earth. They wondered whether the inhabitants of the Moon might fall off as it orbits overhead, and whether they might suffer or be roasted by the heat of the Sun. They argued that just as there are plants that grow in deserts on Earth, there might exist plants and woods on the Moon that do not require rain, but only some periodic dew. They pondered whether the Moon's inhabitants wondered about whether there is life on Earth or whether it only holds Hell and Tartarus.

Christians against the Belief in Other Worlds

Cicero, Pliny, and Lucian spoke about the belief in other worlds as if it were ridiculous or worthy of censure. The early Christians agreed. Around 225 CE, Hippolytus was a theologian of the Church of Rome. He ridiculed those who believed in many worlds. In particular, Hippolytus complained about Democritus:

> He claimed that worlds are infinite and of various sizes; that in some there is no Sun or Moon, whereas in others they are larger than ours, and in others more numerous. And the separations between worlds are unequal . . . . Some worlds are destitute of animals and plants and every kind of liquid. And that the earth of our world was created before that of the stars, and that the Moon is underneath; next to it the Sun; then the fixed stars.[424]

This passage implies that multiple worlds have living beings. Hippolytus then criticized Democritus, saying that he "ridiculed everything, as if everything about humanity were laughable."[425] Similarly, Hippolytus discussed the beliefs of Xenophanes of Colophon, who allegedly believed that "nothing is generated or perishes," the universe is endowed with perception, that "there are infinitely many Suns and Moons, and that all things spring from

[424] Hippolytus [traditionally misattributed to Origen], Ὁ κατὰ πασῶν αιρέσεων ἔλεγχος (ca. 225 CE), in Hippolytus, *Refutatio Omnium Haeresium,* ed. Miroslav Marcovich (Berlin: Walter De Gruyter, 1986), bk. 1, sec. 13, pp. 72-73, trans. Martínez.
[425] Ibid.

the Earth."[426] These beliefs attributed to Democritus and Xenophanes became later attributed to Pythagoras, even if perhaps they did not yet seem Pythagorean to all writers. Hippolytus also spoke about philosophers who believed in more than one "world," though in abstract ways. He said that Pythagoras believed in "two worlds: one intelligible, which arises from the monad, and the other sensible."[427] Supposedly there existed incorporeal but divine substances that could be perceived only through the intellect. Also, Anaximander spoke of heavens and worlds being generated from the Infinite, and, Leucippus claimed that worlds are produced when many bodies congregate together.[428] However, none of these vague claims referred explicitly to material worlds resembling our Earth. But such claims were voiced by some Pythagoreans, as well as Democritus, Epicurus, Varro, and others.

In 248 CE, in Alexandria, the Christian theologian Origen Adamantius tried to import the notion of many worlds into Christianity. Origen wrote: "The fact is that prior to this world there have existed others, as Ecclesiastes says: "What is it that has been done? the same as is the future. And what is it that has been created? the same that will be created: and there is nothing new under the Sun."[429] (Centuries, later, these lines became the motto of Giordano Bruno.) Origen said that omnipotence led God to create worlds prior to ours; and God will create worlds after ours. Origen also wrote about souls after death getting new, different bodies. For one, he said that after the resurrection wicked souls "may be clothed with dark and black bodies."[430] His insistence on the eternity of souls suggested that such souls might live in future worlds. Origen's speculations did not work; he was eventually declared a heretic.

Around 260 CE, Pope Dionysius of Alexandria composed a work against the Epicureans, mainly to criticize their theory that all things are composed of atoms that came together without divine Providence. In it, Pope Dionysius briefly dismissed one of the corollaries of the atomistic theory: that the atoms in the void clash and combine by chance "and thus

---

[426] Ibid., sec. 14, p. 74.
[427] Ibid., bk. 6, sec. 24, p. 231.
[428] Ibid., bk. 1, sec. 6, p. 64; and sec. 12, p. 72.
[429] Origen, *Peri Archon*, bk. 3, trans. Rufinus [400 CE], in Origenis Adamantii, *Operum Origenis Adamantii, quorum Tertius complectitur, post Apologiam Explicanda*, Vols. 3-4 (n.p.: Iacobo Giunti, 1536), 205; see also bk. 1, chap. 6, trans. Martínez.
[430] Ibid., bk. 2, chap. 10.

gradually form this world and all objects in it; and more, that they construct infinite worlds."[431] He attributed this theory to Epicurus and Democritus, while he credited Pythagoras and Plato with the wiser view that the universe is one coherent whole. Later, Lactantius attributed the theory of "innumerable worlds" to Leucippus, as a necessary byproduct of atoms. Lactantius complained that Leucippus was therefore "perfectly insane" and "raved with impunity."[432]

Discussions of pagan beliefs combined religion with cosmology. According to the Pythagoreans, the Sun, the Moon, the planets, the stars, and the Milky Way all had religious significance pertaining to polytheism and the transmigration of souls. Around 430 CE, the Roman philosopher Macrobius made remarks about the Pythagorean cosmology in his "Commentary on the Dream of Scipio." He wrote: "Pythagoras also thinks that the infernal regions [or the empire of death] of Dis [Pluto] begin with the Milky Way, and extend downwards because souls falling away from it seem to have withdrawn from the heavens. He says that the reason why milk is the first nourishment offered to the newborn infant is that the first movement of souls slipping into earthly bodies is from the Milky Way."[433] Allegedly, Pythagoras taught that human souls come from the Milky Way, where the infernal regions begin, and, that animal souls come from the stars.

Earlier, the *Placita* had said that the Pythagoreans, Heraclides, and the followers of Orpheus all believed that every star is a world. The *Placita* said that the Moon was terrestrial and inhabioted; it was the world nearest to Earth. In later antiquity, around 300 CE, Iamblichus said that some people viewed Pythagoras as an exceedingly good daemon, and some others considered him to be "one of the daemons that inhabit the Moon."[434] This notion of daemons or demons inhabiting the Moon is unusual. Another example is found in Saint Augustine. He criticized Porphyry as a polytheist

---

[431] Dionysius of Alexandria, "Against the Epicureans," in Roberts and Donaldson, *Ante-Nicene Christian Library*, Vol. 20: *The Writings of Gregory Thaumaturgus, Dionysius of Alexandria, and Archelaus* (1871), p. 171.

[432] Lactantii, *De Ira Dei* (ca. 313), published with *Divianae Institutiones* (Lugduni: Thomam Soubron, 1594), chap. 10, p. 700, trans. Martínez.

[433] [Ambrosius Aurelius Theodosius] Macrobius, *Commentarii in Somnium Scipionis* (ca. 430? CE); *Commentary on the Dream of Scipio*, trans. William Harris Stahl (New York: Columbia University Press, 1952), p. 134.

[434] Iamblichi, *De Vita Pythagorica* (ca. 300 CE), reissued as Iamblichus, *On the Pythagorean Way of Life*, ed. and trans. John Dillon and Jackson Hershbell (Atlanta: Scholars Press, 1991), chap. 6, p. 14.

who advocated the illicit and sacrilegious arts of communicating with de-mons, though at least, said Augustine, Porphyry repudiated some demons living in the air and on the Moon.[435] He added that Porphyry had admitted that humans are not purified by sacrificing to the Sun and the Moon, both allegedly gods.[436] Philostratus said that Pythagoras was "the man who came from Jupiter," meaning either the god Zeus, or the planet, or the realm of Zeus.[437]

Patristic philosophers increasingly debated whether the Earth is the only world that exists. Around 320 CE, Athanasius of Alexandria, soon its bishop, insisted that the world is one and not many, which *proves* that God is only one and not many. He said that to believe otherwise was "impious," "grotesque," and "totally nefarious." He also stated: "if many gods exist, then many worlds would necessarily exist."[438]

Epiphanius complained that the Manichaeans too believed in the trans-migration of souls, even into animals. After death, souls could also travel to the Moon or the Sun.[439] The Moon became periodically "full" when it was full of souls. He further complained that the Manichaeans believed that there exist other worlds, and that air is the soul of men, animals, and eve-rything.[440] Epiphanius wrote: "They pretendedly speak of Christ but wor-ship the Sun and the Moon, and invoke stars, powers and daemons."[441]

Soon, some Christian theologians denounced the notion that there ex-ist many worlds as *heretical.* Hippolytus, Pope Dionysius, and Athanasius had criticized it —but it was explicitly categorized as heretical by Philaster, the Bishop of Brescia, Italy. Around 384 CE, in a *Book of Heresies,* Philaster explicitly denounced certain pagan philosophical beliefs as heretical. In par-ticular, he wrote:

---

[435] Augustine of Hippo, *De Civitate Dei Contra Paganos* (ca. 412-427 CE); *City of God Against the Pagans,* bk. 10, chap. 11.

[436] Ibid., bk. 10, chap. 23.

[437] Philostratus, *The Life of Apollonius of Tyana,* trans. Edward Berwick (London: T. Payne, 1809), bk. 1, chap. 2, p. 4.

[438] Athanasius, *Contra Gentiles* (ca. 320), in *Divi Athanasii Alexandrini Vero Episcopi Opera Omnia* (Lugduni: Melchioriis et Gasparis Trechsel, 1532), bk. 1, p. 217, trans. Mar-tínez.

[439] Epiphanius, *The Panarion of Epiphanius of Salamis: De Fide. Books II and III,* trans. Frank Williams (Leiden: Brill, 2012), 237, 275-277.

[440] Ibid., 258.

[441] Ibid., 215.

Another heresy is to say that worlds are infinite and innumerable, following the asinine opinion of the philosophers, whereas Scriptures say that the world is one and it teaches us that it is one. This is also about the prophets' apocrypha (that is, secrets), who said that those who believe this are pagans; such as Democritus who asserted that many worlds exist, with which he proclaimed his wisdom, he stirred many souls to experience various doubtful errors.[442]

Philaster became a very famous bishop for confuting heresies, converting Jews and pagans, and for defending orthodoxy. Consequently, other theologians reified his critiques.

In the year 385, the bishop of Milan, Aurelius Ambrosius, wrote a letter discussing the nature of Paradise and he too dismissed the idea of many worlds: "Therefore it is clear that God is the author of man, & that there is one God, not many gods, but there is one who wrought the world, & one world, not many worlds, as the philosophers say."[443] In another work, Ambrosius noted that, "Pythagoras said that the world is one; but others say that worlds are innumerable, as written by Democritus."[444] Similarly, Hermias the Christian attributed to Epicurus the notion that "there are many and endless worlds," and that one can travel between them. Hermias complained that such things "are the darkness of ignorance to me, and black error, and endless wandering, and unprofitable fancy," because such endless inquiry is useless and unconfirmed by facts.[445]

The question of whether there are many worlds was linked to whether there are many heavens. Ioannes Chrysostom was a priest from Antioch, known as the greatest preacher of the early Church. He became Archbishop of Constantinople in 397 CE. In popular homilies, Chrysostom preached against the ancient Greek philosophers, belittling them as ridiculous and evil. While discussing *Genesis*, Saint Chrysostom argued that it is a mistake

---

[442] Philastrius, *De Haeresibus Liber* (ca. 384 CE), in Franciscus Oehler, ed., *Corporis Haereseologici*, Vol. 2 (Berolini: A. Asher et Socios, 1860), p. 121, trans. Martínez.
[443] Saint Ambrose, "Ad Sabinum Enarratio" (385 CE), in *Operum Sancti Ambrosii Mediolanensis Episcopi*, Vol. 1 (Rome: Dominici Basae, 1580), p. 332, trans. Martínez.
[444] Saint Ambrose, *Hexameron* (ca. 389), bk. 1, preface; and bk. 2, chap. 2; both in Ibid., pp. 1, 13, trans. Martínez.
[445] Hermias the Philosopher, *Irrisio Gentilium Philosophorum* (ca. 250-550? CE), in *The Writings of the Early Christians of the Second Century*, edited by Rev. Dr. Giles (London: John Russell Smith, 1857), p.199.

to imagine many heavens: "How is it, you will say, some people want to claim many heavens were created? They don't get this teaching from Sacred Scripture, but base it on their own reasoning." He said that the divinely inspired Moses taught that "God made heaven and Earth," nothing more. Chrysostom argued that the word heaven is often rendered as "heavens" merely as an idiom. He wrote:

> ...because it is idiomatic in Hebrew to use the name of a single thing in the plural; if there were several heavens the Holy Spirit would not have neglected to teach us through the tongue of this blessed author [Moses] about the creation of the other ones. Keep a close grasp on these matters, I beg you, so as to be able to curb those people wanting to come up with objections against the Church, and be quite sure in your knowledge of the efficacy of what is contained in the Sacred Scriptures.[446]

Chrysostom criticized Greek philosophy as a main root of heresies. He complained that some people still did not believe in the Resurrection because they suffered "the disease of Grecian foolishness. For indeed all these things were the progeny of the madness which belongs to Heathen Philosophy, and she was the mother of all mischief."[447]

Meanwhile, one of Origen's works in particular had been vigorously denounced as very heretical and full of poisonous errors: his treatise *On Principles*. Saint Jerome and Pope Anastasius condemned Rufinus of Aquileia for translating it from the Greek in 400 CE, in Rome. In it Origen had argued, among other things, that the Sun, Moon and stars are living beings and that many worlds exist. In 402 CE, Saint Jerome complained that among the many bad things that Origen had said, some things were "the most heretical: that God's Son is a creature, the Holy Spirit a servant, worlds innumerable, succeeding one another eternally, angels become human souls," and so forth, and he explained how the notion of other worlds related to the transmigration of souls. Jerome rebuked Origen's opinion that, after death, departed souls:

---

[446] Ioannes Chrysostom, "Fourth Homily on Genesis," in *The Fathers of the Church: St. John Chrysostom*, trans. Robert C. Hill (Washington DC: Catholic University of America Press, 1986), Homily 4, secs. 8-10, pp. 55-57.

[447] Chrysostom, *Homilies of St. John Chrysostom, Archbishop of Constantinople, on the First Epistle of S. Paul the Apostle to the Corinhtians* (Oxford: John Henry Parker, 1845), Argument [Introduction], sec. 2, p. 3; see also p. 92.

will then have another beginning in a different world, and other bodies, which will clothe the souls falling from heaven; and that we who are now men may fear that afterwards we might be born as women, and that today's virgin might then be a prostitute. These things I point out as heresies in Origen's books.[448]

In other works, Saint Jerome repeated his designation of "worlds innumerable, succeeding one another eternally" as two of Origen's most heretical propositions.[449] Copies and editions of Jerome's works circulated for centuries.

But above all, Saint Augustine validated Bishop Philaster's categorization. In 427 CE, a deacon of the church of Carthage asked Augustine to compose a succinct catalog of all heresies. Augustine eventually compiled a selection. He noted that Philaster listed 156 heresies, many more than the eminent Epiphanius, who had compiled 80. Augustine explained that the proper application of the word 'heresy' was difficult to define.[450] Hence, some of the items on Philaster's list were merely questionable or erroneous opinions. Nonetheless, Augustine composed a list with 88 heresies—and he included "that worlds are innumerable" as the "Seventy-seventh heresy."[451] In his *City of God Against the Pagans*, Augustine blamed this nightmare on Anaximander and Epicurus.[452]

Around 430, the Bishop of Cyrus in Syria, Theodoret, wrote the *Cure of Greek Maladies*. In it, he blamed philosophers for the opinion of many or infinite worlds, namely, Anaximander, Anaximenes, Archelaus, Xenophanes, Diogenes, Leucippus, Democritus, and Epicurus. He added that, "Heraclides among others of the Pythagorean sect said that each of the stars are

---

[448] Jerome, *Ad Pammachium et Marcellinum Apologia Hieronymi adversum Ruffinum*, bk. 2 (402 CE), in Sancti Hieronymi Stridoniensis, *Opera Omnia*, ed. Mariani Victorii (1624), p. 511, trans. Martínez.

[449] Jerome, *Confessio Hieronymiana, ex Omnibus Germanis B. Hieronymi Operibus Optima Fide Collecta*, ed. Cornelii Schultingi Steinuvichii (Paris: Michaelem Sonnium, 1585), pp. 41, 45, 236.

[450] Augustine to deacon Quodvultdeus, ca. 427 CE, in Saint Augustine, *Letters 211-270*, ed. Edmund Hill and John E. Rotelle (New York: New City Press, 2005), Letter 222, p. 81.

[451] Augustine, *De Haeresibus Liber* (ca. 430? CE), in Oehler, ed., *Corporis Haereseologici*, Vol. 2, bk. 1, pp. 195, 218, trans. Martínez.

[452] Augustine, *De Civitate Dei*, bk. 8 chap. 2, and bk. 11, chap. 5.

individual worlds, which contain land and air."[453] For Theodoret, such beliefs showed the extent to which the Greek philosophers engaged in "discord" and nonsense.

In a much more positive light, the philosopher Proclus sympathetically
echoed statements about the Pythagoreans. Around 450 CE, Proclus credited the Pythagoreans with the notion that the Moon is another world. He
said that they believed that the elements can be surveyed in the heavens
because the Moon is "ethereal earth." Right then, Proclus quoted Greek
lines by the ancient poet Orpheus, writing about God:

> He created another boundless Earth,
> which the immortals call Selene, and humans call Moon,
> with many mountains, many cities, many dwellings.[454]

Centuries later, one of Galileo's enemies criticized this very passage. Orpheus was a legendary poet who allegedly greatly influenced Pythagoras.
Thus some of the early Christians sensed a threat in his seductive fictions.
For example, the Platonic philosopher Clement of Alexandria, who embraced Christianity around 200 CE, complained that Orpheus was a Thracian unworthy of the name 'man,' because he was a deceiver who "under
the pretense of poetry corrupts human life, possessed by a spirit of artful
sorcery for purposes of destruction, celebrating crimes in their orgies, and
making human woes the materials of religious worship," to entice men to
worship false idols, by incantations.[455] Even so, Proclus also explained that
according to Plato, not all souls were placed on Earth, some existed on the
Moon.

Sometime around 540 CE, Emperor Justinian wrote an edict *Against
Origen*, in which, among other things, he denounced Origen's belief in many

---

[453] Theodoreti, *Graecarum Afectionum Curatio* (ca. 430), ed. Thomas Gaisford (Oxford:
Typographeo Academico, 1839), bk. 4, p. 162.

[454] Proclus, *Σισ τον του Πλατωνοσ Τιμαιον; In Platonis Timaeon Commentariorum Procli Libri
Quinque* (n.p., 1534), bk. Γ (i.e., bk. 3), p. 154, lines 6-7; see also bk. Δ (bk. 4), p. 283,
lines 11-12, trans. Martínez.

[455] Clement of Alexandria, *Protrepticus* (ca. 195 CE), trans. as *Exhortation to the Heathen*,
in Roberts and Donaldson, eds., *Ante-Nicene Christian Library*, Vol. 4: *Clement of Alexandria*, trans. William Wilson (1884), chap. 1, p. 19.

worlds.[456] The Emperor wanted to condemn Origen for adopting doctrines of Pythagoras and Plato that human souls pre-exist in the heavens and descend to be born in mortal bodies. In 553 the Fifth Ecumenical Council posthumously condemned Origen as a heretic.

Other churchmen echoed Philaster, Jerome, and Augustine. Consider Isidore, a Spaniard who was the Archbishop of Seville. From the late 610s until he died in 636, Isidore worked on an encyclopedia of Greco-Roman and Christian knowledge, which includes a discussion of the meaning and kinds of heresy. Bishop Isidore explained that a heretic is someone who willfully chooses what personally seems appealing yet who in so doing ponders perverse notions and thus withdraws from the Church. Instead, Isidore argued that as Catholic individuals "we are permitted to introduce nothing based on our own judgment, nor to choose what someone else has introduced from his own judgment. We have the apostles of God as authorities, who did not choose anything themselves to introduce from their own judgment, but faithfully bestowed on the world the teaching received from Christ."[457] Instead of merely listing heresies of the Christians, Isidore also attributed heresies to Jews and pagans. Like his predecessors, he listed dozens of heretical sects by name. And while still enumerating Christian heresies and before listing pagan beliefs he noted other heresies "without a founder and without names; others convert souls into daemons and into all sorts of animals in existence; others dissent about the state of the world; some have the opinion that there are innumerable worlds."[458]

Lest there be any doubt about the status of such beliefs in Christendom, Isidore immediately explained: "These are heresies that have arisen in opposition to the Catholic faith, and have been condemned by the apostles and Holy Fathers, or by the Councils." He insisted that anyone who interprets Holy Scriptures in any deviant way should be considered a heretic. As for Pythagoras, he was the first philosopher mentioned by Isidore in the following section, titled: "Pagan philosophers." Isidore claimed that the errors of the philosophers had introduced heresies within the Church. This Archbishop became so famous for his extensive knowledge that he became

---

[456] Justiniani Imperatoris, Λογος κατα Ὠριγενους (*Liber Adversus Origenem*) (ca. 538-543 CE), in *Patrologiae Cursus Completus: sive Bibliotheca Universalis*, Vol. 2, edited by J. Migne (Paris: Editorem in Via Dicta D'Amboise, 1848), p. 182.

[457] *The Etymologies of Isidore of Seville*, edited by Stephen Barney, W. Lewis, J. Beach, Oliver Berghof (Cambridge: Cambridge University Press, 2006), Vol. 8, sec. iii, p. 178.

[458] Ibid., sec. v.

known as the last of the ancient Church Fathers. Almost a thousand years after his death, Isidore was canonized in 1598 by the same Pope who judged Giordano Bruno.

Heresies were often known by the name of the heretical Christian sects that advocated them. The heresy of many worlds was usually attributed to no sect, as noted by Isidore. However, this nameless heresy was sometimes attributed to two utterly obscure heretical sects: the *Ametritae* and the *Ophitae*.[459] Some writers later conjectured that the latter name referred to Orpheus, since apparently he was the first to claim that the Moon was inhabited.[460]

There is evidence that the rejection of the plurality of worlds was taken seriously. In 748, the abbot of St. Peter's monastery in Salzburg somehow upset Pope Zacharias such that the Pope denounced the notion that there exists more than one world. The abbot was an Irishman named Feargal, known in Latin as Virgilius. Apparently he had said that the Earth was spherical and was inhabited everywhere, even in points diametrically opposite, known as the "antipodes." In the *Timaeus*, Plato had mentioned the antipodes, which were subsequently discussed by Aristotle and others. Hence Diogenes Laertius said that Alexander Polyhistor found that the "Commentaries of Pythagoras" asserted the existence of the antipodes.

But Virgilius's superior, Bishop Bonifacio misunderstood him. Bonifacio was the primate of Germany, at Mainz. He complained to Pope Zacharias that Virgilius has argued that there exists another world, and that it is inhabited. Fortunately the Pope's reply was preserved, because it is noteworthy. Pope Zacharias wrote that Virgilius "has lied to himself: out of the perverse doctrine, which is spoken against the Lord and his own soul too, namely that there is another world & other men beneath the earth, another Sun & Moon; if he is convicted by the summoned council of the Church

---

[459] Praedestinatus (ca. 461) attributed this heresy to the *Ametritae*. See Oehler, ed., *Corporis Haereseologici*, Vol. 2, bk. 1, p. 261. One commentator on Augustine's list of heresies wrote: "In the index attached to his [Augustine's] work, those who have embraced this madness are called Ophei, or who originated from the Ophitis heretics, or of whom Opheus was their author, or which may have originated from the Valentinians or the Basilidians, I think, who envisioned 365 heavens." Lamberti Danaeum, ed., *D. Aurelii Augustini Hipponensis Episcopi Liber De Haeresibus ad Qoudvultdeum* (Geneva: Haered. Eustachij Vignon, 1595), 223, trans. Martínez.

[460] Christian Gottlieb Joecher, *De Opheorum vel Orpheorum Haeresi Disserit* (Literis Breitkopfianis, 1730), pp. 3-4.

for confessing this, he will be deprived of the honor of the priesthood."[461]

The complaint by Pope Zacharias is very significant. It shows that the notion that there is more than one world, Sun, and Moon seemed intolerable and was addressed severely by the highest authority of the Church. Moreover the Pope's complaint was set in writing and disseminated. Thus clergymen had another precedent, in addition to objections by Hippolytus, Ambrosius, Hermias, Pope Dionysius, Lactantius, Epiphanius, Philaster, Jerome, Augustine, Bishop Theodoret, Bishop Isidore, and Bishop Bonifacio against the idea that there exists more than one world. Now another Pope had personally denounced that idea.

Likewise, in Constantinople, the influential monk Photius disparaged that idea. His statements later became significant because he became an archbishop and the Ecumenical Patriarch of Constantinople. Around 850, Photius criticized a work by Clement of Alexandria. According to Photius, Clement had fairly interpreted some passages of the Old and New Testaments but in some instances had indulged in "absolutely impious and incredible" claims. Photius complained that Clement argued that matter is eternal whereas Jesus Christ was merely created and was not really the Word of God incarnate. Photius further complained that Clement "says prodigious nonsense about the transmigration of souls and about many worlds before Adam." Photius declared that it was all "monstrous blasphemies," part of "six hundred ridiculous blasphemies."[462]

Around 1120, another clergyman who classified the notion of many worlds as a heresy was the Benedictine theologian Rupert of Deutz (now part of Cologne, Germany). Rupert praised God's Creation as described in the Bible, in which one world includes the waters and all of its living inhabitants. And then he remarked: "Therefore the heretical Epicureans will perish, who say that there are many worlds, or they were lying, saying that the

[461] Pope Zacharias to Bishop Bonifacio, 1 May 748, in F. Laurentio Surio Carthusiano, *De Vitis Sanctorum ab Aloysio Lipomano, Episcopo Veronæ, viro Doctissimo olim Conscriptis*, Vol. 3 (Venice, 1581), p. 160, trans. Martínez. Apparently there are no records of what happened immediately afterward, how Virgilius replied to such accusations. But he seems to have defended himself convincingly, because he was not removed from the priesthood. Presumably he had to explain that Bonifacio had misunderstood or misrepresented his remarks. Later, he became a bishop and was eventually canonized in 1233.

[462] Photius, "Clementis Alexandrini Presbyteri Scripta," (ca. 850), in Photii, *Myriobiblon, sive Bibliotheca*, trans. Andreas Schottus (Antwerp: Oliva Pauli Stephani, 1611), pp. 286-287, trans. Martínez.

souls of the dead always pass into other bodies, and live again. Thus Pythagoras, according to their invention, transmigrated into a peacock, and [later] the soul of Pythagoras into [Quintus] Ennius, and in the sixth place rested in Virgil."[463] The Benedictine theologian then asked his readers to reject vanities and praise God's Creation. Also at Cologne, but a century later, Albertus Magnus discussed and rejected the notion of many worlds. Albertus was a Dominican friar and later a famous bishop and saint. Around 1250, he argued that although God could certainly create many worlds, in fact there exists only one.[464]

Thomas Aquinas discussed the same issue. He said that Chrysostom was correct inasmuch as 'heaven' referred to *everything* that is above the Earth and its waters. But, nevertheless he deemed it acceptable to divide all of that into parts, and therefore to speak of several heavens, such as the atmosphere, the spheres of the seven planets (including the Sun and the Moon), and the sphere of the stars. But even then, his account clashed with the Pythagorean claims, because Thomas required that there is only *one* Earth: "The Earth stands in relation to the heaven as the center of a circle to its circumference. But as one center may have many circumferences, so, though there is but one Earth, there may be many heavens."[465]

Furthermore, Thomas specifically discussed the question: "*Whether there is only one World.*" He discussed reasons why multiple worlds might seem to exist. One such reason, he argued, was as follows: "It would seem that there is not only one world, but many. Because, as Augustine says in 1. 83 q., it is inappropriate to say that God created things without reason: but the same reason why He created one, He could create many, since His power is not limited to the creation of one world, but is infinite, as was shown above. Therefore God has produced many worlds." This argument, based on God's infinite power, is similar to what Bruno later argued. But Thomas gave clear denials:

---

[463] Rupert, "In Librum Ecclesiastes, Sancti Laurentii extra Muros Leodienses," bk. 1 (ca. 1120?), in R. D. D. Ruperti Abbatis Monasterij S. Heriberti Tuitiensis, *Opera* (Moguntiae: Hermanni Mylii Birckmanni, 1631), p. 1200, trans. Martínez.

[464] Albertus Magnus, *De Caelo et Mundo* (commentary on Aristotle) (ca. 1250) in Alberti Magni, *Opera Omnia*, ed. Augusti Borgnet, Vol. 4 (Paris: Ludovicum Vivès, 1890), bk. 1, chaps. 1, 6, pp. 66, 80-81.

[465] Thomas Aquinas, *Summa Theologica*, Part 1: *Treatise on the Work of the Six Days*, "Question 68: On the Work of the Second Day," article 4, Reply to Objection 1.

On the contrary, as it says in John 1:10: *"The world was made by Him."* Where the world is named as one, as if only one world existed. I answer by saying that the very order of things created by God shows the unity of the world. *The world is called one by the unity of order,* whereby some things are ordered to others. But whatever things come from God are organized with each other and in relation to God himself, as was shown above. Hence it is necessary that all things belong to one world. Therefore those who posited many worlds were only they who did not acknowledge any ordaining wisdom, but rather believed in chance: as did Democritus, who said that the concourse of atoms made this world, & infinitely many others.

Thomas also argued that "It is not possible for an Earth to exist other than this one: since every Earth would naturally be carried to the center, wherever it be."[466] Other theologians explained problematic consequences of the claim: we cannot assert that there exist "two or many worlds, since neither do we assert two or many Christs."[467] In his commentaries on Aristotle's *On the Heavens,* Thomas insisted: "it is not possible" that many worlds exist.[468] Aristotle had insisted that this is not possible, since it would require more than one "First Cause."[469]

Thus some very prominent clergymen denounced the notion that there are many worlds as ridiculous, perverse, impious, blasphemy, and heresy. Eventually, as we will see, it became labeled "Pythagorean." As we have seen, many stories in the development of so-called Pythagorean ideas seem to have arisen from misunderstandings. Herodotus said that Salmoxis the slave pretended to have resurrected. But later Hermippus, Celsus and Tertullian said that it was Pythagoras who pretended to have resurrected. Aristotle wrote that some Pythagoreans said that the Earth moves. But later

---

[466] Thomae Aqvinatis, *Svmmae Theologiae,* Part 1 (Venetiis: Dominicum Nicolinum & Socios, 1593), "Distinction of Things in General," Question 47, Art. 3, folio 165, trans. Martínez.

[467] Rustici Diaconi, *Contra Acephalos* (ca. 560), in *Antidotum Contra Diversas Omnium Fere Seculorum Haereses* (Basel: Henricus Petrus, 1528), p. 248 reverso. Also in Ludovico Ricchieri, *Haereseologia, hoc est Opus Veterum tam Græcorum quam Latinorum Theologorum, per quos omnes, quæ per Catholicam Christi Ecclesiam grassatae sunt* (Basil: Henrichum Petri, 1556), 715, trans. Martínez.

[468] Thomae Aquinatis, *In Quatuor Libros Arsitotelis De Coelo, & Mundo Commentaria* (Venice: Hieronymum Scotum, 1555), bk. 1, lesson 16, pp. 16-17.

[469] For a discussion of Aristotle's denial that more than one world can exist, see Dick, *Plurality of Worlds,* pp. 12-19.

interpreters claimed that Pythagoras himself discovered that the Earth moves. Aristotle said that some Pythagoreans taught that the Earth and the Sun move around a central fire. Others later claimed that Pythagoras himself taught that Earth circles the Sun. Aristotle wrote that some Pythagoreans said that the Earth is one of the stars. Later writers said that stars are worlds. The eccentric friar Giordano Bruno was one of those writers, and he paid with his life for his beliefs.

Kepler's Tribulations

Among the astronomers in the Renaissance, Johannes Kepler became fascinated by aspects of Pythagorean ideas. Unlike Giordano Bruno and Galileo, Kepler's eccentric beliefs did not lead him to a trial by any Catholic Inquisition, yet that was only because he lived in Protestant lands. At the same time, however, he did endure multiple opressions both from Protestants and Catholics.

Kepler did not believe in any Pythagorean number mysticism. He wrote: "I do not wish to prove anything by the mysticism of numbers, nor do I consider it possible to do so."[470] Yet Kepler had studied old writings that showed how Plato, and supposedly the early Pythagoreans, ascribed great importance to the five regular solids in the order of the universe. The regular solids are figures that are each made of only identical sides and each side has identical side-lengths: four, six, eight, twelve, and twenty sides. According to Proclus, Pythagoras himself had discovered "the structure of the cosmic figures."[471] Impressed by such ideas, Kepler believed that he could explain the quantity of planets and their relative separations by inferring that their orbits were interspaced by the five regular solids. Between the orbits of the six planets, he interspersed the five regular solids in the sequence of 6, 4, 12, 20, 8, which roughly gave the relative separations between the planets. Kepler thought he had found evidence of God's divine

---

[470] Max Caspar, *Kepler*, trans. (1959), p. 93.
[471] Proclus, *A Commentary on the First Book of Euclid's Elements* (ca. 460 CE), trans. Glenn R. Morrow (Princeton: Princeton University Press, 1970), 53. The claim seems doubtful because Proclus wrote more than a thousand years after Pythagoras died and there are no early accounts.

plan of the universe. He published it in his *Cosmographical Mystery*, in 1596.

Kepler thought that the ancient Pythagoreans had known and hidden the connection between the five regular solids and the order of the six planets, but had kept it secret: "Therefore that in the secrets of the Pythagoreans on this basis the five figures were distributed not among the elements, as Aristotle believed, but among the planets themselves is very strongly confirmed by the fact that Proclus tells us that the aim of geometry is to tell how the heaven has received appropriate figures for definite parts of itself."

Kepler wanted to include a chapter explaining the consistency of Copernicus' theory with the holy Bible. Yet the senate of the University of Tübingen required that he omit that part. So Kepler quietly acquiesced: "we shall imitate the Pythagoreans also in their customs. If someone asks us for our opinion in private, then we wish to analyze our theory clearly for him. In public, though, we wish to be silent."[472]

Kepler also noted the claim that Pythagoras could hear a universal harmony, a "music of the spheres" emitted by the motions of the planets.[473] And if anything did not quite work, in his analysis, Kepler hoped that Pythagoras might rise from the dead to help him—which did not happen, he wrote, "unless perhaps his soul has transmigrated into me."[474]

Like some of the Pythagoreans, Kepler argued that the Earth is a living animal, animated by rational soul. He recognized similarities between Pythagorean claims and those of the legendary Hermes Trismegistus. Kepler commented, "either Pythagoras hermeticizes, or Hermes pythagorizes."[475]

At a time of increasing orthodoxies, Kepler openly voiced his opinions on astronomy, religion, and mysticism. Personally, Kepler endured a series of tragedies. In 1598, his newborn son, Heinrich, promptly died. Then in

[472] Kepler, letter to Maestlin, quoted in Max Caspar, *Kepler*, translated by C. Doris Hellman (London: Abelard-Schuman, 1959), 69.

[473] Iamblichus, *On the Pythagorean Life* (ca. 300 CE), translated and edited by Gillian Clark (Liverpool: Liverpool University Press, 1989) Sections 64-66, pp. 27-28. Johannes Kepler, *The Harmony of the World* [1619], trans. E. J. Aiton, A. M. Duncan, J. V. Field (Philadelphia: American Philosophical Society, 1997), pp. 2, 130.

[474] Caspar, *Kepler*, translation, 96; Max Caspar, *Johannes Kepler*, 4th ed. (Stuttgart: Verlag für Geschichte der Naturwissenschaften und der Technik, 1995), 109.

[475] Johannes Kepler, *Harmonices Mundi, Libri V* (Lincii Austriae: Godofredi Tambachii, 1619), bk. 3, in Joannis Kepler, *Astonomi Opera Omnia*, Vol. 5, ed. C. Frisch (Frankfurt: Heyder & Zimmer, 1864), 132: "quin aut Pythagoras hermetiset, aut Hermes pythagoriset."

ca. 350 BCE	Aristotle	The Pythagoreans wrongly say that the Earth is one of the stars, and that moving in a circle around a central fire it produces night and day.
ca. 220 BCE	Archimedes	Aristarchus wrongly hypothesized that the fixed stars and the Sun remain unmoved while the Earth revolves about the Sun.
ca. 150 CE	Ptolemy	The Earth is at the center of the universe and the planets move around it in eccentric circles and epicycles. There exists a discernible celestial harmony.
ca. 150 CE	"Plutarch"	Some Pythagoreans claimed that stars are worlds in infinite space.
ca. 300 CE	Iamblichus	Through Pythagoras there came to be a true understanding of everything in the universe, including movements of the spheres and stars, eclipses, eccentrics and epicycles. Pythagoras could hear the universal harmony and music of the spheres and of the stars.
twelve centuries later…		
ca. 1540	Copernicus	The secretive Pythagoreans rightly argued that the Earth moves around the Sun.
1572	Thomas Digges	The Pythagoreans had a perfect description of the celestial orbs.
ca. 1570	Giordano Bruno	The Pythagoreans argued that souls are repeatedly reborn, even into animals. Stars are worlds in infinite space. The Earth moves because it has a soul.
ca. 1590	Tycho Brahe	The Pythagoreans wrongly believed that solid impenetrable orbs separate the planets' orbits.
1590s	Johannes Kepler	The Pythagoreans sensed the five regular solids in the cosmos. There is harmony in the planets' motions. The Earth moves because it has a soul. And "perhaps his soul [Pythagoras] has transmigrated into me."
1611, 1632	Galileo Galilei	Pythagoras rightly believed that the Earth and planets orbit the Sun.
1616, 1630s	Catholic theologians	Pythagorean ideas are vile, dangerous and should be condemned.

Table 1. *Critiques and praise: sometimes the Pythagoreans were portrayed as utterly wrong on astronomy, or alternatively, as ancient authorities who knew the true structure of the universe.*

September that year, the new Archduke of the region, Ferdinand II, a Catholic who had recently met with Pope Clement VIII in Rome, required that all Lutheran preachers and teachers had to leave the city of Graz, or be executed. These events are significant because they show that like Bruno and later Galileo, Kepler too endured difficulties under Catholic governments. Kepler and his wife were banished from the city. A month later he was allowed to return thanks to an individual exemption, to continue his duties not as a teacher but as district mathematician. The next summer, his daughter Susanna was born, but just a month later, she died. Kepler refused to bury her in the way that Catholics required, so he was fined. Other Catholic rituals were mandated, and many "heretical" books were seized, including copies of Luther's German translation of the Bible, and many books were burned in a huge bonfire in Graz.[476]

In July 1600, the archduke of Graz decreed that individuals should take and pass an exam of Catholic faith. All citizens were required to present themselves before an ecclesiastical commission at a Church, on July 31. Everyone had to declare their allegiance to Catholicism or at least pledge that they would convert, or therefore be expelled from the country. After approaching the large table of the commissioners, Kepler declared that he was a Lutheran and would not convert. Hence they inscribed his name into the list of banished persons, he lost his job, and was required to soon leave the country.[477]

Meanwhile, the prominent astronomer Tycho Brahe left his observatory in the island of Hven, between Denmark and Sweden, in order to become Imperial Mathematician at Prague, Bohemia. Hence, Kepler joined him there. However, in October 1601, Brahe died, so Kepler became appointed Imperial Mathematician to Rudolf II, Emperor of the Holy Roman Empire. Rudolf II had been raised Catholic in Spain but fortunately for Kepler this Emperor had withdrawn from Catholic observances and was tolerant of the Protestants.

Right then, Kepler became intensely busy with legal struggles because his mother was sued for witchcraft, and she was arrested and imprisoned. The incident is relevant because it illustrates how Christians had become increasingly concerned with the literal interpretation of Scriptures. Several passages in the Hebrew Bible, as well as in the New Testament, seemed to refer to witches.[478] For example, Exodus 22:18 states "Thou shalt not suffer a witch to live." This sentence seems to condone the execution of individuals labeled as witches, but if so, much weight is placed on the exact meaning of that one translated word: witch.

The ancient Hebrew word was *Chasaph*, meaning someone who is a

[476] James R. Voelkel, *Johannes Kepler and the New Astronomy* (New York: Oxford University Press, 1999), pp. 42-45.
[477] Voelkel, *Kepler*, p. 54.
[478] Exodus 22:18, 1 Samuel 15:23, 1 Samuel 28, John 15:16, Revelation 12:12.

diviner, poisoner, mutterer, an evildoer, or a juggler. In the early 1600s, in German Protestant lands there was not much ambiguity about the meaning of that word; for example, in his translation of the Bible, Martin Luther did use the German word for witch: *hexerai*. In the Hebrew Bible, the book of Samuel involves a long account of an interaction with a witch.[479] Saul had exiled wizards (or mediums) and "those with familiar spirits" from Israel, but God was no longer communicating with him through prophets or dreams, so he wanted help from a medium or witch. In disguise, he found one, and asked her to consult a spirit for him, so she summoned the spirit of Samuel, who told him that Saul had failed to execute God's wrath. Therefore, the spirit predicted that Saul would die. Just as in the pagan stories about Apollonius of Tyana, this story involves familiars (or daemons), allusion to the practice of divination from dreams, and the consultation of the dead.

Likewise, for years Kepler had been drafting a story about a dream in which an old mother teaches her son about conjuring spirits, and hence they then travel with a daemon up to the Moon, to meet its inhabitants. Kepler there wrote that the mother knew the secret of conjuring spirits, and that the daemon preferred such women, essentially witches: "dried-up old women, experienced since young in riding he-goats at night or forked sticks or threadbare cloaks." That fictional story links the true story of the witchcraft trial of Kepler's mother to Kepler's works and speculations in so-called Pythagorean astronomy.

In 1484, Pope Innocent VIII had sanctioned the hunt against witches, in view of the enormity of these allegedly spiritual crimes against God. Hence in the 1480s, Heinrich Kramers and others enacted a systematic hunt. Later, German Lutherans and others likewise sought to find and execute witches. Whereas the Catholics used the host in exorcisms, that is, they showed "the body of Christ" as a way to confront evil spirits, the Protestants rejected such rituals, so they were left in a seemingly vulnerable position; their main solution was to pray. To help themselves, they developed a system to identify and prosecute witches, as heretics. The usual charge was that the person had done *maleficio*, that is, using black magic to harm someone. Preachers gave sermons against demonology, and they conveyed the reality and immediacy of the Devil's power. Tens of thousands of women were put on trial, executed, and many who were declared

[479] 1 Samuel 28.

innocent by a judge were subsequently lynched by mobs in their hometowns. In German lands, there was no appeals process, and most of the accused were killed. The usual outcome was death by fire, following an allegedly literal interpretation of the words of Jesus according to John 15:16: "if a man not abide in me, he is cast off as a branch that is withered; and men gather them and cast them into the fire, and they are burned." But most witches were not burned alive; in Germany they were first executed by using the spike of a garrote, before the flames burned them.

Kepler's mother was accused of harming a girl, poisoning a woman, denying belief in heaven or hell, riding a calf to death, affecting pigs and cows to become mad and kick, and more. But it was a weak case inasmuch as there was no declaration of a pact with the Devil, a key accusation at the time. Usually, witches were accused of apostasy, that is, having rejected God to join Satan, even engaging in sexual relations with Satan. No such accusations were raised against Kepler's mother. Nevertheless, in 1620 she was arrested; she waited for ten weeks until in 1621 she was interrogated and threatened by showing her the instruments of torture. They held her captive for more than four hundred days, while her famous son carried out legal maneuvers to defend her. The trial finally ended in 1621. She was released from prison, but she soon died, just several months later. At least she was not burned by the Christians.

Meanwhile, Kepler had refused to sign "the Formula of Concord," the beliefs ostensibly required of all Lutherans (though actually, almost half of the ministers who prepared the document did not sign it). He rejected the claim that in the ceremony of the Eucharist the physical body and blood of Jesus Christ combine with the bread and wine. Instead he sympathized with the Calvinist idea that the Eucharist was a symbolic commemoration infused by the spiritual presence of Christ. Therefore, in 1619, the Lutheran ministers excommunicated him from their Church, to his chagrin.[480]

That same year, the Catholics banned Kepler's Copernican writings. Not only had Kepler affirmed the reality of the Copernican system, he affirmed that the Moon is another world and that the Earth is animated by a soul. He argued that mathematics contains hidden divine knowledge: "Plato teaches us many remarkable things about the nature of the gods through the appearance of mathematical things; and the Pythagorean philosophy

---

[480] James A. Connor, *Kepler's Witch* (2004), pp. 242, 287, 320-321.

disguises its teaching on divine matters with these, so to speak, veils."[481]

For years, Kepler planned to publish his belated but much expanded "dream" about life on the Moon. But he died in 1630, survived by his second wife and six children.

Ten Censures
against Giordano Bruno

The Roman Inquisition censured ten propositions in Giordano Bruno's books. Such propositions have something in common: that these beliefs had been attributed to the cult of Pythagoras. The Roman Inquisition censured Bruno's books not merely because he advocated erroneous philosophical views but because he defended pagan heresies.

In 1595, theologians of the Roman Inquisition began to inspect Bruno's books to find propositions to censure. They only had some of his books, but by late 1596 the censures were ready. In December the Inquisitors visited Bruno's cell and ordered "that he be interrogated as soon as possible about the propositions extracted from his writings and about the censures."[482] The list survives in "The Summary of the Trial" discovered by Angelo Mercati in 1940. It consists of ten propositions.[483] Regarding the ten propositions Frances Yates admitted: "I find this document very confused and confusing."[484]

---

[481] Johannes Kepler, *Harmonices Mundi Libri V* (Lincii, Austria: Godofredi Tampachii, 1619); Kepler, *The Harmony of the World*, trans. and ed. E. J. Aiton, Alistair Duncan, Judith Field (Philadelphia: American Philosophical Society, 1997), book III, 127.

[482] Visita dei Carcerati, 16 December 1596, in L. Firpo, *Il Proceso di Giordano Bruno*, Rome, Salerno Editrice, 1993, p. 241. Unless otherwise noted, all translations in the present article are by A. Martínez.

[483] Firpo adds two from Gaspar Schoppe's later account. Ibid., pp. 304, and 80-85. Maurice Finocchiaro follows Firpo but adds another: "the individual immortality of the human soul is a questionable proposition." M. Finocchiaro, *Philosophy versus Religion and Science versus Religion: The Trials of Bruno and Galileo*, in H. Gatti, ed., *Giordano Bruno: Philosopher of the Renaissance*, Burlington, Ashgate, 2002, 61. This is an interpolation. Instead Bruno said: "I hold that souls are immortal." Bruno, in Firpo, *Proceso*, p. 284.

[484] F. Yates, *Giordano Bruno and the Hermetic Tradition*, London: Routledge, 2002, chap. 19, p. 388.

I will explain it. I'll show which propositions were heretical and that nearly all had something in common: they embodied beliefs attributed to the Pythagoreans. This finding shows that the Inquisition censured Bruno's books because he defended *pagan beliefs*.

A few historians have rightly discussed Pythagoras and Pythagorean notions in Bruno's works.[485] The Pythagoreans had anti-Christian beliefs: transmigration of souls, denials of the uniqueness of Jesus, etc. So I'll analyze the censures in this context.

Ten Censured Propositions

The shortest proposition (the 10th) occupies three lines of print in Mercati's edition. The longest (the 4th) occupies 53 lines plus 55 lines of footnotes. I quote the initial lines:

Summary of replies by Brother Giordano to the censures of Propositions extracted from his books.[486]

> [*1st censured proposition*] Concerns the generation of things since he [Bruno] admitted the eternal existence of two real principles from which all things are done, and which are the soul of the world, and primal matter; Interrogated whether they are eternal.
>
> [*2nd censured proposition*] Concerns the conditional, namely, that the nature of God is finite, if it does not in fact produce infinity, or the infinite. [… And Bruno insisted] that as a consequence of my philosophy, since God's power is infinite it must necessarily produce effects that are equally infinite.
>
> [*3rd censured proposition*] Concerns the mode of creation of human souls stated by these words: Deriving from that universal principle, from general to particular.

---

485 E.g., see: R. Mendoza, *Metmpsychosis and Monism in Bruno's nova filosofia*, in Gatti, *Giordano Bruno*, pp. 272-297. H. Gatti, *Giordano Bruno and Renaissance Science*, Ithaca, Cornell University Press, 1999, pp. 13-28. D. Tessicini, *I Dintorni dell'Infinito: Giordano Bruno e l'Astronomia del Cinquecento*, Pisa, Serra, 2007. M. Ciliberto, *Lessico di Giordano Bruno*, II, Rome, Ateneo & Bizarri, 1979, pp. 929-932.
486 *Summarium*, in A. Mercati, *Il Sommario del Processo di Giordano Bruno*, in *Studi e Testi*, Vol. 101, Vatican, Biblioteca Apostolica, 1942, pp. 113-119.

[*4th censured proposition*] Concerning that proposition, indeed. In this world nothing is generated, or corrupted in substance, unless we want to refer to alteration in this way; a product, whatever may be its alteration, it always maintains the same substance. [...Bruno replied:] As Solomon does not contradict this, now saying [Ecclesiastes 1:4] "a generation passes away, and a generation arrives, [but the Earth remains forever]" and now also with: [Ecclesiastes 1:9] "Nothing new under the Sun," that is, what is now is what was.

[*5th censured proposition*] Concerning Earth's motion he states: First, I generally say that the manner and cause of the motion of the Earth, and of the immobility of the firmament and heaven are to me produced with the proper reasons and authority, which are certain and not harmful to the authority of divine Scriptures [...]

[*6th censured proposition*] Likewise folio 292 face 2 states that Stars are Angels, in these words: the Stars are actually Angels, animated rational bodies, which while they praise God, and reveal the power and greatness of that by which light, its writings etched in the firmament, "the Heavens declare the glory of God"; Angels do not mean anything other than the messengers and interpreters of the divine voice, and of nature, and these are sensible Angels, visible, while others are invisible, and insensible.

[*7th censured proposition*] Likewise, folio 293 posits the Earth is alive, not only with a sensitive soul, but also rational, and God expressly attributed a soul to it, by saying "Earth produce a living soul," which is how animals are constituted with the body from a part of its body, and its [Earth's] universal spirit comes to animate each particular one of them, by transmitting to them from its spirit. [...] That it [the Earth] is a rational animal is manifest by its rational intellectual acts, which are seen in the regularity of its motion around its own center, another around the Sun...

[*8th censured proposition*] Likewise on folio 294 states that the intelligent soul is not form, in these words: "I do not intend to support by my philosophy the ordinance that the soul is form, as in no place of divine Scriptures is it so called, but the spirit which is now in the body as the inhabitant in his house, a traveler in his pilgrimage, as the inner man in the outer man, as a captive in a prison."

[*9th censured proposition*] Likewise, he denies that individuals' true being, what they are, is but vanity, according to the dictate of Solomon [Ecclesiastes

1:14], "I saw everything that is done under the Sun, and all is vanity," but that true substances are species of primal nature, that truly are that which they are.

[*10th censured proposition*] Again, he posits many worlds, many Suns, necessarily containing similar things in kind and in species as in this world, and even men, as in folio 139 and the subsequent long digression.

These last two propositions are brief: they don't have Bruno's replies. The 10th cites a folio number out of sequence with the rest. Apparently Bruno replied to eight propositions, then the censors added two more.

Do the ten propositions form a coherent group? Some match Pythagorean beliefs: such as (10) that many worlds exist. But at first it seems that several are not Pythagorean: (2), (3), (4), (6), (8), (9). However, we'll see that Bruno's transgressions were essentially "Pythagorean." The term does not necessarily mean that Pythagoras or his early followers held such views. Instead, it means that, throughout the centuries, such views had been variously attributed to the Pythagoreans.[487] For each censured proposition from Bruno's books, I will note which specific works attributed such notions to the Pythagoreans.

Bruno's first censured proposition was that things arise from two principles: the world soul and primal matter—both eternal. "The world" means either Earth or universe. The *Placita Philosophorum* said that Pythagoras believed that the world has a soul.[488] It said that he thought the universe could never be destroyed.[489] Porphyry—enemy of Christians but advocate of Pythagoras—also asserted the universe's eternity. He denied Creation and spoke of the "soul of the world."[490]

---

[487] For accounts of how notions in mathematics, astronomy, religion, and alchemy were misattributed to Pythagoras over time, see: A. Martinez, *The Cult of Pythagoras*, Pittsburgh, University of Pittsburgh, 2012, pp. 1-28, 125-127, 201-224; Martinez, *Science Secrets*, Pittsburgh, U. Pittsburgh, 2011, pp. 13-42, 55-57, 70-76, 229-230, 261-280; and, Martinez, *Pythagoras, Bruno, Galileo*, Cambridge, SaltshadowCastle, 2014, pp. 11-120, 135-158, 193-207.

[488] [falsely attributed to Plutarch], *Placita Philosophorum* [based on a work by Aetius, ca. 50 BC], in H. Daiber, ed., *Aetius Arabus: Die Vorsokratiker in Arabischer Überlieferung*, Wiesbaden, Steiner, 1980, bk. 4, chap. 7.

[489] Ibid., bk. 2, chap. 14.

[490] Porphyry, *On the Abstinence of Animal Food*, bk. 2, in *Select Works of Porphyry*, ed. and trans. T. Taylor, London, Rodd, 1823, p. 74.

Saint Hippolytus complained that Pythagoras said the world is eternal.[491] In the 1270s the Bishop of Paris Étienne Tempier condemned the proposition "the world is eternal" as heretical; with authority granted by Pope John XXI.[492] Bishop Tempier argued that members of the faculty of the University of Paris transgressed the limits of philosophy to speak erroneously about theology. Anyone stating the world's eternity would be excommunicated and subject to the Inquisition. Tempier also deemed heretical "That the substance of the soul is eternal."[493] Yet Bruno said that souls are made from the eternal substance of the world soul.

In 1553 the Divinity Faculty of the University of Paris censured the claim "That the World was never made."[494] It was a denial of Genesis. In short, any belief in the eternity of the world was a heresy, if voiced by a Catholic. For example, in the 1580s a compendium of heresies specified: "One heresy is to say that elementary Matter, from which the world is made, was not made by God, but is coeternal with God."[495] This tome was published in Venice and Florence, and its author was Sebastiano Medici, a distant relative of the first Grand Duke of Tuscany, Cosimo de Medici.

Justin Martyr quoted Pythagoras as saying God is the "animating soul of the universe, the movement of all orbits."[496] The Pythagorean philosopher Apollonius also said the world has a soul.[497] This notion derived popularity from Plato's *Timaeus*. Likewise, the Roman writer Marcus Varro (ca. 50 BC) said the true gods are the soul of the world and its parts. Saint Augustine attacked this at length in *City of God Against the Pagans*.

Augustine complained that the various souls that allegedly were parts of God, were of two kinds: the mortal ones that live on Earth, and the immortal souls that live in the air and the ether:

[491] Hippolytus, Ὁ κατὰ πασῶν αἱρέσεων ἔλεγχος (ca. 225 CE), in *Refutatio Omnium Haeresium,* ed. M. Marcovich, Berlin, De Gruyter, 1986, bk. 4, sec. 14; bk. 6, sec. 23.

[492] É Tempier, *Tredecim errores a Stephano episcopo Parisiensi condemnati, 1270,* Prop. 5, and *Sequntur Errores Annotati in Rotulo, 1277,* Props. 87, 98; in H. Deinfle, *Chartularium Universitatis Parisiensis,* I, Paris, Delalain, 1889, pp. 487, 548.

[493] Tempier (1277), Prop. 109, *Chartularium,* p. 549.

[494] Faculty of Divinity of Paris, Censures of 1 August 1553, quoted in L. Dupin, *A New Ecclesiastical History of the Sixteenth Century,* II, London, Churchill, 1706, p. 441.

[495] S. Medice, *Summa Omnium Haeresum,* Florence, Officina Sermartelliana, 1581, p. 647. S. Medicis, *Summa Omnium Hæresum,* Venice, Iuntas, 1587, Pt. 1, p. 37 rev.

[496] Justin Martyr [apocryphal?], *Justin's Hortatory Address to the Greeks,* in A. Roberts and J. Donaldson, eds., *Ante-Nicene Christian Library,* II (1867), chap. 19, p. 305.

[497] Philostratus, *The Life of Apollonius of Tyana,* Cambridge, Harvard U., 1948, bk. 3, chap. 34, p. 308.

from the highest part of the heavens to the orbit of the Moon there are souls, namely, the stars and planets, and these are not only understood to be gods, but are seen as such. And between the orbit of the Moon and the commencement of the region of clouds and winds there are aerial souls; but these are seen with the mind, not with the eyes, and are called Heroes, and Lares, and Genii.[498]

Augustine attributed this theology to "not only Varro, but many philosophers." Augustine argued that their belief that there exists a soul of the world led them to imagine that this soul pervades the Earth, that it penetrates into living bodies and nourishes trees, and "the stones and earth in the world, which we see, and which are not pervaded by the power of sensation, are, as it were, the bones and nails of God."[499] Augustine argued that this belief in the divine soul of the living Earth led to the false belief in multiple gods.

Augustine denounced this polytheistic notion of an *anima mundi* as contradictory. He complained that pagans who believed such notions were "possessed by many demons."[500] Saint Jerome too rejected "the error of heretics, who suppose that everything is animated."[501]

To further understand the first censure against Bruno, we must discuss the French theologian Peter Abelard. In 1121 he was convicted of misinterpreting the Holy Trinity. Still he later argued that ancient philosophers called the Holy Spirit the "soul of the world," a Spirit that infuses all and "vivifies creatures."[502] He cited Salvian who "quoted" Pythagoras: "A soul is intermixed or diffused in all parts of the world, from which all animals when born receive their life."[503]

---

[498] Augustine, *De Civitate Dei*, bk. 7, chap. 6.

[499] Augustine, *De Civitate Dei*, bk. 7, chap. 23.

[500] Augustine, *De Civitate Dei*, bk. 7, chaps. 6, 22.

[501] Jerome, *Commentariorum Hieronymi in Matthaeum Evangelistam, Liber Primus*, in *Operum Divi Hieronymi Eusebii Stridonensis*, IX, Paris, Chevallonium, 1534, chap. 8, p. 12 rev.

[502] Abelardus, *Epitome Theologiæ Christianæ*, in *Sæculum XII Petri Abælardi Abbatis Rugensis Opera Omnia*, ed. J. Migne, Paris, D'Amboise, 1855, chap. 18, pp. 1720-1721.

[503] Abelard, *Introductio ad Theologiam*, bk. 1, in *Opera Omnia*, p. 1019. Original in Salvianus, *De Gubernatione Dei, Octo Libri dati ad S. Salonium Episcoum* (ca. 440 CE), bk. 1, in *Salviani, Opera Omnia*, ed. Migne, Paris, D'Amboise, 1859, p. 29. Abelard discussed the World Soul not as strictly real, but as a metaphor for the Holy Spirit.

In 1139 Abelard's claims about the Holy Spirit angered William of St. Thierry. He denounced Abelard to the Bishop of Chartres and the Abbot of Clairvaux, complaining that Abelard endangered faith in the Trinity. Among the thirteen "monstrous doctrines" was: "That the Holy Spirit is the soul of the world."[504] The Council of Sens condemned Abelard's doctrines as heretical.[505] Pope Innocent II confirmed their ruling. About Abelard's books, he ordered: "wherever you find them, burn them."[506] Abelard died the next year, in 1142.

Henceforth some treatises on heresies included the heresy that the Holy Spirit is the world soul. For example, the Franciscan theologian Alfonso de Castro enumerated heresies about God, including "The eleventh heresy: that the Holy Spirit is the soul of the world."[507] Castro's treatise was published in thirteen editions until 1578. Another book too specified how Pythagoras defined God: a soul that permeates the world and vivifies animals.[508]

Giordano Bruno wrote about God, who "for the Pythagoreans is an infinite spirit that penetrates everything, comprehending and vivifying."[509] Interrogated by Venetian Inquisitors, he said that he didn't understand the Trinity or "the Holy Spirit as a third person," except "by following the Pythagorean way" as soul of the universe.[510] He quoted the Bible, "Solomon: "For the spirit of God fills the Earthly orb: and therefore he who contains everything," which conforms entirely to the Pythagorean doctrine."[511]

[504] G. de Saint-Thierry to the Bishop of Chartres and B. of Clarivaux, late 1139, in J. Leclercq, ed., *Receuil d'Études sur Saint Bernard et ses Écrits*, IV, Rome, Storia, 1987, p. 352.
[505] J. Morrison, *The Life and Times of Saint Bernard, Abbot of Clairvaux, A.D. 1091-1153*, London, Macmillan, 1894, pp. 301-311.
[506] Pope Innocent II, 1141, *Conciliorum Generalium Ecclesiae Catholicae*, IV, Rome, Camerae Apostolicae, 1612, p. 23.
[507] A. de Castro, *Adversus Omnes Hæreses. Libri XIIII*, Paris, Gaultherot, 1543, bk. 5, p. 80. See also T. Deciani, *Tractatus Criminalis Omnium Hæresum*, I, Venice, Zenarios, 1590, pp. 236-237.
[508] Medicis, *Summa Omnium Hæresum* (1581), p. 647, and (1587), Part 1, p. 62 verso.
[509] *Camoeracenis Acrotismus*, in J. Bruni, *Opera Latine Conscripta*, ed. F. Fiorentino, I, Naples, Morano, 1879, Article LXV, p. 177.
[510] Bruno, in Firpo, *Processo*, p. 169.
[511] Ibid., p. 254. *Bible*, Book of Wisdom 1:7.

Bruno's first censure was Pythagorean: the world soul as a generating principle.[512] About primal matter, see below.

The second censure was Bruno's claim that since God is infinite the universe He created is infinite too. Bruno had argued: "So great is God's excellence, that it is manifested in the greatness of his empire: it is not glorified in one, but in innumerable suns: not in one Earth, one world: but in ten-hundred thousand, I say in infinite."[513] In another book he ridiculed a finite universe as a stupid dream of a confused imagination.[514] His infinite universe was Pythagorean in that they believed that stars are worlds in an infinite aether.[515] Thomas Digges too said the universe is infinite, crediting the Pythagoreans.[516]

The third censure was that each human soul is *derived* from a universal principle, the world soul. Aristotle denied the Pythagoreans' claim that any soul can be clothed in any body.[517] Justin rejected the claim that souls are not created, when explaining how he left Pythagoras and Plato for Christ.[518] Hippolytus and Origen criticized the Pythagoreans for saying that souls of come from the stars. According to the *Placita*, Pythagoras taught that the eternal rational part of human souls is derived from an eternal Deity.[519] Porphyry and Macrobius said that Pythagoras taught that souls, immortal, come from the Milky Way.[520] Tertullian, Lactantius and Epiphanius said

---

[512] See also Bruno, *De la Causa, Principio et Uno* (1584), Dialogue 5, p. 124; reissued in G. Gentile, ed., *Opere Italiane di Giordano Bruno*, I, Bari, 1908, p. 253. See also: D. Knox, *Bruno: Immanence and Transcendence in De la Causa, Principio et Uno, Dialogue II*, in "*Bruniana & Campanelliana*," XIX, 2013, 2, pp. 466, 473. É. Namer, *Les Aspects de Dieu dans la Philosophie de Giordano Bruno*, Paris, 1926, pp. 35-98. Ciliberto, *Lessico*, II, p. 929. For a discussion of the Stoics, see T. Gregory, *Anima Mundi*, Florence, Sansoni, 1955, pp. 123-127.

[513] *De l'Infinito Universo et Mondi*, n.p., 1584, p. [xxix].

[514] *De Immenso et Innumerabilibus, seu de Universo et Mundis* (1591), in Bruni, *Opera Latine Conscripta*, ed. F. Fiorentino, I,II, pp. 171, 291. See also M. Granada, *Bruno, Digges, Palingenio: Omogeneità ed Eterogeneità nella Concezione dell'Universo Infinito*, in "*Rivista di Storia della Filosofia*," XLVII, 1992, 1, p. 67.

[515] *Placita*, bk. 2, chap. 13.

[516] T. Digges, *A Perfit Description of the Caelestiall Orbes according to the most aunciente Doctrine of the Pythagoreans*, in L. Digges, *A Prognostication Everlastinge* (1576), The Addition.

[517] Aristotle, *De Anima* (ca. 350?), in W. Ross, ed., *Works of Aristotle*, III, Oxford, Clarendon, 1928, bk. 1, pp. 3 verso, 8 rev.

[518] Justin, *Dialogue with Trypho*, chap. 2, in *Ante-Nicene*, II, chap. 4, pp. 93-94.

[519] *Placita*, bk. 4, chap. 7.

[520] Macrobius, *Commentary on the Dream of Scipio* (ca. 430? CE), trans. W. Stahl, New York, Columbia U. Press, 1952, 134.

Pythagoras misunderstood the soul's immortality.[521] Saint Jerome said that Pythagoras taught that souls go from bodies to bodies.[522] Thus the Pythagoreans thought that human souls are *derived* from a previous state, whether fragments of the world soul, or immortal souls in the heavens. Instead Christians said that God creates a soul for each person.

Bruno's fourth proposition was that nothing is created: things are only *transformed*. Was it distinctly Pythagorean? Other ancient writers emphasized change, such as Heraclitus. Hippolytus discussed Xenophanes' belief that, "nothing is generated or perishes."[523] He also quoted Epicurus: "nothing was generated, except from atoms."[524] Yet in Bruno's self-education, Pythagoras became the most prominent proponent that nothing is new. Interrogated by Venetian Inquisitors, Bruno quoted Ecclesiastes 1:9.[525] In the Bible it's about the past and the future:

> What has been will be again,
> what has been done will be done again;
> there is nothing new under the Sun.

But Bruno spoke about the past and the present, as a personal motto:

> Solomon and Pythagoras.
> What is that which is? That which was.
> What is that which was? That which is.
> Nothing new under the Sun.[526]

---

[521] Tertullian, *De Anima* (ca. 215 CE), in J. Waszink, ed., *Tertulliani Opera*, II, Turnholti: Brepols Editores Pontificii, 1954, chaps. 28-32, 54. Lactantius, *The Divine Institutes*, bk. III, chap. 18, in *Ante-Nicene Christian Library*, XXI (1871), pp. 182-183. Epiphanius, *Panarion* (ca. 374-377), in Epiphanius, *The Panarion of Epiphanius of Salamis: Book 1*, 2nd ed., trans. F. Williams, Leiden, Brill, 2009, Sect. 7, p. 24.

[522] Jerome, *Ad Pammachium et Marcellinum Apologia Hieronymi Adversum Ruffinum*, bk. III, in Hieronymi, *Opera Omnia*, ed. M. Victorii, Paris, Bibliopolas, 1624, p. 537. See also pp. 20-21, 30, 380, 411-412, 444, 551.

[523] Hippolytus, *Refutatio*, bk. 1, sec. 14, p. 74.

[524] Ibid., bk. 1, sec. 22, p. 84.

[525] Bruno, 2 June 1592, in Firpo, *Processo*, 190.

[526] Bruno, ca. 1587, ibid., plate 5 after p. 86.

He often said "nothing new under the Sun."[527] His words echo the Pythagorean concern for memories of past lives—instead of the Christian afterlife. Ancient tales said that the divine Pythagoras had lived many lives.

The *Placita* stated: "Matter is that first being which is substrate for generation, corruption, and all other alterations. The disciples of Thales and Pythagoras, with the Stoics, are of opinion that matter is changeable, mutable, convertible, and sliding through all things."[528] Ovid portrayed Pythagoras as the master of transmutations, teaching that everything in the world transforms, and the soul "passes into ever-changing bodies."[529]

Not only could the soul of Pythagoras move from one body to others, he could allegedly transform matter. An important medieval text on alchemy, *The Convention of Philosophers*, featured Pythagoras. It tells of a gathering of nine philosophers convened by Pythagoras to clarify obscurities in ancient alchemical books. Their Master, Pythagoras spoke of "the stone that is not a stone," common but hidden, and known by many names: Spume of the Moon and Heart of the Sun. The philosophers discussed how to produce this stone, to "roast it in a fire even more intense, until it gains the color of blood, when it is placed on coins and changes them into gold, according to Divine desire."[530] Pythagoras argued that the philosophers used strange expressions to convey the secret art, to hide it from the vulgar and foolish. Regardless, the Catholic Church condemned alchemy and denounced it as forgery.

Porphyry wrote that Pythagoras "taught that the soul was immortal and that after death it transmigrated into other animated bodies. After certain specified periods, the same events occur again; that nothing was entirely new."[531] Saint Jerome too said that Pythagoras taught immortality and that:

---

[527] H. von Warnsdorf Family Album, 18 September [1587], in ibid., pp. 169, 301, 304, plate 4, after p. 86. See also E. Canone, ed., *Giordano Bruno: gli Anni Napoletani e la 'Peregrinato' Europea*, Cassino, Universita degli Studi, 1992, pp. 121-125. See also F. Tocco, *Un Nuovo Autografo di G. Bruno*, in "*La Bibliofilia*," IX, Florence, 1906, pp. 342-345.

[528] *Placita*, bk. 1, chap. 9, p. 123.

[529] Ovid, *Metamorphoses*, trans. F. Miller, II, London, Heinemann, 1916, pp. 375-377.

[530] *Turba Philosophorum;* this Arabic manuscript seems to date from about 900 CE, as shown by Martin Plessner. It partly derives from Greek sources; its earliest printed edition was published in 1572: *Auriferae Artis, quam Chemiam Vocant, Antiquissimi Authores, sive Turba Philosophorum* (Basel, 1572), Dictums 13, 49, 32, trans. Martínez.

[531] Porphyry, *Life of Pythagoras* (ca. 300? CE), *The Pythagorean Sourcebook and Library*, trans. K. Guthrie, ed. D. Fideler, Grand Rapids, Phanes, 1987, sec. 19.

"those things which had existed, after certain revolutions of time, came into being again; so that nothing in the world should be thought of as new."[532]

Bruno's fifth censured proposition was that Earth moves. It was a Pythagorean idea. Aristotle complained that the Pythagoreans believed it.[533] In the *Placita*, "Philolaus the Pythagorean" and "Ecphantus the Pythagorean" said that Earth orbits a central fire. Hippolytus noted that Ecphantus said that Earth moves.[534] Porphyry argued that the world soul is self-movable and can "move the body of the world."[535] Laertius and Joannes Stobaeus also credited a moving Earth to Philolaus. Copernicus, Digges, Bruno, and Zúñiga credited the theory of Earth's motion to the Pythagoreans.[536]

A moving Earth seemed to oppose phrases in the Bible. Moreover, it was linked to Bruno's other censures: Earth moves because of its soul.

The sixth censured proposition was that stars are angels: animated rational bodies that convey God's voice. The Pythagoreans did not write about angels, so this was not their belief. However, Digges framed the "Doctrine of the Pythagoreans" as involving stars as angels: "glorious lights innumerable. Far excelling our Sun both in quantity and quality the very court of celestial angels devoid of grief."[537] Bruno briefly referred to "angels, which are stars, announcing the divine infinite majesty."[538] He also wrote that angels flow into heavenly bodies, the elements flow to the heavens and then "into daemons or angels."[539] Bruno used the terms 'angels' and 'daemons' synonymously, as Christian and pagan terms.[540] He wrote:

---

[532] Jerome, *Ad Pammachium*, bk. 3, sec. 40.

[533] Aristotle, *De Caelo* (ca. 340? BCE), bk. 2, sec. 13.

[534] Hippolytus, *Refutatio*, bk. 1, sec. 15, p. 74.

[535] Porphyry, *Abstinence*, p. 74.

[536] Bruno, *La Cena delle Ceneri* (London, 1584).

[537] Digges, *Description*, folio 43.

[538] *De Immenso*, in Bruni, *Opera Latine Conscripta*, ed. F. Fiorentino I,II, p. 377.

[539] Bruno, *De Magia Mathematica*, in Bruno, *Opere Magiche*, ed. M. Ciliberto, et al., Milan, 2000, sec. 1.

[540] F. Tocco, *Le Opere Inedite di Giordano Bruno*, in *Atti della Realle Accademia di Scienze Morali e Politiche*, XXV, Naples, Società Reale, 1892, p. 146. A. von Nettesheim, *De Occulta Philosophia*, ed. V. Compagni, Leiden, Brill, 1992, p. 85. Bruno echoes Agrippa, but Bruno's identification of "daemons or angels" and the infusion of angels into stars are his interpolations. Bruno also linked stars and daemons in W. Lutoslawski, *Jordani Bruni Nolani Opera Inedita, Manu Propria Scripta*, in L. Stein, ed., *Archiv für Geschichte der Philosophie*, II, Berlin, Reimer, 1889, p. 541. Regarding Bruno's sources for *De Magia*, see S. Ricci, *Giordano Bruno nell'Europa del Cinquecento*, Rome, Salerno, 2000, p. 426. See also Bruno, *Opere Magiche*, ed. M. Ciliberto.

"How to attract both good and bad angels: Good daemons are enticed in diverse ways."[541]

To the Pythagoreans, daemons mediated between humans and gods. Some portrayed Pythagoras as a daemon, perhaps from the Moon or from Jupiter. Philostratus said that a daemon guided Apollonius. Saint Hippolytus complained that Pythagoras said the souls of animals come from the stars, and can become human souls. Pythagoras theorized: "the Sun, and the Moon, and the stars were all gods," said Diogenes Laertius. Likewise, Porphyry said that the heavenly bodies were visible gods: "the world, the fixed stars, the wandering stars, who are visible Gods, consisting of soul and body."[542] (Porphyry also spoke of the many invisible daemons. He said that they are the progeny of the soul of the universe, and they govern the region under the Moon, and announce the will of the gods to men.[543])

Yet many astrological books construed stars or planets as divine beings. So Bruno's sixth proposition is compatible with the so-called Pythagorean beliefs, but it cannot be described as distinctly Pythagorean. And Bruno did not attribute it to them, at least in writing, such as *On Mathematical Magic*.

Was it a heresy? Yes. In 553 CE the Fifth Ecumenical Council at Constantinople issued "Anathemas Against Origen." The sixth states: "If anyone says that the heaven & Sun & Moon & stars and the waters that are above the heavens, are animated [have souls] & material powers, he is anathema," i.e., a heretic.[544] Origen's heresies were well known in the 1590s.[545]

The seventh censured proposition was that Earth is a living animal with a rational, sensitive soul that embodies a universal spirit that animates animals. In various Pythagorean accounts it is more common to read that animal souls come from the stars, not explicitly from the Earth itself, though one might infer (like Bruno) that since some writers specified that the Earth is a star then this implies that some souls come from the Earth. Moreover, the idea of the Earth's vitality and rationality involves another Pythagorean connection inasmuch as it was linked, in Bruno's account, to the claim that the Earth moves.

---

[541] *De Magia*, sec. 17, in Bruno, *Opere Magiche*, ed. M. Ciliberto.
[542] Porphyry, *On the Abstinence from Animal Foods*, ed. Taylor, bk. 2, sec. 37, p. 74; translation modified.
[543] Ibid., pp. 74-75.
[544] N. Callisti, *Ecclesiasticæ Historiæ Libri Decem & Octo*, Basel, Oporini, 1553, p. 893.
[545] E.g., C. Baronio, *Annales Ecclesiastici*, VII, Rome, Typographia Vaticana, 1596, p. 289

The belief that Earth is alive appears in *Timaeus*: "the world became a living creature truly endowed with soul and intelligence by the providence of God....one visible animal comprehending within itself all other animals of a kindred nature."[546] Some commentators thought that Timaeus was a Pythagorean and that Plato based his book on impressions about Pythagoras.[547] The *Placita* spoke of the "respiration" of the Earth.[548] Laertius said that Pythagoras taught that the world "is endowed with life, and intellect." Plotinus (Porphyry's teacher) argued that Earth's soul transmits growth to its parts.[549] Apollonius reportedly thought that Earth is a soulful animal.[550] Iamblichus too argued that its a great animal.[551]

Some of the Stoics advocated similar beliefs.[552] But Saint Augustine denied that the Earth is a living being.[553] He said that belief in the divine soul of the living Earth led to false belief in many gods. Bishop Tempier condemned the notion that the heavenly bodies are moved by a soul "like an animal." So this too was a heresy, forbidden under penalty of excommunication.[554]

In Ovid's *Metamorphoses*, Pythagoras declared: "the Earth is of the nature of an animal, living."[555] In 1584 an Italian translation discussed in great length this "Pythagorean doctrine."[556] Bellarmino served on the Index of Forbidden Books. In 1592, he wrote that the original *Metamorphoses* could be "tolerated" as a model of proper Latin, but its Italian editions should be censored.[557]

---

[546] Plato, *Timaeus* (ca. 360 BC), *The Dialogues of Plato*, II, trans. B. Jowett, Oxford, Clarendon, 1871, paragraphs 30-31, pp. 525-526.

[547] Hippolytus, *Refutatio*, bk. 6, sec. 21, p. 229.

[548] *Placita*, bk. 2, chap. 9, pp. 136-137.

[549] Plotinus, *The Six Enneads* (ca. 255-270 CE), trans. S. MacKenna, London, Warner, 1917-1930, 4th Ennead, Treatise 4, chap. 27.

[550] Philostratus, *Life of Apollonius*, bk. 3, chap. 34, p. 308.

[551] Iamblichus, *De Mysteriis Aegyptiorum, Chaldæorum, Assyriorum*, ed. M. Ficinus, London, Tornæaesium, 1549, pp. 108-109, 114.

[552] Gregory, *Anima Mundi*, pp. 123-127.

[553] Augustine, *De Civitate*, bk. 7, chap. 23.

[554] Tempier (1277), in G. Klima et al., *Medieval Philosophy: Essential Readings*, Malden, Blackell, 2007, p. 184.

[555] Ovid, *Metamorphoses*, II, p. 389.

[556] G. Dell'Anguillara, *Le Metamorfosi di Ovidio*, revised by G. Horologgi, Venice, Zoppini, 1584, pp. 255 rev., 271 verso.

[557] R. Bellarmini, *Auctores addendi ad tertiam classem Indicis Pii IV*, 1592, in P. Godman, *The Saint as Censor: Robert Bellarmine between Inquisition and Index*, Leiden, Brill, 2000, p. 273.

The eighth censure opposed Bruno's statement that soul is not "form." He thus rejected Aristotle's theory of souls, describing it as incomprehensible. But in so doing, he was also enabling the Inquisition to declare him a heretic, because, in 1312, that definition of soul had been decreed by the Council of Vienna, stating that anyone who denies or doubts that "soul is the form of the human body" is "a heretic." The Council decreed:

> we reject as erroneous and contrary to the truth of the Catholic faith every doctrine or proposition rashly asserting that the substance of the rational or intellectual soul is not of itself and essentially the form of the human body, or casting doubt on this matter. In order that all may know the truth of the faith in its purity and all error may be excluded, we define that anyone who presumes henceforth to assert, defend or hold stubbornly that the rational or intellectual soul is not the form of the human body of itself and essentially, is to be considered a heretic.

Therefore, Bruno was a heretic. In order to determine whether Bruno's heresy was Pythagorean, we must specify his definition of soul. He claimed that souls are immortal intellective substances that inhabit bodies that are human or other. Under interrogation he explained:

> "Speaking as a Catholic, they [souls] do not pass from body to body, but go to Paradise, Purgatory or Hell. But I have reasoned deeply, and, speaking as a philosopher, since soul is not found without body and yet is not body, it may be in one body or another, and pass from body to body. This, if it be not true, seems at least verisimilar, according to the opinion of Pythagoras."[558]

In several books Bruno wrote about transmigration.[559] He beseeched God: "We beg that in our transfusion, or transit, or metempsychosis we shall

---

[558] Firpo, *Processo*, 284.
[559] Most scholars agree that Bruno believed in some kind of transmigration, given his writings, though he denied it to the Inquisitors. Some writers now argue Bruno believed in some kind of metempsychosis but not in the transmigration of souls into various bodies. Yet Bruno used such words interchangeably. He wrote about "nella nostra transffusione, ó transito, ó metampsicosi," in *Spaccio de la Bestia Trionfante*, 1584, p. 20. He also wrote: "metamphisicosi, cioé transformatione, ó transcorporatione de tutte

receive contented genii [daemons]: since however inexorable He be, we must attend him with pleas, either to be kept in our present state, or to enter into a better one, or a similar one, or a little worse."[560] Bruno argued that death does not affect souls, so that following the saintly Pythagoras we should not fear death, a transition.[561]

Aristotle denied the "Pythagorean myths; that any soul could be clothed upon with any body—an absurd view, for each body seems to have a form and shape of its own. It is absurd as to say that the art of carpentry could embody itself in flutes; each art must use its tools, each soul its body."[562] Justin Martyr too denied transmigration. Tertullian said that Pythagoras used shameful lies to advocate transmigration, which corrupted Christianity.[563] Epiphanius criticized Pythagoras for proclaiming "the wicked, extremely impious doctrine of the immortalizations and

l'anime," in *Cabala del Cavallo Pegaseo*, 1585), p. 52. He also wrote about the conversion by which Jove "s'investice de diverse figure dovenendo in forma de bestie, et cossi gl' altri dei transmigrano in forme basse et aliene," in *De gli Heroici Furori*, 1585, 3rd Dialogue, p. 80. In his 11th deposition, Inquisitors asked him whether "animam unius hominis posse transmigrare de uno corpore in aliud." Bruno replied that he posited "la transmigratione," not as a fact, but only as possible; see Firpo, *Processo*, p. 285. Then they asked whether he believed in the "transmigrationem" of human souls into *animal* bodies, but he denied it. Yet he had repeatedly written about it and three witnesses accused him of it. Three witnesses also accused him of believing in transmigration among human bodies. However, Roger Mendoza argues that the soul/body dualism implied by Pythagorean transmigration is incompatible with Bruno's monism (which united corporeal matter and incorporeal matter such as the universal soul). Such distinctions do not affect my argument, which requires only that Bruno's readers sensed a reiterated support for some kind of transmigration in Bruno's writings, and that he repeatedly credited Pythagoras. Note also that there did not exist a unified version of Pythagorean transmigration as Mendoza seems to imply. It stems from not reviewing, at least in his article, the various Pythagorean sources across the centuries. Still, Mendoza argues that Bruno rigorously abandoned the notion that souls migrate from body to body. Mendoza makes this interpretation by dismissing the multiple instances in which Bruno wrote about process, while emphasizing instances in which he did not. See Mendoza, *Metempsychosis*, pp. 272-297. He argues that Bruno modified metempsychosis and thus "made Pythagoras's transmigration obsolete." Actually, accounts of Pythagorean transmigration varied, and Bruno frequently praised such views.

[560] Bruno, *Spaccio*, p. 20.

[561] Bruno, *De Triplici Minimo et Mensura* (1591), bk. 1, chap. 3. See also *The New Atomism*, in H. Gatti, *Essays on Giordano Bruno*, Princeton, Princeton University Press, 2011, pp. 76-77.

[562] Aristotle, *De Anima*, bk. 1, p. 8 reverso.

[563] Tertullian, *De Anima*, chaps. 34-35, pp. 835-837.

transmigrations of souls and the dissolution of bodies."[564] Augustine rebuked Porphyry on transmigration.[565] Thomas Aquinas rejected it too.[566]

Thus again, Bruno's denial of the standard Catholic doctrine about souls involved his philosophical preference for the opinion that he attributed to Pythagoras, one that allowed the possibility of the transmigration of souls.

Under interrogation, Bruno said that the false claim that the soul is the form of the body is not found in Scriptures. Instead he said that the soul, "in its pilgrimage" inhabits the body "as a captive in a prison" and controls it like a ship.[567] He said the soul subsists outside the body, against Aristotle.[568] Bruno's analogy to a "prison" was not rare but the Pythagoreans used it. For example, according to Philostratus, Apollonius said: "Whilst we live, we are all men in prison. Our soul, attached to this mortal body, suffers much, and is subject to all the vicissitudes of mortality."[569] Lactantius and Jerome both attributed it to Pythagoras.[570] Lactantius wrote that Pythagoras himself claimed that the aim of the true philosophy is to struggle to free the soul from "the prison of the body."[571] Erasmus too said that when Pythagoras saw "his disciples taking care of his their bodies, to be obese or to have a clean skin, he said: *This is his prison which never ceases to sense pain. Or man is*

---

[564] Epiphanius, *Panarion* Sect. 7, p. 24.

[565] Augustine, bk. 10, chaps. 24, 29-30; bk. 13, chap. 19; bk. 22, chaps. 12, 26-28.

[566] Thomæ Aquinatis, *Tertia Pars: Summæ Theologicæ* (ca. 1274?), reissued ,Venetiis, Bindoni, 1585, p. 241.

[567] For discussion, see Eugenio Canone, *Il Dorso e il Grembo dell'Eterno. Percorsi della Filosofia di Giordano Bruno*, Pisa, Istituti Editoriali e Poligrafici Internazionali, 2003, pp. 7, 54, 65, 242-243.

[568] 8th Censured Proposition with Bruno's reply; and 5th deposition; in Firpo, *Processo*, pp. 304, 285. Aristotle said the soul is inseparable from its body, but that "it is uncertain whether the soul is the actuality of its body as a sailor of a ship," *De Anima*, bk. 2, pt. 1.

[569] E.g., Philostratus, *Life of Apollonius*, Vol. 2, bk. 7, chap. 26, p. 222.

[570] Lactantius, *Divine Institutes*, bk. 6, chap. 8, p. 447. Jerome, *Adverus Ruffinum*, 88, in Divi Eusebii Hieronymi, *Opera Omnia*, ed. Erasmus of Rotterdam (Paris: Claudium Chevallonium, 1534).

[571] Lucius Lactantius, *De Divino Praemio*, chap. 8, pp. 103-104, in L. Coelii Lactantii, *Divinarum Institutionum Libri VII* (Basel: Andream Cratandrum & Io. Bebelium, 1532).

a soul enclosed in a bodily prison.[572] Saint Basil quoted Pythagoras on people who eat a lot: "*Can you not stop planning for a heavier prison?*"[573]

It was not a Christian notion. It implied the heresy of the mobility of souls from body to body. Saint Irenaeus (ca. 180 CE) denounced that doctrine as false, saying that its insane believers relied partly on the Devil to supposedly help transfer their souls into new bodies, new "prisons."[574]

So Bruno's eighth proposition was Pythagorean. The Fifth Ecumenical Council denounced Origen's heresy that souls are "condemned to punishment in bodies" like prisons.[575] They also condemned: "That the intellect is not a bodily form, except as a captain is the form of a ship."[576] Plus, Tempier condemned the thesis "That the intellect can transit from body to body."[577] In 1553, theologians of the University of Paris censured claims "That the transmigration of souls is an argument for the Resurrection."[578]

The ninth censure was that Bruno denied Solomon's statement that individuals' true being is vanity. Consider Bruno's *De la Causa*:

> Every production, of any kind, is an alteration, while substance always remains the same, since there is only one substance, as there is but one divine, immortal being. Pythagoras, who did not fear death but saw it as a transformation, reached this conclusion. [...] Solomon inferred this as well, saying, "there is nothing new under the Sun, but what is, has already been." You see, then, how the universe is [....] eternal, while every aspect, every face, every other thing is vanity and nothingness.[579]

Here, Bruno was drawing a distinction between the underlying eternal substance, which "always remains the same," and every apparent, individual, and transient thing. He argued that the latter was really "vanity and

---

[572] Erasmus, *Apophthegms*, bk. 8, sec. 60, p. 283. Erasmus, *Apophthegmatum*, bk. 8, in Erasmi, [*Opera Omnia*] *Quartos Tomus quae ad Morum Institutionem Pertinent Complectens*, Basel, Frobeniana, 1560, p. 340.

[573] Basilii, *Oratio VIII: De Temperantia & Incontinentia*, in *Omnia quae in Hunc Diem Latino Sermone Donata Sunt Opera*, Antwerp, Nutium, 1570, p. 819.

[574] Irenaei, Adversus Haereses Libri Quinque [ca. 180 AD], ed. Ubaldo Mannucci (Rome, 1907), bk. 1, chap. 25, sec. 4, pp. 264-5.

[575] Callisti, *Ecclesiasticæ Historiæ*, p. 893.

[576] Tempier (1277), Prop. 7, *Chartularium*, Vol. 1 (1889), p. 544.

[577] Ibid., Prop. 193, p. 554.

[578] Censures of August 1, 1553, in Dupin, *New Ecclesiastical History*, Vol. 2, p. 441.

[579] *Causa*, 5th dialogue, p. 90.

nothingness," while the primal substance was incorruptible and eternal unity. Bruno echoed this point in another work, *On the Heroic Frenzies*, where the character of Tansillo argued: "In this manner the wise holds all mutable things as things which do not exist, and he believes these are nothing else but vanity and nothingness, because the same proportion exists between finite time and eternity that exists between mere point and the line."[580] Bruno's proposition was Pythagorean because he credited it to Pythagoras. He was ostensibly echoing the ancient, deep wisdom of Pythagoras himself. The main source for such claims was Ovid's *Metamorphoses*.

For Bruno, primal substance was not vanity, it was eternal like God. The Inquisitors disagreed. Ecclesiastes 1:14 states: "I have seen all that is done under the Sun, and behold: all is vanity and an affliction of the spirit." To the Inquisitors it meant that *every thing* is vanity. They censured Bruno's belief "that true substances are species of primal nature, that truly are what they are."

Finally, the tenth proposition: many inhabited worlds and Suns exist. Historians have argued that the accusation of many worlds was "too vague to be defined as formally heretical."[581] I'll show that it was heretical.

Aristotle had complained that the Pythagoreans said that, "Earth is one of the stars."[582] Lucian wrote that Pythagoras lived in such starry worlds. The *Placita* said that the Pythagoreans thought that the Moon and the stars are worlds, with soil, air and animals. Bruno told the Inquisitors: "I have indeed asserted infinite particular worlds similar to the Earth, which with Pythagoras I consider a star, similar to which is the Moon, other planets and other stars, which are infinitely many."[583]

Was it a heresy? Hippolytus ridiculed the doctrine of infinitely many worlds, Suns and Moons, some inhabited.[584] Saint Philaster categorized the notion of "innumerable worlds" as heretical. Augustine agreed, so

[580] Giordano Bruno, *De Gli Eroici Furore* (Paris: Antonio Baio, 1585), Second Dialogue.
[581] L. Spruit, *Una Rilettura del Processo di Giordano Bruno: Procedure e Aspetti Giuridico-Formali*, in P. Giustiniani, et al., eds., *Giordano Bruno. Oltre il Mito e le Opposte Passioni*, Naples, Biblioteca Teologica, 2002), p. 225.
[582] *De Caelo*, bk. 2, sec. 13.
[583] Bruno, 2 June 1592, in Firpo, *Processo*, pp. 167, 269.
[584] Hippolytus, *Refutatio*, bk. 1, secs. 13-14, pp. 72-74.

theologians cited this heresy for centuries.[585] They explained the problem: we cannot assert that there exist "two or many worlds, since neither do we assert two or many Christs."[586] Aristotle had insisted that many worlds cannot exist since it would require more than one First Cause. The belief in many worlds seemed to entail belief in many gods. Saint Isidore too listed it as heretical.

The highest authority proves that Bruno's belief in many worlds was heretical. In 1582 Pope Gregory XIII issued a compilation of laws of the Catholic Church and ordered that it be used in all church courts and schools of canon law. Expanded in 1591, the *Corpus of Canon Law* includes long discussions of what are heresies and who shall be considered a heretic. Echoing Isidore, its list of heresies includes: "having the opinion of innumerable worlds."[587] The *Canon Law* embodied the fundamental laws of the Catholic Church; all inquisitorial laws and courts had to comply with the Pope's canon laws.[588] Even the Roman Inquisition's condemnation of Bruno refers to the "sacred Canons" three times.[589]

In his depositions Bruno did not mention Democritus or other philosophers associated with belief in many worlds. He only credited Pythagoras.

Finally, there is a link between worlds and transmigration in Bruno's motto about "Solomon and Pythagoras." Centuries before Bruno highlighted "nothing new under the Sun," others had linked that phrase to claims about transmigration and many worlds. This had been done by one

---

[585] Alphonsum Alvarez Guerrero, *Thesaurus Christianae Religionis*, Venetiis, 1559, p. 261. Lamberti Danei, *Aurelii Augustini Hipponensis Episcopi Liber De Haeresibus*, Genevae, Vignon, 1578, p. [M.v] rev. G. Valentia, *Commentariorum Theologicorum Tomi Quatuor*, I, Ingolstadt, Sartorius, 1591, p. 991.

[586] R. Diaconi, *Contra Acephalos* (ca. 560), in *Antidotum Contra Diversas Omnium Fere Seculorum Haereses*, Basel, H. Petrus, 1528, p. 248; rev. L. Ricchieri, *Haereseologia*, Basil, Petri, 1556, p. 715.

[587] *Decretum Gratiani Emendatum et Notationibus Illustratum, unà cum glossis, Gregorii XIII. Pont. Max. iussu editum*, Rome, Aedibus Populi Romani, 1582, Pt. 2, Causa 24, Question 3, column 1895. Reissued: *Corpus Iuris Canonici Emendatum et Notis Illustratum: Gregorii XIII. Pont. Max. iussu editum*, additions by P. Lanceloti, Lugduni, Cum Licentia, 1591, column 877. See also: N. Eymerici, *Directorium Inquisitorium* (1378), with commentaries by F. Pegñae, Venice, Simeonis, 1595, p. 246.

[588] J. Wickersham, *Rituals of Prosecution: The Roman Inquisition and the Prosecution of Philo-Protestants in Sixteenth-Century Italy* (Toronto: U. of Toronto, 2012), 56-58. Inquisitors commonly had degrees in both canon and civil law.

[589] Firpo, *Processo*, pp. 341-342. These were standard expressions in court documents. Prior to 1582, they referred to various canons, including those that were later included in the *Corpus*.

of the most infamous early heretics: Origen. He argued: "The fact is that prior to this world there have existed others, as Ecclesiastes says: 'What is it that has been done? the same as is the future. And what is it that has been created? the same that will be created: and there is nothing new under the Sun.'"[590] Origen said that omnipotence led God to create worlds prior to ours, and after it. He said that our souls might live in future worlds. The claim of transmigration of souls is not explicit here, but readers could infer it, since Origen spoke about souls after death getting bodies that might seem different from their former bodies. For one, he said that after the resurrection wicked souls "may be clothed with dark and black bodies."[591] His insistence on the immortality and eternity of souls also suggested that such souls might live in future worlds.

Jerome complained that Origen's notion of innumerable worlds is clearly heretical.[592] Other commentatorss stressed the link between many worlds and transmigration. For example, at around 1120, the Benedictine theologian Rupert of Deutz discussed Ecclesiastes 1:9, which he rendered as: "What is it that was? that which the future is. What is it that is done? that which will be done again. Nothing new under the Sun."[593] Rupert argued that this does not mean that many worlds exist, and therefore, that the "heretics" who claimed that there are many worlds were deathly wrong to think that Pythagoras's soul transmigrated to many bodies.[594]

Remarkably, Bruno's Pythagorean ideas echoed Origen's heresies: eternally many worlds and transmigration. For Bruno, the existence of many worlds and the transmigration of souls were part of an eternally ongoing process of transmutations. Had he read Origen's censored book *On Principles*? Yes, and Bruno praised him as "the only theologian, who like the great philosophers" dared to voice "after the reproved sects" the truth of revolutions and eternal change.[595]

---

[590] Origen, *Peri Archon*, bk. 3, trans. Rufinus, in Origenis, *Operum Origenis Adamantii*, Vols. 3-4, Giunti, 1536, p. 205.

[591] Ibid., bk. 2, chap. 10.

[592] E.g., Jerome, *Confessio Hieronymiana, ex Omnibus Germanis B. Hieronymi Operibus Optima Fide Collecta*, ed. C. Steinuvichii, Paris, Sonnium, 1585, pp. 41, 45, 236.

[593] Rupert, "In Librum Ecclesiastes, Sancti Laurentii extra Muros Leodienses," bk. 1 (ca. 1120?), in R. D. D. Ruperti Abbatis Monasterij S. Heriberti Tuitiensis, *Opera* (Moguntiae: Hermanni Mylii Birckmanni, 1631), 1200, trans. Martínez.

[594] Ibid.

[595] *Furori*, p. 20. See also, Gatti, *Essays*, p. 272.

1. Two eternal principles generate everything: primal matter and the soul of the world.

2. Since God is infinite, He must have produced infinity.

3. Human souls are derived from a general principle.

4. Nothing is generated or corrupted in substance.

5. The Earth moves.

6. Stars are Angels, animated rational bodies.

7. Earth is alive, it has a sensitive and rational soul.

8. The human soul is not form.

9. He denies Solomon's dictate: 'all is vanity,' saying that primal substance is not vanity.

10. He posits many Suns and worlds, even inhabited.

Table 2. *Summary of the Ten Propositions Censured in Bruno's Books.*

Having analyzed the ten propositions, we can see that they are a coherent set of interconnected beliefs. These ones were clearly heretical: the first, sixth, seventh, eighth, and tenth. These five propositions involve at least six formal heresies: the eternity of the world, the world soul, the heavenly bodies are animated, transmigration, the human soul is not form, and many worlds. The other propositions could be considered "errors" or "nearly heretical." Any such proposition, once identified, could constitute a heresy if the suspect persisted in not abandoning it. And Bruno did defend such propositions.

Such heresies do not challenge the divinity of Christ. They are not about magic or Hermeticism. Yet without exaggeration they can be described as *Pythagorean heresies*. Only the sixth censured proposition, about angels, is not quite Pythagorean, though it has some relevant aspects. The rest, *nine out of ten* of Bruno's heresies as a writer were Pythagorean propositions inasmuch as either ancient writers famously attributed such ideas to Pythagoras or his followers, Church Fathers denounced those beliefs as Pythagorean, and foremost, that Bruno himself presented such notions as derived from Pythagorean sources. Bruno learned many of these notions from the *Placita*, Lucian, Virgil, Erasmus, and Ovid. Bruno appreciated the Pythagorean tradition as one of the alternative, ancient traditions that challenged the philosophy of Aristotle. And Bruno did not discuss Pythagoras merely as a philosopher, but as a contributor to theology. Bruno argued: "the negative theology of Pythagoras and Dionysus [the Aeropagite] is much more renowned, above the demonstrative one of Aristotle and the scholastic doctors."[596]

In 1599 Bellarmino presented "eight heretical propositions collected from the books and trial" of Bruno. The list is not extant, but apparently Bruno did not know that those propositions were really heretical. He asked whether the Pope deemed such propositions heretical.[597] The Pope replied that the eight propositions had been declared heretical "by the most ancient Fathers of the Church and the Apostolic See."[598]

From the previous historical context, it seems fitting that some of Bruno's beliefs appeared in the works of advocates of the Pythagoreans, including Ovid, Apollonius, Porphyry, Iamblichus, Philostratus. Church Fathers such as Irenaeus, Tertullian, Athanasius, Chrysostom, Jerome, Augustine, and Isidore had denounced claims about transmigration, eternity, many worlds, and Pythagorean denials of the uniqueness of Jesus. The Church Fathers vehemently denied that Pythagoras's soul had been reborn or lived in Hell.[599] They accused Pythagoras and his disciples of faking their deaths and resurrections. They denied the "Pythagorean doctrine" that living men are formed from dead men, and that souls are imprisoned in bodies.[600] Such "perverse falsehoods" threatened people's faith in Jesus Christ.[601] Those early confrontations against pagans were not forgotten in the Renaissance.

Inquisitors adhered to many writings by the ancient Church Fathers. Some of the accusations against Bruno are unknown, six of eight heresies selected by Bellarmino.[602]

Two of the propositions are mentioned in a Decree of 24 August 1599: "prima videlicet, ubi de haeresi Novatiana, et VII, ubi tractat an anima sit

---

[596] *Furori*, unnumbered pages, end of the Fourth Dialogue. For discussion of Bruno's departures from Aristotle, see Ricci, *Giordano Bruno nell'Europa*, e.g., pp. 257-261, 281-298, 358-360.

[597] Copia Parziale della Sentenza, 8 February 1600, in Firpo, *Processo*, p. 341.

[598] Decreto, 4 February 1599, in ibid., p. 314.

[599] E.g., Tertullian, *De Anima*, chap. 28, p. 824.

[600] Ibid., chap. 29, p. 479.

[601] Lactantius, *Divine Institutes*, bk. III, chap. 18, p. 185.

[602] L. Boschetti, *Sul Processo di Giordano Bruno: Indagini attorno all'Eresia Novaziana, "Rinascimento; Rivista dell'Istituto Nazionale di Studi sul Rinascimento,"* 2nd Ser., XLVI (2006), pp. 93-130. See also: Martínez, *Burned Alive: Giordano Bruno, Galileo, and the Inquisition.*

in corpore sicut nauta in navi." The "Novatian heresy" seems to pertain to the soul of the world as the Holy Spirit, as explained by Lucia Boschetti. The heresy about the soul "as a sailor" is about transmigration. But, some writers claim that the first proposition in Bellarmino's list was denying transubstantiation. This is mistaken. First, because the first proposition is specified in the Decree above. Second, Bellarmino extracted such propositions from Bruno's books and depositions yet in neither did Bruno deny transubstantiation; he affirmed it. Third, writers infer that the first proposition was about transubstantiation because it shows up in the "Copia Parziale," which cites transubstantiation at the start of a truncated list *of the earliest accusations*, those by Mocenigo. Fourth, the Copia omits but subsequently refers to Bellarmino's propositions; there is no reason to suppose that the top theologian in Rome simply echoed the same accusations by Mocenigo. Fifth, the denial of transubstantiation was permissible in Rome, in the 1590s, because (as reported by Schoppe) the Pope had ordered that Protestants should be treated with civility in Rome instead of being prosecuted for their beliefs, to encourage them to return to Catholicism.

But we know which beliefs Bruno repeatedly refused to recant: the Pythagorean beliefs about souls and the universe. Since he refused to repudiate the final list of heresies, it seems that it included some of those beliefs. After Bruno's execution, Schoppe reported Bruno's awful doctrines, starting with five Pythagorean beliefs: *worlds are innumerable, souls transmigrate to such worlds, one soul can take two bodies, the Holy Spirit is the soul of the world, and the world exists eternally.*[603]

Some writers mischaracterize Schoppe's list as starting with: denying transubstantiation, doubting Mary's virginity, living in heretical places, etc. Such writers mix Schoppe's chronological account of early accusations with the list of Bruno's "doctrines." However, Schoppe specified that Lutherans were *not* executed for their teachings (e.g., about transubstantiation) so it is unjustified to construe the early accusations as the doctrines for which Bruno died. He was not obstinate or impenitent about Mary, transubstantiation, or about living where Protestants lived.

Bruno's crime was that he obstinately advocated pagan heresies that Christians had denounced. The Catholics who hated the reforms of Luther

---

[603] G. Schoppe to K. Rittershausen, 17 February 1600, *Epistola, in qua haereticos jure infelicibus lignis cremari concludit*, in *Machiavellizatio*, Saragossae, Ibarra, 1621, p. 31.

and Calvin rejected Bruno's more eccentric effort to interpret Scriptures and Catholic doctrines on the basis of pagan Pythagorean beliefs.

4

Giordano Bruno's heresy of Many Worlds

As an academic discipline, the history of science provides insights that are not just significant to history but also to discussions about science and religion. For decades, one of those claims has been the clear conviction that the Catholic Church did not condemn Giordano Bruno for any astronomical beliefs but for religious heresies. Some persons claimed that the Roman Inquisition condemned Bruno partly because of cosmology. But historians insisted that it was a myth, that it wasn't true.

But were they right? It's an explosive topic in the alleged conflict between Christianity and science. Scholars defused that bomb by saying Bruno was no scientist and that the Inquisition condemned him for religious transgressions, not cosmology. He was burned alive in Rome, in February 1600, as a heretic. As someone who debunks myths in the history of science, I too had learned that Bruno did not die because of his beliefs about Earth or the universe. However, after spending much time analyzing primary sources, in Italian and Latin, my impressions began to change.

But consider first the academic consensus. In 1908, *The Catholic Encyclopedia* stated "Bruno was not condemned for his defence of the Copernican system of astronomy, nor for his doctrine of the plurality of inhabited worlds, but for his theological errors..."[604] Similarly, in 1964, historian Frances Yates declared: "the legend that Bruno was prosecuted as a philosophical thinker, was burned for his daring views on innumerable worlds or on the movement of the Earth, can no longer stand."[605] Yates was enormously influential in convincing many historians to construe Bruno as a Hermeticist who focused on esoteric notions and magic.

And likewise, in the 1980s the historians of astronomy considered the question of whether Bruno was condemned for his beliefs that the planets and star systems are distant worlds and they too dismissed it as a myth. In his groundbreaking history of the *Plurality of Worlds*, Steven J. Dick wrote: "It is true that he [Bruno] was burned at the stake in Rome in 1600, but the church authorities were almost certainly more distressed at his denial of Christ's divinity and alleged diabolism than his cosmological doctrines."[606] Accordingly, Michael J. Crowe later echoed that it is a "myth that Giordano Bruno was martyred for his pluralistic convictions" about many worlds.[607]

In short, there was consensus that Bruno was not condemned for his cosmological beliefs. However, there was no consensus about why he was condemned. The *Catholic Encyclopedia*, for example, claimed that Bruno was condemned for beliefs such as "that Christ was not God but merely an unusually skillful magician, that the Holy Ghost is the soul of the world, that the Devil will be saved, etc." Professor Yates claimed that Bruno was condemned because the Roman Inquisition considered him a Hermeticist and a magician. More recently, however, Professor Maurice Finocchiaro has

---

[604] Gabriel Meier, "Bruno, Giordano," in Charles G. Herbermann, et al., *The Catholic Encyclopedia: An International Work of Reference on the Constitution, Doctrine, Discipline, and History of the Catholic Church*, Vol. 3 (New York: The Encyclopedia Press, 1913), p. 17.

[605] Frances Yates, *Giordano Bruno and the Hermetic Tradition*, Vol. 2 (1964; reissued, Abingdon: Routledge, 1999), p. 355.

[606] Steven J. Dick, *Plurality of Worlds: The Origins of the Extraterrestrial Life Debate from Democritus to Kant* (Cambridge: Cambridge University Press, 1982), p. 10, see also p. 69. However, in later writings Dick moved away from that opinion, without much discussion; see Steven J. Dick, *Extraterrestrial Life and Our World View at the Turn of the Millennium* (Washington, DC: Smithsonian Institution Libraries, 2000), p. 9; and Dick, *Life on Other Worlds: the 20th-Century Extraterrestrial Life Debate* (Cambridge: Cambridge University Press, 1998), p. 10.

[607] Michael J. Crowe, *The Extraterrestrial Life Debate 1750-1900: The Idea of a Plurality of Worlds from Kant to Lowell* (Cambridge: Cambridge University Press, 1986), p. 8. Crowe's important book focused on the period from 1750 onwards, so he did not take into account any of the evidence presently discussed; he mainly echoed Dick's impression in *Plurality of Worlds*.

rightly argued that the problem with Yates's thesis is that "there is little trace of Hermeticism and magic in the trial proceedings."[608]

Overview:
Bruno's Principal Crime

For decades, historians, writers, and astronomers said that the Roman Inquisition did not execute Giordano Bruno for his belief in many worlds. In 2014, television stations aired the remake of the famous TV series *Cosmos*. The very first episode dedicated a quarter of its airtime to Giordano Bruno. The narrator, the famous astrophysicist Neil DeGrasse Tyson, said that Bruno risked his life by voicing his vision of the cosmos: "the penalty for doing so, in his world, was the most vicious form of cruel and unusual punishment." Roughly seven million viewers in the U.S. saw that first episode when it first aired. Subsequently, many commentators and news blogs complained that *Cosmos* had misrepresented Bruno by echoing the myth that the Inquisition killed him for his cosmological views. However, the matter is not so simple. The commentators who criticized *Cosmos* online showed no acquaintance with the extant primary source documents.

For example, some commenters asked: if Bruno got in trouble for his belief in many worlds, why did the Church not prosecute previous writers who considered such beliefs?

In 1440, the German theologian Nicholas of Cusa briefly argued that the Earth moves a little bit (around a center that is not the Sun, but God) and he wrote that there might well exist beings in the regions of heaven. Cusa did not say that the stars are Suns surrounded by planets, although he used the word star (apparently to mean heavenly bodies including the Sun). Similarly, the French Franciscan theologian Guillame de Vaurouillon (or William of Vorilong) pondered whether sinful men might exist in another world, but he replied no.

Cusa and others did not get in trouble because the Catholic Church was a very different institution before the Protestant Reformation. When Cusa wrote, in 1440, Catholics were in the midst of Renaissance humanism, when

[608] Finocchiaro, 2002, 78.

old pagan ideas were discussed with curiosity and sympathy. Plus, his ideas were not the same as Bruno's. Later, when Bruno wrote in the 1580s, Catholics had lost much of Europe because of the Protestants; so heresies were a far graver concern. In 1542 Pope Paul III had established the Supreme Inquisition. There was no similar mechanism for the prosecution of unorthodox thoughts in the 1440s.

Likewise, Nicholas Oresme had died in 1382. He did not assert the same things as Bruno; Oresme argued that omnipotence enabled God to create many worlds, but that in fact "there has never been nor will there be more than one corporeal world." To the contrary, Bruno argued that because of God's omnipotence there must exist innumerable worlds, and that in fact they do exist: star systems surrounded by planets such as the Earth, made of the same elements and some of them inhabited.

We sometimes hear that unfortunately the documents from Bruno's trial were lost, so we just cannot know what really happened. This impression has a seed of truth: that during the Napoleonic occupation of Rome many Inquisition documents were removed, shipped to France, and in the process, many were lost, including the file of proceedings against Bruno.

But actually, however, very many documents pertaining to Bruno's trial do exist and have been gradually uncovered over time. We have the virtually complete transcripts of the initial proceedings in Venice, from 1592. Plus, we have a most important and revealing document, discovered in 1940, the so-called "Sommario" which is a long and systematic official summary of the ~300 folios (= 600 pages) that were transcripts of the complete proceedings in Rome until around 1598. Plus, we have numerous other individual documents, including the Censures of propositions excerpted from Bruno's books, and a partial copy of the Sententia of 1600. Most of these documents are reproduced in Luigi Firpo's valuable book, *Il Processo di Giordano Bruno* (1993). And there are others.

Thus, among the dozens of known accusations against Bruno, Professor Finocchiaro fairly noted that questions of Hermeticism or magic arise only in three charges: that he practiced magical arts, and that he allegedly wrongly believed that Jesus and Moses practiced magic. Yet such charges did not stick, since Bruno promptly and vigorously denied them. Therefore, contrary to Frances Yates' very influential opinion, issues of Hermeticism and magic were of minor importance in Bruno's trial.

So why did the Romans kill Bruno? In 2014, a historian of the Inquisition, Thomas F. Mayer, claimed causal ignorance. He admitted: "The simple fact is that we do not know why he was executed."[609]

Meanwhile, I was systematically analyzing the primary sources. In Bruno's seven-year trial, I identified fifty-four distinct accusations. Thirty-nine of them, let's call them Type A, were alleged departures from Catholic dogma and practices, plus alleged blasphemies against God, Christ, the Virgin Mary, the Prophets, the Church Fathers, etc. The fifteen other accusations, let's call them Type B, were about Bruno's philosophical notions about souls, primal substance, and worlds, including the Earth.

Historians had assumed that the worst kinds of accusations were what I here call Type A: transgressions such as that Bruno allegedly questioned transubstantiation or the virginity of Mary. However, when I analyzed the evidence for each of the fifty-four accusations against Bruno, I found something surprising. The case against him in terms of accusations of Type A was weak; the case in terms of accusations of Type B was very strong.

At the time, the Roman Inquisition was a highly procedural and bureaucratic institution. To execute someone they relied on specific procedures. Hearsay was not enough. For example, Bruno was accused of having doubted the virginity of Mary, but only one witness made the accusation: Giovanni Mocenigo, in Venice. Nobody confirmed it. When the Venetian Inquisitors confronted Bruno about it, Bruno replied that he never spoke against the virginity of Mary, and that certainly Mary did conceive Jesus thanks to a miracle of the Holy Spirit. Likewise, he did not question Mary's virginity in any of his many books. Hence, in the seven year trial proceedings, the Inquisitors in Rome *did not* accuse Bruno of denying Mary's virginity. They accused him of other things.

Similarly, some historians claimed that one of Bruno's big crimes was that he questioned transubstantiation: that bread becomes the body of Christ in the ceremony of the Eucharist. Three witnesses accused him of this: Mocenigo, Francisco Gratianus (quoting Francisco Vaia) and Matteo de Silvestris. This sounds serious, but let me give seven objections, seven reasons to the contrary.

First, Gratianus, Vaia, and Silvestris were all prisoners in Venice, so they lacked the credibility of Mocenigo. Second, under interrogation Bruno repudiated the accusation of denying transubstantiation, saying, "I have not doubted this sacrament."[610] Third, he did not deny transubstantiation in

---

[609] Mayer, *Roman Inquisition* (2014), p. 124.
[610] Firpo, 1993, 265.

his books. Fourth, he said that he wanted to take communion.

Fifth, at that time in Rome it was not a crime to deny transubstantiation. Gaspar Schoppe was present when Bruno was condemned, because, Schoppe lived in the palace of the "supreme Inquisitor" in Bruno's trial, Cardinal Lodovico Madruzzi. Schoppe was also present when Bruno was burned alive. In a letter describing those events, Schoppe noted that some laypersons wrongly thought that "a Lutheran" had been burned. Yet he explained that Lutherans and Calvinists were really not in any danger in Rome because the Pope had ordered that they be treated with extraordinary civility. Both the Lutherans and the Calvinists denied transubstantiation, in different ways. Why would Bruno be burned for denying transubstantiation since he did not deny it, when denying it was not a crime?

Historians and writers had one more apparent reason to think that one of Bruno's major transgressions was denying transubstantiation. Namely, that the issue of transubstantiation appears in the Inquisition's condemnation (Sententia) of 1600. However, this document is incomplete, it's only a "partial copy" of Bruno's final condemnation. Unfortunately it omits material with an "etc." It was common that copies of inquisitorial condemnations, issued to the Governor of Rome, omitted the Inquisition's list of accusations. The document gives a brief historical account of how Bruno came to be incarcerated, and it specifies that Bruno was denounced by Mocenigo (a mere layman) in Venice, with accusations such as "that you had said that it is a great blasphemy to say that the bread transubstantiates into flesh, etc."[611] This was the very first of Mocenigo's extant and initial list of twenty-one accusations from "eight years ago" (1592), as noted in the Sententia, yet this incomplete copy of the Sententia mentions no other initial or subsequent accusations because it is truncated at the word "etc."

Then, the copy mentions "these eight propositions," clearly meaning the eight heretical propositions formulated by Cardinal Bellarmino in 1599. Thus, my sixth objection is that by conflating Mocenigo's initial accusations of 1592 with Bellarmino's 1599 official list of eight heresies, writers such as Ingrid Rowland mistakenly concluded that Bruno was killed partly because of a denial of transubstantiation.[612] Why would the top theologian in Rome, Inquisitor Bellarmino, merely echo the accusations of the layman Mocenigo? This is a mistake also because (my seventh objection) we actually

611 Firpo, 1993.
612 Rowland, 2008, 259.

have a primary source from 1599 that specifies the very first accusation in Bellarmino's list and it was not Mocenigo's claim of denying transubstantiation. It specifies: "prima videlicet, ubi de haeresi Novatiana."[613] The so-called Novatian heresy was not about transubstantiation, it was either about the claim that the Church cannot forgive certain sins, or about bishop Novatian's conflation of the Holy Spirit as a being created thing, like air, as explained by historian Lucia Boschetti in 2006.

But back to the point: the evidence led me to conclude that issues such as transubstantiation or Mary's virginity were not of major importance in Bruno's trial. Schoppe reported that Bruno was something *far worse* than a Lutheran, he was a "monster," who taught and believed opinions of the ancient philosophers. Among them, the first one listed by Schoppe was "that worlds are innumerable."[614] Surprisingly, when I analyzed the fifty-four accusations against Bruno I found that there was far more evidence for this accusation than any other. I will review the evidence in a moment, but first I must state the most important point: that I discovered that contrary to historians' impressions, Bruno's belief in many worlds was officially heretical.

Decades ago, a very few historians, such as Michael Crowe, had noted that belief in many worlds had been classified as heretical by Saint Philastrius in 384 CE. Personally, I was stunned to learn this. And moreover, this classification was echoed in the early 5th century by Saint Jerome and Saint Augustine, and by Saint Isidore around 620 AD. Still, none of this necessarily meant that it was also a heresy centuries later.

Yet I discovered that during Bruno's life, treatises of heresies also listed the heresy of believing in many or innumerable worlds, even in the 1590s. Most importantly, above all, I discovered that the Corpus of Canon Law of Pope Gregory XIII includes the heresy of "having the opinion of innumerable worlds."[615] The Corpus was first published in 1582, and expanded in 1591, and it was the Catholic code of law that ruled over all Church courts and over the courts of the Inquisition.

Historians and writers had assumed that Bruno's cosmological beliefs

---

[613] Firpo, 1993, 324.
[614] Schoppe, 1600, 34.
[615] *Corpus Iuris Canonici Emendatum et Notis Illustratum: Gregorii XIII. Pont. Max. iussu editum*, with new indices and appendices by Pauli Lanceloti (Lugduni: [n. p.] "Cum Licentia," 1591), Part 2, Cause 24, Question 3, column 877 [unnumbered pages].

—that planets are worlds like the Earth and stars are solar planetary systems like our own — were not heresies. He didn't defend an esoteric belief in immaterial worlds. Instead, he asserted parts of our modern cosmology: our acentric universe has innumerable suns, surrounded by planets, even some that may resemble our inhabited Earth. Yet it turned out that his belief in such "innumerable worlds," as he repeatedly called them, was literally heretical. Many dead and living authorities had denounced it, including theologians, jurists, bishops, one emperor, three popes, five Church Fathers and nine saints.

Why? Because it conflicted with the literal interpretation of Genesis, and apparently it led to horrible theological absurdities. Theologians explained: "we cannot assert that two or many worlds exist, since neither do we assert two or many Christs."[616] Completely unlike the spurious accusations such as about Christ or the Virgin Mary, Bruno actually asserted his belief in many worlds in his books, in at least nine of his books. Bruno inferred the existence of worlds from God's omnipotence: by having infinite power God made innumerable worlds. More than the Copernican Sun-centered universe, Bruno's conception of a far larger cosmos resembles our own: the stars are suns. And it stemmed from both astronomical and religious beliefs.

From 1595 until 1596, the Consultors of the Roman Inquisition examined Bruno's books until they extracted ten propositions that they censured. One of the ten censures stated: "Again, he posits many worlds, many Suns, necessarily containing similar things in kind and in species as in this world, and even men, as in folio 139 and the subsequent long digression."[617]

Furthermore, during Bruno's trial, six witnesses accused him of believing in many worlds; thirteen times, in ten depositions. No other accusation was invoked even half as much. It was the most frequently recurring charge. For example, one accuser testified that in prison one night Bruno brought a fellow prisoner "to the window and showed him a star, saying that it was a world and that all the stars were worlds."

For an accusation to count as a formal heresy, the Inquisitors required a confession: a self-incriminating testimony showing that the accused intentionally contradicted Church doctrine. Otherwise, the accused could well recant the transgression. Yet in at least four depositions, Bruno refused

[616] Ricchieri et al., 1556, 715.
[617] Firpo, 1993, 304.

to recant: in his third deposition (in 1592 in Venice), the twelfth (in 1593 in Rome), the fourteenth (also in 1593) and the seventeenth (around 1598). He repeatedly insisted: Earth is a star (an archaic term for any heavenly body), and the stars include innumerable worlds.

In 1597, Bruno was confronted by Inquisitors and Consultors, including the authoritative theologian Roberto Bellarmino. The Inquisition's record for that meeting states: Bruno "was admonished to thus abandon his delusions of diverse worlds."[618] To be admonished was a serious disciplinary measure. And later, the Inquisitors confronted Bruno about his belief in many worlds: "About this reply he was interrogated in the 17th Deposition, but does not seem to satisfy, because he relapsed into the same reply."[619] According to inquisitorial manuals, to relapse was to be a heretic. Thus, Giordano Bruno was a heretic.

Right after Bruno was executed, Gaspar Schoppe penned two letters about it and in them he noted Bruno's belief in many worlds not just once but four times. Schoppe wrote that "the Lutherans neither teach nor believe such things, and therefore should be treated otherwise. I agree with you, & therefore, precisely no Lutherans do we [Catholics] burn."[620] The clear and direct implication is that Bruno burned for his pagan, philosophical teachings, and foremost among them Schoppe listed Bruno's belief in many worlds. Thus Schoppe used the exact wording in which it was categorized as a heresy in Latin: "*mundos esse innumerabilis.*"

Bruno was condemned for several heresies, but the one about multiple worlds was the strongest case against him. Still, there are other ways in which the accusations against Bruno overlapped cosmology. The Inquisitors didn't condemn him for believing in Copernicus. Nevertheless, Bruno's belief in the Earth's motion really did annoy them. In 1596, when the Consultors of the Inquisition censured ten propositions in Bruno's books, one of them was Bruno's claim that the Earth moves. Exactly twenty years later, in 1616, one of the same clergymen, Bellarmino, officially admonished Galileo for that belief. Moreover, in that process, three other members of the Inquisition who weighed Galileo's transgression had participated in the trial against Bruno.

Bruno's belief in the Earth's motion was not a heresy. However, it was

---

[618] Firpo, 1993, 244.
[619] Firpo, 1993, 269.
[620] Schoppe, 1600, 34.

rooted in heresies. First, it was a consequence of his belief that the stars (heavenly bodies) are worlds. Since the Earth is one such star, and all the stars move, then the Earth moves too. Second, it's based on the idea that the Earth was a living being, a kind of animal, which has a soul and therefore it moves. In 1277, this kind of belief had been indirectly denounced as a heresy, for heavenly bodies in general, by the Bishop of Paris, Étienne Tempier: "That the heavenly bodies are moved by an intrinsic principle, which is the soul, and that they are moved by a soul and an appetitive power, like an animal." This was one of the "loathsome," pagan "errors" and "insane lies" that the Bishop of Paris then strictly prohibited under penalty of excommunication.[621]

But more importantly, Bruno believed that the Earth and the universe are animated by a universal soul, the *anima mundi*. This was a heresy if the accused claimed that the soul of the world is the Holy Spirit. And Bruno did tell his Inquisitors precisely that. In 1139, William of Saint-Thierry had denounced Peter Abelard for the belief "That the Holy Spirit is the soul of the world," as one of thirteen heresies, "monstrous doctrines," that were confirmed and condemned by Pope Innocent II.[622] Hence, even in Bruno's time, some Inquisitorial manuals listed that heresy. For example, a *Criminal Treatise on All Heresies*, published in Venice in 1590, specified that it is a heresy to "assert that the Holy Spirit is the soul of the world, as taught by Peter Abelard."[623]

And that is what Bruno told his Inquisitors in Venice: "Regarding the Holy Spirit . . . I construe it as the soul of the universe." Later these words were quoted verbatim in Rome, when Inquisitors prepared the Sommario of Bruno's trial. There again, he was interrogated about it and relapsed into that heresy: "About these replies by him, he was interrogated [again] in the 17th Deposition, folio 257, where he affirmed the same replies in which he relapses [reincidit]."

When I first learned about Giordano Bruno, many years ago, he was portrayed as an eccentric non-scientist who was executed by the Church because he repeatedly repudiated Catholic doctrines that had nothing to do

---

[621] Bishop Tempier, "Condemnation of 219 Propositions" (1277), in Gyula Klima, et al., eds., Medieval Philosophy: Essential Readings with Commentary (Malden, Massachusetts: Blackell Publishing, 2007), Condemnation 74, p. 184.
[622] Saint-Thierry, 1139, 352.
[623] Deciani, 1590, 236.

with astronomy. That old story served a purpose: it demarcated science from esoteric nonsense, and claimed that Bruno died not for natural philosophy but for impertinence.

He believed in ideas we reject: that Earth is a living animal with a soul. Nonetheless, some famous Copernican scientists believed that too, including Johannes Kepler and William Gilbert.

Ultimately, Bruno's beliefs about the universe were more correct than those of famous astronomers. He reasoned that the universe is unbounded, with no center, and he insisted that stars are suns, surrounded by planets and moons. Remarkably, Bruno thus outlined large-scale aspects of our cosmology, while Copernicus and Kepler mistakenly thought that the universe is spherical, the Sun is its center, unmoving, and that stars are not suns, which are not surrounded by planets with moons. Bruno wrote that innumerably many unseen stars exist, moons other than ours; he wrote that mountains exist on the Moon, and the Sun moves, long before Galileo detected all of that with a telescope.

The historical evidence shows that Bruno's cosmological claims about the universe, stars, planets, and Earth did get him into trouble. Apparently he did not know that belief in many worlds was heretical, just as historians of science did not know it either, centuries later. While a few clergymen entertained the possibility of other worlds, others vehemently denied it and called it a heresy: that in fact such worlds do exist, not that God lacks power to create them. Since the Catholic Church was losing Christians to the Protestants, the Church became increasingly militant in its opposition to certain unorthodox beliefs. Hence the belief in alien worlds became "totally condemned" in Rome, and this rejection was part of an increasingly intolerant Catholic atmosphere against a resurgence of certain ancient pagan beliefs that were far more alien that anything proclaimed by the Lutherans.

Scholars analyze Bruno's trial closely do notice the relevance of the many worlds issue. For example, in a recent scholarly book that debunks myths about the conflicts between science and religion, Jole Shackelford argued that although Bruno indeed was not executed for his belief in the Earth's motion, the record of the interrogations of Bruno by the Venetian and Roman Inquisitions "reveals a nagging concern on the part of Bruno's inquisitors about his idea that there may be innumerable inhabited earth-like worlds." Shackelford concludes: "Bruno probably was burned alive for resolutely maintaining a series of heresies, among which his teaching of the

	Copernicus 1543	Bruno 1584-92	Kepler 1609	Galileo 1610-13	science in 2021
the Earth moves	√	√	√	√	√
planets orbit the Sun	√	√	√	√	√
other moons orbit planets		√	G	√	√
many invisible stars exist		√	G	√	√
the Moon has mountains		√	G	√	√
the Sun moves		√	G	*it spins*	√
planets' orbits are not circular		√	1619		√
relativity: processes on a smoothly moving ship happen as on land		√		1632	√
the Sun is a star		√		1632?	√
the Sun is not the center of the universe		√			√
the stars move		√			√
exoplanets orbit the stars		√			√
exoplanets have moons		√			√
the universe is acentric, unbounded		√			√
the universe is infinite		√			?
there are living beings in other worlds		√	√	1632?	?

Table 3. *Comparing claims: Who was right? Bruno wrote claims that are now considered correct, which others did not. Kepler accepted 'G' claims after Galileo's telescopic discoveries of 1609-13. Galileo wrote some claims in 1632, in the voice of a character in his Dialogue.*

plurality of worlds was prominent but by no means singular."[624]

Like other researchers, I too expected that the story that Bruno died for his belief in many worlds would indeed be another myth. However, a systematic analysis of the extant primary sources, along with previously unknown documents, shows that the opposite is true. I will argue that— surprisingly, and contrary to all scholarly expectations— Bruno's belief in many worlds was the principal accusation leading to his execution.

Bruno died more than 400 years ago. For 340 years, very little was

<hr>

[624] Jole Shackelford, "Giordano Bruno as the First Scientific Martyr," in *Galileo Goes to Jail, and Other Myths about Science and Religion,* edited by Ronald L. Numbers (Cambridge, MA: Harvard University Press, 2009), pp. 59-67 (pp. 65, 66).

known about the Roman Inquisition's proceedings against him. In 1925 Angelo Mercati became Prefect of the Secret Vatican Archives and soon learned that in 1887 a document had been discovered regarding the Inquisition's proceedings against Bruno. But, on its discovery, Pope Leo XIII had ordered that it be sent immediately to him and that he "absolutely did not want these proceedings to be given to anyone." Hence Mercati began an extensive archival search that continued for fifteen years to find that document. Finally, in November 1940, Mercati found the long lost "Summary of the Trial of Giordano Bruno," in the personal archives of Pope Pius IX. It consists of 261 paragraphs, including 34 articles of accusations, embedded in summaries of Bruno's interrogations in Venice and Rome.[625] The "Summary" was published in 1942. Only then did historians realize that the accusation that Bruno believed that many worlds exist, recurred throughout his prolonged trial, both in Venice and Rome.[626]

the Crime of (Dany Worlds

Following the efforts of Martin Luther and John Calvin to reform Christianity in northern Europe, the Roman Catholic Church became increasingly intolerant of unorthodox beliefs. In 1542, Pope Paul III established the Supreme Sacred Congregation of the Roman and Universal Inquisition. Its official function was "to maintain and defend the integrity of the faith and to examine and proscribe errors and false doctrines." It served as the final court of appeal in trials of heresy. With the Council of Trent (1545-1563), the Catholic Church reintroduced the medieval persecution of heresy in a severe but highly bureaucratic way. In the late 1550s, the Roman Catholic

---

[625] It was common to prepare an official "sommario" of a trial. However, it is unclear whether the present document was that final "sommario" or another internal summary. For discussion, see Francesco Beretta, "Giordano Bruno e l'Inquisizione Romana. Considerazioni sul Processo," *Bruniana & Campanelliana*, 7 (1), (2001), 15-49 (pp. 6, 14).

[626] For example, see Jean Seidengart, "L'Infinitisme Brunien devant l'Inquisition," in *Cosmología, Teología, y Religión en la Obra y en el Proceso de Giordano Bruno* (Barcelona: Universidad de Barcelona, 2001), pp. 21-38; and Maurice A. Finocchiaro, "Philosophy versus Religion and Science versus Religion: The Trials of Bruno and Galileo," in *Giordano Bruno: Philosopher of the Renaissance*, edited by Hilary Gatti (Burlington, VT: Ashgate: 2002), pp. 51-85.

Church established also the Index of Forbidden Books, in order to prohibit or censure offensive works to prevent the spread of heresies, including the spread of Protestant beliefs. The precise definition of heresy became a subject of debate after the Council of Trent had led to the systematic establishment of the Inquisitional courts and the Index of Forbidden Books. Only officially proclaimed heresies justified the death penalty. Erroneous or distasteful opinions usually led to an abjuration.

Historians thought that the belief in many worlds was not a heresy when Bruno was executed. For example, Leen Spruit has argued that "the multiplicity of worlds" was an accusation against Bruno that was "too vague to be defined as formally heretical," so that, instead, maybe it was merely viewed as "erroneous," "scandalous," or "injurious."[627] However, I will now show that it was actually heretical.

Bishop Isidore's encyclopedic work was so admired that it was printed in at least twelve editions between 1470 and 1595. Isidore's list of heresies was also echoed in a *Thesaurus of the Christian Religion* of 1559, which listed hundreds of heresies, and, in an edition of Philaster's *Book of Heresies* in 1578.[628] Furthermore, editions of Saint Jerome's works included his complaint that Origen's notion of innumerable worlds is clearly heretical.[629] Saint Jerome was especially famous in the Renaissance, because at the Council of Trent the Catholic Church had selected his translation of the Bible as the official version, known as the Latin Vulgate Bible. Above all, Augustine had rebuked the plurality of worlds in his authoritative compendium of heresies. Catholics duly cited "the 77th heresy." For example, in 1591 the Jesuit theologian Gregorius de Valentia cautioned: "There is no need of heretics among Christians, who follow Democritus and other ancient philosophers in saying that there exists not one but innumerable worlds, as the divine Augustine reports in his book on heresies, namely the

---

[627] Leen Spruit, "Una Rilettura del Processo di Giordano Bruno: Procedure e Aspetti Giuridico-Formali," in *Giordano Bruno. Oltre il Mito e le Opposte Passioni*, edited by P. Giustiniani, et al., (Naples: Biblioteca Teologica Napolitana, 2002), p. 225.

[628] Alphonsum Alvarez Guerrero, *Thesaurus Christianae Religionis et Speculum Sacrorum Summorum* (Venetiis, 1559), p. 261. Lamberti Danei, *D. Aurelii Augustini Hippon Ensis Episcopi Liber De Haeresibus, ad Quodvultdeum* (Genevae: Eustathium Vignon, 1578) p. [M.v] reverso.

[629] For example: Jerome, *Confessio Hieronymiana, ex Omnibus Germanis B. Hieronymi Operibus Optima Fide Collecta*, ed. Cornelii Schultingi Steinuvichii (Paris: Michaelem Sonnium, 1585), pp. 41, 45, 236.

seventy-seventh heresy."[630]

Some historians have shown that during the sixteenth century the Church lacked a centralized authority on censorship.[631] Instead there were multiple competing authorities, including bishops, the Inquisition, and the Congregation of the Index. For example, some bishops sympathized with humanist ideas, however, by the 1590s "the Inquisition had seized control of the whole machinery of censorship, and it used its powers of investigation and censorship to crush the humanist reforming movements."[632]

Historian Neil Tarrant has rightly argued that ecclesiastical censors did not recognize a single type of activity, what we call "science," that they sought to regulate. Instead, Tarrant asks: "Why at particular moments in history did ecclesiastical censors define as heretical, certain intellectual ideas, practices or philosophical teachings relating to the natural world?"[633] In the present case, I reply that the censors regarded the idea of many worlds as heretical because ancient authorities including Church Fathers had denounced it, partly for being linked to polytheism, atomism, and the transmigration of souls.

Finally, I found the most highly authoritative source that underlines the fact that Bruno's belief in many worlds was officially a heresy. During the rule of Pope Gregory XIII, from 1572 to 1585, the Pope reformed the Church by centralizing its authority and enacting the recommendations of the Council of Trent. Among his major projects, the Pope sponsored an expansive and updated edition of the *Corpus of Canon Law*, a compilation of laws of the Roman Catholic Church that would serve as its chief source of legislation. In 1582, when Pope Gregory XIII introduced the Gregorian calendar, he also issued the completed system of laws and ordered that it

---

[630] Gregorii de Valentia, *Commentariorum Theologicorum Tomi Quatuor: in quibus Omnes Materiae quae continentur in Summa Theologica Divi Thomae Aquinatis Ordine Explicatur*, Vol. 1 (Ingolstadt: David Sartorius, 1591), p. 991, trans. Martínez.

[631] Vittorio Frajese, "La Revoca dell' Index Sistino e la Curia Romana (1588-1596)," *Nouvelles de la République des Lettres*, 1 (1986), 15-49; Frajese, "La Politica dell'Indice dal Tridentino al Clementino (1571-1596)," *Archivio Italiano per la Storia della Pietà*, XI (1998), 304-354. Gigliola Fragnito, *La Bibbia al Rogo: La censura Ecclesiastica e i Volgarizzamenti della Scrittura* (Bologna: Il Mulino, 1997); Fragnito, "La Censura Libraria tra Congregazione dell'Indice, Congregazione dell'Inquisizione e Maestro del Sacro Palazzo (1570-1596)," in *La Censura Libraria nell'Europa del Secolo XVI*, edited by Ugo Rozzo (Udine: Forum, 1997), 163-175.

[632] Neil Tarrant, "Censoring Science in Sixteenth-Century Italy: Recent (and Not-So-Recent) Research," *History of Science*, 52 (1) (2014), 1–27, (p.12).

[633] Ibid., 17.

be used in schools of canon law and in church courts. It became the preponderant code of law in the Roman Catholic Church (for centuries, until it was replaced in 1917 by the *Code of Canon Law*). Fundamentally, Inquisition law had to comply with canon law. And the *Corpus* was reprinted soon, in 1591, and regularly thereafter. In it, the Second Part includes long discussions of what exactly constitutes heresy and who shall be considered a heretic. Echoing Isidore, a long list of heretical sects ends with a paragraph that begins: "There are also other heresies without author and without names," among which is included "having the opinion of innumerable worlds."[634]

The same expression appeared in the *Directorium Inquisitorum*, authored by the Dominican theologian Nicholas Eymerich in the 1370s, and published again in 1578 and 1595, with new commentaries by Francisco Peña, the foremost expert on inquisitorial law by 1595, in Rome.[635] Hence, the *Directorium Inquisitorum* was "as close as anything to being the official handbook of the Roman Inquisition."[636]

Table 4 lists Christian authorities that denounced the claim that many worlds exist. It includes various theologians, jurists, bishops, archbishops,

[634] *Decretum Gratiani Emendatum et Notationibus Illustratum, unà cum glossis, Gregorii XIII. Pont. Max. iussu editum* (Rome: Aedibus Populi Romani, 1582) Part 2, Causa 24, Question 3, column 1895 [unnumbered p. 1011], trans. Martínez. The title *Decretum Gratiani* shows that this work began as a revised edition of the work of the theologian Franciscus Gratianus, *Concordia Discordantium Canonum* (ca. 1150), which in subsequent editions became known as the *Decretum Gratiani*; for example, see Bartolomeus da Brescia and Franciscus Moneliensis, *Decretum Gratiani* (Venice: Johann Herbort, 1482); for the passage on "innumerable worlds" which echoes Isidore, see Causa 24, Questio 3. The much-revised *Decretum* issued by Pope Gregory XIII in 1582 became reissued later as: *Corpus Iuris Canonici Emendatum et Notis Illustratum: Gregorii XIII. Pont. Max. iussu editum*, with new indices and appendices by Pauli Lanceloti (Lugduni: [n. p.] "Cum Licentia," 1591), Part 2, Cause 24, Question 3, column 877 [unnumbered pages].

[635] Nicolai Eymerici, *Directorium Inquisitorium* (1378), corrected edition, with commentaries by Francisci Pegñae (Venice: Simeonis, 1595), p. 246. For information on Peña, see Vincenzo Lavenia, "Francisco Peña," in *Dizionario Storico dell'Inquisizione*, ed. Adriano Prosperi, Vol. III (Pisa: Scuola Normale Superiore, 2010), pp. 1186–1189. Since 1588, Peña was auditor (judge) in the Rota (the papal supreme court); see, Thomas F. Mayer, *The Roman Inquisition: A Papal Bureaucracy and Its Laws in the Age of Galileo* (Philadelphia: University of Pennsylvania Press, 2013), pp. 152-159. The Roman advocate, Quintiliano Mandosio, for example, stated: "the Rota speaking, all other tribunals fall silent," quoted in ibid., p. 157. See also Quintilliani Mandosij, ed., *Repertorium Inquisitorum Pravitatis Haereticae* (Venice: Damianum Zenarum, 1588), p. 396: "Aliae innumerabiles mundos opinantur."

[636] Mayer, *The Roman Inquisition: A Papal Bureaucracy*, p. 159.

ca. 225	Bishop Hippolytus	*Refutatio Omnium Haeresium*
ca. 260	Pope Dionysius	"Contra Epicureis"
ca. 313	Lactantius	*De Ira Dei*, and, *De Falsa Sapientia*
ca. 320	Saint Athanasius	*Contra Gentiles*
ca. 384	**Saint Philaster**	**De Haeresibus Liber**
385	Saint Ambrose	"Ad Sabinum Enarratio"
ca. 375	Saint Epiphanius	*Panarion*
402	**Saint Jerome**	**Ad Pammachium et Marcellinum Apologia**
427	**Saint Augustine**	**De Haeresibus Liber**
ca. 430	Bishop Theodoret	*Graecarum Afectionum Curatio*
ca. 461	**Praedestinatus**	**Praedestinatorum Haeresis**
ca. 540	Emperor Justinian	*Liber Adversus Origenem*
pre-550	Hermias	*Irrisio Gentilium Philosophorum*
560	Diaconus Rusticus	*Contra Acephalos*
ca. 630	**Saint Isidore**	**Etymologiae**
748	Pope Zacharias	"Ad Episcopo Bonifacio"
ca. 850	Archbishop Photius	"Clementis Alexandrini Presbyteri Scripta"
ca. 1120	**Rupert of Deutz**	**"In Librum Ecclesiastes, Sancti Laurentii"**
ca. 1150	**Franciscus Gratianus**	**Concordia Discordantium Canonum**
ca. 1250	Saint Albertus Magnus	*De Caelo et Mundo*
ca. 1274	Saint Thomas Aquinas	*Summa Theologica*
1370s	**Nicholas Eymerich**	**Directorium Inquisitorum**
1482	**Bartolomeus da Brescia**	**Decretum Gratiani**
1540	Bishop Agostino Steuco	*De Perenni Philosophia Libri X*
1559	**Alfonso Guerrero**	**Thesaurus Christianae Religionis**
1578	**Lambert Daneus, ed.**	**Liber De Haeresibus, ad Quodvultdeum**
1582	**Pope Gregory XIII**	**Decretum Gratiani Emendatum**
1588	**Quintillian Mandosi, ed.**	**Repert. Inquisitorum Pravitatis Haereticae**
1591	**Gregorius de Valentia, S.J.**	**Commentariorum Theologicorum**
1591	**Pope Gregory XIII**	**Corpus Iuris Canonici Emendatum**
1595	**Francisco Peña, ed.**	**Directorium Inquisitorum**

Table 4. *This is a selection of prominent Christian authorities who denounced the claim that many worlds exist. Authors and works that describe that belief as a "**heresy**" are in bold.*

one Emperor, three Popes, five Church Fathers, and nine Saints. Roughly half of them claimed that it was a heresy, including three Church Fathers, four saints, and one Pope. In this context, finally, it is clearly understandable why various participants in the trial of Giordano Bruno accused him of believing in many worlds. That belief belonged to pagan worldviews that Christians had condemned for over a thousand years, since the rise of Christianity. It was linked to offensive beliefs about atomism, transmigration of souls, many gods, and many Christs. So even in the 1590s, it was a heresy for a Catholic to believe in other worlds. Catholics viewed heresies as the worst kind of crimes. They were viewed as crimes against God. It was illegal to say the stars are worlds. But Bruno repeatedly said it.

It is well known that at least a couple of Bruno's books made this claim, but it is surprising to find that Bruno made the claim that the Moon, planets, and stars, are worlds in at least nine separate books.

1584	*La Cena de le Ceneri*
1584	*De l'Infinito Universo et Mondi*
1584	*De la Causa, Principio, et Uno*
1584	*Spaccio de la Bestia Trionfante*
1585	*De gli Heroici Furori*
1585	*Cabala del Cavallo Pegaseo*
1588	*Oratio Valedictoria*
1588	*Camoeracensis Acrotismus*
1591	*De Innumerabilibus, Immenso, & Infigurabili*

Table 5. *Books in which Bruno asserted that many worlds exist, including the Moon, the planets, the stars, or the Sun. In later editions, some of these books' titles varied.*

Captivated by the theory that Earth moves around the Sun, Bruno studied ancient texts on cosmology, including the *Placita* allegedly by Plutarch, in which the author or authors discussed "Pythagorean" ideas that greatly impressed Bruno: that stars are worlds, the universe is infinite, and other worlds exist similar to Earth. Following the Pythagoreans, he also pondered their major religious belief: that human souls are reborn, even in animals.

In 1584, Bruno published *The Ash Wednesday Supper*, a post-Copernican dialogue on the structure of universe. In the *Supper*, Bruno described himself in the third person as "the Nolan," and he used a character named

Theophil, a philosopher, to convey his views. Through this mouthpiece, Bruno argued that there exist "innumerable worlds," similar to Earth, and that the Earth is actually a living being. Bruno even referred to the Moon's *inhabitants.*[637] Like Thomas Digges, Bruno argued that the universe is infinite.[638] He even bragged about this finding, as it gave evidence of the majesty of God's infinite power: "Thus we shall advance to the discovery of the infinite effect of the infinite cause, the true and living evidence of the infinite vigor." And he added that "it consists of an infinite ethereal region," the same claim that Aristotle had attributed to the Pythagoreans.

Also, in another book of 1584, *On the Infinite Universe and Worlds*, Bruno argued that God's omnipotence and greatness entailed the existence of his infinite dominion: "So great is God's excellence, that it is manifested in the greatness of his empire: it is not glorified in one, but in innumerable suns: not in one Earth, one world: but in ten-hundred thousand, I say in infinite."[639] Bruno wrote about "the Moon (which is another Earth)," he said, made of earth, water, air, and fire, with seas, rocks, mountains, and valleys.[640] Bruno gave reasons why the universe is infinite, and he quoted passages from Lucretius" *On the Nature of Things* (ca. 50 BCE), in which the author elaborated the views of Democritus and Epicurus. Like them, Lucretius had remarked that, "it is in the highest degree unlikely that this Earth and sky is the only one to have been created."[641] Bruno's book was a dialogue, and the character that spoke for him voiced this argument about the stars:

> the universe being infinite, there must ultimately be more suns: because it is impossible that the heat and light from a particular one can spread

[637] Bruno, *La Cena de le Ceneri* (London: n. p., 1584), pp. 10-11, 55, 65, 69-70.
[638] There seems to be no clear evidence as to whether Bruno read the work by Digges. However, both Digges and Bruno read Marcello Palingenio Stellato's *Zodiacus Vitae* (1543), which argued that the universe is infinite but has a hierarchical structure: there exists life and misery only on the Earth while the unchangeable heavens are illuminated by spiritual and immaterial lights, unlike the Sun. For discussion, see Miguel A. Granada, "Bruno, Digges, Palingenio: Omogeneità ed Eterogeneità nella Concezione dell'Universo Infinito," in *Rivista di Storia della Filosofia*, 47(1) (1992), 47-73.
[639] Giordano Bruno Nolano, *De l'Infinito Universo et Mondi* ('Venice' [London]: n.p., 1584), p. [xxix], trans. Martínez.
[640] Ibid., pp. 71, 87, 111.
[641] Lucretius, *De Rerum Natura* (ca. 50 BCE), in *On the Nature of the Universe*, trans b y Ronald Latham (Baltimore: Penguin, 1951), p 91.

throughout immensity, as Epicurus could imagine, if what others report of him is true. Therefore it necessarily follows that there exist innumerable suns, of which many are visible as sorts of small bodies: but such an apparently minor star can be much larger than the one that seems the greatest.[642]

Bruno argued that despite their heat, such suns might be inhabited by some beings or animals. Such beings would "vegetate" by virtue of the surrounding cooling bodies, analogously to how those in our world depend on the Sun's heat. The Earth seemed to be a relatively opaque star, whereas some other stars are bright. He also argued that some stars are moons. He argued that all stars are worlds, and furthermore, that stars are rational, moving animals, which, like the Earth, have waters that move within their caverns as blood through veins. He spoke about a soul that embraces and infuses all things. He referred to the Earth as a "divinity." Furthermore, Bruno praised the views voiced in Plato's *Timaeus* and by Nicholas of Cusa. Against Aristotle, Bruno argued that the accepted concept of the order of the elements and the heavenly bodies was a vain fantasy.

In another book, Bruno again referred to the Moon "which we regard as another Earth."[643] Bruno claimed that the Moon was the world closest to the Earth and similar to the Earth. Likewise, in *On the Immense and the Innumerable*, published in 1591, Bruno again insisted that "There are innumerable distinct worlds, which we call stars."[644] He disdained the traditional notion of a finite universe as a stupid dream produced by a confused and delirious imagination.[645]

Bruno published all of these works outside of Italy, beyond the reach of Catholic censors. In order to give them more prestige, his books included false imprints, such as "Venice," and no publisher. In 1591, however, Bruno took the risk of traveling through Italy, on the way to Venice, to teach philosophy to a Venetian aristocrat, Giovanni Mocenigo.

---

[642] Bruno, *De l'Infinito Universo*, Dialogue 3, pp. 74-75, trans. Martínez.

[643] Bruno, *De gli Heroici Furori* ('Paris' [London]: Ant. Baio, 1585), Fifth Dialogue (unnumbered pages).

[644] Bruno, *De Immenso et Innumerabilibus, seu de Universo et Mundis* (1591), bk. 3, in *Opera Latine Conscripta*, ed. Francesco Fiorentino and Felice Tocco, Vol. 1, Part 1 (Naples: Dom. Morano, 1879), p. 324, trans. Martínez.

[645] Ibid., Vol. 1, Part 2 (Stuttgart-Bad Canstatt: F. Frommann Verlag, 1961), pp. 171, 291. For discussion, see Miguel A. Granada, "Bruno, Digges, Palingenio," p. 67.

Right at that time, unbeknownst to Bruno, someone in Venice was trying to publish a book that discussed the idea of many worlds. Juan "Giovanni" da Gara was a Christian printer who served the Hebrew printing market in Venice.[646] Da Gara prepared the text of a work published a century earlier, by Rabbi Abarbanel, and submitted the project to the Venetian Inquisitor Sebastiano Barbadico. The text was evaluated, and finally a special consultant for the Inquisition complained: "In this book I have found the following false conclusions: that there have been and shall be many worlds," and several other claims, "and these are things that are repugnant to our Catholic faith."[647]

The recurring heresy in Bruno's trial

In May 1592, Mocenigo sent a written complaint to the Venetian Inquisition, with twenty-one accusations against Bruno. The seventh on the list is that Bruno believed "that there are infinite worlds." One historian rightly remarks that it seems as if this proposition "did not present to the eyes of the Venetian accuser any character of novelty."[648] Mocenigo did not claim to list Bruno's transgressions in any particular order. For example, he listed some seemingly awful offenses after the many worlds issue, such as that Bruno denied Christ's miracles and denied that the Virgin Mary could have given birth.

Some of the interrogations were attended and "licensed" by the Inquisitor mentioned above, Sebastiano Barbadico.[649] The Venetian Inquisition found several witnesses to testify against Bruno. Five of them repeated the accusation that he believed in many worlds: Friar Celestino of Verona, Iulius de Salodio, Francisco Vaia, Francisco Gratianus, and Matteo de

---

[646] Elisheva Carlbach, *Palaces of Time* (Cambridge: Harvard University Press, 2011), pp. 60, 65.

[647] Deposition of the Reverend Father Sebastiano Taiapetra, professor of Hebrew, Venice, Archivio di Stato, Sant'Uffizio 69, Case 25, June 9, 1592; quoted in Ingrid Rowland, *Giordano Bruno: Philosopher/Heretic* (New York: Farrar, Strauss and Giroux, 2008), p. 235.

[648] Seidengart, "L'Infinitisme Brunien," p. 23, trans. Martínez.

[649] Third Deposition, 2 June 1592; Fourth Deposition, 2 June 1592; Fifth Deposition, 3 June 1592; Sixth Deposition, 4 June 1592; in Luigi Firpo, *Il Proceso di Giordano Bruno* (Rome: Salerno Editrice, 1993), pp. 165, 172, 184, 192.

Silvestris. However, all five were imprisoned at the time, they only knew Bruno from the Inquisition's prisons, so their testimony did not carry enough weight.

The Venetian proceedings were interrupted by the Inquisition of Rome. The central office of the Inquisition determined that the case was so important that it should be handled directly. The "Supreme Inquisitor" in Rome, Cardinal Giulio Santori of Santa Severina, ordered that Bruno be transferred because he was not merely a heretic, he was something worse: a *heresiarch*, someone who leads and converts Catholics into heretics, and can become their intellectual patriarch.[650] They complained that this "public heresiarch" had fraternized with heretics, he had written heretical books, published them "in heretical places."[651] In 1593, Bruno was transferred to Rome. The Roman Inquisitors managed to get four of the previous witnesses to testify about Bruno again. All four of them: Mocenico, Celestino, Gratianus, and Silvestries repeated the accusation that Bruno believed in many worlds. Celestino's second accusation has special significance, because at the time he was no longer a prisoner, so then his claims had more validity.[652]

Moreover, in connection with Bruno's claims about the transmigration of souls, Celestino (twice) and Gratiano (once) accused Bruno of claiming that souls are reborn in multiple worlds. For example, Celestino recalled: "When discussing the plurality of worlds, [Bruno] said that the soul travels from one world to another and from one body to another, and that he remembered having been in another world at another time, and that being a boy he was approached by a viper, which scared him, and that his mother defended him."[653]

In sum, six witnesses accused Bruno of believing in many worlds on no less than thirteen separate instances, in ten depositions. In fact, it was the one accusation leveled more often than any other against Bruno, throughout the protracted seven and a half year trial in Venice and Rome.

---

[650] "Verbale di Seduta dell'Eccellentissimo Collegio fi Venezia," 28 September 1592, in Firpo, *Il Proceso*, p. 202.

[651] Ibid., and "Verbale di Seduta dell'Eccellentissimo Collegio di Venezia," 22 December 1592, in Firpo, *Il Proceso*, 207.

[652] Celestino seemingly confirmed only three of Mocenigo's accusations: that Bruno said that "Christ was a wretch," that many worlds exist, and that souls transmigrate from body to body. See *Firpo, Il Proceso*, pp. 259-260, 267-268, 283-284.

[653] Celestino, in Firpo, *Il Proceso*, p. 284, trans. Martínez.

At the time, any Catholic person who was confronted by an Inquisitor was expected to deny or renounce any errors, blasphemies, or heresies. If the accused admitted that such beliefs were mistaken, the Roman Inquisitors often granted leniency, because they understood that their function was not merely punitive. For example, in the Fourth Deposition in Venice, in 1592, the Inquisitors asked Bruno "whether the miracles that were done by Christ and the apostles were apparent miracles and made by magical arts and not true." Bruno replied: "What is this thing? Who is it that has contrived such devilry? I have not said any such thing, nor did any such thing pass through my imagination. Oh God, what is this thing? I would rather sooner be dead than to have such a thing proposed to me."[654] Afterward, the Inquisitors in Rome and Venice did not ask Bruno about that accusation again.

Bruno's reactions to being accused of believing in many worlds were quite the opposite. It was one of the very few doctrines that Bruno asserted as true. He repeatedly refused to recant this opinion. He refused at least four times, in four out of the total of seventeen depositions: in the 3rd (in 1592 in Venice), the 12th (in 1593 in Rome), the 14th (also in 1593), and the 17th (around 1596). Bruno repeatedly *insisted* that the Earth is a star, what we call a heavenly body, the Sun is a star, radiant stars are orbited by planets such as the Earth, which are all worlds made of the same elements as the Earth. He insisted that "innumerably many worlds" exist.

For example, in his Third Deposition in Venice, Bruno said: "I have not taught anything against the Catholic Christian religion," but he acknowledged that philosophical arguments could be misinterpreted as being indirectly opposed to the Catholic faith. He then summarized his views:

> "In these books particularly my intention can be seen and that which I have held; which, in sum is that I affirm an infinite universe, which is the consequence of the infinite divine power, because I regard it as unworthy of the divine goodness and power that, being able to produce in addition to our world another and infinitely many others, to produce one finite world. Yes I have asserted infinite particular worlds similar to the Earth, which with Pythagoras I consider a star, similar to which is the Moon, other planets and other stars, which are infinite; and that all those bodies are worlds and numberless, which thus constitute the infinite universality in an infinite space; and this is called the infinite universe, in which are

654 Bruno, Fourth Deposition, in Firpo, *Il Proceso*, p. 181, trans. Martínez.

innumerable worlds. Thus the fortune that is double from the infinitude and greatness of the universe and the multitude of worlds, but without indirectly meaning to reject the truth according to the faith."[655]

In this one statement, Bruno affirmed the existence of many worlds at least five times! Despite his intentions, Bruno's "philosophical" opinions had theological significance because they referred to "the divine power" and the nature of God's Creation. Bruno seems utterly unaware that it was a heresy to posit many worlds.

He apparently thought that it was acceptable to defend philosophical views that were distinct from theological doctrines.[656] But actually, according to some manuals on heresies it was forbidden to hold philosophical views contrary to the faith because they could lead to heresy.[657] In 1513, the Fifth Lateran Council, headed by Pope Leo X, had strictly decreed that all philosophers who teach principles that deviate from the Catholic faith were obligated "to make every effort to manifest the truth of the Christian religion" to their listeners and to invest all energies in *refuting* any contrary philosophical arguments.[658] The Council specified that "truth cannot contradict truth," so any statement contrary to the faith was totally false and strictly prohibited from being taught. It decreed that anyone who clings to such erroneous statements should be "punished as detestable and abominable heretics."[659] More recently, the prominent jurist of Inquisition law Francisco Peña had reasserted this decree of the Fifth Lateran Council, insisting that professors should manifest the truth of Catholic doctrine to refute any opinions of pagan philosophers contrary to the faith. And Peña quoted

---

[655] Bruno, "Terzo Constituto del Brun," in Firpo, *Il Proceso*, pp. 167-168. Originally published as Jordanus Brunus, deposition of 2 June 1592, in Domenico Berti, ed., *Vita di Giordano Bruno da Nola* (Firenze: G. Paravia, 1868), doc. 9, p. 353, trans. Martínez.

[656] Beretta, "Giordano Bruno e l'Inquisizione Romana," p. 35.

[657] Ibid., and Francesco Beretta, "Orthodoxie Philosophique et Inquisition Romaine au 16e-17e Siècles. Un Essai d'Interprétation," *Historia Philosophica* 3 (2005), 82-96 at p. 90. E.g., see Francisco Peña, "Schol. XXIII. In quaestionem iiij. de erroribus Philosophorum Priscorum," in N. Eymerich, *Directorium Inquisitorum; cum Scholiis seu Annotationibus Eruditissimis D. Francisci Pegnae* (Rome: Aedibus Pop., 1578), pp. 53-54; and p. 242 in the edition of 1587.

[658] Fifth Lateran Council, session 8 (19 December 1513), in *Bullarum Diplomatum et Privilegiorum Sanctorum Romanorum Pontificum*, Vol. 5 (Turin: Seb. Franco et Henrico Dalmazzo, 1860), 602.

[659] Ibid.

Tertullian: "philosophers are the Patriarchs of heretics."[660]

Bruno did not merely assert the plurality of worlds as a philosophical possibility, an interesting hypothesis. He boldly asserted it as actually true. In his 12th deposition, in Rome, Bruno insisted: "It is evident that in all my writings and the reports by intelligent and trustworthy persons, that I hold that the world and the worlds," including the Earth and stars, all had a beginning and could have an end. Moreover, in the "Summary" of Bruno's trial, right where his Third Deposition is summarized, where Bruno said that the Earth is a star, an officer of the Inquisition noted on the margin: "About this reply he was interrogated [yet again] in the 17th Deposition, folio 261, but does not seem to satisfy, because he relapsed [*reincidit*] into the same reply."[661] The word *reincidit* was a technical term for Inquisitors. It was part of the definition of someone who has "relapsed" into heresy.[662] Again, this shows that Bruno's belief about the plurality of worlds was heretical, and worse: that he obstinately repeated it after being instructed to abandon it.

In early 1595, the Inquisition decided that its theologians should systematically inspect Bruno's books to pinpoint heretical statements that should be censured. They only managed to gather some of his books, not

---

[660] Peña, "Schol. XXIII," p. 53. Tertullian, *Adversus Hermogenem*, in J. Waszink, ed., *Tertulliani Opera*, Vol. 1 (Turnholti: Brepols Editores Pontificii, 1954), Vol. 1, chap. 8, p. 404. Tertullian, *De Anima* (ca. 215 CE), in *Tertulliani Opera*, Vol. 2, chap. 28, pp. 824-825. See also: Roberto Bellarmino, *De Amissione Gratiae et Statu Peccati Libri Sex* (1613); reissued in *Disputationum Roberti Bellarmini Politiani S. J., S. R. E. Cardinalis, De Controversiis Christianae Fidei Adversus Huius Temporis Haereticos*, Vol. 4 (Naples: Josephum Giuliano, 1858), bk. 4, chap. 11, p. 161.

[661] Bruno, 17th Deposition, in Firpo, *Il Proceso*, p. 269, trans. Martínez.

[662] Iacobi Menochij, *De Arbitrarii Iudicum Quaestionibus & Causis Libri Duo* (Frankfurt am Main, 1576), Casus 374: "Est relapsus, qui bis in eandem haeresim reincidit." Ioannis Bernardi Diaz de Luco, *Practica Criminalis Canonica* (Rome: Vincentium Accoltum, 1581), 225: "quando fuerit inventus in haeresi, aut abiuravit eam, & fuit relapsus, aut quando se compurgavit, & reincidit eam…." Quintilliani Mandosij, ed., *Repertorium Inquisitorum Pravitatis Haereticae* (Venice: Damianum Zenarum, 1588), 676: "verè relapsus dicitur ille, qui per confessionem, vel veram probationé primò fuit convictus de haeresi, & ipsam abiuravit, deinde reincidit in errorem illum." Caesare Carena, *Tractatus de Officio Sanctissimae Inquisitionis et Modo Procedendi in Causis Fidei* (Cremonae: Marc Antonium Belpierum, 1641), p. 253: "qui haeresim in Juditio abiurauerat, & postea reincidit in ipsa, censeri debeat iuris fictione haereticus relapsus."

all.[663] (The identity of the theologians is unknown, but it seems plausible that Roberto Bellarmino joined them after February 1596, when he became a Consultor for the Inquisition.) By late 1596 the list of censured propositions from Bruno's books was nearly ready.[664] On December 16th, the Inquisitors visited Bruno in his cell, and ordered "that he be interrogated as soon as possible about the propositions excerpted from his writings and about the censures."[665]

The list of ten censured propositions is included in the Summary of Bruno"s trial. It includes this censure: "Again, he posits many worlds, many Suns, necessarily containing similar things in kind and in species as in this world, and even men, as in folio 139 and the subsequent long digression."[666] This was the tenth and last censured proposition on the list. There are at least four reasons for believing that it was added later than the rest: its numbering, and, that by comparison to the first eight, the last two are very brief; those two do not include Bruno's replies; and, this last proposition includes a cited page number, "fol. 139," which is out of sequence with all the other cited page numbers. It seems that after the first eight propositions were composed and presented to Bruno, and after his replies were recorded, the censors added two more propositions. The fact that the issue had arisen several times in the trial, previously, shows that this addition was a matter

[663] It seems that the list of books that were obtained is not extant. However, several titles of Bruno's books appear in the trial accusations, depositions, etc. I list the titles as they appear in the trial documents, with transcription defects, and in the sequence in which they were mentioned. I have marked each book that claims the existence of many worlds with an asterisk: *De Minimo, Magno et Mensura*; **Li Heroici Furori*; **Dell'Infinito, Universo et Mondi*; *Cantus Circeus*; *De Memoria*; *De Lampade Combinatoria*; *De Umbris Idearum*; *De Numero, Monade et Figura*; *Delle Sette Arte Liberali*; *De Sigillis Hermetis, Ptolemei et Aliorum*; *Centovinti Articuli contra li Peripatetici*; **De Immenso et Innumerabilibus*; *De Compositione Imaginum*; **De Causa, Principio et Uno*; **La Cene delle Cenere*; *De' Segni de' Tempi*; **Trionfante Bestia*.

[664] Theologian consultors drafted the list of censured propositions. In Sept. 1596 the list was submitted to three reviewers: Master [Garcia?] Guerra, Fra Pedro Juan Zaragoza (a consultor of the Index since 1592), both Dominicans, and a Jesuit presbyter named Gallo. See Firpo, *Il Proceso*, 235, and Thomas F. Mayer, *The Roman Inquisition on the Stage of Italy c. 1590-1640* (Philadelphia: University of Pennsylvania Press, 2014), pp. 121, 289. Apparently nothing else is known about Guerra or Gallo.

[665] Visita dei Carcerati nel Sant'Uffizio Romano, 16 December 1596, in Firpo, 241, trans. Martínez.

[666] "Item, ponit plures mundos, plures soles, continentes necessario res similes in genere et in specie sicut iste mundus, ac etiam homines, ut supra fol. 139, et sequentibus, longo digress," in Firpo, *Il Proceso*, p.304.

of completeness: he had already testified about it repeatedly, yet it was in his books, so it had to be included in the list of censures.

Incidentally, the fifth censured proposition from Bruno's books was that the Earth moves.

On March 24, 1597, the Inquisitors and theologians visited Bruno in his cell. This meeting is significant for two reasons. It is the first extant record that shows the participation of "Robertus Bellarminius," the famous Jesuit theologian who would exert important influence in the Inquisition's proceedings against both Bruno and Galileo. Bellarmino was a highly accomplished professor of theology for twenty years and the personal theologian to Pope Clement VIII.[667] Bellarmino had become *the* authority in the analysis and persecution of heresies, especially against the Protestants. He wrote: "heresy is a more serious perversity than all other crimes and atrocities, just as the plague is more formidable and fearsome than common diseases."[668] Bellarmino now served as a Consultor in Bruno's trial.

The second important point about the meeting of 24 March is that the official record states a single demand against Bruno: "He was admonished to thus abandon his delusions [*vanitates*] of diverse worlds, and ordered that he should be interrogated sternly. Later he was given the censure."[669] Consultors and Inquisitors such as Bellarmino knew well the authoritative works on heresies, such as Philaster's treatise and Saint Augustine's book *On Heresies*.[670] Hence they knew that it was heretical to claim that there are many worlds. Moreover, Bellarmino's presence is significant because he

---

[667] Bellarmino made his vow of secrecy as Consultor to the Holy Office on 5 February 1597, see the document reproduced in Peter Godman, *The Saint as Censor: Robert Bellarmine between Inquisition and Index* (Leiden: Brill, 2000), 456,

[668] Roberti Bellarmini, *Disputationes de Controversis Christianae Fidei, Adversus hujus Temporis Hæreticos*, Vol. 1 (1575), "Præfatio," reissued in (Venice: Joannem Malachinum, 1721), x, trans. Martínez.

[669] "Deinde fuit admonitus ad relinquendum huiusmodi eius vanitates diversorum mundorum, atque ordinatum quod interrogetur stricte. Postea detur ei censura," Visita dei Carcerati nel Sant'Uffizio Romano, 24 March 1597, in Firpo, *Il Proceso*, p. 244, trans. Martínez.

[670] Bellarmino showed that he knew Philaster's *Diversarum Hereseon Liber* and Augustine's *De Haeresibus*, for example, in Bellarmino, *Disputationes; De Controversiis Christianae Fidei Adversus Huius Temporis Haereticos*, Second ed. (Ingolstadii: Davidis Sartorii, 1588), 14, 20, 145, 343, 359. Bellarmino, *Disputationum; De Controversiis Christianae Fidei Adversus Huius Temporis Haereticos*, Vol. 4 (Naples: Josephum Giuliano, 1858), pp. 33, 122, 136, 161, 164, 278, 384, 398, 639, 654, 678, 683. Bellarmino was also very familiar with works on heresies by Tertullian, Epiphanius, Irenaeus, and others, which he also cited often.

knew that certain heresies were rooted in *pagan* notions. For example, in a book of 1594, titled *On the Need for Caution When Reading Pagan Philosophers*, its author noted that "Father Roberto Bellarmino" had advised that, "certain Catholics who are too pleased with a burgeoning Pagan sense should be subjected to censorship, by admonishing the Author."[671]

Bruno assumed that by insisting on his identity as a philosopher he had some latitude in how far he could entertain speculative opinions. Catholic authorities had recently confronted other philosophers without deadly consequences.[672] In 1583, the philosopher Girolamo Borri at Siena was imprisoned for a year (apparently for having claimed that the soul is mortal), and again, under suspicion of Protestant beliefs and for possessing prohibited books.[673] But Borri was repeatedly released. From 1592 until 1594, the Congregation of the Index interrogated the philosopher Francesco Patrizi, yet he was allowed to continue teaching Platonic philosophy at the University of Rome. [674] They censored his magnum opus, but later allowed him to make changes to it. Around 1598, the Pope asked Bellarmino whether the University of Rome should keep its professorship on Platonic philosophy. Bellarmino warned against it, arguing that it more easily led to dangerous views than other pagan philosophies. Hence the Pope terminated that position in 1598.[675] Catholic authorities reaffirmed their commitment to Aristotelian neo-Scholasticism and rejected Platonic and Pythagorean philosophies.[676]

Bruno's "admonition" of 1597 was a serious warning. Historian Peter Godman explains that from Bellarmino's perspective it was common to treat secular scholars less severely than clergymen. Godman writes:

---

[671] Io. Baptistae Crispi, *De Ethnicis Philosophis Caute Legendis Disputationum* (Rome: Aloysij Zannetti, 1594), [p. xi], trans. Martínez.

[672] For primary sources, see, Ugo Baldini and Leen Spruit, eds., *Catholic Church and Modern Science: Documents from the Archives of the Roman Congregations of the Holy Office and the Index*, Vol. 1 (Rome: Libreria Editrice Vaticana, 2010).

[673] Paul F. Grendler, *The Universities of the Italian Renaissance* (Baltimore: Johns Hopkins University Press), 190, 294.

[674] Ibid., 300-309. Beretta, pp. 82-96.

[675] Grendler, *The Universities of the Italian Renaissance*, 306-309. Between 1604 and 1626, the Paduan Inquisition interrogated the philosopher Cesare Cremonini several times, but they did not imprison him. Antonino Poppi, "Cremonini, Galileo e gli Inquisitori del Santo a Padova', *Il Santo: Rivista Antoniana di Storia Dottrina Arte*, Ser. 2, Vol. 33 (1-2), pp. 5-112.

[676] I have found that, during Bruno's trial, nine of the ten propositions that were censured in his books were Pythagorean. See the previous chapter.

"Discipline and authority were at stake and, if learned laymen might be spared, no quarter would be given to the rank and file of the *Ecclesia militans* who presumed to step out of line."[677] This applied to deviant clergymen, such as Bruno. He presented himself as a philosopher, but the Inquisitors perceived him as an apostate priest; so his punishments would be worse than if he were merely a layperson or a philosopher.

By March of 1598, the Congregation of the Holy Roman Office consisted of several cardinals, several coadjutors or Consultors, plus an Assessor of the Holy Office, a General Commissary, and the official notary. Father Alberto Tragagliolo was the General Commissary of the Holy Office. Tragagliolo and Bellarmino agreed to produce another list of propositions that would synthesize Bruno's principal heresies. Hence on 14 January 1599, Tragagliolo and Bellarmino presented "eight heretical propositions collected from the books and trial" of Bruno.[678] The Inquisitors agreed that Bruno would be required to solemnly abjure such propositions. Unfortunately, the list is not extant, or researchers have not found it despite many efforts.

Since that document is missing, some historians claim causal ignorance. For example, Thomas F. Mayer writes: "The simple fact is that we do not know why he was executed. Nevertheless, Francesco Beretta must be right that the articles could not have included any Copernican charges because they were all specified in the sentence as heretical."[679] Mayer neglected to point out that charges of heresy did not need to correspond to any preexisting list of heresies. They could be so declared by the Pope. They could also include any propositions that Consultors and Cardinals concluded were contrary to Church dogma. Also, some of Bruno's propositions were semi-Copernican, pertaining to astronomy or cosmology, and yet were censured. Unlike recent historians and writers, Consultors and Inquisitors knew that it was heretical to claim that many worlds exist.

On February 4, 1599, Pope Clement VIII sent a message to the prisoner: "Our most Holy Lord decrees and ordains that it be intimated to the apostate brother Giordano Bruno of Nola by the theologian Fathers,

---

[677] Godman, *The Saint as Censor*, p. 219.
[678] "Decreto de la Congregazione del Sant'Ufficio," Rome, 14 January 1599, in Firpo, *Il Proceso*, p.312.
[679] Mayer, *Roman Inquisition*, p. 124. Beretta, "Giordano Bruno e l'Inquisizione Romana," pp. 46-47.

namely Father Bellarmino and the Father Commissary, that these propositions are heretical, and not only heretical as now declared, but by the most ancient Fathers of the Church and the Apostolic See."[680] By not knowing the history of the heresy of many worlds, historians have conjectured that since Bellarmino's list presumably included Bruno's cosmological views then the Pope acted inappropriately here.[681] But actually, the Pope's statement is remarkably consonant with the heresy of many worlds. As I showed, several Church Fathers and Popes had denounced the heresy of many worlds, namely, Saint Jerome, Saint Augustine, Saint Isidore, Pope Dionysius, Pope Zacharias, and Pope Gregory XIII. So indeed, this belief had been declared heretical by the Apostolic See.

Bruno had already spent six years in the Inquisitions' prisons, yet they then gave him forty more days to recant the heresies in Bellarmino's list. But Bruno did not recant. In March 1599, Bellarmino was promoted to cardinal and Inquisitor. And on April 30, one of the early members of the Roman Inquisition in the proceedings against Bruno, Ferdinando Taverna, became governor of Rome. Taverna soon became infamous for being ruthlessly cruel toward criminals. He personally extracted the confession of a young woman who killed her incestuous father. Consequently Taverna's officers beheaded her, and her mother, and they tore off flesh from her brother with pincers (while forcing a younger brother to watch), then they bludgeoned him, and tore his body to pieces. People rioted because of such brutally cruel executions but Taverna crushed them. They said that the governor and the Pope did not care for justice.[682]

In August 1599, a Decree of the Inquisitors noted that Bruno had "clearly revoked in writing" most of the propositions that had been

---

[680] Adrianus, notary, "Decreto della Congregazione del Sant'Uffizio," 4 February 1599, in Firpo, *Il Proceso*, p. 314, trans. Martínez. Two more documents echoed this claim; and one of them added that these propositions were "heretical and contrary to the Catholic faith" and that the ancient Church Fathers had "rejected and condemned" them; in Firpo, *Il Proceso*, pp. 314-315.

[681] For example, F. Beretta, *Galilée devant le Tribunal de l'Inquisition*; Doctoral Dissertation, Faculty of Theology, University of Fribourg, Switzerland (1998), 210-211; and Leen Spruit, "The Invention of Solitude: Giordano Bruno's Self-Presentation in Speech, Works and Trial," *Fragmenta*, 4 (2011), 169-170.

[682] Andrew Graham-Dixon, *Caravaggio: A Life Sacred and Profane* (New York: W.W. Norton: 2011), pp. 253-254.

presented to him in April.[683] In December, the Cardinals of the Inquisition, including Bellarmino, confronted Bruno again. They asked if he would recant. They recorded his answer: "He said that he neither wants nor should repent, and has nothing to repent, nor has matters of repentance, and does not know about what he should repent."[684] So they gave him even more time to recant. They submitted his books to the Index of Forbidden Books, for heresies and errors.[685]

On January 20, 1600, a Decree of the Congregation of the Holy Office reported that Bruno had been asked to "recognize, detest, and abjure" the "heretical propositions that were contained in his books and that he had voiced in his depositions." However, the Decree reported: "Bruno did not want to agree, asserting that he never said or wrote heretical propositions, but that the excerpts were done wrongly by the ministers of the Holy Office, conveying the opposite. Because, he was prepared to give an account of all his writings, to defend them against any theologians."[686]

Since he did not admit his heresies, the Decree stated that he would be sentenced and delivered to the secular Roman Court for punishment. On February 8, the Inquisitors sentenced Bruno. They also declared: "we condemn, reprove and prohibit all your books and writings mentioned above and others as heretical and erroneous and containing many heresies and errors." They ordered that his works be publicly burned at St. Peter's square and listed in the Index of Forbidden Books. Hence in that document, the cardinals condemned Bruno as an "obstinate and impenitent heretic." Nine cardinals, including Bellarmino, approved the final judgment, and it was sent to the Governor of Rome, Taverna. On the same day, the Congregation of the Index duly noted that Bruno's books and writings would be prohibited.

---

[683] Adrianus, notary "Decreto della Congregazione del Sant'Uffizio," 24 August 1599, in Firpo, *Il Proceso*, p. 324. This same statement is reiterated in another document, the "Bella Copia Sommaria," of 24 August 1599, in ibid., p. 325. Bruno did not revoke two propositions: "namely the first, about the Novatian heresy, and the 7th, which treats the soul being in the body as a sailor in a ship." Neither heresy was explained in this Decree.

[684] "Visita dei Carcerati nel Sant'Uffizio," 21 December 1599, in Firpo, *Il Proceso*, 133.

[685] For a discussion of the differences between kinds of heresies and errors, in connection with Bruno's trial, see Spruit, "Una Rilettura del Proceso di Giordano Bruno," pp. 217-234.

[686] "Decreto della Congregazione del Sant'Uffizio," 20 January 1600, in Firpo, *Il Proceso*, p. 338, trans. Martínez.

In 2010, a remarkable document was discovered in the Archivio Storico Capitolino, which shows the importance of the heresy of many worlds. It is from February 12, 1600, just five days before Bruno's execution. It says:

> The Proceedings were burned, those in which the curate [parish priest] already noted had specified so many ☉ [suns?] and for which he was burned, and soon will be burned an obstinate *relasso* [someone who re-lapsed into heresy] called Tadeo [*sic*] Bruno of Nola, a famous writer...[687]

So, apparently, someone else, as well as Bruno, died for believing in many suns.

Federica Favino infers that the clergyman in question was actually Friar Celestino of Verona (born Giovanni Antonio Arrigoni).[688] Her conjecture seems compelling for several reasons. Friar Celestino and the "curate" mentioned in the document were both clergyman, both were from Verona, both were burned in Rome, both were executed shortly before Bruno, both knew of the notion of many suns or worlds.[689] Also, the Inquisition "ordered" that: "silence be imposed to not make disclosures."[690] This seems to match the extreme secrecy in the act of burning the curate's trial proceedings. Celestino was burned alive at the Campo dei Fiori on September 16, 1599. In addition to the surprising document about "many suns," only one accusation is known for why Celestino was executed. A letter from Rome states: "he was killed. . . at the Campo di Fiore, a Veronese Capuchin friar Antonio [Celestino] burned at night, an extremely wicked man who insisted that Our

---

[687] "Fu brugiato il Processo co'l quale quel curato già scritto haveva nominato tanti ☉ et per questo brugiato, et sta per brugiarsi un relasso ostinato chiamato Tadeo Bruno da Nola grandissimo letterato...," Report, [12 February 1600, Rome], Archivio Orsini. I. Corrispondenza, b. 380, n. 385 Archivio Storico Capitolino, Roma, trans. Martínez. The ☉ was the astronomical symbol for Sun. See also Federica Favino, " 'Et Sta per Brugiarsi un Relasso Ostinato': Una Testimonianza Inedita intorno a la Condanna di Giordano Bruno," *Galilæana: Journal of Galilean Studies*, 7 (2010), 85–95 (pp. 85-86).

[688] See Favino, pp. 91-93. On May 1599, Celestino wrote to the Roman Inquisition, to turn himself in for some reason. Soon, they arrested and interrogated him in Rome. See Firpo, *Il Proceso*, pp. 43-46, 126-127. Most records of his trials seem to be lost.

[689] The fact that the curate was from Verona is noted in another letter, dated 29 January 1600, in Orsini I, Corrispondenza, 280, n. 304, in the Archivio Storico Capitolino; quoted in Favino, p. 91.

[690] Roman Inquisition, document of 24 August 1599, in Firpo, *Il Proceso*, p. 126.

Lord Christ did not redeem the human race."[691]

Next, we have an eyewitness report about Bruno's execution. Gaspar Schoppe was a young German humanist, almost twenty-four years old, who was a convert Catholic and a critic of the Protestants. In February 1600, Schoppe lived in the palace of Cardinal Madruzzi, one of the Inquisitors who judged Bruno. Schoppe wrote: "Perhaps I too would believe the vulgar rumors that Bruno was burned for Lutheranism, but I was present at the Holy Office of the Inquisition when the condemnation against him was voiced, & so I know what heresy he professed."[692] In fact, it is true that the category of "Lutheran" was misused in Italy to cover a great many practices and beliefs.[693] Schoppe described the site of the condemnation as "the Palace of the supreme Inquisitor," and indeed, it was Cardinal Madruzzi's home. Madruzzi was the first to sign Bruno's condemnation on that very day. Schoppe listed twelve accusations against Bruno, "horrendous and utter absurdities," he said, deserving of death. The very first one on the list is "That Worlds are Innumerable."[694] Schoppe echoed the precise wording in which it was known as a heresy in Latin: *"Mundos esse innumerabiles."*[695]

---

[691] Francisco Vialardo, 27 September 1599, Archivio Mediceo, Collezione di Avvisi già dell' Archivio Urbinate, Biblioteca Apostolica Vaticana; quoted in Luigi Amabile, *Fra Tommaso Campanella*, Vol. 1 (Naples: Antonio Morano, 1882), p. 69, trans. Martínez.

[692] Gaspar Schoppe to Konrad Rittershausen, 17 February 1600, printed in Gaspari Scioppii, "Epistola, in qua haereticos jure infelicibus lignis cremari concludit," [also titled: "Epistola, in qua sententiam de Lutheranis tanquam haereticis atram Romae fieri asserit & probat"], in *Machiavellizatio* (Saragossae: Didacus Ibarra, 1621), p. 31, trans. Martínez.

[693] See John Tedeschi, *The Prosecution of Heresy* (Binghamton, NY: Medieval & Renaissance Texts and Studies, 1991), pp. 94-95.

[694] Some writers (but not all) characterize Schoppe's list as beginning with other items: denying transubstantiation, doubting Mary's virginity, having lived in heretical places, etc. Such writers mix Schoppe's narrative account of Bruno's early transgressions with the subsequent and separate list of Bruno's "doctrines." Note, however, that Schoppe specified that Lutherans were *not* executed for their teachings (such as about transubstantiation) so it is unjustified to construe Bruno's transgressions, in Schoppe's narrative, as the doctrines for which he was found to be an impenitent and obstinate heretic, and for which he was executed. Bruno was neither obstinate nor impenitent about transubstantiation, or about Mary's virginity, or about having lived in countries where Protestants lived.

[695] Cicero and Lactantius disdained the claim that "mundos esse innumerabiles" as insane. Valerius Maximus and Seneca quoted the expression, attributing it to Democritus. Philaster declared that "mundos esse infinitos et innumerabiles" was a heresy.

Comparing Bruno's teachings to those of the Lutherans, Schoppe argued: "But perhaps you might add: *the Lutherans neither teach nor believe such things, and therefore should be treated otherwise.* I agree with you, & therefore, precisely no Lutherans do we [Catholics] burn." [emphasis added] This passage plainly means that if only the Lutherans held Bruno's teachings or beliefs, "*docere neque credere,*" they too would be burned. It also requires that Bruno was burned for his teachings and beliefs, and Schoppe specifically referred to Bruno's absurdly horrible claims as "what he teaches": "*quibus horrenda prorsus absurdissima docet.*"

Schoppe exaggerated Bruno's crimes: "In a word, whatever was affirmed by the pagan philosophers or by ancient and recent heretics, he defended it all." Finally, Schoppe concluded that therefore Bruno "perished miserably by burning, departing, I think, so that he might tell them in the other worlds, imagined, the manner in which blasphemous and impious men are usually treated by the Romans."[696]

This striking, last sentence highlights the importance of Bruno's pagan heresy of the plurality of worlds. We have seen that it appeared from the start, in Mocenigo's initial accusations against Bruno. It was reiterated by five other witnesses against him. And importantly, it was singled out as the one belief that Bruno was required to relinquish on the very first report that cites the presence of Bellarmino. It was included in the Summary of ten censures extracted from his books. It appeared again in Schoppe's eyewitness account.

Furthermore, Schoppe wrote another account. Johann Wackher was an Imperial Ambassador in Rome. He had been a patron of Bruno in Prague, in 1588. And he was a patron of Schoppe. On February 19, two days after Bruno's death, Schoppe sent a letter to Wackher, telling him:

on Thursday. . . , Giordano Bruno was adopted into the family of the

Jerome too criticized Origen for asserting "mundos esse innumerabiles." Augustine described this heresy as "Alia dicit esse innumerabiles mundos." Likewise, Praedestinatus denounced the heresy of "innumerabiles esse mundos." Echoing Valerius Maximus, both Ficino and Erasmus quoted the expression "mundos esse innumerabiles." Among various critics, the Lutheran Jacob Schegk "refuted" this belief in 1550. Among the various other expressions that were used instead, especially by philosophers, to discuss the notion of many worlds, are the following: "multos mundos," "mundos alios," "pluribus mundis," "plures esse mundos," "mundos asserit innumerabiles"; and in Italian, "innumerabili mondi," "molti mondi," "infiniti mondi," etc.
[696] Scioppii, "Epistola," p. 34, trans. Martínez.

Baron of Atoms. When the fire began, the image of the crucified Christ was offered to him to kiss it, [but] he turned away from it with a scowling face. Now, I think, he shall announce to the innumerable worlds and the Simonians how things are done in this one [world] of ours.[697]

The Simonians were a heretical Christian sect that followed Simon Magus, reputed magician who was rebuked by tmphe apostles. The Simonians were some of the earliest Gnostics. They were denounced as heretics who believed in transmigration.

I have found more evidence showing that in 1600 the Catholic Church in Rome did condemn the belief in many of worlds. First, while the Inquisitors were deliberating Bruno's final fate, Cardinal Baronio, was finishing the ninth volume of his *Ecclesiastical Annals*. That volume was published in 1600, and it discusses, among many things, how Pope Zacharias reacted against Virgilius in the year 748. Cardinal Baronio conveyed Zacharias's critique as follows:

Regarding the perverse doctrine, which he [Virgilius] has spoken against the Lord & his own soul, namely that there is † another world, and other men beneath the earth, another sun & moon, if he is convicted of confessing this: the summoned Council will deprive him of the honor of being a priest of the Church. But we also communicate with the Duke mentioned above, regarding the aforementioned Virgilius we send a letter as we have presented this, & request a thorough investigation, [and] if an error is found, [we will] condemn it in canonical decrees.[698]

On the margin of the page, Baronio added a note corresponding to the dagger or cross that he placed next to the expression "another world"—he wrote: "To doubt the Antipodes is not heresy, but to posit many worlds is

---

[697] Gaspar Schoppe to Johann Wackher, 19 February 1600, in *Giordano Bruno, Documents: Le Procès*, edited by L. Firpo and P. Segonds (Paris: Les Belles Lettres, 2000), p. 521, trans. Martínez. Other extant primary sources show that Bruno was executed on Thursday the 17th. Schoppe's letter mistakenly says that it was on Thursday the 16th.
[698] Pope Zacharias (748 CE), paraphrased by Cardinal Baronio, in Caesare Baronio, *Annales Ecclesiastici*, Vol. 9 (Rome: Typographia Vaticana, 1600), p. 191, trans. Martínez.

repugnant to divine scriptures, and therefore is proven to be a heresy."[699] Cardinal Baronio was librarian of the Vatican. He was a close colleague of Cardinal Bellarmino, and both had brought Schoppe to Rome. Baronio held a privileged position as one of the closest clergymen to Pope Clement VIII: he was the Pope's personal confessor. Moreover, in another book, Cardinal Baronio reproduced Emperor Justinian's attack against Origen, including these lines:

> Moreover, he [Origen] posits various established & constituent worlds, some past, some future. And who is so stupid, upon hearing this, who is not shocked by this uttermost impiety? Who would not abhor the insane Origen, who thus fashioned in writing such blasphemies against God? Which are forbidden to all Christians, having manifestly impious arguments, it is superfluous to dignify them with a refutation.[700]

In other works, Baronio abundantly cited the treatises against heresies by Epiphanius, Jerome, Theodoret, Augustine, and especially, Philaster.[701] All of them had denounced the heresy of innumerable worlds.

It is not surprising that Baronio and his friend Bellarmino both condemned the notion of many worlds. To do so was consonant with how both men approached the Protestant Reformation. Thus, Baronio's monumental, historical volumes on *Ecclesiastical Annals*, and Bellarmino's authoritative multi-volume *Disputations on the Controversies of the Christian Faith*, all attacked the Protestants by meticulously reviewing the long lineage of the Catholic tradition, to prove its doctrinal legitimacy since antiquity.

Next, we consider a document produced by Johann van Heck, a Catholic physician, originally from the Netherlands, who lived in Rome at the time of Bruno's execution (and subsequently, he became one of the four founders of the scientific Academy of the Lynx in Rome, in 1603). In 1600 or 1601, Heck drafted a manuscript commentary on Pliny's *Natural Histories*. Recall that Pliny had discussed, from the outset, the question of

---

[699] "...plures statuisse mundos, divina repugnat scriptura, ac proinde haeresis esse convincitur." Ibid., trans. Martínez.

[700] Baronio, *Annales Ecclesiastici*, Vol. 7 (Rome: Typographia Vaticana, 1596), p. 282

[701] Caesare Baronio, *Annales Ecclesiastici*, Vol. 1 (Rome: Typographia Vaticana, 1588), pp. 54, 183, 309, 314, 318, 363, 582-583, 612, 663, 665, 695. Baronio, *Annales Ecclesiastici*, Vol. 3 (Rome: Typographia Vaticana, 1592), pp. 51, 137, 564, 721-722, 734. Baronio, *Martyrologium Romanum* (Venice: Minimam Societatem, 1593), pp. 60, 391.

whether there exist many worlds; Pliny had written that it was "madness" to believe that there are innumerable stars and worlds. Hence, Heck too discussed "whether the world is infinite and [whether it is] one."[702] He rejected the notion that the universe is infinite, and he attributed the thesis of the plurality of worlds to several writers: Democritus, followed by "Archelaus, Metrodorus, Anaximenes, Diogenes, Leucippus, Epicurus, and some others." Heck did not specify it, but his list echoed an account by Stobaeus, ca. 425 CE.[703] Heck quoted the critical statements by Saint Albertus Magnus against the belief in many worlds. Heck added that this false belief was one also asserted by the Manicheans, who were "truly heretics." Heck did not explain this reference, but I find that the *Kitâb al Fihrist*, a history of Arabic literature ca. 987, attributes to the Manichaeans a belief in the existence of "five worlds" inhabited by devilish, lustful creatures.[704] And here is the most significant point: Heck then wrote a timely remark that echoed the outcome of Bruno's trial some months prior: "to posit a plurality of worlds is totally condemned by the Holy Roman Church."[705]

In 1603 the Index of Forbidden Books prohibited all of Bruno's works.[706] It prohibited such works for including "false doctrines, heretical, erroneous, scandalous, corrupting," and "against God."[707]

---

[702] Joannis Heckij [Joannes Heckius], "Super Plinij. ii. Historias Na[tura]les," (Archivio Linceo, Rome, manuscript 21), 11 verso, trans. Martínez. The title page seems to superimpose two dates: "Incepi die i9a, Septembris anno i600" or "i60i."

[703] Stobaeus had written that "Metrodorus [of Chios], the teacher of Epicurus," spoke of the production of the infinite, and Stobaeus then noted that "Anaximander, Anaximenes, Archelaus, Xenophanes, Diogenes [of Apollonia], Leucippus, Democritus, Epicurus, [posited] infinitely many in infinity according to the entire circuit." See Ioannis Stobaei, *Eclogarum Physicarum et Ethicarum* (Göttingen: Vandenhoek et Ruprecht, 1792), bk. 1, pp. 497-498, trans. Martínez. See also, pp. 57, 293, 491. Also, Metrodorus had reportedly argued: "It would be strange if a single ear of corn grew in a large plain or if there were only one world in the infinite," according to Simplicius, quoted in Francis Cornford, "Innumerable Worlds in Presocratic Philosophy," *Classical Quarterly*, 28 (1) (1934), 1–16 (p. 13).

[704] See also, Iain Gardner and Samuel N. C. Lieu, *Manichaean Texts from the Roman Empire* (Cambridge: Cambridge University Press, 2004), pp. 12, 16, 57, 85, 88, 199-208, 218, 221, 224. I have found an account of 1626 that reports that one of the heresies that led to Bruno's conviction was Manichaean.

[705] "...ab Ecclesia S. Romana damnatur omnino mundorum ponere pluralitatem," Heckius, "Super Plinij," 18 verso, trans. Martínez.

[706] For discussion, see Eugenio Canone, "L'Editto di Proibizione delle Opere di Bruno e Campanella," in *Bruniana & Campanelliana*, 1(1-2) (1995), 43-61.

[707] Io. Brisichellen, "Magistri Sacri Palatij," 7 August 1603, in Alexandri VII, ed., *Index Librorum Prohibitorum* (Rome: Cameræ Apostolicæ, 1664), pp. 321-322, trans. Martínez.

Which heresies mattered most in Bruno's Trial?

Having presented abundant evidence about Bruno's heresy of worlds, we should now compare it to other transgressions. I will not compare it to all of his transgressions because the witnesses against Bruno made many varied allegations against him: I count more than fifty distinct accusations, most of which were not taken up by the Inquisitors at any length. Most of those allegations were immediately and clearly denied by Bruno.[708]

For example, Mocenigo accused Bruno of saying that the Virgin Mary could not have given birth. Bruno defended himself to the Inquisitors by saying that he never spoke against the virginity of Mary, and that certainly she did conceive Jesus thanks to a miracle of the Holy Spirit.[709] No other witnesses made that accusation against him. Afterward, the Inquisitors in Venice or Rome did not accuse Bruno of this unconfirmed allegation again. For an accusation to count as a formal heresy, the Inquisitors required a confession: that the accused intentionally wished to contradict Church doctrine.[710] But Bruno said no such thing about Mary's virginity. Thus, in the present context, it is easy to see that this accusation did not matter as much as the accusation of many worlds. Without the present context, it would be easy to imagine that the accusation about the Virgin was of greater consequence than any "philosophical" or cosmological views.

Therefore, I will focus on a few accusations that have often been discussed in the literature about Bruno, in order to show how such accusations compared in importance to the heresy of many worlds.

---

[708] Thomas F. Mayer overstates Bruno's compliance: "Unlike Galileo, Bruno did not need accusers. He was perfectly happy to incriminate himself." Mayer, *The Roman Inquisition on the Stage of Italy*, p. 117. But no, Bruno's depositions show that he was very concerned with the accusations and directly denied nearly all of them; acknowledging almost only those very few that he construed as not opposing Catholicism.

[709] Mocenigo, in Firpo, *Il Proceso*, p. 279. Bruno (unspecified deposition), in Firpo, *Il Proceso*, p. 280.

[710] Beretta, "Giordano Bruno e l'Inquisizione Romana," p. 5.

	denying transubstantiation	*denying the Virgin Mary gave birth*	*denying Christ's incarnation*	*doubting the Holy Trinity*	*many worlds exist*
Was it a heresy for a Catholic?	yes	yes	yes	yes	**yes**
Was it forbidden in Rome in 1600?	–	yes	yes	yes	**yes**
Books in which Bruno said this:	–	–	–	–	**9**
Witnesses who accused Bruno of this:	3	1	–	1	**6**
Instances in which they accused him of this:	4	2	–	2	**13**
Depositions in which Bruno said this:	–	–	–	2	**4**
Was Bruno admonished for this reason?	–	–	–	–	**yes**
Did Bruno "relapse" into this heresy?	–	–	–	yes	**yes**
Was it included in the ten censures of Bruno's books?	–	–	–	–	**yes**
Included in Bruno's Final Condemnation?	yes	?	?	?	**?**
Included in Schoppe's account?	yes	yes	yes	yes	**yes**

Table 6. *This selection of accusations against Bruno clearly illustrates that the heresy of many worlds was of primary significance: in Bruno's books, in the accusations against him, and throughout his trial and condemnation. The dashes mean 'no' or 'none.'*

Table 6 compares some of the accusations against Bruno. To start, one of the accusations commonly highlighted in discussions of Bruno's trial is his alleged denial of transubstantiation. For a Catholic, it was certainly a heresy. It is easy to imagine that Catholic clergymen were offended by the claim of Protestants that, during the ceremony of the Eucharist, the bread of the host does *not* become the body of Christ. The Lutherans claimed instead that the body of Christ becomes mixed with the substance of the bread. The Calvinists argued, instead, that the transformation of bread into Christ was symbolic. Someone might nowadays imagine that Protestants were frequently burned in Rome for this. But that did not happen.

Looking at primary sources, some writers have claimed that the accusation of transubstantiation was especially important because it shows up in Bruno's final condemnation by the Inquisitors, the "Sentenzia" destined for the Governor of Rome. However, this conjecture is defective.

The first problem is that this document is a "Copia Parziale," that is, an incomplete copy of the condemnation. It omits, precisely, the list of accusations, listing only: "That you have said that it was a great blasphemy to say that the bread transubstantiates into flesh, etc., and below." This accusation was the very first accusation that Giovanni Mocenigo had raised against Bruno. The "Partial Copy" of Bruno's final sentence omits his obstinate heresies with the "etc. et infra." I suspect that the original, long list began with Mocenigo's accusations, plus others, and concluded with the last eight propositions selected from Bruno's books and trial. Indeed, the preceding sentence refers to the accusations from "eight years ago" (Mocenigo), and it is followed by a paragraph that mentions "these eight propositions," meaning clearly the ones by Bellarmino.[711]

The case against Bruno on the matter of transubstantiation was very weak. Only one credible witness, Mocenigo, had accused him of denying it, but the Inquisition needed two credible witnesses. Two others accused him of it, but they were not credible, because both were prisoners[712] (Gratianus and Silvestris; and Gratianus was merely quoting Vaia, another prisoner). Also, Bruno clearly denied having ever doubted transubstantiation, in his second, fourth, and fifth depositions in Venice.[713] Instead he affirmed it. Plus, he did not deny it in any of his books. To the Venetian Inquisitors, Bruno asserted: "I have always upheld and believed, as I hold and believe, that the transubstantiation of the bread and wine into the body and blood

---

[711] Indeed, Luigi Firpo points out that the partial document omits Mocenigo's accusations, Celestino's accusations, the censures, and Bellarmino's eight propositions; Firpo, *Il Proceso*, 99. Ingrid Rowland, however, conjectures that since the "Copia Parziale" quotes Mocenigo's first accusation against Bruno, about transubstantiation, then the eight propositions were probably all from Mocenigo's initial list. However, this cannot be, mainly because an Inquisition Decree of 24 August 1599 specifies the 1st and 7th of the eight propositions, and neither of them are in Mocenigo's accusations: "prima videlicet, ubi de haeresi Novatiana, et VII, ubi tractat an anima sit in corpore sicut nauta in navi."

[712] E.g., see Firpo, *Il Proceso*, 78.

[713] In Firpo, *Il Proceso*, 265.

of Christ is effected really and substantially, as is upheld by the Church."[714] Moreover, in the extant long summary of Bruno's depositions in Rome, transubstantiation was not even discussed.

Furthermore, Gaspar Schoppe clearly reported that Lutherans and Calvinists were *not* in any danger in Rome because the Pope had requested that they be treated with extraordinary civility and exhorted to investigate the truth. Indeed, by the 1590s the Italian Inquisitions processed relatively fewer Protestants than previously.[715] Yet both Lutherans and Calvinists denied the Catholic account of transubstantiation. They could respectfully discuss their opinions in Rome, as long as they did not cause a public spectacle. Bruno had done something worse. Schoppe ruthlessly criticized the Protestants, yet he explained that most people did not recognize that the impenitent Bruno was not "a Lutheran," he said, but something far worse: a "Monster."[716]

Bruno's unusually "horrendous" beliefs, reported by Schoppe, included: *that worlds are innumerable, souls go from body to body, souls migrate to other worlds, the world has a soul, souls can migrate into the soul of the world, one soul can shape two bodies, the world is eternal,* etc. These beliefs had been voiced by pagans and heretics yet criticized by theologians, Church Fathers, and saints. Accordingly, much of the trial proceedings against Bruno, both in Venice and Rome, discuss the pagan notions of many worlds, the soul of the world, and the transmigration of souls. The Protestants had diverged from the Catholics in the interpretation of Christian scriptures and rituals. In contradistinction, pagan beliefs constituted far greater deviations from Christianity: such as the belief in polytheism, the belief that the Resurrection of Jesus was comparable to anybody's reincarnation or transmigration, that magic could effect things similar to Christ's miracles, etc.

Concerning the Holy Trinity, again, only one witness accused Bruno about it: Mocenigo. The accusation was not even that Bruno had denied

---

[714] Still, the Inquisitors asked Bruno whether he had asserted, "that Christ was not God but a wretch." Bruno waved his arms, agitated, and replied: "I am amazed that this interrogation is brought to me, not having had any such opinions, having said no such thing, nor thought anything against that which I just said about the person of Christ, which is that I uphold that which is upheld by the holy mother Church." Bruno, Fourth Deposition, in Firpo, *Il Proceso*, p. 174, trans. Martínez.

[715] See Tedeschi, *The Prosecution of Heresy*, pp. 94-95.

[716] Scioppii, "Epistola," February 1600, in *Machiavellizatio* (1621), 34, "imò Monstra." Also in Firpo, *Il Proceso*, p. 352.

the Trinity, but merely that he had expressed doubts about it. Then, the Inquisitors asked Celestino, if Bruno had spoken about the Trinity. Celestino said yes, but did not recall any particular statement at all. In his depositions, Bruno expressed doubts about the Trinity twice, and in another deposition he just said that he had doubts about the "name" of the Trinity. Still, Bruno's beliefs about the Trinity were more offensive than he realized: they were clearly heretical. In his Third Deposition, Bruno frankly admitted that he did not understand the Catholic notion of the Trinity, or of "the Holy Spirit as a third person," that is, *except* "by following the Pythagorean way": *as the soul of the universe*. He argued that all things have life and soul.[717] He argued that such conjectures were merely philosophical. Apparently he did not know that Catholic treatises on heresies specifically condemned the belief that the Holy Spirit is the soul of the world. It was a heresy.[718] Bruno's misinterpretation of the Trinity is one of the most recurrent issues in his trial, second only to his belief in many worlds.

Since the Holy Trinity consists of God, Christ, and the Holy Spirit, some writers conflate Bruno's obstinate and heretical remarks about the Holy Spirit with his questions about Christ. But no witnesses accused Bruno of doubting that Christ was the incarnation of God. However, on five separate occasions in his depositions, Bruno himself expressed "doubts" about *how* the incarnation happened.[719] He insisted that this did not mean that he doubted Christ's incarnation at all, but only that he was curious to learn how it transpired. Wanting to know how something happened could certainly seem inappropriate or audacious, but it was not a heresy. Despite various offensive allegations and grotesque blasphemies voiced by some "witnesses," Bruno repeatedly insisted: "I have held everything that is held by the holy mother Catholic Church."[720]

Bruno's condemnation is unusual by comparison to the trials of other philosophers. Having analyzed the extant Inquisition documents of such trials, Ugo Baldini and Leen Spruit conclude: "In the majority of cases the

---

[717] Ibid., in Firpo, *Il Proceso*, p. 169, trans. Martínez.

[718] Fratris Alfonsi de Castro, *Adversus Omnes Hæreses. Libri XIIII* (Paris: Vivantium Gaultherot, 1543), bk. 5, p. 80. Sebastiani Medicis, *Summa Omnium Hæresum* (1581), pp. 134, 647, and *Summa Omnium Hæresum* (1587), Part 1, p. 62 verso. Tiberii, Deciani, *Tractatus Criminalis Omnium Hæresum*, Vol. 1 (Venice: Ioannem & Andream Zenarios, 1590), 236-237.

[719] Third Deposition and Fourth Deposition, in Firpo, *Il Proceso*, pp. 170, 172.

[720] Fourth Deposition, in Firpo, *Il Proceso*, p. 174, trans. Martínez.

trials of philosophers and scientists did not sensibly affect their later careers."[721] Most received very mild sentences and returned soon to writing or teaching, even at universities. Still, Baldini and Spruit acknowledge that such trials and censorship created a climate of terror and intimidation.

In order to find out how usual or unusual Bruno's execution was, we should compare it to other executions in Rome. The Arch-Confraternity of Saint John the Beheaded carried out the duty of accompanying all convicts to their deaths, and it kept records of such events.[722] Consider, for example, the executions carried out from 1598 until 1604.[723] During those seven years, 189 persons were executed in Rome. Table 7 conveys the numbers and methods of torture and execution.

By far, the majority of executions in Rome were by hanging. Other convicts were executed by decapitation or bludgeoning. Most convicts were executed at the Piazza di Ponte, and then their corpses were exhibited at the Sant'Angelo bridge. The death records do not specify whether bodies were quartered only after death, or whether some individuals were still alive when their bodies were torn to pieces. In any case, the rarest kind of execution was being "roasted and burned alive." It was feared as the most painful kind of punishment, inflicted for the gravest offenses.[724]

The most surprising point about the records of executions, over those years, is that only two men were killed as "heretics": Celestino and Bruno.[725]

[721] Ugo Baldini and Leen Spruit, "Catholic Church and Modern Science. Prolegomena to the Edition of Inquisition and Index Documents," in *Verbotene Bücher. Zur Geschichte des Index im 18. und 19. Jahrhundert*, edited by Hubert Wolf (Paderborn: Ferdinand Schöningh, 2008), pp. 391-426 (p. 410).

[722] "Giornale' dell'Arciconfraternita di San Giovanni Decollato (Rome), busta 8, num. 16 (5/1/1598 – 9/1/1602), Archivio di Stato di Roma. Summaries of records for the missing months and years are available in the inventory by Luigi De Santis and Giovanni Ricci Parracciani, "Nomi dei Giustiziati Assistiti negli Ultimi Momenti a dall' Archiconfraternita di S. Giovanni Decollato in Roma," 285/II (1878), also titled "Repertorio dei Giustiziati," at the Archivio di Stato di Roma.

[723] The time frame is arbitrary: I considered counting how many people were executed in Rome only during the rule of Governor Taverna, from April 1599 until June 1604. However, since Bruno was executed soon after Taverna began as governor, I expanded the scope a bit more, from January 1598 until December 1604.

[724] Christopher F. Black, *The Italian Inquisition* (New Haven: Yale University Press, 2010), p. 90.

[725] Likewise, for an even broader timeframe, from 1596 until 1606, the extant records seem to show that no other heretics were burned in Rome. And, for the twenty-year period from April 1590 until the July 1610, the city of Rome executed eleven heretics,

136	*hanged*	
24	*hanged and quartered*	*169*
8	*hanged and burned*	
1	*tortured with pincers, hanged, and quartered*	
5	*decapitated*	
2	*decapitated and quartered*	*8*
1	*decapitated and burned*	
5	*bludgeoned and quartered*	
3	*tortured with pincers, bludgeoned, quartered*	*10*
2	*pincers, bludgeoned, decapitated, and quartered*	
2	*burned alive*	*2*
	Total executions:	***189***

Table 7. *Executions in Rome: January 1, 1598 to December 31, 1604. Data gathered from records of the Arch-Confraternity of Saint John the Beheaded, at the Archivio di Stato di Roma.*

Only the two of them were burned alive. Both were executed at the Campo di Fiore.[726] Both of them were described as "heretics," both "obstinate and impenitent."[727] Bruno had asserted to the Inquisitors that many suns exist, and apparently Celestino too.

Summing up, the extant evidence shows that the heresy of many worlds was the most recurring issue in Bruno's trial. At the time, this pagan belief

apparently, four of which were burned alive: Lorenzo dell'Aglio (1590), Chuplenich Pietro di Carniola and Merse Gualtieri (1595, both burned alive), Giovanni Antonio "Celestino" (1599, burned alive), Giordano Bruno (1600, burned alive), Gio. Pietro di Tunis (1607), Antonio di Jacopo, Fortunati Aniello, Vincenti Pietro, and Uberti Marcantonio (1609), and Manfredi Fulgenzio (1610). "Giornale" dell'Arciconfraternita di San Giovanni Decollato, busta 7-8, num. 16-17, Archivio di Stato di Roma.

[726] It was common to refer to the marketplace square as the "Campo di Fiore" or "Campo di Fiori," while now it is known as the "Campo de' Fiori." From 1598 until 1604, only two men, Celestino and Bruno were burned alive at the Campo di Fiore. One other, Ottaviano Cesaroni, was hanged and then burned there, in 1603. Meanwhile, 130 were executed at Ponte, while roughly 45 others were executed in other places.

[727] "Giornale," busta 8, num. 16, pp. 69 verso, 87 verso, trans. Martínez.

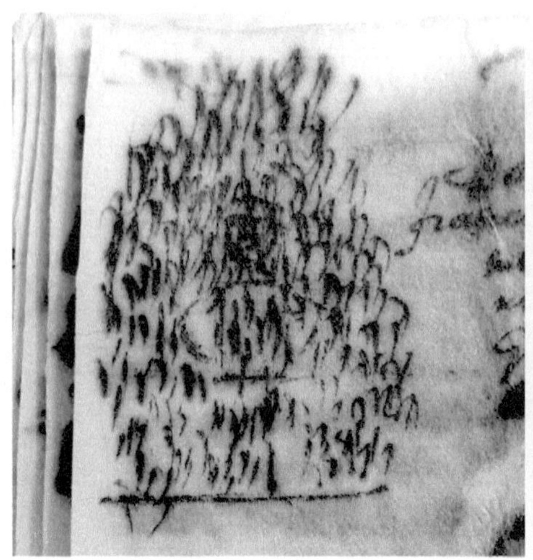

Figure 1. When Celestino (left) and Bruno (right) were burned alive, the Roman notary Giuseppe de Angelis was present, and he sketched their images, on September 16, 1599, and on February 17, 1600, respectively. *Tribunale Criminale del Governatore, Registrazioni d'Atti*, Archivio di Stato, Rome. (Photos by A. Martínez)

was more bizarre and unusual than the claims of the Protestants. This ancient heresy had been affirmed by both infamous and obscure heretics, including Origen, and some of the Gnostics, the Manichaeans, the Ametritae, and the Ophitae. It constituted an intrusion of pagan beliefs into Christianity, beliefs that had been advocated by Pythagoreans, atomists, polytheists, atheists, and others.

Even the Protestants denied the belief in many worlds. For example, Philipp Melanchthon argued that the doctrine of "innumerable worlds" was "execrable."[728] It was one of the "abhorrent pagan frenzies."[729] He condemned the doctrine of many worlds: "It is such audacity to effect monstrous detestable opinions, & which are pernicious to life, & condemned by

[728] Philipp Melanchthon, *Initia Doctrinae Physica, Dicta in Academia Vuitebergensi* (Wittenberg: Iohannem Lufft, 1549), 22 reverso. Melanchthon blamed the opinion of many worlds on Democritus, Epicurus, Archelaeus, the Stoics, and Empedocles.
[729] Melanchthon, "Preface," *In Genesim Enarrationum Reverendi Patris, Domini Doctoris Martini Luteri* (Nuremberg, 1555), p. 1. See also Iacobi Schegij (Lutheran), *Reliquos Naturalium Aristotelis Libros Commentaria Plane Philosophica* (Basel: Ioannem Harvagium, 1550), pp. 25, 547.

God, who said: *Do not bear false witness.*"[730] Melanchthon then denied repeatedly that other humans live in such other worlds. And he wrote: "For us within the Church, it is easy & necessary to assert that the world is one," partly because Christ was only one, and was born and resurrected only once. "Therefore do not imagine that many worlds exist, which is to imagine that frequently Christ dies and is resurrected, in any other world."[731]

Even decades after Bruno's death, some Catholic commentators remarked that the belief in many worlds was more offensive than the heresies of the Protestants. Consider the French scholar Gabriel Naudé. He had been a prominent librarian in Paris, until in 1629 he became the librarian for Cardinal Guidi di Bagno in Rome. In 1640, Naudé wrote a letter to the astronomer Ismaël Boulliau, in which he argued:

I'm afraid that the old theological heresies are nothing by comparison to the new ones, which the Astronomers want to introduce with their worlds, or rather the lunar and celestial Earths. Because the consequence of these will be much more perilous than the previous ones, and will introduce some very strange revolutions. God help, above all, those who would say about Lucian that what he gave us as extravagant fables, and which he professed to not exist and to not be true, that it would be verified to be the truth itself, what do you think that he would say? This reminds me of the Antipodes, which nobody could believe for some two or three hundred years without being declared a Heretic.[732]

Note that Bruno himself had said that Lucian had made the mistake of not realizing that the Moon and planets really are inhabited. Like others, Naudé thought that the belief in other worlds was a heresy. In a previous book, Naudé had complained about recent "innovators" who followed Bernardino Telesio, Bruno, and Tommaso Campanella, "who truly have no other intention but to strike this Philosophy with an elbow, & to ruin this great building that Aristotle & more than twelve thousand others who have

---

[730] Melanchthon, *Initia Doctrinae Physica*, 23 verso, trans. Martínez.

[731] Ibid., 53 verso.

[732] Gabriel Naudé to Ismaël Boulliau, 15 August 1640, in René Pintard, *Le Libertinage Érudit dans la Première Moitié du XVIIe Siècle* (Geneva: Éditions Slatkine, 2000), pp. 473-474, trans. Martínez. See also, Petrus Cazraeus to Pierre Gassendi, 3 November 1642, in Petri Gassendi, *Epistolae* [*Opera Omnia*], Vol. 6 (Lugduni: Laurentii Anisson, 1658), p. 451.

interpreted him have struggled to build over a long span of years."[733]

My present argument, that Bruno died for his cosmological beliefs, may seem surprising to us. But it was quite clear to some early commentators. In the 1680s, for example, Daniel Morhof, a German professor of history and the chief librarian at the University of Kiel, wrote an authoritative historical encyclopedia in which he included a chapter on Bruno and other "recent innovators." Morhof's first paragraph plainly stated why the Romans killed Bruno. Morhof wrote:

> Giordano Bruno, asserted a multitude of innumerable Worlds & Suns, and he paid for this opinion by being burned alive. A plurality of Worlds, and Moons, other Planets, homogeneous to the Earth, was defended before him by Nic. of Cusa & Nic. Copernicus, and after him by Galileo Galilei (forced to voice a Recantation), Johannes Kepler, Athan. Kircher, Tomm. Campanella, and other mathematicians.[734]

Also, while discussing the followers of Epicurus, Morhof noted again and again that Bruno was burned for his belief in other worlds, "although there are not lacking some who think that he was executed for some other reason."[735] After summarizing Bruno's opinion that many worlds exist, Morhof immediately reiterated: "this miserable man [Bruno] paid for his audacious opinion by burning alive; which greatly injured that belief; for it made his writings become suspected of the crime of Atheism."[736]

In a book of 1705, a German librarian and theologian, Johann Albert Fabricius, also discussed the claim that the Moon and the stars are inhabited. He said that Orpheus was the first to assert this belief, followed by the Pythagoreans and others. Fabricius noted that Philaster, Augustine, and Praedestinatus declared that this belief was a heresy, and he added that, "in the [Corpus of] Canon Law, Cause 24, question 3, column 39, it is ascribed as a heresy, the *Ophic* heresy which some write as *Orphic*." Fabricius added

---

[733] Gabriel Naudé, *Apologie pour Tous les Grands Personnages qui Ont Esté Faussement Soupçonnez* (Targa, 1625); Second ed. (La Haye: Adrian Vlac, 1653), 331, trans. Martínez.

[734] Dan. Georgi Morhofi, *Polyhistoris Continuatio, Tomum Philosophicum & Practicum*, ed. Johanne Möllero (Lubecæ: Petri Böckmanni, 1708), 239, trans. Martínez. Morhof lived from 1639 to 1691; this volume was published posthumously. His *Polyhistor* volumes grew from lectures he gave at the University of Kiel around 1666.

[735] Ibid., p. 26; see also pp. 303, 343.

[736] Ibid., p. 260, see also p. 303.

that Praedestinatus "called this the heresy of the *Ametritarum*, namely that which to an infinite power attributes infinite effects, introducing infinite worlds. The same was taught by the Manicheans, about which see Archelaeus with Epiphanius, Vol. 1, p. 645."[737]

Immediately, Johann Fabricius listed the "recent writers who in some sense said that the stars are inhabited," namely: "Nicolas of Cusa, the miserable Giordano Bruno, Tycho Brahe, Tommaso Campanella, William Gilbert, René Descartes, and those who follow him, and Johannes Kepler, Galileo Galilei, and David Fabricius, those who with their own eyes have dared to see the inhabitants of the Moon..." About Bruno, he added a footnote: "Burned in Rome on 9 February Year 1600. His teachings were first expounded in his eight books on the innumerable, the immense & shapeless or the universe & the worlds."[738]

The trial of Giordano Bruno is one of the most infamous events in the volatile and contested borders between science and religion. The Roman Inquisition succeeded in nearly obliterating the memory of Bruno's martyrdom. Centuries after Bruno's execution, some writers doubted and denied that the Inquisition prosecuted or killed him. They argued that it was a myth. When Schoppe's account was finally noticed, some scholars then argued that it was fake.[739] When discoveries of multiple documents clearly confirmed the accuracy of Schoppe's account, historians still conjectured that Bruno was not executed for his cosmological beliefs. Even today, some people who have never read even one of Bruno's books nonetheless dismiss him as a foolish and "pre-modern" nonscientist who perhaps deserved to die, because, after all, he had been criticized and excommunicated by Catholics, Lutherans, and Calvinists. If many disliked him, shouldn't we dislike him too?

Despite the frequency with which recent writers have disdained Bruno

---

[737] Jo. Alberti Fabricii, *Bibliotheca Græca* (Hamburg: Christiani Liebezeit, 1705), bk. 1, chap. 20, pp. 132-133, trans. Martínez.

[738] Ibid., p. 133.

[739] For example, in 1803, Niccolò Haym claimed that only "a portrait" of Bruno had been burned. Niccolò Haym, *Biblioteca Italian, o sia Notizia dei Libri Rari nella Lingua Italiani* (Milan, 1803), 184. In 1885 a professor of philosophy at Versailles, Théophile Desdouits, argued that the claim that the Inquisition burned Bruno was "a legend." He argued that Schoppe's letter was not authentic, and that Schoppe was not its author. Desdouits concluded: "Absolutely nothing proves that Giordano Bruno was burned in Rome." Théophile Desdouits, *La Légende Tragique de Jordano Bruno* (Paris: Ernest Thorin, 1885), pp. 8-24, trans. Martínez.

as an occultist or a hermeticist, he instead described himself proudly as "a philosopher." And he told the Venetian Inquisition that his books included beliefs that should have been attributed to God and the Christian faith, but that instead he had not proceeded entirely as a good Christian, because "I founded my doctrine upon sense and reason, and not upon faith."

Unlike Galileo, Bruno has been repeatedly belittled as being neither a scientist nor a martyr for cosmology.[740] Nevertheless, for decades, specialists on Bruno have increasingly acknowledged that his belief in many worlds was an important factor in his trial, owing to the growing evidence. Now, having shown the severity of the accusation of many worlds — that it was a *heresy* denounced by bishops, saints, Church Fathers, Popes, Inquisitors, and the Corpus of Canon Law — it is clear that Bruno indeed was a martyr for cosmology. The alleged myth is not a myth after all.

Still, the conflict between Bruno and the Inquisition can hardly be described as a conflict between science and religion. Instead, recent historians have recognized that it is better to describe it as a conflict between philosophy and religion.[741] There were certainly substantial conflicts between Catholic doctrine and Bruno's philosophy. Yet the question was: Why?

Why did the Roman Inquisition concern itself with philosophy or science at a time when it was busy responding to a plethora of Protestant heresies? The present analysis reveals a neglected dimension: some of Bruno's main heresies were directly rooted in ancient *pagan religious beliefs* and their interpretations in the Renaissance. Seemingly scientific notions, such as the Earth's motion, were linked to Pythagorean ideas such as that the Earth has a soul. The idea that there are many worlds like Earth was linked to the Pythagorean belief that the beings living in such worlds can embody the souls of persons who previously lived on Earth.

The Catholics who denounced, feared and hated the Christian reforms of Luther and Calvin, likewise rejected Bruno's more eccentric efforts to interpret Biblical scriptures and Catholic doctrines on the basis of pagan beliefs. The Venetian and Roman Inquisitions' reaction against the cosmology of many worlds was not merely provoked by a growing sensitivity

---

[740] For example, Hans Blumenberg, "Not a Martyr for Copernicanism: Giordano Bruno," in his *The Genesis of the Copernican World* (Cambridge: MIT Press, 1987), Chapter 5, (p. 366).
[741] Finocchiaro, "Philosophy versus Religion," pp. 81-82; Beretta, "Orthodoxie Philosophique et Inquisition," pp. 88-94.

against the Protestants. It was also a continuation of a much older tradition whereby Christians had worked to suppress pagan religious beliefs for over a thousand years. Therefore, the Romans finally gagged Bruno and burned him alive.

5

The Soul of the World

We can plunge into a series of obscure considerations, and the lineage of ideas that led from pagan beliefs to astronomical heresies in the Renaissance: from the ancient belief *that the Earth has a soul*, to the thesis denied and condemned by the Roman Inquisition, *that the Earth moves*. But before reviewing this tangle of thorns, I think it's good to give a brief overview of the story, and to explain why it matters. So let's do that first.

Before Galileo did anything in astronomy, the Italian philosopher Giordano Bruno argued that the Earth moves around the Sun. Bruno believed that the Earth is a living being, with a soul. Yet these were unusual beliefs for a Christian.

In 1592, Bruno was captured by the Inquisition in Venice and imprisoned. The next year he was transferred to the Inquisition's prison in Rome. After seven and a half years of interrogations, he was finally condemned to what was widely feared as the worst kind of punishment: he was gagged, taken to a public place, tied to a post, and burned alive. Historians are quick to point out that Bruno was not killed for his belief in the Earth's motion, but for heretical religious beliefs.

For years I investigated this story and what I found really surprised me. It turns out that Giordano Bruno's belief in the moving Earth was directly connected to some of his beliefs that were heretical. To Catholics, heresies were willful departures from Catholic dogma. Heresies were the worst kinds of crimes, worse than murder. Heresies were crimes against God.

Bruno's final condemnation by the Inquisition exists only in a partial copy, prepared for the Governor of Rome. Unfortunately, it omits the list of accusations against Bruno, that is, his alleged heresies. But there is some good evidence of what they were. On February 8, 1600, the Roman Inquisition condemned Bruno at the palace of the "Supreme Inquisitor," Cardinal Ludovico Madruzzi. On that day, one of the witnesses present was a young German humanist, Gaspar Schoppe, a guest living at Cardinal Madruzzi's palace. Days later, Schoppe also witnessed Bruno's execution at a public marketplace, an open intersection of city streets in Rome known as the Campo de' Fiori: the "Field of Flowers."

The day Bruno was burned, Schoppe wrote a detailed letter to a friend explaining what had just happened. Schoppe complained that ordinary people in Rome were saying that a Lutheran was burned. But Schoppe explained that that was not true at all. Bruno wasn't a Lutheran, but something far worse—a "monster." Schoppe wrote: "Perhaps I too would believe the vulgar rumors that Bruno was burned for Lutheranism, but I was present at the Holy Office of the Inquisition when the sentence against him was pronounced, & so I know what heresy he professed."

Schoppe listed twelve of Bruno's "the completely horrendous most absurd things that he teaches." I quote just the first and fifth:

(1) "Worlds are innumerable,"…

(5) "the Holy Spirit is nothing other than the soul of the world,"…
Schoppe commented: "perhaps you might add: the Lutherans neither teach nor believe such things, and therefore should be treated otherwise. I agree with you, & therefore, precisely no Lutherans do we [Catholics] burn." This means that if the Lutherans held these teachings or beliefs, *docere neque credere*, they would be burned. It also means that Bruno was burned for these teachings and beliefs.

The two accusations above recur throughout Bruno's trial, from its beginning to the end. It turns out that both were directly connected to Bruno's conviction that the Earth moves. And most importantly, surprisingly, I found that these beliefs were heresies.

First, Bruno had said in nine books that many worlds exist: not just the Earth, but the Moon, the planets and the stars: "innumerably many worlds." Apparently he didn't know it was a heresy to claim that "innumerably many worlds exist." This belief had been denounced as a heresy by many authorities including Saint Philaster, Saint Jerome, Saint Augustine, and Pope Gregory XIII. Catholics were horrified by this idea, because if many worlds exist then Jesus Christ would have to be born and crucified in each of those worlds to offer salvation to the beings in such worlds.

Second, Bruno said that the Earth has a soul. In twelve of his books he repeatedly asserted that the world has a soul, the Earth has a soul, or the universe has a spirit. According to Bruno, the Earth was alive, an animal. Just as our bodies are made from matter, from bits of the Earth, so too he said that our individual souls come from soul of the Earth. Yet this belief that heavenly bodies are animated had been declared heretical by the Fifth Ecumenical Council in the year 553. Similarly, in 1277, Bishop Etienne Tempier in Paris had condemned as a heresy the belief that the heavenly bodies are animated, like animals. This was viewed as a belief of ancient pagans, not Christians.

When Bruno was interrogated by Inquisitors, he said that the Holy Spirit is the soul of the world. Apparently he didn't know that in 1141 the Council of Sens had condemned as heretical the claim that "the Holy Spirit is the soul of the world."

Books on heresies echoed this statement. For example, in 1590, Tiberio Deciani published a *Criminal Treatise on All Heresies*, in Venice, including the heresy that the Holy Spirit is the soul of the world. Yet Bruno said that to the Inquisitors in Venice when he was interrogated in 1592. And Bruno repeated it to the Roman Inquisitors; he "relapsed" into this heresy. Anyone who relapsed into a heresy, after being instructed to abandon it, was a proven to be an obstinate heretic.

So these heresies about many worlds and about the universal soul were linked to Bruno's conviction that the Earth moves. It moves because it's a heavenly body. It moves because it has a soul.

Still, is there any direct evidence that the Inquisitors were aware, concerned, or annoyed, specifically, by Bruno's claim, in three books, that the Earth moves around the Sun?

Yes. By 1597, theologians working for the Roman Inquisition had extracted ten propositions from Bruno's books. The propositions were censured and Bruno had to recant. Two were about the "world soul" or "universal spirit." One was about the planets being animated. One was about the existence of many worlds. And yes—Bruno's fifth censured proposition was: "About the Earth's motion."

This all means that Bruno's belief in a moving Earth was part of the heretical worldview that he advocated both in his books and in his trial. His ideas about many worlds and about the soul of the world convinced him that Copernicus was right: the Earth moves. Those same ideas about worlds and souls led Bruno to his death, in 1600.

Sixteen years later, in 1616, when Galileo first got in trouble with the Inquisition in Rome, four of the same Inquisitors and Consultors from Bruno's trial also met with Galileo. One of them was now the head of the Inquisition. Another one was now the head of the Index of Forbidden Books. And another was now the Pope.

Yet Galileo was more cautious than Bruno.

Galileo denied that the Moon was another world, even though he discovered—he saw with a telescope—that the Moon has mountains and valleys. Bruno had actually predicted that, whereas Copernicus had not. Galileo didn't say that "innumerably many worlds exist," though he proudly wrote that he had discovered "innumerably many stars." Bruno, not Copernicus, had predicted that too. Galileo discovered moons around Jupiter. And again, Bruno had predicted that some planets have moons, like the Earth, while Copernicus had not.

In 1615, Galileo wrote a letter to a friend, Benedetto Castelli, in which Galileo argued that the Earth's motion is compatible with the Bible. Several passages in the Bible seem to say that the Sun moves but the Earth does not, for example:

> Ecclesiastes 1:5: The Sun rises and the Sun goes down, and hastens to the place where it rises.

> Psalm 93:1 (Latin Vulgate 92:1): …the world [or orb] is established; it shall not be moved.

> Psalm 104:5 (Latin Vulgate 103:5): …[God] established the Earth on its foundations, it cannot be moved forever and ever.

> Joshua 10:12-13: Then spoke Joshua to the Lord in the day when the Lord gave the Amorites over to the men of Israel; and he said in the sight of Israel, "Sun, stand thou still at Gibeon, and thou Moon in the valley of Aijalon." And the Sun stood still, and the Moon stayed, until the nation took vengeance on their enemies.

Galileo argued that such passages do not necessarily mean what they seem to say. But in doing so, Galileo was inadvertently violating Catholic rules on the interpretation of Scriptures. Giordano Bruno had committed the same indiscretion. Since they were not designated representatives of the Church, they could hardly claim the right to make sense of the Bible against its canonical interpretation. Yet handwritten copies of Galileo's letter to Castelli soon circulated in Florence.

1584	Bruno	*De la Causa, Principio et Uno*
1591	Bruno	*De Triplici Minimo et Mensura*
1591	Campanella	*Philosophia Sensibus Demonstrata*
1590s	Bruno	manuscripts
1592	Bruno	3rd deposition to the Venetian Inquisition
1593	Bruno	14th deposition to the Roman Inquisition
1596	Bruno	17th deposition to the Roman Inquisition
1600	Gilbert	*De Magnete, ... et de Magno Magnete Tellure*
1606	Kepler	*De Stella Nova in Pede Serpentarii*
1615	Galilei	"Lettera a Piero Dini"
1615	Galilei	"Lettera a Madama Cristina"
1620	Campanella	*De Sensu Rerum et Magia*
1620	Kepler	*Epitome Astronomiae Copernicanae, Liber IV*
1622	Kepler	*Pro Suo Opere Harmonices Mundi Apologia*
1630	Lansberge	*Commentationes in Motum Terræ*

Table 8. *Copernicans who affirmed the existence of a Soul of the World or a Living Earth, including when they made such cl.*

Soon, Galileo was discussing his views with Inquisitors. He did not tell the Inquisitors about any soul or universal spirit that moves the Earth either. But in two private letters, in 1615, as we will see, he guardedly admitted that he believed that the Sun can be described as the soul of the world and that it transmits a spirit throughout the universe, a spirit that gives life and movement to all things. Even the Earth?

After meeting with the Inquisitors in Rome, Galileo never again wrote about the universal spirit that vivifies and moves all things. We don't even know if the Inquisitors knew that, in private, secretly, quietly, Galileo too entertained such ideas.

Bruno was not killed for his belief in the Earth's motion. But this belief was directly linked to key heresies that led to his execution. The trial of Bruno was in the background of Galileo's troubles with the Inquisition. Galileo lived in the haunting shadow of the burning man.

A Spirit
moves the Earth

Surprisingly, the notion of the soul of the world is of critical importance. It connects the ancient Pythagorean beliefs to neo-Platonist interpretations of the Copernican theory. It helped lead to the conviction of heresy of Peter Abelard. It was categorized as a heresy by Alfonso de Castro. It was advocated by Bruno, and even seems to be the meaning of the "Novatian heresy" that he refused to recant. It was also advocated by Cornelius Gemma, William Gilbert, and Johannes Kepler. It was criticized by the Dominican preacher Augustino Petreto as well as the Jesuit Cardinal Roberto Bellarmino.[742] Therefore, we should investigate its roots.

Bruno, Gemma, and Kepler all linked the idea of the soul of the world to Virgil's *Aeneid*, and to one line in particular: *Spirit nourishes within*. I have tried to find who was the earliest Christian writer who, like them, linked book 6 of Virgil's *Aeneid* to claims about Pythagoras' notion of God. To date, the earliest such writer I have found is Lucius Lactantius. In his Christian tract on "The False Religion," around 312 CE, Lactantius spoke approvingly but cautiously of Virgil Maro as someone who came close to understanding some truth about God. Lactantius noted that Virgil referred to God as "Spirit," and then he quoted Virgil's lines from the *Aeneid*:

> First the sky, and lands, watery plains
> shining globe of the Moon Titanic star,
> the spirit nourishes within the totality infused through the limbs
> mind agitates the mass, and mingles with the great body.[743]

These were the exact lines quoted by Bruno to the Venetian Inquisition! Lactantius then added that if anyone were ignorant about the identity of

---

[742] For discussions on Gilbert, Gemma, Petreto, Bellarmino, see Martínez, *Burned Alive*, pp. 101-103, 108, 144-45, 223-226.

[743] Virgil's *Aeneid*, quoted in Lucius Lactantius, "De Falsa Religione," bk. 1 of *Divinarum Institutionum*, reissued in Lucii Coelii Lactantii, *Opera quae Extant, ad Fidem MSS. Recognita et Commentariis Illustrata*, ed. Tho. Spark (Oxford: Theatro Sheldoniano, 1684), p. 17, trans. Martínez.

this great Spirit that has so much power, Virgil himself had clarified it in another work, saying:

. . . . . . for God permeates all
lands and tracts of the sea, the depth of heaven.
Hence the cattle, herds, men, every kind of beasts,
each so faint at birth, receive their lives from him.[744]

Yet Lactantius noted that Virgil, like Ovid and Orpheus, had not quite learned the full truth because they had not always followed the guidance of nature. He did not explain this remark, but we might well recall that book 6 of the *Aeneid* describes the soul of the world and the transmigration of souls, which were not Christian beliefs.

Then, noting that poets were not as authoritative as philosophers, Lactantius promptly discussed the Greek philosophers' views of God. He then said that "Pythagoras thus defined God: a Soul that pervades universally by all parts of the world, and diffused; from which all that are born, animals receive their life."[745] His words paraphrase the account given in Cicero's *On the Nature of the Gods*, but adding the word 'animals.' Lactantius did not dwell on this account, he just proceeded to convey views of other Greek philosophers; but nonetheless, the similarity is evident between the views attributed to Pythagoras and Virgil in these specific passages. By 402 CE, Saint Jerome linked Pythagoras and Virgil's sixth in just two sentences about the immortality and transmigrations of souls: "among the Greeks Pythagoras was the first to find: that the soul is immortal, and transits from some bodies into others. That which Virgil followed in the sixth volume of the *Aeneid*."[746]

There are two earlier Christian writers who also referred to Pythagoras as having taught that God somehow infuses and animates everything. In

[744] Ibid. This passage is from Virgil's *Georgics* (ca. 30 BCE), bk. 4. Even in 1613, the the very same passages in Virgil's *Aeneid* and his *Georgics* were quoted to illustrate the "Pythagorean opinion" that God is the soul of the world; see Ioannis Ludovici Vivis, Commentary on bk 8, chap. 5 of Augustine's *City of God*, in Augustini, *De Civitate Dei, Libri XXII*, with Commentaries by Leonardi Coquaei and Ioa. Lud. Vivis (Paris: n.p., 1613), column 1660.

[745] Ibid., p. 18.

[746] Jerome, *Ad Pammachium et Marcellinum Apologia Hieronymi Adversum Ruffinum* (402 CE), bk. III, in Sancti Hieronymi Stridoniensis, *Opera Omnia*, (1624), p. 537.

his "Exhortation to the Greeks or Gentiles," around 150 CE, Justin Martyr described the Greek philosophers' views of God. And Justin gave a quotation allegedly by Pythagoras himself:

> [Pythagoras said:] "It is true that God is one: but he is not, as some have suspected, an adornment outside the world, but he is infused in everything, in the whole circle of generations he sees everyone, in all ages he is the regulator, artificer of all his virtues and works, the first principle of all, the one light of heaven and parent of all, universal mind and soul [*animatio*], the motion of all the circles."[747]

But Justin did not refer to Virgil's *Aeneid*. A few decades later, around 195 CE, Clement of Alexandria gave the same quotation about God being infused in everything as the soul or animation of all things, but he attributed it to "the Pythagoreans," not explicitly to Pythagoras himself.[748]

The notions linked by Lactantius eventually developed into sophisticated and more appreciative accounts, especially as advocated by Bruno, and before him, by the humanist and astrologer Marsilio Ficino.

In the 1480s, Ficino too discussed the ancient notion of the soul of the world. From 1484 until 1490, Ficino produced a Latin translation of the *Enneads* of Plotinus, with commentaries, which was finally published in 1492, in Florence. Previously, the works of Plotinus has been unavailable since late antiquity. But he had been an influential philosopher, and was Porphyry's teacher. Plotinus had argued that the "Soul of the World" has a "vital and sensual breath" that infuses all things and beings in the world. Hence Ficino described the World Soul as a body or being that "vivifies" beings everywhere, and he too quoted the poetic line *Spirit nourishes within*—explaining that this knowledge had been acquired by Iarchas and Apollonius of Tyana.[749]

---

[747] Justin Martyr, "Ad Graecos sive Gentiles Cohortatoria Oratio" (ca. 150 CE), in Iustini, *Operum, quae Extant, Omnium*, Vol. 3, ed, and trans. from the Greek by Ioannem Langum, (Basel: Ambrosium et Aurelium, 1565) p. 58, trans. Martínez.

[748] Clement of Alexandria, *Protrepticus* (ca. 195 CE), trans. as *Exhortation to the Heathen*, in Alexander Roberts and James Donaldson, eds., *Ante-Nicene Christian Library*, Vol. 4: *Clement of Alexandria*, trans. William Wilson (Edinburgh: T. & T. Clark, 1884), chap. 6, p. 72.

[749] Marsilii Ficini, *Librum Tertium de Vita Coelitus Comparanda* [1489], *compositus ab eodem inter Commentaria eiusdem in Plotinum* 1490], in Marsilii Ficini, *Opera & quae Hactenus Extitére*, Vol. 1 (Basileae: Henricum Petri, 1561), bk. 3, p. 535.

Here Ficino did not specify who had written the brief phrase, *Spirit nourishes within*, but in a similar passage in another work, he clearly referred to the *Aeneid*:

[Virgil] Maro in a Platonist way seems to judge rightly. When he said: "Spirit nourishes all from within": that the spirit in itself disperses & rules fortuitous nature with stable ordinances, adding: "the totality infused by the frame, mind agitates the mass." And by mentioning 'the frame,' and 'limbs,' one signifies that the world is an animal, one in which spirit lives everywhere, one rightly likewise intelligent.[750]

Thus Ficino associated the spirit in the *Aeneid* with the universal breath of life in the works of Plotinus.[751] Plotinus had asked souls to "remember" that the great World Soul is the author of all living things, as it breathed life into them all; it made the Sun, ordered the heavens and drives its motions.[752] Plotinus also claimed that human souls come from the stars.[753]

Furthermore, like the mythical Indian sage Iarchas who allegedly taught Apollonius the Pythagorean, Ficino too believed that the Earth is an animal, as he insisted: "And that is the greatest, the world in itself is an animal, more than any other animal, only as it is the most perfect animal."[754] He argued that "in order that this world would be absolutely similar to an animal, from given that it would be the only one, thus neither two nor innumerably many are begotten, but only one world parentage, which was made and will be.

---

[750] Marsilii Ficini, *In Plotini Epitomae, seu Argumenta, Commentaris & Annotationes* [1490], in Ficini, *Operum* [*Opera*]: *in quo compraehenduntur ea, quae ex Graeco in Latinum Sermonem doctrissime transtulit, exceptis Platone atque Plotino Philosophis*, Vol. 2 (Basileae: Henricum Petri, 1561): "In Librum De Coelo [Plotinus], Comment. Summa Totius Libri," p. 1597; trans. Martínez.

[751] Ficino was thus subtly subverting the original meaning of Plotinus, because the idea that the World Soul, as a substance, infuses everything is alien and contradictory to the views of Plotinus, as he required that it was not possible for one body of any kind to totally permeate another body; for discussion, see Riccardo Chiaradonna, "Voce 'Plotino' in Tommaso Campanella," *Bruniana e Campanelliana*, 14, no. 2 (Pisa: Fabrizio Serra, 2008), p. 524.

[752] Plotinus, *The Fifth Ennead*, First Treatise, Sec. 2.

[753] Plotinus, *The Second Ennead*, Third Treatise, Sec. 9.

[754] Ficini, *Vita Coelitus Comparanda*, in *Opera*, Vol. 1 (1561), bk. 3, p. 533; trans. Martínez.

But listen to Timaeus the Pythagorean, who was Plato's teacher…"[755] In Plato's *Timaeus*, the protagonist said: "the world became a living creature truly endowed with soul and intelligence by the providence of God," because God wanted to create the most perfect beings.[756]

Ficino and Bruno were also influenced by Hermetic notions that matter nourishes bodies while spirit nourishes souls. Hermes Trismegistus was the alleged and mythical author of the *Corpus Hermeticum*: ancient Greek or Egyptian works on spiritual wisdom and alchemy. Marsilio Ficino translated many of those works into Latin by 1463. However, the most influential work was already available in Latin since late Antiquity: *Asclepius*, a dialogue between Hermes Trismegistus and his disciple Asclepius. Lactantius and Augustine cited this work. Some of the teachings discussed in *Asclepius* match some of the notions developed later by Ficino and Bruno: that God infused all primal matter with spirit, which nourishes souls, and that the world is eternal. For example, Hermes claims: "But the Spirit agitates or governs all species in the world, as distributed from God to each of them according to their natures. . . . Therefore the world nourishes bodies, spirits, and souls."[757]

Note, however, that some other translators of the same passage, from Greek into Latin, used the word *vivificatur* instead of *gubernatur*: "the Spirit agitates or vivifies all species in the world."[758] One such writer was Agostino Steuco, in 1540, who seems particularly significant because some of his arguments are similar to those of Bruno. That is, Bruno seems to echo or respond to Steuco more than Ficino, though he did not quote Steuco, as far as I know. Ficino had attributed the notions of the soul of the world and that the world is an animal to Apollonius of Tyana and "Timaeus the Pythagorean." As far as I know, however, Ficino stopped short of attributing those notions to Pythagoras himself. He also did not interpret the

[755] Marsilius Ficinus to Ioanni Cavalcanti, 30 March 1474, in Marsilii Ficini, *Epistolarum*, Liber 1, in Ficini, *Opera*, Vol. 1 (1561), p. 630; trans. Martínez.

[756] Plato, *Timaeus* (ca. 360 BCE), in *The Dialogues of Plato*, trans. Benjamin Jowett, Vol. 2 (Oxford: Clarendon Press, 1871), paragraphs 30-31, pp. 525-526, translation modified slightly.

[757] See *Asclepius Hermetis Trismegisti Dialogus ab Apuleio Madaurense Platonico, in Latinum Conversus*, reissued in Francisci Patricii, *Nova de Universis Philosophia* (Ferrariae: Benedictum Mammarellum, 1591), p. 3, trans. Martínez.

[758] Augustini Steuchi, *De Perenni Philosophia Libri X* (Lugduni: Gryphius Excudebat, 1540), p. 87; reissued in Steuchi, *Opera Omnia*, Vol. 3 (Dominicum Nicolinum, 1591), p. 31.

soul of the world as the Holy Spirit. Yet these notions appear in the subsequent works of Agostino Steuco, a few decades before being voiced by Bruno.

Steuco was a librarian in a monastery in Venice, and he was a critic of Luther and Erasmus. Steuco became a Bishop in 1538, and also librarian of the Papal collection of manuscripts and books in the Vatican. In 1540, he published a book titled: *On the Perennial Philosophy*, analyzing to what extent the famous ancient philosophers had grasped true, sacred knowledge in accordance with Christianity. For example, Steuco discussed views on the immortality of the soul, such as by Plotinus. He discussed the "error" of thinking that souls fall from the heavens. He discussed Plato's claim, in the *Timaeus*, that stars have souls. Steuco also discussed: "Whether the statement is true: that particulars [souls] return to the soul of the universe. This mystery is perversely misunderstood by recent philosophers. What do Sacred Scriptures say about it? About which Plato and Pythagoras say that souls return to God."[759] Steuco also analyzed the question of whether there exist "many worlds, or innumerably many," and whether "innumerable stars exist." But he concluded that although God is eternal, the world is not eternal, all infinities are absurd, and "God did not make many worlds, nor many Suns, nor moons, nor Earths."[760]

In addition to these "errors," Steuco discussed whether the "soul of the universe" is God. Steuco noted that in an ancient commentary on the *Timaeus*, Calcidius had said that what Platonic poets called the soul of the world is what the Christians called the Holy Spirit. Steuco quoted Calcidius: "Plato calls it the Soul of the world, and the Soul of the world is called the Spirit that vegetates and rules the world. Of which the Poet says: *First the sky, and lands*. Until *Spirit nourishes within*. Of Him too, the Apostle says, *In whom we live, move, & are*."[761] With the latter phrase, Calcidius was quoting the Acts of the Apostles, 17:28. Calcidius finished his translation and commentary on the *Timaeus* at around 321 CE. It became the only extensive text of Plato known to scholars in the Latin West, for about 800 years.[762]

---

[759] Steuchi, *De Perenni Philosophia Libri X* (1540), p. [vii], trans. Martínez.
[760] Ibid., pp. 289-290, 301, 306, trans. Martínez.
[761] Ibid., p. 88, trans. Martínez, italics added to designate quotations.
[762] Edward Grant, *Science and Religion, 400 B.C. to A.D. 1550* (Westport: Greenwood Publishing Group, 2004), pp. 93-94.

In itself, the slight similarity between the *Aeneid* and the Bible seemed worthy of discussion, but Steuco did not mention that, recently, in 1534, the Franciscan theologian Alfonso de Castro had categorized the claim that the soul of the world is the Holy Spirit as a heresy, in his *Fourteen Books Against All Heresies*. Steuco then said that Pythagoras had learned about this *Spirit* from the Egyptians but had "construed it to be a Soul, which pervades all natural things, and of which our souls are fragments."[763] Here he explicitly quoted Cicero's claim about Pythagoras, in *Nature of the Gods*. Steuco had also read the works of Lactantius. Next, Steuco also attributed the notion of the soul of the world to Plotinus. As a humanist, Steuco tried to harmonize ancient wisdom and Catholic beliefs. Hence he did not strongly favor the Pythagorean notions but he viewed them in a positive light, where feasible. Steuco said that God is present everywhere, "as Pythagoras said is necessary, and thus he sounded:

Spirit nourishes within, the totality infused through the limbs,
Mind agitates the mass, & mingles with the great body."[764]

Thus Steuco attributed these lines to both Virgil *and Pythagoras!* Fifty years later, Bruno did the same thing.[765]

As for Kepler, he specifically cited yet another author: "Scaliger." He did not specify the first name, but in his writings Kepler sometimes made references to Julius Caesar Scaliger and to Joseph Justus Scaliger. The former, Julius Caesar Scaliger had indeed elaborated upon Aristotle's discussion *On the Generation of Animals*, to the effect that heat generates living things, such as plants and animacules; especially the Sun's heat, all of which "leads the soul into the hidden mysteries of Nature."[766]

Still, the search for Kepler's reference to a particular Scaliger led me to another: Paul Skalich, or "Scaliger," a humanist and encyclopedist born in Croatia but who had lived throughout Europe. In a commentary on astronomy, in 1570, Scaliger discussed various ancient notions, including the soul

---

[763] Steuchi, *De Perenni Philosophia Libri X* (1540), p. 167, see also pp. 198, 246.

[764] Steuchi, *De Perenni Philosophia Libri X* (1540), p. see also p. 198.

[765] I have not yet found evidence of whether Bruno actually read Steuco's *De Perenii*.

[766] Iulii Caesaris Scaligeri, *Exotericarum Exercitationum Liber Quintus Decimus, de Subtilitate, ad Hieronymum Cardanum* (Lutetiae: Michaelis Vascosani, 1557), Exercitatio 26, pp. 50 reverso to 51 reverso. See also Aristotle, *On the Generation of Animals*, bk. 3, chap. 11, in Aristoteles, [*Opera*] *Latine Interpretibus Variis*, Vol. 3 (Berolini: Georgium Reimerum, 1831), p. 372.

of the world. Scaliger praised Pythagoras, Moses, and Orpheus for penetrating into the secrets of philosophy, and he then declared: "In Ancient Theology, this is the supremely good father; the mind of the son & the artificer; the Spirit is truly called the soul of the world; as accordingly the poet said: *Spirit nourishes within, the totality infused through the limbs, Mind agitates the mass, & mingles with the great body.*"[767]

Scaliger said that Virgil, Asclepius, and the Bible all confirmed that the soul of the world is the same as "the Spirit of God." He therefore quoted Psalm 103:30 in the Vulgate Bible: "You send forth your spirit, and create them, and renew the face of the Earth," as if it gave evidence for his argument. He also quoted Mercurius (Hermes) in his "sermon" to Asclepius, paraphrasing that "Spirit agitates & vivifies all Species in the world; then the Spirit fills all. Again, the World nourishes bodies; the Spirit [nourishes] souls. And the Spirit administrates all & vegetates in the world..."[768] This particular Scaliger is interesting for the explicit way in which he interconnected the seemingly converging notions from Orpheus, the Bible, the *Aeneid*, and the Hermetic *Asclepius*. Moreover, like Ficino, this Scaliger used such notions to try to explain the phrase in Genesis "the spirit of God hovered over the waters," as a process in which the Holy Spirit animated all living beings. He argued: "In this way generation was produced: the heat of the Holy Spirit was confused with the bodies in heaven & Earth, heating them & animating them, the waters too, flowing as the dispositions of matter, and really as the causal agent, & existing as the organ of the divine art, it moves."[769]

Like Ficino and Scaliger, years later Giordano Bruno too tried to explain "the spirit of God" hovering over the waters, or "nourishing" them, as he said. Bruno tried to further validate the ancient pagan notions by construing Virgil's deity as the Holy Spirit.

Furthermore, Bernardino Telesio too had written a book about similar notions, titled: *That the Universal Animal is Governed by a Unique Soul Substance.* This work was placed on the Index of Forbidden Books in 1596, "until expunged." Telesio had written this work already by 1565, but he didn't

---

[767] Pauli Scaliger, *Pauli Principis de la Scala et Hvn. Marchionis Veronae, &c. Domini Creutzburgi in Prusia. Miscellaneourum de Rerum Causis & Successibus* (1570), bk. 4, chap. 1, p. 161 verso, trans. Martínez; italics added.
[768] Ibid., p. 161 reverso, trans. Martínez.
[769] Ibid., p. 177 verso, trans. Martínez.

publish it during his lifetime. He died in 1588, but his manuscript circulated in handwritten copies, until it was finally published.[770]

But not everyone appreciated the mixture of pagan notions with Christianity. Aside from devout Catholics and Inquisitors, an interesting example is the Italian Protestant, Girolamo Zanchi, because he rejected that notion in 1591, the same year as Bruno argued the opposite in print. Zanchi remarked: "What the Platonists called the soul of the world, properly speaking, does not mean (so to speak), formally, that the Holy Spirit is the soul of the world: for this is blasphemous." Zanchi too explained this notion as the claim that the Holy Spirit had "vivified the World and everything," and he even quoted Virgil's passage about how the "Spirit nourishes within."[771] At the very same time, however, a Catholic friar defended the contrary view, someone who later became Galileo's advocate: Tommaso Campanella.

In my previous book, *Burned Alive*, I already discussed how Campanella advocated for Galileo, Pythagoras, and the notion of the soul of the world. In a book of 1591, Campanella approvingly quoted Ficino's views on the soul of the world, which led the Inquisition to interrogate and torture him, in the 1590s.[772] Still, I can elaborate on how Campanella tried to legitimize the views of Pythagoras by making conjectures about his ancestry.

Campanella argued that the theory of Copernicus and Galileo had originated from Moses himself, and that "Pythagoras, who was of Jewish stock although he was born in a Greek city," brought these ideas "to Greece and to Italy, and taught it at Croton in Calabria."[773] He further explained:

[Saint] Ambrose testifies that Pythagoras was a Jew, …. one of the commentators on Ambrose wondered how Pythagoras could be a Jew when others say that he was from Samos in Greece (Gabriele Barrio of Francica says he moved from Samos to Calabria, which was Magna Graecia at the time), and answered that Ambrose would not have said this without clear

---

[770] Bernardini Telesii, *Quod Animal Vniversvm ab Vnica Animae Substantia Gubernatur, Adversvs Galenvm Liber Vnicus*, ed. Antonio Persio (Venice: Felicem Valgrisium, 1590).

[771] Hieron. Zanchii, *De Operibus Dei intra Sex Dierum Creatis Opus: Tres in Partes Distinctum* (Neostadii Palatinorum: Matthaei Harnisii, 1591), bk. 1, p. 208-209, trans. Martínez; see also bk. 1, p. 197, and bk. 2, p. 599.

[772] Alberto Martínez, *Burned Alive: Giordano Bruno, Galileo and the Inquisition* (Reaktion: London, 2018), p. 117; see also p. 166.

[773] F. Tomæ Campanellæ, *Apologia Pro Galileo, Mathematico Florentino* (Francofvrti: Godefridi Tamachii, 1623); reissued as *Defense of Galileo, the Mathematician from Florence*, trans. Richard J. Blackwell (Notre Dame: University of Notre Dame, 1994), 49.

historical evidence. This is justified not only by Ambrose's sanctity and reputation but also by arguments. For Pythagoras taught that we should abstain from certain foods, that there is only one God even though he said that the angels are second gods, and that all things are numbers (as did Moses in the construction of the tabernacle and Solomon who said [Wisdom 11:21] all things were created "in numbers, weight, and measure"). Also, Pythagoras rivaled Moses as a lawgiver; on this point see my *Metaphysica*. But all these things were known also to the Jews.

Campanella added that, "Pliny rightly says that Pythagoras was the wisest of philosophers."[774] Yet the biggest compliment was the implication that the Pythagorean knowledge was truly from God. In a seemingly deeper Pythagorean tone, Campanella praised the "noble verses of Ovid," and he confidently asserted that "the soul is immortal and capable of being divine."[775]

In his book, Campanella did not mention some opinions that he himself had previously voiced, and which he attributed to Pythagoras: that the world (or universe) has a soul, and that the Earth is a living animal. Bruno had been judged for these Pythagorean doctrines, among others.

Campanella then summarized how the theory of the Earth's motions (allegedly) developed. Following Pythagoras, Campanella said that "my compatriot Timaeus Locri, a disciple of Pythagoras," had demonstrated mathematically the Earth's daily motion. Then, Philolaus the Pythagorean, at Croton, proved the Earth's annual motion. And finally, Copernicus had studied "the prior teachings of the Pythagoreans," and hence he "seems to have added" a third motion for the Earth: the supposed motion that held the Earth's axis in the same orientation relative to the universe as it orbits around the Sun.[776] Campanella complained that Aristotle and others had wrongly attacked such ideas, "But Galileo has saved our ancestors from the damage caused by the Greeks. This same view was held by Numa Pompilius, a student of Pythagoras and the wisest king of the Romans."[777]

After having proposed his convenient story about the Jewish Pythagoras, Campanella argued that even if Pythagoras were not Jewish, he still

[774] Ibid., p. 49.
[775] Ibid., 115.
[776] Ibid., 120-121.
[777] Ibid., 49.

visited the priests of Egypt, along with Pherecydes (his teacher, according to some accounts), and met with the Jews, and "Thus it was from them that he heard the law and the philosophy which locates water and earths in the heavens, and mountains on the Moon, and similar things, which we have shown are found in the Holy Bible."[778] Thus Campanella tried to rehabilitate Pythagorean ideas by attributing them to ancient authorities, beginning with Moses.

Campanella argued that there should be a more accurate way, instead of Aristotle, to interpret Scriptures to match the new science. Against Catholic tradition, Campanella argued that the teachings of Moses should not be interpreted in reference to the philosophy of Aristotle, but instead "according to the philosophy of Pythagoras," which had rightly been accepted by Plato.[779] Thus he tried to promote the Pythagorean views as a key to understanding the Bible.

Ending his book, Campanella stressed: "In conclusion, the views of Galileo and Empedocles, who derived his teachings from the Pythagoreans more than any other philosophers, as St. Thomas says, are in agreement with ancient and modern interpretations of Sacred Scriptures. Therefore, they are also in agreement with the Sacred Scriptures themselves on astronomical matters." Campanella said: "it is clear that not only Moses but also Solomon and experience agree with Empedocles and Galileo."[780]

He advised that Galileo's writings should not be prohibited. He noted that Cardinal Bellarmino had stated that presently heretics (Protestants) disagreed with everything voiced by Roman theologians, which Campanella construed as relevant to his own claim that to censure Galileo would undermine the credibility of Catholics. Finally, Campanella noted that he submitted himself as always to the censure of the Holy Mother Catholic Church.

Despite his attempt to defend and legitimize Galileo and the Pythagorean theory, publication of Campanella's *Defense of Galileo* was promptly forbidden in Italy, and he was forced to disavow the edition that was published in Frankfurt. Campanella's *Defense of Galileo* was banned in 1623.

[778] Ibid., 121.
[779] Ibid., 106.
[780] Ibid., 122, 108.

Summing up, some writers in the Renaissance boldly echoed the notions of some ancient pagans, to the effect that the Earth has a soul, and that since it is animated it is alive. And hence, one way to demonstrate that the Earth *really* is a soulful being, a rational animal, was to show a startling and counterintuitive fact: *that it moves.*

the Jesuit against the New Pythagoreans

Following Galileo's trial of 1633, the Jesuit theologian Melchior Inchofer, author of the most negative reports used by the Roman Inquisition against Galileo, repudiated the Copernicans for the "heresy" of the soul of the world (*anima mundi*), in an unpublished manuscript. I show that Inchofer's arguments applied far more to the beliefs of Giordano Bruno than to those of Galileo. Since antiquity, various Christian authorities had repudiated several beliefs about the *anima mundi* as "heretical," hence I review their critiques against Pythagoras, Origen, and Peter Abelard, for allegedly asserting animistic beliefs about the Earth, or a universal spirit, or that souls move the heavenly bodies. Still, in the Renaissance such beliefs were defended by several advocates of Copernicus, including Bruno, William Gilbert, Johannes Kepler, and Philippe van Lansberge, who all claimed that Earth moves because it has a soul.

By comparing Inchofer's works and some of the Roman Inquisition's earlier censures against Bruno, I argue that prominent Catholic theologians' repudiation of pagan notions of the *anima mundi* as heretical contributed partly to theologians' opposition against the Copernicans.

To some of its early readers, *De Revolutionibus* implied certain extraordinary meanings that actually Copernicus had not really asserted. They surmised, in particular, that if the Earth were really *self-moving* then it was an animated being, a body with a soul. This ancient, pagan implication was endorsed even by several prominent proponents of Copernicus, especially Giordano Bruno and Johannes Kepler, but it was also denounced by critics, because throughout the centuries multiple Catholic theologians had repudiated notions of the *anima mundi*, and worse, some had categorized such notions as *heretical.*

553	5th Ecumenical Council	Anathemas Against Origen	
1141	Bernard of Clairvaux	Council of Sens against Peter Abelard	
1277	Bishop Tempier	Condemnation of 217 Propositions	
1533	Alfonso de Castro	*Adversus Omnes Hæreses. Libri XIIII*	Paris
1539	Alfonso de Castro	*Adversus Omnes Hæreses. Libri XIIII*	Cologne
1541	Alfonso de Castro	*Adversus Omnes Hæreses. Libri XIIII*	Paris
1543	Alfonso de Castro	*Adversus Omnes Hæreses. Libri XIIII*	Cologne
1546	Alfonso de Castro	*Adversus Omnes Hæreses. Libri XIIII*	Venice
1548	Alfonso de Castro	*Adversus Omnes Hæreses. Libri XIIII*	Cologne
1555	Alfonso de Castro	*Adversus Omnes Hæreses. Libri XIIII*	Lyon
1556	Alfonso de Castro	*Adversus Omnes Hæreses. Libri XIIII*	Antwerp
1558	Alfonso de Castro	*Adversus Omnes Hæreses. Libri XIIII*	Cologne
1560	Alfonso de Castro	*Adversus Omnes Hæreses. Libri XIIII*	Paris
1564	Alfonso de Castro	*Adversus Omnes Hæreses. Libri XIIII*	Paris
1565	Alfonso de Castro	*Adversus Omnes Hæreses. Libri XIIII*	Paris
1565	Alfonso de Castro	*Adversus Omnes Hæreses. Libri XIIII*	Antwerp
1566	Bernard of Clairvaux	*Conciliorum Generalium Eccl. Catholica*	(1141)
1578	Alfonso de Castro	*Opera Omnia (Adversus Omnes Hæreses)*	Paris
1581	Sebastiano Medici	*Summa Omnium Hæresum*	Florence
1587	Sebastiano Medici	*Summa Omnium Hæresum*	Venice
1590	Tiberio Deciani	*Tractatus Criminalis Omnium Hæresum*	Venice
1601	Augustino Petreto	*Babilonis Haeresos Vasta Destructio*	Reg.Emilia
1627	Livio Galante	*Christianae Theologiae cum Platonica Comparatio*	Bonn
1635	Melchior Inchofer	*V. Adversus Neo-Pythagoraeos Terrae Motores*	Rome
1637	Athanasius Rhetor	*Anticampanella in Compendium*	Paris

Table 9. *Selected works that categorized the Soul of the World as a "**heresy**."*

It is remarkable that during the Renaissance, in any country, the strongest repudiation that I have found against the belief in the *anima mundi*, as a heresy, appears in a manuscript treatise against the Earth's motion, written in Rome by Melchior Inchofer, the one Jesuit theologian now infamous for having authored the longest and most damning reports against Galileo. In April 1633, Pope Urban VIII solicited official reports by three Catholic theologians analyzing whether Galileo taught, defended, or held that the Earth moves. Inchofer responded that he "vehemently suspected" that Galileo really believed it. The reports were promptly used by the Roman Inquisition against Galileo, such that, two months later the Inquisitors declared Galileo guilty of "vehement suspicion of heresy," a punishable offence.[781] The reports by Inchofer and the two other theologians do not specify *why* the view of Earth's motion was offensive. Yet just two months later, Inchofer published his *Tractatus Syllepticus* justifying the official Catholic opposition to belief in a moving Earth.[782] Among various objections, Inchofer denied the Earth's motion by repudiating animism: he argued that the Earth was not moved by a soul. His book was approved by the Pope and his prominent nephew the Cardinal Inquisitor Francesco Barberini: it bears their family coat of arms and it was published by Ludovico Grignani, the printer who specialised on authors attached to the Barberini papal court.

During Galileo's trial, Inchofer had also begun writing a second, much longer treatise justifying why the Copernicans should be condemned. I first learned about this unpublished manuscript in a book by Domenico Berti from 1876.[783] Since I had been investigating Pythagorean aspects of the Copernican revolution, the manuscript's title drew my attention: *Vindication of the Holy Apostolic See, the Sacred Tribunal and Authorities Against the Neo-Pythagoreans' Moving Earth, and Stationary Sun.*[784] It consists of two "books" bound as one. Inchofer finished it in 1635. Apparently, nobody has published an analysis of this revealing Latin manuscript.[785] The neatly

[781] For discussion of different kinds of heresy, in relation to Galileo's trial, see Jules Speller, *Galileo's Inquisition Trial Revisited* (Frankfurt am Main, 2008), e.g., pp. 21-50. See also, Maurice A. Finocchiaro, *Retrying Galileo, 1633-1992* (Berkeley, 2005), pp. 12-16, 47, 272-274.

[782] Melchioris Inchofer, *Tractatvs Syllepticvs, in quo, Qvid de Terrae, Solisq. Motv, vel Statione, secundum S. Scripturam, & Sanctos Patres sentiendum, quaque certitudine alterutra sentential tenenda sit, breuiter ostenditur* (Rome, 1633), pp. 77-78, 86; trans. in Richard J. Blackwell, ed., *Behind the Scenes at Galileo's Trial: Including the First English Translation of Melchior Inchofer's Tractatus Syllepticus* (Notre Dame, 2006), pp. 108, 123, 167.

[783] Domenico Berti, *Il Processo Originale di Galileo Galilei* (Rome, 1876), pp. xci–xcii.

[784] Melchiorre Inchofer, *Vindiciarum S. Sedis Apostolicae, Sacrorum Tribunalium et Authoritatum Adversus Neo-Pythagoraeos Terrae Motores, et Solis Statores* [Libri Duo], unpublished manuscript (1635), at the Biblioteca Casanatense, Rome, MS 182.

[785] Richard J. Blackwell and Maurice Finocchiaro list this manuscript's title in bibliographies, but without having personally seen it, as they told me. Rafael Martínez consulted it around 1999, not to read its contents but just to use it as a reference for Inchofer's handwriting: to ascertain whether Inchofer had authored a brief document known as EE 291. Francesco Beretta too consulted Inchofer's *Vindiciarum*, but characterized it only very briefly in just six sentences, in Beretta, "Melchior Inchofer et

handwritten and bound text is 210 pages long, roughly 49,000 words. By comparison, Inchofer's *Tractatus Syllepticus* is much shorter: 94 pages of printed text, roughly 33,000 words. In some respects, the *Tractatus* does summarise (as its title implies) a small portion of the material contained in the *Vindication*, but each work includes abundant material that is not mentioned in the other. The scope of the *Vindication* is much too large to be covered in one journal article, so in the present article, I confine myself to discussing just one of the main reasons why Inchofer here condemned the theory of the Earth's motion, namely, his denial that Earth is animated by a soul.

I will explain Inchofer's objections in relation to earlier instances in which the Copernicans, especially Giordano Bruno, had affirmed that the Earth is animated by a soul, but were denounced by Catholic censors and Inquisitors. Interestingly, Inchofer's critiques applied less to what Galileo had written and far more closely to what Giordano Bruno wrote. By analyzing accusations against Bruno, I will show that his Inquisitors and censors in Venice and Rome were similarly concerned by his assertions of heresies about the *anima mundi*. Therefore, I will argue that interpolated, pagan notions of animism factored into some of the Catholic opposition against Copernicanism. The neglected evidence will show that certain Catholic authorities were disturbed by notions about a soulful moving Earth from the 1590s until the 1630s; from Bruno's trial to Inchofer's condemnation of the Copernicans.

In his manuscript *Vindication*, Inchofer repeatedly and abundantly referred to Galileo and the Copernicans as "New-Pythagoreans." As scholars know, the ancient Pythagorean philosophy had been used to characterise the Copernican theory for two main reasons: first, that according to ancient sources the Pythagoreans believed that the Earth moves, and second, that it circles a "central fire." But presently, I will focus on a third (and neglected) reason: that Pythagoras reputedly taught that the Earth is animated by a soul. Thus, in his manuscript Inchofer complained that Copernicus and his followers echoed certain false pagan doctrines of the ancient

l'hérésie de Galilée: censure doctrinale et hiérarchie intellectuelle," *Journal of Modern European History*, 3 (1), (2005), 41-42. For reasons why the *Vindiciarum* was not published, see Michael Gorman, "A Matter of Faith? Christoph Scheiner, Jesuit Censorship, and the Trial of Galileo," *Perspectives on Science* 4 (3), (1996), p. 305.

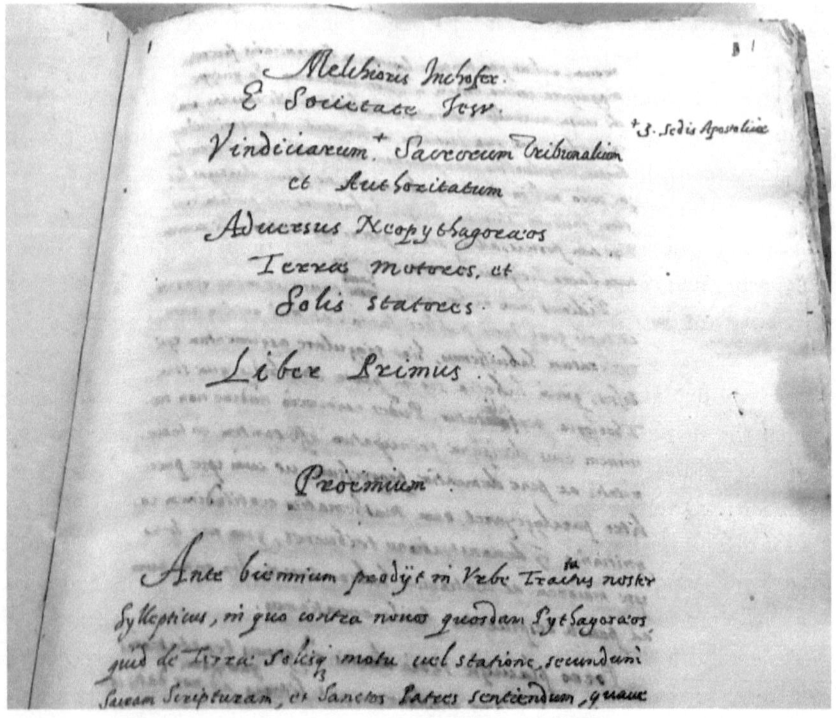

Figure 2. Title page of Melchior Inchofer's manuscript treatise on the *Vindication of the Holy Apostolic See, the Sacred Tribunal and Authorities Against the Neo-Pythagoreans' Moving Earth and Stationary Sun* (1635), MS 182 at the Biblioteca Casanatense, Rome. (Photo by A. Martínez)

Pythagoreans: the Earth moves, it is a living being animated by a soul, there exist many worlds, and human souls can transmigrate from body to body. These beliefs do not all match the beliefs of Copernicus or Galileo, but such beliefs were discussed or defended extensively by Giordano Bruno, above all, and to lesser extents, by William Gilbert, Johannes Kepler, Tommaso Campanella, and Philippe van Lansberge.

Writing in Rome, Inchofer explicitly attacked several Copernicans in his *Vindication*: Gilbert, Kepler, and Lansberge—and they were all foreign Protestants. In contradistinction, Inchofer hardly mentioned the several Italian, Spanish, or Catholic advocates of Copernicus who had been censored or condemned in Rome. Inchofer did not name Bruno; and he just briefly quoted the names of Diego de Zúñiga and Paolo Antonio Foscarini (only because Inchofer quoted the anti-Copernican decree of the Index of Forbidden Books of 1616, which includes their names); and he mentioned Galileo too only very briefly. Inchofer's arguments clearly show that he knew about all of them (Bruno, Zúñiga, Foscarini, Galileo), as we will see, so he chose to focus his critique on Protestant Copernicans, not on Catholic Copernicans. At any rate, Inchofer accused the "New-Pythagoreans" of believing in the *anima mundi*.

To be sure, historians often associate the *anima mundi* not with Pythagoras but with Plato, the Stoics, and others.[786] In Plato's *Timaeus*, for example, the protagonist proclaims: "the world became a living creature truly endowed with soul and intelligence by the providence of God."[787] Likewise, in a work now lost (ca. 50 BCE), Marcus Terentius Varro argued that the true gods are the soul of the world and its various parts. Nevertheless, some writers in the Renaissance, including Bruno and Inchofer, attributed the theory of the *anima mundi* more often to Pythagoras, and they had reasons to do so; consider the following precedents. Around 50 BCE, the *Placita Philosophorum* claimed that Pythagoras thought the world has a soul.[788] It also claimed that Pythagoras thought that when bodies die, their souls join the *anima mundi*.[789] In Ovid's *Metamorphoses*, the character of Pythagoras declared that the Earth is a great animal, living and breathing. Around 150 CE, Justin Martyr claimed that Pythagoras taught that God was the "universal mind and soul [*animatio*], the motion of all the circles."[790] Later, Apollonius of Tyana, a Pythagorean, allegedly learned that the world is an animal

---

[786] For discussion of the Stoic tradition, see Tullio Gregory, *Anima Mundi: La Filosofia di Guglielmo di Conches e la Scuola di Chartres* (Florence: Sansoni, 1955), e.g., pp. 123-27.

[787] Plato, *Timaeus* (ca. 360 BCE), in *The Dialogues of Plato*, trans. Benjamin Jowett, vol. 2 (Oxford, 1871), paragraphs 30-31, pp. 525-26, translation modified slightly.

[788] *De placita philosophorum*, IV, chap. 7. This work, known in Greek as *Peri ton areskonton philosophois, physikon dogmaton*. Falsely attributed to Plutarch, it was based on a work by Aetius (c. 50 BCE), as noted by Theodoret of Cyrus (c. 393–c. 458/466 CE). It was falsely attributed to Qusta ibn Luqa by Ibn al-Nadim; see Hans Daiber, ed., *Aetius Arabus: Die Vorsokratiker in arabischer Uberlieferung* (Wiesbaden, 1980).

[789] Ibid., bk. 1, chap. 3; bk. 4, chaps. 4 and 7.

[790] Justin Martyr, "Ad Graecos sive Gentiles Cohortatoria Oratio" (ca. 150 CE), in Iustini, *Operum, quae Extant, Omnium*, vol. 3, ed, and trans. from the Greek by Ioannem Langum (Basel, 1565), p. 58. Clement of Alexandria echoed the same claim, attributing it the Pythagoreans. Clement of Alexandria, *Protrepticus* (ca. 195 CE), trans. as *Exhortation to the Heathen*, in Roberts and Donaldson, eds., *Ante-Nicene Christian Library*, vol. 4: *Clement of Alexandria*, trans. William Wilson (1884), chap. 6, p. 72.

and it has a soul.[791] Around 300 CE, Porphyry, the infamous author of *Fif-teen Books against the Christians* but great advocate of Pythagoras, also spoke about the "soul of the world."[792] Porphyry claimed that the *anima mundi* "is adapted to be moved in a beautiful and orderly manner, and also to move the body of the world."[793] Likewise, the Christian theologian Lactantius wrote: "Pythagoras thus defined God: a Soul that pervades universally in all parts of the world, and diffused; from which all animals that are born receive their life."[794] By the expression "the world" writers usually meant either the Earth or the universe.[795]

However, there is no evidence that any such claims were historically accurate, mainly because there exist no extant works by Pythagoras, and the extant works by the earliest commentators (Heraclitus of Ephesus, Plato, Herodotus, Isocrates, Aristotle, etc.) make no such claims about Pythagoras. However, the accounts from late antiquity became influential in the Renaissance. Notably, Bruno credited Pythagoras with the notion that the moving Earth has a soul, as we will see.

But consider first the fact that Inchofer described the theory of the Earth's motion as a Pythagorean "*heresy.*" When he was criticizing Gilbert, Kepler, and Lansberge (without naming also Bruno, Zúñiga, Foscarini, Campanella, or Galileo), Inchofer traced the lineage of their pagan "heresy":

> Orpheus, then Aglaophamus, who Pythagoras follows, [and then] Plato's teacher Philolaus following Pythagoras, and we omit others, but

---

[791] Philostratus, *Life of Apollonius of Tyana* (Cambridge, 1948), bk. 3, chap. 34, p. 308.

[792] Porphyry, *On the Abstinence from Animal Food*, bk. 2, in Porphyry, *Select Works of Porphyry*, ed. and trans. Thomas Taylor (London, 1823), bk. 2, sec. 37, p. 74.

[793] Ibid.

[794] Lucius Lactantius, "De Falsa Religione," bk. 1 of *Divinarum Institutionum*, reissued in Lucii Coelii Lactantii, *Opera quae Extant, ad Fidem MSS. Recognita et Commentariis Illus-trata*, ed. Tho. Spark (Oxford, 1684), p. 18. His words paraphrase the account given in Cicero's *De Natura Deorum*, but adding the word "animals."

[795] For example, regarding the "anima del mondo," Giordano Bruno recognized this ambiguity and made this distinction: "the world" commonly meant the universe (which to him was spacious, infinite, shapeless, and immobile), or, it could also mean the Earth and all other heavenly bodies all constantly moving, animated. Bruno, *De gl' Heroici Furori* ('Paris', 1585), Dialogo 4, unnumbered pages, [pp. 107-08]; also in Bruno, *Opere Italiane* 2, ed. Giovanni Aquilecchia (Turin: UTET Libreria, 2007), pp. 597-98. Bruno, *The Heroic Frenzies*, ed. Eugenio Canone, trans. Ingrid Rowland (Toronto: University of Toronto Press, 2013), pt. 1, p. 139.

Pythagoras rather badly *departing* from the example and doctrine of his teachers, with Philolaus, [was] the first of anyone who asserted the heresy of the Earth's motion, certainly promoting impiety (just as Cleanthes of Samos later), unless he were wary.[796]

Inchofer also discussed the Hermetic *Asclepius*, rejecting Hermes's notion of the soul of the world.

Moreover, Inchofer was not the only Jesuit to refer to the Earth's motion as a heresy; in 1610 it had been called a heresy by Nicolaus Serarius.[797] Why did they describe the Earth's motion as a *heresy*? Historians argue that it was not officially a heresy in 1616 or in 1632, yet Galileo was condemned of "vehement suspicion of heresy" in April 1633. To be sure, in 1616, eleven Consultors of the Inquisition agreed unanimously that the Sun's immobility was "formally heretical" because it contradicted Sacred Scriptures; yet they did not declare the Earth's motion to be heretical. Were there any earlier theological precedents for construing the Earth's motion as a heresy?

Inchofer argued that the errors of the New-Pythagoreans (Copernicans) resembled the heresies of certain early Christian heretics: the Manichæans. Although such early heretics did not discuss the Earth's motion, they did advocate notions of the transmigration of souls (metempsychosis) and reportedly their leader Mani had claimed that "soul is diffused in all things," including all animals, plants, wood, wind, Moon, the Sun, light, and God.[798] Such beliefs were discussed by some of the Copernicans. Bruno, Kepler, and Campanella had written repeatedly about transmigration. For example, Campanella affirmed a kind of universal transmigration or resurrection, in one of his poems:

---

[796] Inchofer, *Vindiciarum*, 149. His erroneous attribution of a moving Earth theory to Cleanthes apparently stemmed from an edition of Plutarch's *Moralia* of 1542, including Plutarch's "The Face of the Moon," which mistakenly switched the names of Cleanthes and Aristarchus.

[797] Nicolai Serarii, *Iosue, ab Utero ad ipsum usque Tumulum* (Paris, 1610), chap. 10, p. 1006.

[798] Saint Epiphanius, *The Panarion of Epiphanius of Salamis: De Fide*. Books II and III [ca. 375], trans. Frank Williams, second ed. (Leiden, 2012), p. 236. Epiphanius, "Epistola Marcelli ad Manichaeum" in *Contra Octoaginta Haereses Opus, Panarium* (Basel: Officina Hervagiana, 1578), bk. 2, p. 205: "Asserebat autem rursus, quod sapientia superna boni Dei consultans secum animam in omnibus diffusam (esse enim dicit ipse & qui ab ipso sunt Manichaei, animam partem Dei & ab ipso avulsam)..."

> If the world were in the happy golden age,
>   being well can happen more than in one turn;
>   that indeed all buried things are revived,
>   as the cycle revolves again to the root.
> Yet the fox with the wolf and the crow
>   are denying this with much perfidy;
>   but God who reigns, and the sky that turns itself,
>   the prophecy and the common desire all say it.[799]

And Bruno, Gilbert, Kepler, Campanella, and Lansberge wrote about a universal spirit or soul that infuses all things and animates the Earth. Even some of the advocates of Copernicus claimed that there was animism in his writings. In particular, Kepler remarked that *Copernicus himself* claimed that the Earth is endowed with a mobile soul. In 1606, Kepler wrote: "Copernicus posits that Earth and all terrestrial things, even if expelled from Earth, are endowed with one and the same mobile soul, which makes its body rotate, the Earth, and makes particles expelled from it rotate along with it."[800] Similarly, Campanella argued that all things have sense, and he claimed that *Copernicus himself* believed that the Earth has sense.[801] Thus, although Copernicus did not really attribute a soul or animism to the Earth, some of his interpreters did.

Twelve centuries earlier, around 375 CE, Saint Epiphanius had denounced the Manichæans as heretics. He complained that Mani taught that each human soul is a fragment of God, imprisoned in a body, and that souls can transmigrate to other bodies, and even to the Moon.[802] According to Epiphanius, Mani taught that after death human souls can go to the Moon and subsequently to the Sun, which are vessels that carry souls. Thus, Inchofer plumbed the history of theology to find authorities who had condemned animistic or Pythagorean beliefs. Inchofer strongly denied that, "the universe has life and sense, the metempsychosis in the opinions of the

---

[799] Tommaso Campanella, "Sonetto III" (undated), in *in Gio. Gaspare Orelli, ed., Poesie Filosofiche di Tomaso Campanella* (Lugano: Gius. Ruggia, 1834), 109, trans. Martínez.
[800] Kepler, *De Stella Nova*, in Kepler, *Gesammelte Werke*, ed. Max Caspar, vol. 3 (Munich, 1938), p. 28. For discussion, see Dilwyn Knox, "Bruno's Doctrine of Gravity, Levity and Natural Circular Motion," *Physis* 38 (2001), p. 206.
[801] Tommaso Campanella, *De Sensu Rerum et Magia, Libri Quatuor* (Frankfurt: Godefridi Tampachij, 1620), pp. 214-15.
[802] Epiphanius, *Panarion*, p. 236.

Pythagoreans and of the Manichæans, as thought commonly by the innovators [the New-Pythagoreans], and also by the institutes of Kepler and Galileo that humans and other animate beings inhabit the orb of the Moon."[803] Thus Inchofer slandered Galileo, as if Galileo had claimed that all things had life and sense, souls migrate from body to body, and there are men living on the Moon. With all accuracy, Inchofer instead could have attributed such beliefs to Bruno, and to a lesser extent, to Kepler, Gilbert, or Campanella.

Moreover, Inchofer spent an entire chapter denying the *anima mundi*. He argued that the notion that Earth has a soul was refuted by Scriptures, Saint Augustine, and Saint Anselm. Meanwhile, Philippe van Lansberge was a Dutch Calvinist minister who in 1629 had published a short treatise in favor of the Earth's motion. It was reissued in 65-pages in Latin translation in 1630, in Middelburg, the capital of the province of Zeeland, in the Netherlands. Although Lansberge had died in December 1632, Inchofer now promptly criticised him too as if he were still a serious threat; after all, his writings had become very popular. Lansberge too (like Bruno, Gilbert, Kepler, and Campanella) had affirmed that the Earth moved because it was a living being.[804] Lansberge even argued that the Holy Spirit somehow corresponds with air.[805] Deeply annoyed, Inchofer included Lansberge among the New-Pythagoreans.[806]

Next, Inchofer ridiculed the ancient philosopher Anaxagoras because William Gilbert had cited him as an authority who claimed that magnets have portions of the soul of the world.[807] At length Inchofer ranted that the alien doctrinc of the New-Pythagoreans was "absurd," and "contrary to the faith."[808] He praised the critics of the New-Pythagoreans, he listed them:

[803] Inchofer, *Vindiciarum*, p. 51.
[804] For discussion, see Rienk Vermij, "Putting the Earth in Heaven: Philips Lansbergen, the Early Dutch Copernicans and the Mechanization of the World Picture," in Massimo Bucciantini, et al., eds., *Mechanics and Cosmology in the Medieval and Early Modern Period* (Florence, 2007), pp. 131-32.
[805] Philippi Lansbergii, *Bedenckinghen, Op den Daghelijckschen, ende Iaerlijckschen loop vanden Aerdt-cloot* (Middelburg, 1629), pp. 58-59. See also, Rienk Vermij, *The Calvinist Copernicans* (Amsterdam, 2002), p. 89.
[806] Inchofer, *Vindiciarum*, 128; Philippi Lansbergii, *Commentationes in Motum Terræ Diurnum, & Annum*, trans. Martino Hortensio (Middelburg, 1630).
[807] Apparently, Gilbert's source for this claim was Diogenes Laertius, *Lives of Eminent Philosophers* (ca. 225 CE), ed. Tiziano Dorandi (Cambridge, 2013), bk. 2, secs. 6-8, pp. 153-54.
[808] Inchofer, *Vindiciarum*, p. 154.

"Marin Mersenne, Libert Froidmont, Christopher Scheiner, Joannes Costeus, and others."[809] In 1589, Joannes Costeus had criticised "Copernicus and others," for that theory.[810] Later, Mersenne sympathized and corresponded with Galileo, but in 1624 he excoriated Bruno as a miscreant, an atheist, and "one of the most evil men that the Earth has ever produced."[811] Mersenne criticised Campanella too. Scheiner criticised Galileo. And Froidmont complained that "the [new] Pythagoreans . . . also known as the Copernicans," were a "particularly alien sect that has invaded the Catholic faith," and he named some of them: Kepler, Michael Maestlin, Gilbert, Foscarini, Galileo.

Inchofer complained that the ancients believed in a universal soul, then he disapprovingly quoted passages by Gilbert that pertained to animism and the *anima mundi* in Gilbert's *De Magnete* of 1600. Gilbert had not mentioned Bruno in that book, but he shared or echoed at least nine of Bruno's beliefs: (1) that Earth moves because it's a living animal (2), with a soul, (3) giving parts of its soul to humans, (4) to vivify them, and that (5) the Sun, (6) Moon, (7) planets, and (8) stars all have souls—and even (9) that God is a soul.[812] None of this was Copernican or Catholic doctrine. Yet in his *Dialogue* of 1632, Galileo dared to discuss and praise Gilbert at length.[813] In

---

[809] Ibid., p. 155.

[810] Ioannis Costaei, *Disquisitionum Physiologicarum* (Bonn: Ioannem Rosium, 1589), pp. 90, 97-100. Who did he mean by "others"? At the time, very few individuals had supported Copernicus in print; e.g., five years earlier, Bruno had published his first books on Earth's motion, *The Ash Wednesday Supper*, and *Infinite Universe and Worlds*, both in 1584.

[811] Marin Mersenne, *L'impieté des déistes, athées, et libertins de ce temps*, vol. 2 (Paris, 1624), p. 299.

[812] Gilbert was present and active in London at the same time that Bruno lived there, and therefore historians argue that Bruno helped to inspire Gilbert's cosmology. For discussion, see Hilary Gatti, *Giordano Bruno and Renaissance Science* (Ithaca, 1999), pp. 33-37. Gilbert died in 1603, but he left a manuscript, *On the World*, in which he did mention Bruno, three times. He discussed two kinds of motion that "the Nolan" had attributed to the Earth "when he was younger." Guilielmi Gilberti, *De Mundo Nostro Sublunari Philosophia Nova. Opus Posthumum* (Amsterdam, 1651), pp. 165, 199-201. In this work Gilbert again wrote about the souls that animate the Earth and the heavenly bodies. See ibid., pp. 84, 124-26, 158, 165, 217-18, 246.

[813] Galileo Galilei, *Dialogo, Doue ne i Congressi di Quattro Giornate si Discorre sopra i due Massimi Sistemi del Mondo Tolemaico, e Copernicano* (Fiorenza, 1632), pp. 393-406. Galileo, *Dialogue Concerning the Two Chief World Systems*, ed. Stillman Drake (1962), pp. 467-71, 477-79. Galileo wrote about whether Earth is really magnetic. He praised Gilbert for

contradistinction, Inchofer spurned Gilbert's claim that "the whole world is animated, all the globes, all stars, and also Earth, each have their own distinct souls that govern them from the start, to maintain their motions."[814] He quoted Gilbert's claim that the Earth is an animal. Inchofer scoffed: "We laugh at him more than at the Stoics, as in a contradictory way he affirms and denies that which is a soul, he identifies it with what has vigor or form."[815] Inchofer protested that one could see "how evil is impiety."[816]

He cited more authorities: Saint Hilary, Augustine, Gregory of Nyssa, Saint John of Damascus, and Chrysostom; all to argue that misinterpretations of Scriptures had generated heresies and irrationality. For one, John of Damascus had discussed philosophers' opinions about the heavens to illustrate their confusion, bemoaning:

> It must not be supposed that the heavens or the luminaries are endowed with life. For they are inanimate and insensible. Thus, when the divine Scripture says, *Let the heavens rejoice and the Earth be glad*, it is the angels in heaven and the men on Earth that are invited to rejoice. For the Scripture is familiar with the figure of personification, and is wont to speak of inanimate things as though they were animate...[817]

"the progress in his manner of philosophizing, with a certain similarity to my own." He urged that one should read Gilbert's book. Galileo highlighted "Gilbert's progress upon philosophizing" in the margin of the page and also in the index of his book. Ibid., pp. 396-97. Drake ed., pp. 467-68.

[814] Guilielmi Gilberti, *De Magnete, magneticisque corporibus, et de magno magnete tellure* (London, 1600), p. 209.

[815] Inchofer, *Vindiciarum*, p. 156.

[816] Ibid. Similarly, this was how Schoppe and Mersenne had disparaged Bruno.

[817] John of Damascus, *De Fide Orthodoxa* (ca. 730?), in *A Select Library of Nicene and Post-Nicene Fathers of the Christian Church*, ser. 2, vol. 9: St. Hilary of Poitiers / John of Damascus (Oxford, 1899), bk. 2, chap. 6, p. 22. As another Example, John wrote: "*the heavens declare the glory of God*, does not mean that they send forth a voice that can be heard by bodily ears, but that from their own greatness they bring before our minds the power of the Creator." Incidentally, in one of Bruno's depositions, the Roman Inquisitors accused him of having said that stars are animated rational beings that speak. Bruno admitted it. He cited Psalms as evidence: "the Heavens declare the glory of God," and that therefore heavenly bodies are rational beings or angels that interpret God's voice. This became also the 6th censured proposition in his books. Bruno (14th deposition), in Luigi Firpo, *Il Processo di Giordano Bruno* (Rome: Salerno, 1993), p. 270. Also, "Summarium": Sixth Censured Proposition, including Bruno's reply, in Firpo, *Processo*, p. 303. Psalms 19:1, or 18:2 in the Latin Vulgate.

Accordingly, Inchofer quoted passages from Scripture that should not be taken literally; for example, Deuteronomy 32:1, "Listen, you heavens, and I will speak"; and Job 38:7 "while the morning stars sang together." Inchofer stressed that there are many such phrases: "six hundred others of this kind, the explanation of which is so easy and obvious, that if by chance they are further opposed by the New-Pythagoreans, it would be necessary for them to be embarrassed by their ineptitude, unless they implore the aid of Hermes, Orpheus, and Pythagoras, bringing to bear things even more obscure."[818] Inchofer argued that if the Sun and Moon have souls and minds, and if the Earth moves, then in the Joshua miracle the Earth would need ears (or some kind of hearing organs) in order to obey. Inchofer pleaded: "Stop the dementia."[819]

He quoted the ancient theologian Origen for falsely asserting: "*Heaven and the Sun and the Moon and the stars and the waters that are above the heavens, have a soul.*"[820] This falsehood, Inchofer said, was echoed by Gilbert, but rightly condemned by Augustine, Saint Anselm, and Boethius. Moreover, Inchofer quoted the Fifth Ecumenical Council (553 CE) condemning those very words as a heresy in Origen's writings, that: "*If someone says* [like Origen] *that Heaven, Sun, and the Moon & stars and the waters that are above the heavens, are animated & have material powers, then he is anathema,*" that is, a heretic.[821] Inchofer then scorned the Pythagoreans, while quoting the Fifth Ecumenical Council:

> "*Anathema to Origen who is Adamantius, who promoted this with his nefarious and entirely execrable doctrine, and anyone* (note the New-Pythagoreans) *who claims or defends that statement, or presumes to protect it in any way or at any time.*" It's all over for the New-Pythagoreans, or as settled according to their own opinion, [they are] Heretics, for if through all philosophy, like heaven and the stars so too they think that the Earth is animated, not to say a monstrous

---

[818] Inchofer, *Vindiciarum*, p. 158.

[819] Ibid.

[820] Inchofer, *Vindiciarum*, p. 159. Origen, *Peri Archon* [ca. 250?], bk. 7, trans. Rufinus [400 CE], in Origen Adamantius, *Operum Origenis Adamantii, quorum Tertius complectitur, post Apologiam Explicanda*, vols. 3-4 (n.p., 1536).

[821] Inchofer, *Vindiciarum*, p. 159. For the statement in the Fifth Ecumenical Council itself, see: Nicephori Callisti, *Ecclesiasticæ Historiæ Libri Decem & Octo* (Basel, 1553), p. 893. The last phrase, *animatas quasdam esse & materiales virtutes, anathema sit* is often translated as "have souls, and are reasonable beings, let him be anathema."

animal, having a soul throughout its entire body, clearly to some degree or other they are refuted by positing an animated Heaven and even more so by affirming this about the Earth.[822]

This condemnation is important because Inchofer was invoking an authority of the highest caliber: not merely the judgment of one important book or bishop, nor even the judgment of a local council of churches, such as the Council of Sens—for Inchofer was quoting an Ecumenical Council, that is, the historic judgment of a major gathering of ecclesiastical authorities, theologians, and many bishops, soon confirmed by Pope Vigilius (and by the Sixth Ecumenical Council), to establish official doctrines to rule over all Christianity.[823] Strictly speaking, the Fifth Council had not condemned the doctrine of the *anima mundi* but the animation of the heavenly bodies and heaven, yet Inchofer deduced that since the Copernicans argued that the Earth too is a heavenly body then that condemnation applied to this belief too.

Although some of Origen's views had been anathematized posthumously and severely by the Fifth Ecumenical Council, he was not declared a heretic, and henceforth some theologians nonetheless esteemed him as a venerable Christian figure, whereas many others viewed him as highly suspect. For example, in 1629 the Jesuit Etienne Binet, published a book in Paris debating the fate of Origen's soul. To illustrate the opinion that Origen was damned in Hell, Binet attributed it to Cardinals Bellarmino and Baronio, who in Binet's imaginary dialogue argued that the "criminal" Origen had been condemned by emperors, popes, saints, the Fifth Ecumenical Council, "and almost by the mouth of God himself," and that hence he was in Hell among other heresiarchs, "damned among the others, & burdened

---

[822] Inchofer, *Vindiciarum*, p. 159, italics in the original.
[823] Pope Vigilius chose not to attend the Fifth Ecumenical Council (May-June 553), and did not send a representative. Moreover, he sent a lengthy *Constitutum* objecting to potential proceedings that might undo decrees of the Fourth Ecumenical Council and arguing that it was not the custom of the Church to condemn dead persons. The Pope's absence and reservations later led to historical doubts about the validity of this Council's decrees, even about Origen. However, actually, Pope Vigilius did finally approve the decrees of the Fifth Ecumenical Council, on December 8, 553 and February 23, 554. Moreover, in the year 680, the Sixth Ecumenical Council (Third Council of Constantinople) reaffirmed the decrees of the Fifth Council.

with the horror, flames, & confusion."[824] According to these literary versions of Bellarmino and Baronio, two of the reasons why Origen was damned in Hell were his beliefs "That the Sun, the Moon, & all the Stars are animated & living," and that "he said the Earth is a great animal."[825] Binet's fictional dialogue thus shows, again, that in the times of Galileo, some theologians regarded views ascribing *animism* to the Earth and heavenly bodies as offensive.

Moreover, Inchofer was not the only person to link Origen with the Copernicans. For example, Giordano Bruno had read, echoed, and praised Origen.[826] Campanella advised Galileo to use Origen as a defence against theologians critical of the Earth's motion, saying that the Earth is an animal. And John Donne had compared Copernicus to Origen while ridiculing the Jesuits. Also, in 1634, the French astronomer Fabri de Peiresc wrote to the secretary of the Inquisition, Cardinal Francesco Barberini, pleading for leniency for Galileo: "posterity will always show great appreciation for his marvelous report of his discoveries in the sky with the telescope and his sharp ingenuity. And since Tertullian and Origen and so many other Fathers," had committed certain errors, the Church had nevertheless appreciated some of their labors, Peiresc said—so instead of "punishing them with the same severity as it punishes the obstinate heretics"—the Church might

---

[824] Etienne Binet, *Du Salut d'Origene, Question 1. A scavoir si Origene est sauvé ou damné...* (Paris: Sebastien Cramoisy, 1629) pp. 157, 196-98. According to Cardinal Baronio himself, Origen's heresies were "pagan errors" for "imbecile minds," see Cesare Baronio, *Annales Ecclesiastici* 7 (Rome, 1596), p. 289. Bellarmino's objections will be discussed below.

[825] Binet, *Du Salut d'Origene*, pp. 161, 169.

[826] Bruno, *Heroici furori* (1585), unnumbered pages [p. 23] (*Opere Italiane* 2, ed. Aquilecchia, p. 513); Bruno, *Cabala del Cavallo Pegaseo. Con l'aggiunta dell'Asino Cillenico* (Paris: Antonio Baio, 1585), unnumbered pages [pp. 2, 17] (*Opere Italiane* 2, ed. Aquilecchia, pp. 408, 421); Bruno, *De triplici minimo et mensura* (Frankfurt, 1591), chap. 3, p. 13; Bruno, *De Magia*, in *Cause, Principle and Unity; and Essays on Magic*, ed. Richard J. Blackwell and Robert de Lucca (Cambridge: Cambridge University Press, 1998), pp. 125, 127. Bruno, *Opera Latine Conscripta*, ed. Felice Tocco and H. Vitelli, vol. 3 (Naples, 1891): *De Magia*, p. 428. Bruno praised Origen for being the only Christian theologian who dared to admit that the revolutions of the world are eternal, and that after death souls travel out of human bodies. He also wrote that Origen had rightly stated that angels are not fully incorporeal, but are animals with subtle bodies made of spiritual substances: fire and flames. Bruno agreed with Origen that the world has a soul, that it is an animal, stars too are living rational beings, human souls are immortal, eternal, and pre-exist their bodies, and might live again in other worlds, and that nothing is really new.

now show compassion toward Galileo as well.[827] Still, other writers cited the condemnations against Origen as reasons to reject the *anima mundi* and the animation of the heavenly bodies.[828]

Next, Inchofer repudiated the theory that God is the *anima mundi*, moving the heavenly bodies. Inchofer noted that Saint Basil, in his *Hexameron*, had rejected the claim that the heavens and stars are animated, said Basil: as "an ancient imposture and a ruinous weakening rotting."[829] And Inchofer repeatedly excoriated Gilbert. He groused that Gilbert's absurd Neo-Pythagorean philosophy revived the ancient "Idolatry or Egyptian paganism," in professing that the Sun is divine.[830] Such beliefs waged war against Catholic philosophy. He said that Gilbert's claim that magnets and the Earth have souls, stemmed from the awful Hermetic philosophy. And right then, Inchofer complained that Galileo had greatly supported Gilbert's philosophy.[831] Then Inchofer further castigated the notion that a spirit animates the magnetic Earth. By the way, in April 1633, when Pope Urban VIII solicited Inchofer's views on Galileo's *Dialogue*, Inchofer submitted his first report, including his complaint that Galileo praised Gilbert, a "perverse heretic."

Finally, on the very last page of Inchofer's extensive manuscript *Vindication*, he again stressed the offensive core of the Pythagorean heresies:

> but even if the pagan Heathen wanderers degenerate, attributing perceptions and comprehension to degenerate the mute nature of things, affirming that the universal world possesses a soul, even the Earth on which we walk, not knowing what kind of strange soul, latching onto the more ridiculous or stupid. Such truly impious arguments, and just as formerly the

---

[827] Niccolò Fabri de Peiresc to Francesco Barberini, 5 December 1634, in Antonio Favaro, ed., *Le Opere di Galileo Galilei: Edizione Nazionale* (Florence, 1890–1909), vol. 16, p. 170. Similarly, other Christian theologians were occasionally denounced by other Christian authorities yet retained respectability; thus the famous Augustine, Albertus Magnus, Thomas Aquinas, and even Bellarmino had endured Christian adversaries and accusations.

[828] For example, see Giovanni Battista Riccioli, *Almagestum Novum, Astronomia Veterem*, vol. 1 (Bonn: Haeredis Victorij Benati, 1651), bk. 9, sec. 1, pp. 245-46.

[829] Ibid. Inchofer further supported this denunciation by citing John of Damascus, Cyril, Ambrosius, and Lactantius.

[830] Ibid., 161.

[831] Ibid., 162. Inchofer added that it was absurd for a stone, magnetic or not, to have sense.

heads of the Church already condemned it in sacred laws, and even in Councils, as we show here, amply repeating it, we do not seem to exaggerate the case, we think not.[832]

Inchofer's anti-Copernican manuscript is remarkable partly because he, more than any other critic, blamed multiple parties for having advocated beliefs about the *anima mundi* and a celestial animation. At the time, apparently nobody else wrote about the *anima mundi* critically in such length. As far as I know, no other authorities involved in Galileo's trial voiced any concerns about whether heresies about animism were linked to the Earth's motion. Still, we find the Jesuit Inchofer, Galileo's most critical judge no less, vehemently accusing the Copernicans of these old and ancient heresies.

Summing up, Inchofer's manuscript reveals that he linked Copernicanism with *pagan heresies*. His *Tractatus Syllepticus* had already argued the *philosophical* absurdity of a soulful Earth, yet in the *Vindication* Inchofer added the *theological* argument: that it involved heresies. As a zealous Jesuit theologian, like the deceased but famous Bellarmino, it was Inchofer's obligation to know the canons of heresies. One way to prove that Earth really is a soulful being was to show a counterintuitive fact: that it moves. For Inchofer the *cause* was false: Earth has a soul. Therefore, its alleged *effect* was false too: that it moves.

the ħeretic
who should not be named

Prior to Inchofer, the most robust Catholic objections against animism in cosmology transpired in the trial of Giordano Bruno of Nola. It is intriguing to see that many of the controversies that Inchofer discussed applied not to Galileo or Copernicus at all, but to Bruno. No Copernican mentioned by Inchofer (not even Kepler or Gilbert) had voiced views so closely related to the many topics that Inchofer criticised. Yet Inchofer did not write Bruno's name at all. Why not? Similarly, in his extensive manuscript

---

[832] Inchofer, *Vindiciarum*, 210.

Vindication, Inchofer scarcely mentioned Galileo at all. Moreover, in his *Tractatus Syllepticus*, which was a sanctioned repudiation of Galileo's beliefs, Inchofer *did not name Galileo at all*. Why not? Because back then it was improper for most Catholics to write about heretics. Bruno had been burned alive for heresies, and worse, his Inquisitors viewed him as a "heresiarch": an intellectual patriarch of heretics. Accordingly, years before Galileo was condemned, Campanella referred only obliquely to Bruno in print, in his *Apologia Pro Galileo*: "This opinion [the existence of many suns and planets] was defended by a person from Nola and by others who, being heretics, we cannot mention by name." Likewise, Galileo himself *never* mentioned Bruno in print. In contradistinction, writing safely from Protestant lands, Kepler repeatedly named Bruno in print—even complaining that Galileo had failed to acknowledge that his telescopic discoveries actually *confirmed* some of Bruno's claims: the existence of innumerable previously invisible stars, new moons, mountains on the Moon, and the probability that beings live on the Moon; none of which had been predicted by Copernicus at all.

Therefore, just as Galileo is clearly implicated but not named in Inchofer's *Tractatus*, I argue that Bruno is implicated in Inchofer's *Vindication*. I will now bring to light the similarities between Inchofer's accusations against 'the New Pythagoreans' and accusations that Inquisitors had raised directly against Bruno's 'Pythagorean' beliefs.

The Venetian Inquisition imprisoned Bruno in 1592. Under interrogation, in his Third Deposition, he admitted to not understanding the Catholic notion of "the Holy Spirit as a third person," *except* "by following the Pythagorean way," he said, by construing the Holy Spirit as the "soul of the universe."[833] To explain himself, Bruno then quoted a biblical line attributed to Solomon:

> "For the spirit of God fills the Earthly orb: and therefore he who contains everything,"[834] which entirely conforms to the Pythagorean doctrine explained by Virgil in the sixth [book] of the *Aeneid*:
>> In the beginning, the spirit nourishes within
>> the sky, and lands, and regions of water,
>> and the shining globe of the Moon, and the Titanic stars,

833 Giordano Bruno, Third Deposition to the Venetian Inquisition, 2 June 1592, in Firpo, *Processo*, p. 254.
834 *Bible*, Book of Wisdom 1:7.

> totally infused through the limbs
> a mind agitates the mass… [835]

and that which follows. Thus from this spirit, that I have called the life
of the universe, I say in my philosophy, there originates the life and the
soul of each thing that has soul and life, which I understand to be immortal; as all other bodies.[836]

Thus, Solomon spoke about a spirit that fills the Earth, and in book 6 of
the *Aeneid*, Virgil had written that an immense fiery spirit fills and animates
the entire world, including Earth, Sun, Moon, and every star.[837] We will
soon see that Bruno's claims about this universal soul or spirit seemed very
offensive. Note that Bruno here used both expressions: universal "spirit"
and "soul of the universe" synonymously.[838]

---

[835] Virgil, *Aeneid*, bk. 6 (ca. 20 BCE), lines 724-727 [Latin numbering].

[836] Firpo, *Processo*, p. 254. In one of his unpublished manuscripts, Bruno had written
Virgil's words followed by a line from the Bible. He wrote: "Principio coelum et terras, camposque liquentes, Lucentemque globum lunae, Titaniaque astra, Spiritus intus
alit, totamque infusa per arctus, Mens agitat molem," followed by Solomon's line
from the Book of Wisdom 1:7: "Spiritus Domini replevit orbem terrarium et hoc
quod contient omnia." See W. Lutoslawski, "Jordani Bruni Nolani Opera Inedita,
Manu Propria Scripta," in Ludwig Stein, ed., *Archiv für Geschichte der Philosophie*, vol. 2
(Berlin, 1889), p. 539. Writers used slightly modified versions of Virgil's words and
punctuation. Virgil's original states: "Principio caelum ac terras camposque liquentis /
lucentemque globum Lunae Titaniaque astra / spiritus intus alit, totamque infusa per
artus / mens agitat molem et magno se corpore miscet," *Aeneid*, 724-27. Some translations interpret the "Titaniaque astra," which seems plural, as the singular Sun, or the
Sun plus the stars. For example, one prominent classicist wrote: "First, / the sky and
the earth and the flowing fields of the sea, / the shining orb of the moon and the Ti-
tan sun, the stars: / an inner spirit feeds them, coursing through all their limbs, /
mind stirs the mass and their fusion brings the world to birth." Virgil, *The Aeneid*,
trans. Robert Fagles (New York: Penguin, 2006), p. 206; but note also that the last
phrase "brings the world to birth" is not in the Latin original. See also, Seamus Hea-
ney, *Aeneid Book VI: A New Verse Translation* (New York: Farrar, Straus and Giroux,
2016), p. 75.

[837] Virgil, *Aeneid*, bk. 6, lines 685-755.

[838] As in his reply to the Inquisitors, Bruno often conflated the two terms (soul of the
world and universal spirit) in his books, or he intentionally treated them as synony-
mous. E.g., in Bruno, *Lampas Triginta Statuarum* (ca. 1590–91), first published in *Opera
Latine Conscripta*, vol. 3, p. 50: "spiritus universalis seu animae mundi." Also in Bruno,
De Magia, in ibid., p. 436: "vinculum est anima mundi seu spiritus universi," also in
Bruno, *Opere Magiche*, ed. M. Ciliberto et al. (Milan, 2000), pp. 22, 244. Similarly, see
De La Causa, Principio et Uno ('Venice' [London], 1584), pp. [iv, vi], 49-50, 76, 110; also

When Bruno was transferred to the Roman Inquisition, the topic arose again. The Inquisitors were annoyed that Bruno identified the Holy Spirit with a universal soul: around 1596, in his Seventeenth Deposition, the Roman Inquisitors interrogated Bruno again about the universal soul.[839] Reviewing the account of Bruno's Third Deposition, describing "the Pythagorean doctrine" that the Holy Spirit is the universal soul, an officer of the Roman Inquisition wrote on the margin of that page: "About these replies by him, he was interrogated [again] in the 17th Deposition, folio 257, where he affirmed the same replies in which he relapses [*reincidit*]." Next, along the paragraph where Bruno voiced doubts about the persons of God, again the margin bears an annotation: "About these words he was

in Bruno, *Opere Italiane* 1, ed. Giovanni Aquilecchia (Turin: UTET Libreria, 2007), pp. 599, 662-63, 687-88, 719. (Note: Aquilecchia's useful edition of Bruno's works is not a verbatim copy of the original texts; it includes many modifications in spellings, punctuation, paragraph breaks, etc.) Bruno also used the expressions *Spiritus universorum, spiritum universi, anima de l'universo, anima del mondo, mundi anima*, etc. His synonymous usage of such terms was common, as Vassányi observes that "in most early modern sources" *anima mundi* meant the same as *anima universalis*. Miklós Vassányi, *Anima Mundi: The Rise of the World Soul Theory in Modern German Philosophy* (Springer: Dordrecht, 2011), pp. 296, 337. According to Bruno the Earth's soul was a distinct part of the universal spirit (*anima mundi*), as were all individual souls. The universal spirit was uncreated, eternal, incorporeal, self-moving, and immanent in everything everywhere, whereby "all" is within every part of the universe. The universal spirit and matter were two aspects of God, and the universal spirit was the active, internal cause of all shapes and motions. To him, the universal spirit had a foremost faculty: the Universal Intellect, which was the efficient cause that produces and shapes all things, from within. Unlike the Neoplatonists, Bruno did not construe the universal spirit as a transcendent reality that produces subordinate individual souls. Instead, he agreed with the Stoics that the universal spirit was *immanent* in everything. But unlike the Stoics, he claimed that it was not corporeal. Following the pneumatic theories of the Stoics and the Neoplatonists, Bruno also discussed the existence of a distinct *spiritus*: a subtle, airy substance mediating the interactions among heavens and Earth. For discussion, see Vassányi, *Anima Mundi*, pp. 329-40; and Dilwyn Knox, "Bruno: Immanence and Transcendence in *De la Causa, Principio et Uno*, Dialogue II," *Bruniana & Campanelliana*, 12 (2), (2013), 463-82. Although Bruno often treated the *spiritus universalis* and the *anima mundi* as synonymous, he also referred to *spiritus* by itself as a *vehiculum* (in *De Monade*, end of chapter IV) between soul and bodies; see Delfina Giovannozzi, "Spirit in Giordano Bruno's Magical Works," in Steffen Schneider, ed., *Aisthetics of the Spirits: Spirits in Early Modern Science, Religion, Literature and Music* (Göttingen: V&R Unipress GmbH, 2015), pp. 133-34. Alfonso Ingegno, *Cosmologia e filosofia nel penseiro di Giordano Bruno* (Florence: La Nuova Italia, 1978), p. 167.
[839] We know about this important deposition because notes about it were added onto the margins of the "Summary" of Bruno's trial. Angelo Mercati, *Il Sommario del Processo di Giordano Bruno*; in *Studi e Testi*, vol. 101 (Vatican, 1942).

interrogated in the 17th Deposition, fol. 257v up to fol. 261, and he gives replies that relapse [*reincidunt*] into the same." The word *reincidit* was a technical term for Inquisitors; it was part of the definition of someone who has "relapsed" into heresy after having been admonished by Inquisitors to abandon that heresy.[840] (Catholics who relapsed into heresies were liable to being executed as heretics; and in Bruno's extant trial documents there are descriptions of him having relapsed only in regard to three beliefs: his belief in many worlds, his opinion on the three persons of God, and his view of the Holy Spirit in particular.)

Therefore, these records show that the Roman Inquisitors viewed Bruno's replies about his "Pythagorean doctrine" of the Holy Spirit as *heretical.*

But why? To answer, we turn again to the history of theology.

As noted by Inchofer, the Fifth Ecumenical Council had issued the "Anathemas Against Origen," the sixth of which states: "If anyone says that the heaven & Sun & Moon & stars and the waters that are above the heavens, are animated," then that person is a heretic.[841] Origen had claimed that the heavenly bodies are living beings, and he insinuated that human souls preexist bodies. Centuries later, Bruno repeatedly affirmed the same claims in print. Moreover, for Bruno the Earth was "a star" (a heavenly body).[842]

---

[840] Iacobi Menochij, *De Arbitrarii Iudicum Quaestionibus & Causis Libri Duo* (Frankfurt am Main, 1576), Casus 374: "Est relapsus, qui bis in eandem haeresim reincidit." Ioannis Bernardi Diaz de Luco, *Practica Criminalis Canonica* (Rome, 1581), p. 225: "quando fuerit inventus in haeresi, aut abiuravit eam, & fuit relapsus, aut quando se compurgavit, & reincidit eam..." Quintilliani Mandosij, ed., *Repertorium Inquisitorum Pravitatis Haereticae* (Venice, 1588), p. 676: "verè relapsus dicitur ille, qui per confessionem, vel veram probationé primò fuit convictus de haeresi, & ipsam abiuravit, deinde reincidit in errorem illum." Caesare Carena, *Tractatus de Officio Sanctissimae Inquisitionis et Modo Procedendi in Causis Fidei* (Cremonae, 1641), p. 253: "qui haeresim in Juditio abiurauerat, & postea reincidit in ipsa, censeri debeat iuris fictione haereticus relapsus."

[841] Callisti, *Ecclesiasticæ Historiæ*, p. 893.

[842] Bruno's 3rd Deposition to the Venetian Inquisition, 2 June 1592, in Firpo, *Processo,* pp. 167–68. In 1620, the Congregation of the Index censured passages in Copernicus' *De Revolutionibus,* censoring the claim that the Earth is a star three times, more than any other claim. In 1630, Inquisitor Francesco Barberini seriously warned Galileo's friend Benedetto Castelli that "if the Earth really has motion, it seems necessary that it be a star, a thing that then seems too contrary to the theological truth." Castelli then warned Galileo. Barberini, quoted in Castelli to Galileo, 9 February 1630, in Antonio Favaro, ed., *Opere di Galileo Galilei: Edizione Nazionale* 14 (Florence, 1890-1909) p. 78.

Therefore, the condemnation of Origen's notion of soulful heavenly bodies might apply to Bruno's claim of the soulful, moving Earth. Decades later Inchofer thus applied that condemnation against the Copernicans.

Also, Origen claimed that God creates a succession of worlds and that souls are reborn, such that "there is nothing new under the Sun."[843] Centuries later, Bruno made strikingly similar claims, and that same phrase became Bruno's personal motto.[844]

Later, another Catholic authority, in olden days, had also condemned the notion that heavenly bodies are animated by souls. In the 1270s, the Bishop of Paris, Étienne Tempier condemned many philosophical propositions as heretical, including: "That the world is eternal."[845] He did so with the official authority granted to him by Pope John XXI. As Chancellor of the Sorbonne, Tempier argued that faculty who taught such claims transgressed the limits of philosophy to speak erroneously about theology. In 1277, Tempier denounced as heretical the idea "That the substance of the soul is eternal," and he condemned the notion "That the heavenly bodies are moved by an intrinsic principle, which is the soul, and that they are moved by a soul and an appetitive power, like an animal."[846] These were

[843] Origen, *Peri Archon* [ca. 250?], bk. 3, trans. Rufinus [400 CE], in Origen, *Operum Origenis Adamantii*, vols. 3-4 (n.p., 1536), p. 205; see also bk. 1, chap. 6; bk. 2, chap 10.

[844] Bruno, Third Deposition, 1592, in Firpo, *Processo*, p. 169; Fourth Censured Proposition, in Firpo, *Processo*, p. 301; also in Hans von Warnsdorf of Wittenberg, Family Album, 18 September [1587], reproduction in Firpo, *Processo*, plate 4, after p. 86. See also Eugenio Canone, ed., *Giordano Bruno: gli Anni Napoletani e la 'Peregrinato' Europea* (Cassino, 1992), pp. 121-25. The same inscription is also in a print of the Siege of Nola, dated 9 March 1588, see F. Tocco, "Un Nuovo Autografo di G. Bruno," *La Bibliofilia*, vol. 9 (Florence, 1906), 342-45.

[845] Étienne Tempier, Condemnation of 1270, and Condemnation of 1277, see "Tredecim errores a Stephano episcopo Parisiensi condemnati, 1270," Proposition 5, and "Sequntur Errores Annotati in Rotulo, 1277" Propositions 87, 98; both reissued in: Faculty of the University of Paris, and Henricus Deinfle, *Chartularium Universitatis Parisiensis*, vol. 1 (Paris, 1889), pp. 487 and 548 respectively. Also in David Piché, ed., *La Condamnation Parisienne de 1277* (Paris: Libraire Philosophique J. Vrin, 1999), pp. 107, 108, 160; and in Roland Hissette, *Enquête sur les 219 Articles Condamnés à Paris le 7 Mars 1277* (Paris: Vander-Oyez, 1977), pp. 149, 152, and on p. 313 Hissette points out that eighteen of the 219 condemned propositions asserted the eternity of the world. Note: various editions of the Condemnations change the numbering and ordering of the propositions.

[846] Tempier, Condemnation of 1277, Props. 73, 109, in Piché, *La Condamnation*, pp. 106, 112; and in Hissette, *Enquête*, pp. 130, 206. Hissette gives a few examples of writers who apparently accepted the notion that heavenly bodies are animated, including

among the "loathsome," pagan "errors" and "insane lies" that Bishop
Tempier sternly listed as heresies under penalty of excommunication.

Centuries later, Bruno advocated all those heresies: the world is eternal,
the heavenly bodies are moved by souls, like animals (e.g., the Earth *is* an
animal), and human souls are constituted from the eternal substance of the
universal soul.[847] The latter claim was also heretical because the Council of
Vienna (1311-1312) had declared that the human soul is the form of the
human body, not something else.[848]

For Bruno, the Earth and the other "stars" (heavenly bodies) were animals of certain species, each having a soul, a rational intellect, a will, and
sense perception.[849] However, Tempier's list of condemned propositions
was pretty much rescinded, in the fourteenth century, after Thomas Aquinas embedded Aristotle's philosophy within Christianity; consequently, Ar-
istotelianism became official scholastic doctrine.[850] Still, I trace the older
Catholic critiques against notions of the *anima mundi* and the animated heavens in order to identify theological precedents that denounced beliefs similar to Bruno's. Moreover, even after the works of Thomas Aquinas, various
pagan philosophical notions continued to concern and annoy certain clergymen in early modern Italy.[851]

two anonymous commentators and Siger de Brabant, who was among the individuals
condemned by Tempier.

[847] For an analysis of Bruno's concept of the Earth and heavenly bodies as animals, by
comparison to ordinary animals, see Knox, "Bruno's Doctrine of Gravity," pp. 171-
209. Knox also shows that Bruno was unsure about whether individual animals are
parts of the *anima mundi* or are distinct from it; pp. 188-89.

[848] For discussion, see Francesco Beretta, *Galilée devant le Tribunal de l'Inquisition* (Fribourg: Université de Fribourg, 1998), pp. 99-100.

[849] For additional evidence and discussion, see Miguel Á. Granada, "Introducción," in
Giordano Bruno, *La Cena de las Cenizas* (Madrid: Editorial Tecnos, 2015), pp. cxliii-
cxlvii.

[850] Nevertheless, plenty of theologians continued to criticize Aristotle, and certain philosophers taught Aristotle's natural philosophy irrespective of Christian theology, especially in Italy. Paul F. Grendler, *The Universities of the Italian Renaissance* (Baltimore:
John Hopkins University Press, 2002), pp. 269-313.

[851] The 18th Ecumenical Council (Fifth Lateran Council, 1512-1517) mandated that
professors of philosophy had to refute the errors of ancient philosophers, to confirm
the truths of Christianity. Beretta, *Galilée devant le Tribunal de l'Inquisition*, pp. 102-04.
Francesco Beretta, "Orthodoxie Philosophique et Inquisition Romaine aux 16e-17e
Siècles: un Essai d'Interpretation," *Historia Philosophica* 3 (2005): 67-97, see pp. 74-82,
86-87, 94-95.

In the 1590s, Bruno's interpretation of the universal soul as the Holy Spirit was unacceptable for a more specific reason: that it had become anathema among clergymen because of the writings of Peter Abelard, the French philosopher and theologian. From 1118 to 1140, Abelard worked on three books on Christian theology, advocating reason in matters of faith. But in 1121 he was accused and convicted of misinterpreting the Holy Trinity. Still he persisted, and in his *Christian Theology* he argued, among other things, that the ancient philosophers referred to the Holy Spirit as the "soul of the world," a Spirit that infuses everything and "vivifies creatures."[852] Abelard attributed this notion to Pythagoras and Plato.[853] Abelard repeatedly quoted Virgil's passage about "Spirit nourishes within."[854] All of these five claims were later voiced by Bruno too.

In 1139, William of St. Thierry became angered by Abelard's claims about the Holy Spirit. William denounced him to the Bishop of Chartres and the Abbot of Clairvaux, complaining that Abelard's teachings endangered faith in the Trinity, constituting a growing evil, he said. Among thirteen "monstrous doctrines" listed by William was Abelard's proposition "That the Holy Spirit is the soul of the world."[855] Soon, in 1141, the Abbot of Clairvaux convened the Council of Sens. The bishops condemned Abelard's thirteen doctrines as heretical.[856] Pope Innocent II confirmed their

[852] Petrus Abelard, *Epitome Theologiæ Christianæ*, in Abelardus, *Sæculum XII Petri Abælardi Abbatis Rugensis Opera* Omnia, ed. J. P. Migne (Paris, 1855), chap. 18, pp. 1720-21. Also in: Petri Abaelardi, *Opera Theologica*, vol. 4: *Sententie [Epitome] Magistri Petri Abaelardi*, in David Luscombe, ed., *Corpus Christianorum: Continuatio Mediaevalis*, vol. 14 (Turnhout: Brepols Publishers, 2006), pp. 63-64.
[853] Regarding Pythagoras, Abelard cited Salvian, who had written that Pythagoras proclaimed: "A soul is intermixed or diffused in all parts of the world, from which all animals that are born receive their life." Salvianus, allegedly quoting Pythagoras, in Petri Abaelardi, *Opera Theologica*, vol. 2: *Theologia Christiana*, in Eligii M. Buytaert, ed., *Corpus Christianorum: Continuatio Mediaevalis*, vol. 12 (Turnholti: Typographi Brepols Editores Pontificii, 1969), p. 110. Original quotation in Salvianus, *De Gubernatione Dei, Octo Libri dati ad S. Salonium Episcopum* (ca. 440 CE), bk. 1, in Salviani Massiliensis Presbyteri, *Opera Omnia*, ed. J. P. Migne (Paris, 1859), p. 29. The alleged quotation seems to paraphrase the account by Cicero's *On The Nature of the Gods*.
[854] Petri Abaelardi, *Opera Theologica*, vol. 3: *Theologia 'Summi Boni' / Theologia 'Scholarium'*, in E. M. Buytaert, ed., *Corpus Christianorum: Continuatio Mediaevalis*, vol. 13 (Turnholti: Typographi Brepols Editores Pontificii, 1987), '*Scholarium*', Part 1, pp. 389-93.
[855] Guillaume de Saint-Thierry to the Geoffroy Bishop of Chartres and Bernard of Clairvaux, late in 1139, in Jean Leclercq, ed., *Receuil d'Études sur Saint Bernard et ses Écrits*, vol. 4 (Rome, 1987), p. 352: "5. Quod Spiritus Sanctus sit anima mundi."
[856] James Cotter Morrison, *The Life and Times of Saint Bernard, Abbot of Clairvaux, A.D. 1091-1153* (London, 1894), pp. 301-11.

ruling and he condemned Abelard's "erroneous books": "wherever you find them, burn them in fire."[857]

Henceforth, for centuries, Christian authorities denounced the "heresy" that the Holy Spirit is the *anima mundi*. One important example is the *Fourteen Books Against All Heresies*, first published in 1533. Its author, the prominent Franciscan theologian and jurist Alfonso de Castro, included a section on heresies against God, including: "The eleventh heresy: that the Holy Spirit is the soul of the world," blaming this heresy on Abelard.[858] Castro's treatise on heresies was published in at least fifteen editions from 1533 until 1578, in Paris, Cologne, Lyon, Antwerp, and Venice. Similarly, a Carmelite Father quoted Virgil's lines about "Spirit nourishes within," and then complained: "And what is a greater madness? What is a greater dementia than to say that this part is alive: all that is truly inanimate? What is this perversity? Indeed, really what is this frenzy? To attribute life to the universe...'[859] Likewise, the compendium of heresies authored by Sebastiano Medici, published in Venice and Florence in the 1580s, specified how Pythagoras defined God: as a soul that permeates all parts of the world, from which all animals receive their life.[860] Even some Protestants

[857] Pope Innocent II to the Archbishops of Sens and of Reims and to the Abbot of Clairvaux, 1141, in *Conciliorum Generalium Ecclesiae Catholicae*, vol. 4 (Rome, 1612), p. 23. Abelard died the following year, in 1142.

[858] But Castro's critique echoes its reputedly Pythagorean roots: "Since the world cannot receive the Holy Spirit, it is not possible that the Holy Spirit is the soul of the world, from which every body receives a soul that nourishes and vivifies it." These words echo Abelard's, which in turn were derived from those of Salvian and Cicero, when they referred to Pythagoras. Fratris Alfonsi de Castro, *Adversus Omnes Hæreses. Libri XIIII* (Paris, 1543), bk. 5, p. 80. Castro's treatise *Against All Heresies* was published in at least twelve more editions until 1578.

[859] Ioannes Pauli Donati, *Gonzagiorum, seu Solutionum Apparentium Contradictionum in dictis Arist. & D. Thomae Aquinatis Libri Quatuor* (Mantuae, 1578), p. 52.

[860] It also specified: "One heresy is to say that elementary Matter, from which the world is made, was not made by God, but is coeternal with God." Sebastiano Medice, *Summa Omnium Haeresum et Catalogus Schismaticorum, Haereticorum, et Idolatrarum* (Florence, 1581), p. 647. Sebastiani Medicis, *Summa Omnium Hæresum, et Catalogus Schismaticorum, & Idolatrorum*, second ed. (Venice, 1587), Part 1, p. 37 reverso; p. 62 verso. The author of this compendium of heresies was Sebastiano Medici, a distant relative of the first Grand Duke of Tuscany, Cosimo de Medici. Note also that in 1553, the Faculty of Divinity of the University of Paris had censured the claim "That the World was never made." It was a denial of Genesis. Any belief in the eternity of the world was a heresy if voiced by a Catholic. See, Faculty of Divinity of Paris, Censures of August 1, 1553, quoted in Louis Ellies Dupin, *A New Ecclesiastical History of the Sixteenth Century*, vol. 2, trans. or ed. William Wotton (London, 1706), p. 441.

repudiated these notions, e.g., a Protestant theologian remarked that these notions of God by Virgil and Pythagoras were "inexcusable" and "culpable," because they did not glorify God, but only a corruptible image that was "impious and blasphemous."[861]

Moreover, a *Criminal Treatise* published in Venice in 1590 specified that it is a heresy to "assert that the Holy Spirit is the soul of the world, as taught by Peter Abelard."[862] At that very same time, Bruno outlined in a book, *Lampas Triginta Statuarum*, that the "animam universi" or "spiritus" is the Holy Spirit.[863] Just two years later, Bruno asserted this very heresy when he was interrogated by Inquisitors in Venice; he replied: "Cosí quanto al Spirito divino per una terza persona, non ho possuto capire secondo il modo che si deve credere; ma secondo il modo Pitagorico, conforme a quel modo che mostra Salomone, ho inteso come anima dell'universo."[864] Fortunately, we have the primary source record of this quotation: the original transcripts of the Venetian proceedings. As far as I know, historians had not pointed out that Bruno's response about the universal soul was officially a heresy.[865]

---

[861] Wolfgang Musculus, *In Divi Ioannis Apostoli Evangelium Commentarii* (Basel, 1580), p. 90. Likewise, the Italian Protestant, Girolamo Zanchi, rejected that notion: Hieron. Zanchii, *De Operibus Dei intra Sex Dierum Creatis Opus: Tres in Partes Distinctum* (Neostadii Palatinorum, 1591), bk. 1, pp. 208-09; see also bk. 1, p. 197, and bk. 2, p. 599.

[862] Tiberii Deciani, *Tractatus Criminalis Omnium Hæresum*, vol. 1 (Venice, 1590), 236-37.

[863] Bruno wrote that 'Mens' = 'pater', 'substantia prima' = 'Filium, alii vero Verbum', and 'animam universi' = 'amor' = 'Spiritus'. Bruno, *Lampas Triginta Statuarum* (ca. 1590–91), in *Opera Latine Conscripta*, vol. 3, pp. 183-84; see also pp. 48, 54-60. In his deposition of 2 June 1592, in Venice, Bruno specified "che vi sia un Dio in Padre in Verbo et in Amore, che è il Spirito divino," in Firpo, *Processo*, 172.

[864] Firpo, *Processo*, p. 169. Bruno's words were understood to mean precisely that the Holy Spirit is the *anima mundi*. Thus, Schoppe complained that Bruno asserted: "Spiritum sanctum non esse aliud nisi *animam mundi*," in Gaspar Schoppe to Konrad Rittershausen, 17 February 1600, printed in Gaspari Scioppii, "Epistola, in qua haereticos jure infelicibus lignis cremari concludit," *Machiavellizatio* (Saragossae, 1621), p. 32. Frances Yates summed it up too: "his view of the Third Person as the *anima mundi*," in Frances Yates, *Giordano Bruno and the Hermetic Tradition* (1999 ed.), p. 350. Firpo too noted: "nell'identificazione dello Spirito Santo con *l'anima mundi*, chiaramente palesata nel III costituto," in Firpo, *Processo*, p. 97. *The Catholic Encyclopedia* claims that one of the reasons why Bruno was condemned was his belief that "the Holy Ghost is the soul of the world." William Turner, "Giordano Bruno," *The Catholic Encyclopedia*, vol. 3 (New York: Robert Appleton Company, 1908); accessed online 9 March 2018 <http://www.newadvent.org/cathen/03016a.htm>

[865] For example, here's how Frances Yates saw it: "his [Bruno's] view of the Third Person as the *anima mundi* would have been orthodox to many Christian

Subsequently, his offensive statement was quoted verbatim in Rome, when Inquisitors prepared a written summary of Bruno's trial.[866] And again, he was interrogated about it in his Seventeenth Deposition, in which he again relapsed into this heresy, apparently twice.[867]

Nevertheless, owing to the rise of humanism in the Renaissance, it was actually tolerable for Catholics to discuss pagan notions such as the *anima mundi*. However, it was less acceptable to use such notions to interpret the Bible, especially following the rise of the Protestants. For instance, in 1535, Agostino Steuco wrote a commentary on Genesis (before he became a Catholic bishop in 1538), in which he interpreted the "spirit of God hovered over the waters" as the *anima mundi* that vivifies all things. He attributed this belief to Pythagoras and Trismegistus, and he quoted Virgil's "*Spirit nourishes within.*"[868] But following the Council of Trent, clergymen became increasingly intolerant towards philosopher's efforts to reinterpret Scriptures in accord with Pythagoreanism or Platonism. Hence in 1583 and 1596,

Neoplatonists." Yates did not state that it was a heresy at all. Later, she.at least noted that Mersenne "condemns the doctrine of the anima mundi," but again, without giving context about the history of why this notion was repudiated by Catholics. Yates, *Giordano Bruno and the Hermetic Tradition* (1999 ed.), pp. 351, 475. Most scholars who study Bruno do not focus primarily on him as a heretic, but on his ideas, use of language, and poetry. Historians have written about Bruno's heresies and his errors in Catholic doctrine, certainly, but I haven't found any who specifies, for example, that Bruno's belief that the *anima mundi* is the Holy Spirit was regarded as a heresy precisely because that particular belief had been declared to be a heresy in 1141 at the Council of Sens, sanctioned by Pope Innocent II, so it became known as the heresy of Peter Abelard and was listed in catalogs of heresies for centuries. Without this kind of statement, it would seem unclear whether Bruno's belief in the *anima mundi* was merely "erroneous," "ill sounding," "offensive," "temerarious," "scandalous," "nearly heretical," or "heretical." Vassányi notes that prior to Bruno, Abelard too asserted that the Holy Spirit is the *anima mundi* "in a less intolerant epoch," but Vassányi did not note that this was condemned as one of Abelard's awful heresies. Vassányi, *Anima Mundi*, p. 330. Firpo reasoned that Bruno's "doctrines of the *anima mundi* and the human soul" were Bruno's "most exposed and dogmatically condemnable" replies, but likewise, without noting that "the Holy Spirit is the *anima mundi*" was officially a heresy; see Firpo, *Processo*, p. 90.

[866] Firpo, *Processo*, p. 254.

[867] Ibid., p. 255.

[868] Augustini Eugubini [Steuco], *Cosmopoeia, vel, de Mundano Opficio, Expositio Trium Capitum Genesis* (Lugduni, 1535), pp. 33-35, 42.

the Index of Forbidden Books banned Steuco's commentary on Genesis.[869] In 1589, in Rome, the Spanish Jesuit Benito Pereira complained that Steuco had defended views about the heavens that were "not only false, but even most absurd, & entirely abhorrent to Christian teachings."[870] And in 1594, while Bruno was imprisoned, Giovan Crispo criticised Steuco and Marsilio Ficino for daring to mix pagan doctrines with Christianity.[871] Among their objectionable pagan views, Crispo denounced the notion of the *anima mundi*, and the claim that human souls are parts of it.[872] Crispo said that most of the Protestants' heresies were rooted in pagan doctrines. In the Preface, Crispo praised Cardinal Bellarmino, saying that Bellarmino had informed him that Catholics who indulged in pagan notions should be censured along with the pagan writings.[873] Soon, in 1596, Bellarmino became a Consultor in Giordano Bruno's trial, and he became an Inquisitor in 1599. I will show that years later Bellarmino rebuked Bruno's various beliefs about souls and the *anima mundi*, in print (but again, without naming Bruno at all).

[869] Several other philosophers and Platonists were also censured or prosecuted. The Inquisition arrested professor Girolamo Cardano and condemned him to abjure in 1571, and Pope Pius V obstructed him from teaching and publishing. In 1575, 1580, and 1596, two works by the Neoplatonist Francesco Giorgio (Zorsi) were subjected to censures and suspended. In 1592, the Congregation of the Index heavily censured a book by the Platonist theologian Francesco Patrizi, until expurgated. In 1596, the *Cosmopoeia* of Steuco was banned. Ugo Baldini, "L'edizione dei documenti relativi a Cardano negli archivi del Sant'Ufficio e dell'Indice: risultati e problemi, in dans Cardano e la tradizione dei saperi," in M. Baldi and G. Canziani, eds., *Cardano e la tradizione dei saperi* (Milan: Franco Angeli, 2003), pp. 457-515. Luigi Firpo, "Filosofia italiana e Controriforma. II. La condanna di F. Patrizi," *Rivista di Filosofia* 41 (1950-51), 150-73. Grendler, *The Universities of the Italian Renaissance*, pp. 297-309. Tullio Gregory, "L'Apologia e le Declarationes di Francesco Patrizi," in *Medioevo e Rinascimento. Studi in onore di Bruno Nardi*, vol. 1 (Florence: Sansoni, 1955), pp. 385-424. Cesare Vasoli, "Intorno a Francesco Giorgio Veneto e all' 'armonia del mondo'," in Cesare Vasoli, *Profezia e ragione. Studi sulla cultura del Cinquecento e del Seicento* (Naples: Morano, 1974), pp. 291-92.
[870] Benedicti Pererii, *Commentariorum et Disputationum in Genesim, Tomi Quatuor*, vol. 1 (Cologne: Hierat, 1601), p. 17. See also Schmitt, "Perennial Philosophy," p. 525. In another work, Pereira specifically rejected the notion of the *anima mundi*: Benedicti Pererii, *De Communibus Omnium Rerum Naturalium Principiis & Affectionibus* (Cologne: Lazari Zetzneri, 1609), pp. 284, 831.
[871] For Ficino's views about the *anima mundi*, see D. P. Walker, *Spiritual and Demonic Magic, from Ficino to Campanella* (London: Warburg Institute, 1958), pp. 12-13.
[872] Io. Baptistae Crispi, *De Ethnicis Philosophis Caute Legendis Disputationum* (Rome, 1594), pp. 47, 59, 62-66, 73, 105-08, 209.
[873] Ibid., [p. xi].

In 1594, the Roman Inquisition imprisoned Tommaso Campanella for four serious accusations. As Campanella himself recorded, one of the Inquisition's accusations was that he had published "a doctrine about the soul of the world, about living beings and objects, contrary to the fundamental dogmas taught by the Church."[874] This evidence confirms that Bruno's Inquisitors were annoyed by claims about the *anima mundi* and the attribution of life to material objects.[875] In other words, both Bruno and Campanella were in the same Roman Inquisition prison, at the same time, for some of the same heresies, plus others. But unlike Bruno, Campanella recanted or denied these accusations. Still, the Roman Inquisitors brutally and bloodily tortured Campanella, while trying to force him to confess having affirmed heresies.

In this hostile atmosphere, Giordano Bruno dared to affirm his belief in the universal soul. Worse, he construed it as the Holy Spirit in front of his Inquisitors. Bruno had first discussed the universal spirit or soul in a book of 1584, *De la Causa, Principio, et Uno*. He wrote that it was "called by the Pythagoreans the motive force and mover of the universe, as said the poet [Virgil]: "Mind agitates the mass and mingles with the great body." In the same book Bruno quoted a longer excerpt of the same passage and attributed it to Pythagoras.[876] Decades later, Mersenne reported that

---

[874] Léon Blanchet, *Campanella* (Paris, 1920), p. 25. Campanella had published this argument in his book *De Sensitiva Rerum Facultate*, now lost. Decades later, Campanella published comments about the *anima mundi* in his revised edition of *De Sensu Rerum*. In the first edition (1620), his remarks appeared in only six pages, in understated ways. But in his revised edition (1637) he reviewed multiple individuals' views on the *anima mundi*, including "Timaeus the Pythagorean" and Virgil, and he argued that the Earth really does vivify all organisms, so that souls do not originate from nothing nor from a substance, but from the *anima mundi*. Campanella, *De Sensu Rerum, & Magia*, 2nd ed. (Paris: Ludovicum Boullenger, 1637), pp. 13, 21-2, 33-4, 37, 51, 56, 67, 94-5, 114-15.
[875] In 1598, the Inquisitors asked Campanella "if indeed an *anima mundi* exists, consequently it can be beatified or blessed, and therefore also the souls of animals and all parts of the world?" But Campanella replied that animals and things would not be beatified, yet he referred to Saint Gregory of Nyssa and Saint Augustine to "attribute to the world a Rational virtue almost as a soul." Campanella, *De Sensu Rerum, & Magia*, 2nd ed. pp. 90-91, also in Luigi Amabile, ed., *Fra Tommaso Campanella. La sua Congiura, I suoi Processi e la sua Pazzia*, Vol. 1, Pt. 1 (Naples: Antonio Morano, 1882), pp. 74-75. In this recollection, Campanella named three Cardinal Inquisitors: d'Ascoli (Girolamo Bernerio), Giulio Antonio Santori, and Costanzo Sarnano, who, at the same time were all confronting Bruno too.
[876] Bruno, *De la Causa*, Dialogue 2, pp. 39, 50; reissued in Giovanni Gentile, ed., *Opere Italiane di Giordano Bruno*, vol. 1 (Bari: Gius. Laterza & Figli, 1907), pp. 173, 183; also in Bruno, *Opere Italiane* 1, ed. Aquilecchia, pp. 652, 663.

Bruno's "evil book" *De la Causa* contained, "the dialogues for which he was burned in Rome, as some individuals have informed me."[877]

While analyzing *De la Causa*, historian Dilwyn Knox fairly remarks: "Bruno, of course, recognised that the World Soul was an essential feature of Plato's and Platonic cosmology. ... For Bruno, however, the doctrine was not Plato's invention, nor was it quintessentially Platonic. Rather, it was Pythagorean."[878] Knox noted that the ancient Stoics had developed such notions previously, but apparently Bruno was unaware of it. In a manuscript, Bruno again attributed Virgil's words to Pythagoras, arguing that heavenly bodies are animated by "one universal spirit ingrained in the universal machine, one mind, infused through the framework, moves the universal mass, as said by Pythagoras."[879] In another work Bruno discussed the divine: "for the Pythagoreans it is an infinite spirit that penetrates everything, comprehending and vivifying."[880] Next, in *The Heroic Frenzies*, Bruno again said that the heavenly bodies are composed of superior powers (that abide with the divinity) along with inferior powers that abide with the "mass" and "vivify" the body, to sustain "the living things in that world." Bruno praised Virgil as "the Pythagorean poet."[881] In sum, at least *twelve* of Bruno's books discussed the *anima mundi*.

Significantly, Bruno supported his notion of the *anima mundi* in all three of his books advocating the Earth's motion: *The Ash Wednesday Supper* (1584), *Infinite Universe and Worlds* (1584), and *On the Immense, or the Universe*

---

[877] Mersenne, *L'impiété des déistes*, vol. 1, pp. 363-64.

[878] Knox, "Bruno: Immanence and Transcendence," 466, 473. See also, Émile Namer, *Les Aspects de Dieu dans la Philosophie de Giordano Bruno* (Paris, 1926), pp. 35-37, 52-55, 63-64, 70, 87-91, 98.

[879] Giordano Bruno, *De Magia Mathematica*, in Bruno, *Opere Magiche*, ed. M. Ciliberto, S. Bassi, E. Scapparone, and N. Tirinnanzi (Milan, 2000), p. 22. Scholars argue that much of Bruno's *De Magia* is copied from various sources. Note, however, that the passage in question is not copied verbatim from any source. All the texts recently republished as the *Opere Magiche* remained in manuscript, presumably among the papers of his pupil, friend, and secretary Jerome Besler (1566-1632), and did not begin to be published until 1891, and therefore were not available to Bruno's readers or critics in the 1590s. See Bruno, *Opera Latine Conscripta*, vol. 3.

[880] Bruno, *Camoeracensis Acrotismus* (1588), in Jordani Bruni Nolani, *Opera Latine Conscripta*, ed. F. Fiorentino, vol. 1 (Naples, 1879), Article LXV, p. 177.

[881] Bruno, *Heroici Furori*, see: "Argomento" and Dialogue 2 [unnumbered pages: pp. xxii, 22]. See also Bruno, *Gli Eroici Furori* (Milan: G. Daelli, 1864), pp. 19, 44; or Aquilecchia, ed., *Opere Italiane* 2, pp. 511, 543.

1583	*Sigillus Sigillorum*
1584	*De la Causa, Principio, et Uno*
1584	*La Cena de le Ceneri*
1584	*De l'Infinito Universo et Mondi*
1584	*Spaccio de la Bestia Trionfante*
1584	*Camoerancis Acrotismus*
1585	*De gli Heroici Furori*
1585	*Cabala del Cavallo Pegaseo*
1591	*De Triplici Minimo et Mensura*
1591	*De Monade, Nimero et Figuraa*
1591	*De Innumerabilibus, Immenso, & Infigurabili*
1595	*Summa Terminorum Metaphysicorum*

Table 10.   *In twelve books, Bruno wrote about the Soul of the World.*

(1591).[882] Thus Bruno amalgamated ancient *pagan animism* with the Copernican thesis of the moving Earth. This is precisely what Inchofer excoriated about the New-Pythagoreans in 1633-35, when he explained at length why their views were theologically offensive and heretical.

In his books, Bruno was not as overt in stating that the Holy Spirit is the *anima mundi*, as he did under interrogation. Still, in addition to making this point in his *Lampas Triginta*, a similar claim appears in his book *Expulsion of the Triumphant Beast*. He there wrote that God "is the soul of the soul of the world, if not the soul itself."[883] (Note that Bruno did not write: *the Father* is the soul of the world; therefore, here the name 'God' could fairly be used to refer to one or all three of the divine persons: Father, Son, or

[882] Giordano Bruno, *La Cena delle Ceneri* (London, 1584), pp. 70-71 (Aquilecchia, ed., *Opere Italiane* 1: *Cena*, pp. 508-509); Bruno, *De l'Infinito Universo et Mondi* (1584), pp. 23-25, 67-69, 89 (*Opere Italiane* 2: *Infinito*, [sic] *Universo*, pp. 54-55, 84-85, 103); *De Innumerabilibus, Immenso, & Infigurabili, seu, De Vniuerso & Mundis libri octo* (Frankfurt: Ioan. Wechelum & Petrum Fischerum, 1591), in Bruno, *Opera Latine Conscripta*, vol. 1, Part 2 (Naples: Morano, 1884), bk. 8, pp. 346-47, 370, 480. Note: "*Infinity, Universe*" is not the correct translation of *Infinito Universo*, a phrase that appears not only in the cover, but eighteen times in the book.

[883] Bruno, *Spaccio de la Bestia Trionfante* (Paris, 1584), Third Dialogue, p. 217; also in Aquilecchia, ed., *Opere Italiane* 2, p. 363. Incidentally, this book was mentioned in his final condemnation. Saint Augustine had denied that God is the *anima mundi* in his *De Civitate Dei contra Paganos*, bk. 7, chaps. 9, 13, 22, 23.

Holy Spirit, but to say that the Holy Spirit in particular is the *anima mundi* was the heresy of Peter Abelard. Moreover, as we will see, in 1611 Cardinal Bellarmino denied that God is the *anima mundi*—which had been proposed by Bruno and William Gilbert.)

By early 1597, several Roman theologians, working as Consultors for the Inquisition, extracted ten heretical propositions from Bruno's books.[884] I must point out that, remarkably, *five of those ten propositions* involved the *anima mundi* (or, soulful heavenly bodies). Bruno's first censured proposition stated that things are generated from primal matter and the eternal "*anima mundi*."[885] His third censured proposition stated that human souls originate from "the universal soul."[886] His seventh censured proposition was that Earth is animated as a rational animal, infused with the "universal spirit" that animates all its animals too.[887] Plus, Bruno's fifth censured proposition: Earth's mobility, was a consequence of Earth being a soulful animal.[888] Also, his sixth censured proposition was that heavenly bodies too are *animated* rational beings, angels.[889] (However, since ancient times various theologians had construed the stars to be in some sense animated or angelic, so it is surprising to see this belief *censured* by the Consultors for the Inquisition in Bruno's trial.)

[884] "Summarium quarundam responsionum Fratris Iordani ad censuras factas super Propositionibus quibusdam ex libris elicitis," in Mercati, *Il Sommario*, pp. 113-19. Also in Firpo, *Processo*, pp. 299-304

[885] Firpo, *Processo*, p. 299. E.g., Bruno made such claims in: *De La Causa, Principio et Uno* ('Venice' [London], 1584), pp. 73-74, 81 (or Aquilecchia ed., *Opere Italiane* 1, pp. 686-87, 691-92). *De Triplici Minimo et Mensura* (Frankfurt, 1591), p. 74 (also in *Opera Latine*, vol. 1, Pt. 3, 209-10).

[886] Firpo, *Processo*, pp. 28, 300. Bruno discussed this subject in *De la Causa*, pp. 39-40, 43, 49-50, 73-74 (Aquilecchia ed., *Opere Italiane* 2, pp. 652-56, 661-63, 686); in *Cabala*, unnumbered pages [pp. 50-51] (Aquilecchia ed., *Opere Italiane* 2, pp. 450-51); etc.

[887] Firpo, *Processo*, p. 303. Bruno argued that Earth is rational in *La Cena*, pp. v, 70-71 (or Aquilecchia ed., vol. 1, pp. 436, 512); *Infinito Universo*, p. 88 (Aquilecchia ed., vol. 2, p. 54-102); *De Immenso*, p. 113, 146, 154, 195. Saint Augustine had denied that Earth is animated by the *anima mundi* in *De Civitate Dei*, bk. 7, chap. 23.

[888] E.g., Bruno, *Infinito Universo*, pp. [ix], 23, 151, 166, 175 (Aquilecchia ed., vol. 2, pp. 16, 54, 149, 159, 167).

[889] Firpo, *Processo*, p. 303. Bruno argued that stars are animated in *La Cena*, pp. v, 70-71 (or Aquilecchia edition, vol. 1, pp. 436, 512), *Infinito Universo*, pp. 23-24 (Aquilecchia ed., vol. 2, pp. 54-55), *Heroici Furori*, Fourth Dialogue unnumbered pages [p. 107] (Aquilecchia ed., vol. 2, p. 597); *De Immenso*, p. 433. Augustine had denied that stars have souls or are divine in *De Civitate Dei*, bk. 7, chaps. 6, 15. Augustine had thus denied these pagan notions of animism, even though he did not categorize them as heresies in *De Civitate*.

Thus, Bruno had affirmed heresies of the Manichæans, Origen, Abelard, and several heresies denounced by Tempier and the Council of Vienna. Did Bruno initially know that his written claims were, or had once been, heretical? His replies to Inquisitors repeatedly suggest that he did not know, because he insisted that he had said nothing contrary to Catholic doctrines. He repeatedly asserted his agreement with Catholic doctrines, and in 1599 he asked whether the Apostolic See had presently declared his propositions to be heretical.[890] The Pope soon replied that "all these propositions are heretical, and not now declared so for the first time, but by the most ancient Fathers of the Church and the Apostolic See."[891] Two more Inquisitorial documents echo this claim, one of them adding that these propositions were "heretical and contrary to the Catholic faith" and that the ancient Church Fathers had "rejected and condemned" them.[892] If we may apply the Pope's reply to Bruno's statements about the *anima mundi*, we find that indeed such statements had been declared heretical by Church Fathers and the Apostolic See, especially by Pope Vigilius and Pope Innocent II.[893]

Again, in 1597 the Consultors of the Roman Inquisition *censured* Bruno's claims that the Earth and the stars are animated beings and that the Earth moves, and Inchofer too denied these claims in 1633-35.

In September 1599, Bruno still had not recanted all his heresies, so officers of the Inquisition voted that he should be tortured. Only one of them specified a reason why: "concerning foremost the holiest Trinity torture him."[894] This confirms that one of Bruno's heresies was his interpretation

---

[890] Bruno, 25 January 1599, quoted in "Copia parziale della sentenza, destinata al governatore di Roma," 8 February 1600, in Firpo, *Processo*, pp. 340-41.

[891] "Decreto della Congregazione del Sant'Uffzio," 4 February 1599, in Firpo, *Processo*, pp. 313-14.

[892] "Bella copia interrota," and "Bella copia sommaria," 4 February 1599, in Firpo, *Processo*, pp. 314-15.

[893] Meanwhile, another early advocate of Copernicus, Thomas Digges, had also supported the belief that the *stars are animated*. Did Digges not know or care that this was one of Origen's heresies? In 1576, Digges had described stars as divine: "the very court of celestial angels devoid of grief." He used this characterization in the diagram that he titled "the most ancient Doctrine of the Pythagoreans." Digges, "A Perfit Description of the Caelestiall Orbes according to the most aunciente Doctrine of the Pythagoreans," in Leonard Digges, *A Prognostication Everlastinge* (1576), [numbered page] folio 43, English words modernised.

[894] Decreto della Congregazione del Sant'Uffizio, 9 September 1599; in Firpo, *Processo*, p. 329. The participants in the unanimous vote were the Prosecutor, the Commissary,

of the Trinity (and again, part of his interpretation was that the third person is the *anima mundi*).[895] Finally, five months later, in February 1600, Bruno was burned alive as an obstinate heretic. Gaspar Schoppe witnessed the fiery pyre, and he had also attended Bruno's condemnation at the palace of the senior Inquisitor Ludovico Madruzzi. Schoppe immediately recorded Bruno's "horrendous" doctrines, worthy of execution, including: that "the Holy Spirit is nothing other than the World Soul, as Moses meant by writing that it nourished the waters."[896]

Thus far, I have shown that animism was a much greater problem in Bruno's trial and condemnation than previously acknowledged. For example, in discussing Bruno's *Ash Wednesday Supper*, historian Miguel Granada had written: "It cannot be said that the concept of the heavens and the stars as animated and intelligent was heterodox or heretical."[897] Yet I have shown the opposite. Still, Granada rightly recognised that ever since the Patristic age some Christians viewed such beliefs as dangerous to the faith. Granada also acknowledged that such beliefs had been "condemned" at least by Bishop Tempier in the 1270s. But furthermore, as we have now seen, such beliefs also had been repudiated by major authorities such as Epiphanius

the Assessor, and three Consultors of the Inquisition. In addition, Pope Clement VIII was present at that meeting along with Cardinal Bellarmino and the other Cardinal Inquisitors. Still, the extant documents do not specify whether in fact Bruno was tortured. The Pope was patient, so more months passed.

[895] Firpo acknowledged that Bruno's dissolution of the dogma of the Trinity involved "l'identificazione dello Spirito Santo con l'anima del mondo." Firpo, *Processo*, p. 89.

[896] Schoppe to Rittershausen, 17 February 1600, in *Machiavellizatio*, p. 32. Also in Firpo, *Processo*, p. 351. The Latin words in Schoppe's account are *fovisse aquas*, which may be literally translated as "nourished the waters." Historians have construed this to be the same as Genesis 1:1, *Spiritus Dei ferebatur super aquas*, that is, "The Spirit of God hovered over the waters." For example, without referring to Bruno or Schoppe, Tullio Gregory noted that *fovebat aquas* is another translation of *ferebatur super aquas*; see Gregory, *Anima Mundi*, p. 126. Bruno's claim had been advanced previously by Ficino: "Hence the saying [by Virgil]: "*the Spirit nourishes within.*" Similarly, again, and containing the soul power, insofar as with itself it is glued (so to speak), like oil that swims on and surrounds the other. Perhaps here this tends to: "the Spirit of God hovered over the waters," or infused in the waters..." Marsilii Ficini, *In Plotini Epitomae, seu Argumenta, Commentaris & Annotationes*, in Ficini, *Operum* [*Opera*]: *in quo compraehenduntur ea, quae ex Graeco in Latinum Sermonem doctrissime transtulit, exceptis Platone atque Plotino Philosophis*, vol. 2 (Basel, 1561): "In Librum De Coelo [Plotinus], Comment. Summa Totius Libri," p. 1597. Bruno had studied the works of Ficino, and during his interrogations, Bruno had used other lines from the Bible and the *Aeneid*—by Bruno's so called "Pythagorean poet," Virgil—to interpret the Holy Spirit as being the soul of the universe.

[897] Granada, "Introducción," in *La Cena de las Cenizas*, pp. cxlv-cxlvi.

and Augustine, and had been deemed *heretical* by multiple others, including Saint Jerome, the Fifth Ecumenical Council (confirmed by Pope Vigilius and by the subsequent Ecumenical Council), the Council of Sens (and hence Pope Innocent II), the Sorbonne (under the authority of Pope John XXI), various treatises on heresies, and the Venetian and Roman Inquisitions in the 1590s.

Thus I'm arguing that Bruno's interpretation of the Holy Spirit as the *anima mundi* was one of the main reasons why he was executed. Compare it to some alleged alternative reasons why he was executed, proposed by historians.

For example, some historians have claimed that Bruno was executed partly because he denied Christ's Incarnation.[898] However, this is a mistake; Bruno did not deny this in his depositions at all. He only stated that he "merely" did not know *how* God became incarnate in Christ, which, to be fair, is something that no Catholic knew. Bruno was incautious or impertinent in raising this "philosophical" issue to Inquisitors, but he did not deny that it did happen: "I have merely doubted how this second person became incarnate, as I said before, and had suffered, but I have never denied this."[899] Moreover, in none of his books did Bruno ever deny that Jesus was the Incarnation of God, and he even testified that he had written no such denial. And no such denial was extracted from his books by Consultors or Inquisitors.

Also, some historians have claimed that Bruno was executed partly because he denied transubstantiation.[900] Their conjecture arose because Bruno's condemnation states "That you had said that it is a great blasphemy to say that the bread transubstantiates into flesh, etc." However, his condemnation specifies that that accusation was "from eight years ago," that is, from the very first list of accusations against Bruno by layman Giovanni Mocenigo in 1592, therefore not necessarily one of the "eight propositions"

---

[898] E.g., Vassányi, *Anima Mundi*, p. 329; Hilary Gatti, *Essays on Giordano Bruno* (Princeton: Princeton University Press, 2010), p. 194; Paul Richard Blum, *Giordano Bruno—An Introduction*, translated by Peter Henneveld (New York: Rudopi, 2012), pp. 5-6. Nonetheless, these writers also propose other reasons, e.g., Vassányi fairly conjectures that "one charge on which his death sentence was probably based was his thesis identifying the Holy Spirit with the universal soul," yet Vassányi did not specify that this was precisely a heresy. Vassányi, *Anima Mundi*, p. 330.

[899] Firpo, *Processo*, p. 170; see also p. 172.

[900] E.g., Ingrid D. Rowland, *Giordano Bruno: Philosopher/Heretic* (New York, 2008), pp. 259-60.

(mentioned also in the condemnation) which constituted the accusations against Bruno by Inquisitor Bellarmino and the Commissary General of the Holy Office. In point of fact, Bruno did not deny transubstantiation in his trial or in any of his books. Therefore, denying transubstantiation could *not* be one of Bellarmino's accusations, precisely because the eight accusations were extracted *from Bruno's depositions and books*.[901] Moreover, Schoppe explained that at the time it *was not* illegal to be a Lutheran in Rome (they who denied transubstantiation). Plus there's no evidence at all that Bruno *relapsed* into saying anything heretical against transubstantiation.

In contradistinction, abundant evidence shows that Bruno's beliefs about the *anima mundi* were a grave problem. Because, (1) he repeatedly asserted the *anima mundi* in his books; (2) he reaffirmed it in his depositions; (3) he echoed Origen's heresies about animated heavenly bodies, (4) he overtly equated the *anima mundi* with the third person of the Trinity—*another heresy*; (5) the Inquisitors confronted him about his view of the Trinity; (6) Inquisitors complained that he *relapsed* into his heretical replies about it; (7) they proposed to torture him over his replies about the Trinity; plus, (8) eyewitness Schoppe quoted Bruno's "horrendous" belief precisely in the form that it was known as Abelard's heresy: "Spiritum S. esse nihil aliud, nisi animam mundi."

Summing up, among various accusations the Inquisitors censured and accused Bruno about the moving Earth and the *anima mundi*, and Inchofer similarly accused the Copernicans about the moving Earth and the *anima mundi*. So what about Galileo?

Galileo Galilei:
between the heretic and the Jesuits

As we have seen, in 1633-35, the critiques about the *anima mundi* that Inchofer raised against the Copernicans had been previously raised by Catholic authorities against Bruno. Inchofer's critiques were aimed not only at Galileo, who Inchofer did not name *in print*, but also at other "New Pythagoreans," who had asserted more egregious and heretical claims. And

---

[901] "...octo propositiones haereticae collectae ex eius libris et processu," in "Decreto della Congregazione del Sant'Uffizio," 14 January 1599, in Firpo, *Processo*, p. 312.

nobody but Bruno had more boldly or frequently asserted, in print, the very doctrines that Inchofer denounced. Bruno was even known as the foremost new advocate of the Pythagoreans.[902]

It is most clearly in the long proceedings against Bruno, that we see the link between the Roman Catholic denial of the Earth's motion alongside other heretical beliefs of the Pythagoreans: the claims about the existence of other worlds, the soul of the world, and the transmigration of souls, and the questioning of the uniqueness or divinity of Christ.

The question is: How does Galileo fit in the period between Bruno's Pythagorean advocacy of the *anima mundi*, and Inchofer's extensive repudiation of such beliefs? In 1616, the Decree of the Index prohibited the "false Pythagorean doctrine' that Earth moves—which prevented Galileo and other Catholics from affirming the Earth's motion.[903] That very same expression, the "Pythagorean doctrine" had been used previously by one heretic who defended the Earth's motion: Bruno. In the 1590s, he told Inquisitors in Venice and Rome about "the Pythagorean doctrine" that a spirit animates the Earth. What I propose is that there is a thread of "Pythagorean" concerns that runs from Bruno's trial to the anti-Copernican censorship Decree of 1616 to Inchofer's *Vindication* upon Galileo's condemnation.

In 1610, Galileo published his telescopic discoveries about the Moon, the planets, and stars. Months later, the imprisoned heretic Campanella praised Galileo for "retrieving for us the glory of the Pythagoreans, stolen from the subtle Greeks, resurrecting their dogmas."[904] Worried that Galileo's claims could arouse clergymen's objections, Campanella warned him that if "theologians might murmur," Galileo could quote ancient theologians to defend himself: "You have Origen, who taught that the Earth is an animal and all the stars, and praises the Pythagorean dogmas and tested by

---

[902] Christiano Longomontano, *Astronomiæ Danicæ appendix de asscititiis coeli phænomenis* (Amsterdam, 1622), p. 3.

[903] "Decretum Sacrae Congregationis," 5 March 1616 (Rome), reproduced in Berti, *Il Processo Originale di Galileo*, pp. 54-56.

[904] Tommaso Campanella to Galilei, Ides [13th] of January 1611, in Campanella, *Lettere*, ed. Vincenzo Spampanato (Bari, 1927), p. 165.

the Scriptures."[905] Campanella did not warn Galileo that Origen's claim that stars are animated had been categorized as heretical.

Meanwhile, in a book of 1605, one of Bruno's Inquisitors had denied that the Earth or the heavenly bodies are divine, soulful, or alive. Cardinal Bellarmino wrote: "God is not an inanimate thing; hence [God] is not the Earth, not Heaven, not the Sun, not the Moon, not the Stars: because all these things are inanimate, & inferior to the animate things."[906] Later, Bellarmino also denied another one of Bruno's main claims: that God is the universal soul.[907] Bellarmino's remarks appear in his commentaries on the Book of Psalms, published in 1611 and 1612. While discussing Psalm 41:5, "These things I remembered, and poured out my soul in me," Bellarmino commented:

> The soul does not move in the body, and entirely moves, rules, and vivifies the body; and gives it sense; we know that in death the soul departs from it, the body gradually falls, & motion, sense, species, & whatever good it had; in a moment the body loses that which is the soul, it is a thing of universal God, but properly speaking, this does not mean that God is the soul of the world, what the Philosophers seem to have thought; but the likeness that souls seem to have: He remains immobile in Himself, the *word carries all* of His power, *and in Him we live, move, & are.*[908]

---

[905] Ibid., p. 167. Campanella also suggested that Galileo read Campanella's own "three books On the Philosophy of the Pythagoreans," which are now lost. Twenty-five years later, Campanella asserted, in his *Metaphysica*, that he fully agreed with Origen that the stars are living beings, "spirits endowed with power and wisdom." Campanella said that the Sun rules over everything "as the Vicar of God," and that its soul is the *anima mundi*. See, Walker, *Spiritual and Demonic Magic*, pp. 226-27.

[906] Roberto Bellarmino, *Dichiaratione del Simbolo*, second ed. (Naples, 1605), p. 12. Previously, Bellarmino had also complained that some of the ancients worshipped the Sun as a god; see Bellarmino, *De Gratia & Libero Arbitrio*, bk. 4, chap. 2, in Bellarmino, [*Disputationes, De Controversiis Christianae Fidei*] *Tertia Controversia Generalis, De Reparatione Gratiae per Iesum Christum Dominum Nostrum* (Ingolstadt, 1593), p. 278.

[907] E.g., in *Spaccio*, Third Dialogue, p. 217; also in Aquilecchia, ed., *Opere Italiane* 2, p. 363. For a discussion of Bruno's occasional but inconsistent claim that God is the *anima mundi*, see Vassányi, *Anima Mundi*, pp. 341-43. Criticizing Varro, Saint Augustine had denied that God is the anima mundi in *Civitate Dei*, bk. 7, chaps. 5-6, 9, 13, 23.

[908] Roberto Bellarmino, *Explanatio in Psalmos* (Rome, 1611), p. 292. Bellarmino, *Explanatio in Psalmos*, second ed. (Lyon, 1612), p. 292. The last phrase quotes the Acts of the Apostles, 17:28, which was quoted by Calcidius and Steuco in discussing the topic.

Bellarmino echoed the characteristic verb, *vivifies*, which had been used by Novatian, Abelard, Ficino, Scaliger, Bruno, Campanella, and Kepler—all to describe the universal spirit. The expression had been used with caution by Steuco, and it was criticized by Zanchi as blasphemous. At the time, some other theologians also denied that God's spirit infuses all bodies.[909] Bellarmino did not specify which philosophers suggested or wrote that God is the *anima mundi*; but among them were: Plotinus, Porphyry, Novatian, Abelard, Ficino, Bruno, and Gilbert.[910] Bellarmino had served in the Index, and in 1592 he prepared a list of "*Heresiarchs, that is, those who invented or*

[909] For example, the French jurist Pierre Grégoire listed "False gods," including the "obstinate reasonings" of "Pythagoras of Samos and M. Varro that soul permeates the entire universe." Petro Gregorio, *Syntaxeon Artis Mirabilis, in Libros XL Digestarum*, vol. 2 (Cologne, 1610), pp. 79-80. Professor Grégoire's encyclopedic work incorporated sciences and mathematics with astrology and demonology, all from a devoutly Catholic perspective. He explained that, "False Gods have originated from the Devil's wickedness or pretentiousness and his pride, and from other fictions and empty reasonings." Still, his book was placed on the Index of Forbidden Books. Next, the theologian Placido Padiglia published a long commentary on Psalm 50: "Unto the end, a psalm of David," where he noted a censured notion: "not that we want to say, with Pythagoras, that God is a soul dispersed throughout all parts of the World, that by this perhaps we mean that which the [Solomon's book of] Wisdom says: For the spirit of God fills the Earthly orb." Placido Padiglia, *David Penitente Lezzioni sopra il Cinquantesimo Salmo di David* (Rome, 1610), p. 143. This same quotation had been used by Bruno, in writing and also under interrogation by Inquisitors, to construe the Holy Spirit as the universal soul. Padiglia didn't mention Bruno, but he dedicated his book to the "most illustrious and most reverend" Cardinal Bellarmino, the Protector of Padiglia's congregation. Accordingly, Bellarmino owned a copy of this book, which is now at the Biblioteca Nazionale Centrale di Roma, item 6.36.E.11; it came from the Library of the Collegio Romano.

[910] For analysis of the link between Novatian, Bruno, and Virgil's *Aeneid*, see Lucia Boschetti, "Sul processo di Giordano Bruno: Indagini attorno all'eresia Novaziana," *Rinascimento: Rivista dell'Istituto Nazionale di Studi sul Rinascimento*, ser. 2, vol. 46 (2006), 93–130. The first heresy in Bellarmino's list of Bruno's eight heresies was "the Novatian heresy," and Boschetti argues that he referred to Novatian's *De Trinitate*, as heretically denying the Catholic notion of the third person, the Holy Spirit. Novatian claimed that there are only two persons of God (the Father and Son) and did not use the word Trinity in his treatise, but argued that the so-called third person is really just God the Father, because the God *is* a spirit. The only other known heresy from Bellarmino's list of eight was Bruno's belief that the human soul is like a sailor in a ship (contrary to what was required by the Council of Vienna, that the soul is the form of the body). See "Decreto della Congregazione del Sant'Uffizio," 24 August 1599, in Firpo, *Processo*, p. 324.

fomented heresies, or were the leaders of heretics." Heresiarchs were worse than heretics, and Bellarmino included Abelard as a heresiarch.[911]

Subsequently, Bellarmino's role in Catholic censorship grew: he became the prefect of the Index in 1605.[912] And he dedicated his book of 1611 to Pope Paul V, another one of Bruno's Inquisitors. Bellarmino there also denied Earth's motion on the basis of Scriptures and he asserted its centrality, contrary to the doctrines of Copernicus and Bruno (although Bellarmino did not name them there).

Also in 1611, John Donne anonymously used Galileo's lunar discoveries combined with Bruno's beliefs to ridicule the Jesuits.[913] Donne mocked the founder of the Jesuits as possessed by the Devil and damned in Hell, on the Moon.[914] He wrote that Copernicus tried to enter the most exclusive chamber of Hell, because "the Papists have extended the name and punishment of *Heresy* to almost everything." Donne's Copernicus bragged: "I

---

[911] Roberto Bellarmino, "Haeresiarchae, id est, qui haereses invenerunt vel suscitarunt, vel dices haereticorum fuerunt" (1592); reproduced in Peter Godman, *The Saint as Censor: Robert Bellarmine between Inquisition and Index* (Leiden: Brill, 2000), p. 286; see also p. 167. The list includes Calvin, Luther, Melanchthon, Andreas Osiander, and others.

[912] Godman, *The Saint as Censor*, pp. 182, 213, 219. Bellarmino served as prefect until 1621, the year he died.

[913] Donne did not name Bruno in his book, but it includes multiple notions that had been advocated in print by Bruno (in London) but *not* by Galileo, including: (1) the Moon is a star, (2) the Moon is an inhabited world, (3) the planets are also worlds, (4) there are worlds in the stars, (5) such worlds are also inhabited by rational beings, (6) humans can travel to such worlds, (7) human souls can travel out of their bodies, plus, (8) the reference to the soul of the world. [John Donne], *Conclave Ignati: sive Eius in Nuperis Inferni Comitiis Inthronisatio* (n.p., 1611), this anonymous first Latin edition was recorded in the Stationer's Register on 24 January 1611 (it was printed in London and on the continent); pp. 5, 8, 28-31. Did Donne know Bruno"s works? For discussion, see Edmund Gosse, *The Life and Letters of John Donne*, vol. 1 (London, 1899), pp. 56, 269. Jack Lindsay conjectured that Donne's use of the circle metaphor as well as lines 7-10 in his "Love's Alchymie" were drawn from Bruno. Jack Lindsay, "Donne and Giordano Bruno," *Times Literary Supplement* (20 June 1936), 523. Richard Ince conjectured that Donne learned of Bruno's works through Henry Percy, Ninth Earl of Northumberland. Richard Ince, "Donne and Giordano Bruno," *Times Literary Supplement* (27 June 1936), 544. Consequently, Frances Yates agreed with Lindsay and Ince that Bruno influenced Donne. Yates, "Donne and Giordano Bruno," *Times Literary Supplement* (4 July 1936), 564. Furthermore, Linsday provided additional similarities to even argue that Donne's "originality" stemmed from the influence of Bruno's works. Lindsay, "Donne and Giordano Bruno," *Times Literary Supplement* (11 July 1936), 580.

[914] Donne, *Conclave Ignati*, pp. 8, 13, 22, all italics in the original. Donne had previously attacked Bellarmino in a book of 1610, *Pseudo-Martyr*. The Jesuits did not reply to Donne's critiques.

was the soul of the Earth."[915] Since Origen inhabited that chamber of Hell, Donne asked whether Copernicus too belonged in that chamber of *"Antichristian Heroes."*[916] Donne also ridiculed Bellarmino for having evil and vow-breaking ambitions, he wrote, and for being *"the Sword of the Roman Church."*[917]

In 1613, one of Galileo's critics, the priest Francesco Ingoli, declared (in a dinner hosted by Galileo's patron, Prince Cesi) that the opinion "the heavens are animated" was "condemned as erroneous by the Sorbonne of Paris," that is, by Bishop Tempier.[918] Also in 1613, Cardinal Bellarmino discussed the "extremely serious" disputes of the origin of the soul, saying that philosophers such as Plato and Origen voiced erroneous views.[919]

---

[915] Donne, *Conclave Ignati*, p. 7.

[916] Ibid., 9. There has been some debate as to whether Donne's references to Copernicus and Galileo somehow suggests that Donne appreciated their works and used them to belittle the Jesuits. However, a close reading of Donne's text shows that he disdained the new astronomers. I entirely agree with the systematic analysis presented by Chris Hassel, "Donne's *Ignatius His Conclave* and the New Astronomy," *Modern Philology*, 68, no. 4 (May 1971), 329-37; which compellingly shows that Donne disliked the Copernican astronomers" arrogance and vainglory. As Hassel wrote, "To Donne the astronomers and the Jesuits are equally foolish and equally dangerous." Another scholar remarks that Donne had a "characteristically negative attitude to innovation" and he thus viewed the Jesuits as "guilty of innovations in religion"; see Achsah Guibbory, *Returning to John Donne* (Farnham, England: Ashgate: 2015), p. 27.

[917] *Conclave Ignati*, pp. 16–17, 22–3.

[918] Francesco Ingoli to Cardinal Bonifacio Caetani, 9 August 1613, in Archivio Caetani, Rome, Fondo Generale, no. 140664. Quoted in Massimo Bucciantini, "Teologia e Nuova Filosofia. Galileo, Federico Cesi, Giovambattista Agucchi e la Discussione sulla Fluidità e Corruttibilità del Cielo," in *Sciences et Religions de Copernic à Galilée (1540-1610), Actes du Colloque International Organisé par l'École Française de Rome* (Romae, 1999), p. 412. Ingoli and Inchofer were not the only theologians who still claimed that the notion of animated heavens was heretical. E.g., in 1627 Livio Galante warned that Christians should approach Plato's doctrines only with caution, rejecting the belief that the world is a soulful animal, "that which is denied by our law," because "if it were allowed, it would give the opportunity to Heretics who hold (wrongly) that the heavens and the elements are animated, an opinion that is false & heretical and is legally condemned & reproved." Galante credited Augustine for repudiating this heresy, and he blamed it on the Manichaeans and "the wicked men who were excommunicated & condemned in Paris." Livio Galante, *Christianae Theologiae cum Platonica Comparatio* (Bonn, 1627), p. 269.

[919] Roberto Bellarmino, *De Amissione Gratiae et Statu Peccati Libri Sex* (1613); reissued in Bellarmino, *Disputationum: De Controversiis Christianae Fidei Adversus Huius Temporis Haereticos*, vol. 4 (Naples, 1858), bk. 4, chap. 11, p. 161. Incidentally, note that Origen had said that heavenly bodies are rational beings, and Saint Jerome had denounced

Bellarmino criticised six propositions by "pagan philosophers" about the origins of human souls. He wrote: "The First proposition is that human souls are fragments of the substance of God, therefore are not properly created," but are somehow breathed [*inspirari*] by God.[920] Bellarmino objected that since God's substance is really immutable and inviolable, whereas souls are not, this proposition had been "rightly condemned [*damnata*] as heretical."[921] Instead, he said, God makes human souls from nothing. Furthermore, in 1615, Bellarmino finished and published a book *On the Ascent of the Mind to God by a Ladder of Created Things*. He took the opportunity to again reject the notion of the *anima mundi*. He wrote: "Since the soul is in the body, & governing, and moving [the body], it necessarily has the form of the body, and so it is conjoined with it, so that from the soul & body one man is made. God does not need, in order to make the soul, a World Soul; neither is there made a composite substance from Himself & the world."[922] Thus, Bellarmino gave an argument absent in his previous critique of 1611. It was the same argument published by a Dominican preacher Augustino Petreto against the two heresies that either God or the Holy Spirit is the *anima mundi*, which is fitting, since Bellarmino owned a copy of Petreto's monograph.[923]

In print, Bellarmino did not name Giordano Bruno, so he did not point out that he was actually rejecting *eight* of Bruno's censured beliefs: (1) the

him for (allegedly) saying that human souls fall from heaven and may be clothed in new bodies. Jerome, *Ad Pammachium et Marcellinum Apologia Hieronymi adversum Ruffinum*, bk. 2 (402 CE), in Sancti Hieronymi Stridoniensis, *Opera Omnia*, ed. Mariani Victorii (1624), p. 511.

[920] Bellarmino, *De Amissione Gratiae*, chap. 11, p. 161.

[921] Note that Latin expressions such as *damnata*, had a stronger meaning than just our judicial sense of *condemned*, they could also mean the stronger, Catholic sense of *damned*.

[922] Roberto Bellarmino, *De Ascensione Mentis in Deum per Scalas Rerum Creaturum Opusculum* (Cologne, 1615), p. 181. Bellarmino included a dedication that specifies September.

[923] One year after Bruno's execution, Petreto listed nand censured several beliefs that Bruno defended, although he too did not name him. Instead, Petreto blamed such heresies on whomever had most infamously asserted them, or on groups such as "the philosophers." Alongside each heresy, he explained why it was false. He too blamed the heresy that "the Holy Spirit is the World Soul" on Peter Abelard. Augustino Petreto, *D. O. M. Turris Babel, et Totius Civitatis Babilonis Haeresos Vasta Destructio* (Reggio nell'Emilia, 1601), unnumbered pages: items 25, 52, 165, 250. Bellarmino's copy is at the Biblioteca Nazionale Centrale di Roma, item MISC.B.705.1, which came from the Library of the Collegio Romano.

Earth has a soul, (2) the Earth moves, (3) heavenly bodies have souls, (4) God infuses the substance of the world, (5) the universal soul is God (or the Holy Spirit), (6) any human soul isn't the form of its body, (7) human souls are fragments of the universal soul, and (8) souls vivify bodies. This cannot be a coincidence because Bellarmino and the other Inquisitors had explicitly denounced *all of these* beliefs during Bruno's trial.

What about Galileo? Since Inchofer accused the New Pythagoreans of asserting heresies about the *anima mundi*, and since he counted Galileo among the New Pythagoreans, then did Galileo too believe in a universal spirit? Historian David Wootton has argued that, secretly, Galileo did believe in it.[924] In April 1615, Galileo confided to Piero Dini, one of his supporters:

> it seems to me that in nature there is found a most spiritual substance, most tenuous and most rapid, which, spreading itself throughout the universe, penetrates into all without distinction, warming, vivifying and giving fecundity to all living creatures; and about this spirit of which the senses themselves show that the body of the Sun is its foremost reservoir, from which an immense light expands throughout the universe, accompanied by this spirit that heats and penetrates into all vegetative bodies, and gives them life and fecundity.[925]

For Galileo, this universal, vivifying spirit was not just light. He paraphrased Genesis 1:1 to characterise this fertilizing spirit as *"nourishing the waters or incubating over the waters."*[926] That very same passage was quoted by Bruno to argue that the Holy Spirit is the *anima mundi*.[927] Still, someone might

---

[924] David Wootton, *Galileo, Watcher of the Skies* (New Haven: Yale University Press, 2010), pp. 240–50.

[925] Galileo to Piero Dini, 23 March 1615, in *Le Opere di Galileo Galilei, Edizione Nazionale*, vol. 5 (Florence: G. Barbèra, 1895), p. 301. Also in Maurice A. Finocchiaro, *The Galileo Affair: A Documentary History* (Berkeley: University of California Press, 1989), pp. 63-64.

[926] Ibid., 302: Galileo wrote: "[Spiritus Dei] *foventem aquas seu incubantem super aquas.*"

[927] Similarly, while discussing errors and heresies, the Jesuit Francisco Suárez rejected philosophers' identification of the Holy Spirit as the *anima mundi*, using both verbs *foveat* and *ferebatur:* "Spiritum sanctum . . . ut foveat, et quasi conservet, et moveat universa juxta illud Gen. 1. *Spiritus Domini ferebatur super aquas:* et ideo aliqui vocabant hunc spiritum, animam Mundi, sicut quidam Philosophi de Deo locuti sunt." Francisco Suárez, *De Sanctissimo Trinitatis Mysterio* (1619), also in *Opera Omnia*, vol. 1 (Paris: Ludovicum Vivès, 1856), p. 584.

interpret Galileo's universal, vivifying spirit to be the element ether, as conveyed in Aristotle's and Galen's works on generation. Yet some authors conflated the ether with the universal spirit, construing the two as the same.

Galileo wrote that the Sun is located at the centre of the universe "because" there it can receive, focus, and strengthen the "fertilizing spirit" to project it. He wrote that sunspots might be "nourishments" or "excrements" of the Sun, as if the Sun were alive. He further wrote: "the vital spirit sustains and vivifies all the limbs," as if echoing Virgil, as if the universe itself were a living being with bodily parts. And Galileo noted: "I could provide many testimonies from philosophers and serious writers, in favor of the marvelous force and energy of this spirit..." He didn't quote them, but among them were: Pythagoras (allegedly), Varro, Virgil, Apollonius, Novatian, Trismegistus, Abelard, Ficino, Steuco, Bruno, Gilbert, Campanella, and Kepler. Yet some of their claims had been repudiated by saints and clergymen such as Saint Jerome, Saint Augustine, Saint Epiphanius, Bishop Tempier, Castro, Petreto, Bruno's Inquisitors, and Bellarmino. Did Galileo know that his views about the universal, vivifying spirit might seem offensive at least to some clergymen? Apparently he did, because in the same letter of 1615, Galileo wrote caveats that he wrote in no other letters: "I know and confess my excessive temerity in opening my mouth, being inexperienced in Sacred Scriptures," so he asked his confidant to excuse him, saying that he did "submit totally to the judgment of my superiors," and he begged: "please do not let this [letter] reach the hands of anyone who, instead of with the sensitivity of the mother tongue, operates with the roughness and sharpness of a bestial fang, instead of polishing this, no, would lacerate and rip it apart entirely."[928]

Similarly, Galileo voiced the same belief in his private letter to the Grand Duchess Christina.[929] Galileo explicitly mentioned the *anima mundi*: while discussing the Sun, he wrote, "I don't think that it is far from good philosophizing to say that he [the Sun], as maximum minister of Nature, and in a certain way as the soul and heart of the World, infuses the other bodies that surround him not only with light, but also with motion..." Thus,

---

[928] Galileo to Dini, 23 March 1615, *Opere, Ed. Nazionale*, vol. 5, p. 305.
[929] Unlike Galileo's "Letter to Castelli," his more expansive letter to Christina remained relatively private: it circulated only among Galileo's close allies.

Galileo referred to the Sun as being the soul of the world.[930] Galileo quoted "Dionysus the Aeropagite," saying that the Sun "gathers together all that is dispersed," and it "renews, nourishes, protects, perfects, divides, marries, fosters, restores fecundity, increases, mutates, strengthens, delivers, moves, and vitalises all."[931] Like many writers in the Renaissance, Galileo apparently didn't know that this "Dionysus" was *not* the saint converted by Saint Paul. He was a theologian around 500 CE who misattributed his writings; and he tried to smuggle pagan beliefs into Christianity. Bruno too had praised this Dionysus as one of "the most profound and divine theologians" who worshipped God with silence, like Pythagoras.[932]

Now, when Galileo was first accused of asserting the Earth's motion, several of the Inquisitors involved had already participated in censoring Giordano Bruno for his belief that Earth moves because it is animated by the *anima mundi*. In early 1615, Father Niccolò Lorini denounced Galileo to the Inquisition, submitting a complaint to the Inquisitor Paolo Sfondrato, saying that the "Galileists" affirmed that Earth moves, etc., and he included a copy of Galileo's letter to Benedetto Castelli.[933] At the time, Inquisitor

[930] Like Galileo and Campanella, some other writers also linked the Sun with the *anima mundi*. For example, Robert Fludd argued that the world has a soul that emanates from the Sun, by the Trinity, which is how God becomes ubiquitous. He argued that this *anima mundi* animates and vivifies beings and he credited this belief to the Platonists, the Pythagoreans, and others, and he quoted Virgil's line "Spirit nourishes within." Roberto Fludd, *Utriusque Cosmi Maioris scilicet et Minoris Metaphysica, Physica atque Technica Historia*, Vol. 1 (Oppenhemii, 1617), pp. 51, 121-22, 146, 167; see also pp. 25, 39, 98, 107. Ten years later, the Index of Forbidden Books prohibited Fludd's *Cosmi Maioris*. Cardinal Carolus Pius and Franciscus Magdalenus Capiferreus, "Sacrae Congregationis Indicis. Decreto," 4 February 1627, reproduced in [Pope] Alexandri VII, ed., *Index Librorum Prohibitorum* (Rome: Camerae Apostolica, 1664), p. 333. In another book, Fludd argued that Jesus Christ is the "Platonic soul of the world," a soul contained in a divine spirit that emanates from the Sun and which is infused in all bodies, and vivifies them; see: Fludd, *Anatomiae Amphitheatrum Effigie Triplici* (Frankfurt, 1623), pp. 36, 254-56, 304.
[931] Galilei, "Lettera a Madama Cristina," in *Opere, Ed. Nazionale*, vol. 5, p. 345: "in certo modo anima e cuore del Mondo…" See also, Dionysus the Aeropagite, *De Divinis Nominibus* (ca. 500), in Colm Luibheid, trans., *Pseudo-Dionysus: The Complete Works* (Mahwah, New Jersey, 1987), pp. 75, 101-02. Ficino had written a *Commentary on De Divinis Nominibus*.
[932] Bruno, *Heroici Furori*, Part 2, end of the Fourth Dialogue [unnumbered page: p. 233]; Aquilecchia, ed., *Opere Italiane* 2, pp. 736-37.
[933] Galileo's letter to Castelli (21 December 1613) was the basis for his subsequent longer letter to Christina; yet the letter to Castelli did not refer to the Sun as "soul of

Sfondrato (also known as Sfondrati) was the most senior member of the Inquisition, under the Pope, and a member of the Congregation of the Index,[934] and Sfondrato had participated in Bruno's trial from 1594 until Bruno's condemnation in 1600—he was now the very Inquisitor who decided that the accusations against Galileo deserved attention. Hence in 1615 and 1616, several Inquisitors and Pope Paul V discussed the works of Copernicus and Galileo.[935] Four of them had participated in Bruno's trial—including Bellarmino and Sfondrato. The third was Inquisitor Ferdinando Taverna, who had served as Consultor in the Roman proceedings against Bruno from late 1593 to early 1595. He became Governor of Rome in 1599, and presided over Bruno's final imprisonment and brutal execution. Immediately after serving as governor of Rome, Taverna became a cardinal in 1604. The fourth authority in the Inquisition's confrontations, both with Bruno and Galileo, had an even higher rank than Bellarmino or Sfondrato: the Pope, Camillo Borghese; he participated in Bruno's trial as a Cardinal Inquisitor, from 1596 until Bruno's death in 1600. In 1605, Borghese became Pope Paul V. The Pope, Sfondrato, Bellarmino, and Taverna all knew that Bruno tied his censured belief in Earth's motion with the *heresy* that Earth is animated by a soul: the Holy Spirit.

Yet Galileo managed to dodge the Inquisition. The Inquisitors demanded that he no longer advocate the Earth's motion, and in 1616, echoing their judgment, the Index of Forbidden Books banned the "false Pythagorean doctrine" that the Earth moves. That Decree was signed by an Inquisitor from Bruno's trial: Sfondrato.[936] He knew that Bruno had defended the "Pythagorean doctrine" that the Earth is animated by a soul. And in 1616, the prefect of the Index was Bellarmino. Therefore, not only did the Decree have Bellarmino's endorsement, but remarkably, he also claimed that it had been decreed by the Pope himself: in the certificate that Bellarmino gave to Galileo in May 1616, Bellarmino noted that the

---

the world" but only as its heart: "strumento massimo della natura, quasi cuore del Mondo..." *Epistolario di Galileo Galilei*, vol. 1 (Livorno: Franc. Vigo., 1897), p. 173.

[934] In the Galileo literature, it is a common mistake to say that Sfondrato was also head of the Index.

[935] Many years later, Galileo recalled that he "discussed the matter with some cardinals who oversaw the Holy Office at the time, especially with Cardinals Bellarmino, Aracoeli, San Eusebio, Bonsi, and d'Ascoli." Galileo, First Depositon, 12 April 1633, in Finocchiaro, *Galileo Affair*, p. 256. "San Eusebio" was an honorary name for Ferdinando Taverna.

[936] Sfondrato signed the Decree as "Bishop of Albano, Cardinal of St. Cecilia."

declaration published by the Index actually had been "made by the Holy Father."[937] Hence the evidence shows that the "false Pythagorean doctrine" was denounced by the Pope, Bellarmino, and Sfondrato in 1616—three top authorities who as Inquisitors had previously rejected Giordano Bruno's false "Pythagorean doctrine" that the "Earthly orb" is animated by a spirit or soul.

I do not mean to imply that the major reason why Copernican works were censured in 1616 was because of worries about the *anima mundi*. However, the evidence does show that the censorship of Copernican works in 1616 echoed the Inquisitors' censorship of Bruno's works in 1597, which had explicitly censured and tied the belief in the Earth's motion with heresies about the *anima mundi*. Therefore, the Christian repudiation of pagan animism was one of the reasons why certain clergymen had longstanding theological concerns about "the Pythagorean doctrine." It is therefore noteworthy that thirty-three years after Bruno's death, Melchior Inchofer explained his own condemnation of Galileo by using arguments that, actually, could best be used against Bruno, since Galileo mostly had asserted no such things. Moreover, some of the Copernicans shared certain pagan interpretations of biblical scriptures, such as when Bruno and Galileo wrote about the universal spirit that "nourishes" the waters. Hence, in the midst of his diatribe against Gilbert, Inchofer briskly touched upon the phrase of pagan poetry that for decades had inspired the "New Pythagoreans." Inchofer disdained Virgil's infectious words:

> But really, the animating power of the Earth, and as the Poet [Virgil] says, *spirit nourishing within*, to ennoble, and nevertheless it is always fixed in place, clinging like an oyster or a sponge, benumbed, this implies several more things contrary to nature, more than can be easily explained. Since all of this lies open to inspection, we need not pursue it more here.[938]

---

[937] Cardinal Bellarmino's Certificate, 26 May 1616, in Finocchiaro, *Galileo Affair*, p. 153.

[938] Inchofer, *Vindiciarum*, p. 165. The cryptic allusion to an oyster or sponge seems reminiscent of an argument voiced by Campanella in *Sense of Things and Magic*. Campanella had there argued that the human soul cannot be transmitted into oysters or sponges because they are utterly different from humans. Campanella, *De Sensu Rerum et Magia* (1620), p. 168. Thus Campanella and Inchofer both critically departed from Bruno, who, in one of his early discussions of the transmigration of souls, had

In the last section of his long manuscript, Inchofer summed up "The Author's Censure against the Neo-Pythagorean Opinion." He itemised and explained seven legal reasons why he condemned the theory of the Earth's motion: because it was "offensive," "scandalous," "temerarious," "ill-sounding," "erroneous," and even worse: "consciously heretical" and "openly heretical'.

Finally, we must wonder whether Inchofer was the only person involved in officially judging Galileo's book of 1632 who was concerned with old heresies about the *anima mundi*.[939] As far as I know, the other consultants and Inquisitors left no personal documents explaining their own reasons for rejecting the Earth's motion. Still, Inchofer appended a note to his manuscript in which he seems to claim that he had consulted certain authorities who had the right to judge such matters. He wrote: "all that which we modestly insinuate without any bias, and not without consulting those who oversee such matters."[940] I don't know who Inchofer consulted; but we must note that he was an ally of Cardinal Barberini, secretary of the Inquisition, and that Inchofer was a close friend and confidant of the Master of the Sacred Palace, Father Niccolò Riccardi. Inchofer's manuscript remained unpublished, because the censors in the Society of Jesus, not the Vatican, did not approve it.

Still, in his *Tractatus Syllepticus*, Inchofer had already complained in print that the Copernicans followed Pythagoras in falsely holding that a soul

specifically said that the substance of human souls "is the same in essence specifically and generally with that of flies, marine oysters, and plants, and of whatever thing that is animated, or having soul..." Bruno boldly affirmed the equivalence of human souls with those of very different beings. The same soul of the world inhabited all living things. Bruno, *Cabala del Cavallo Pegaseo*, Second Dialogue [unnumbered pages: pp. 22-25]; and Aquilecchia, ed., *Opere Italiane* 2: *Cabala*, pp. 450-53.

[939] The other consultants were Agostino Oreggi and Zaccaria Pasqualigo. I write "consultants" and not "Consultors' because they were tasked directly by the Pope, not appointed officially by the Inquisition. For one, Pasqualigo too later noted (like Inchofer and Bellarmino) his denial of the notion that "Deum esse Animam Mundi," see Zaccaria Pasqualigo, *Sacra Specultive Doctrina de Deo coeterisque Divinitus Revelatis* (Venice: Bertanos, 1650), p. 20.

[940] "quae omnia nos modeste insinuamus sine cuiusquam praeiudicio, idque non inconsultu eorum ad quos spectat." Inchofer, *Vindiciarum*, p. 1.

moves the Earth; and that book certainly had been approved by Riccardi and the Barberinis.[941]

Summing up, I have shown that heresies about the *anima mundi* were of major importance in Bruno's trial, and were an important reason why Melchior Inchofer repudiated the Copernicans. I do not suggest that such heresies were of major importance in Galileo's condemnation of 1633, yet such heresies contributed to why, for centuries, some theologians repudiated claims that Earth is *animated*, even during Galileo's confrontations with Inquisitors in 1616 and 1633. The evidence presently reviewed suggests that historians should consider the importance of pagan notions of animism as one of the extrinsic, interpolated factors that made Copernicanism repulsive to some of its Catholic critics. If we focus on Copernicus's own work as the locus of geo-kinetic theories, it seems that animism was needlessly superimposed on it by others, such as Digges, Bruno, Gilbert, Kepler, and Lansberge. However, if we take a longer historical view, focusing instead on the Pythagoreans, the notion that the Earth was mobile preceded Copernicus's account and *included* the soulful aspect. Hence, to certain Catholic theologians Copernicus's theory of a mobile Earth was a modified, mathematical version of a Pythagorean or Platonic doctrine: that Earth was a divine being or a moving animal with a soul. Centuries later, following the popular success of Cartesian dualism and scientific materialism, recent commentators scarcely noticed that in the 1590s and 1630s the question of Earth's motion, or its self-motion, had animistic or pantheistic connotations. Thus, the theologians who originally complained about Copernicanism were not arbitrarily trying to expand their domain of authority into astronomy; instead some of them were reacting to the fact that the

---

[941] Riccardi had recommended Inchofer to the Pope to review Galileo's *Dialogue*, and Riccardi himself granted the Imprimatur to Inchofer's *Tractatus*, on behalf of the Pope's residence the Sacred Apostolic Palace, and the book was also approved by Lucas Waddingus of the Roman Curia, acting on behalf of the Pope as usual, and also by Antonio Tornielli, Vicegerent of the Vicar of Rome (the Pope), consultor of the Inquisition and Patri Magistro of the Sacred Apostolic Palace. Moreover, Inchofer's *Tractatus* was honored with the Barberinis' coat of arms in its frontispiece, and was issued by the printer who published authors sponsored by the Barberinis. It was also approved by three Jesuit censors. Melchior Inchofer, *Tractatus Syllepticus, in quo, quid de terrae, solisq. motu, vel statione, secundum S. Scripturam, & Sanctos Patres sentiendum* (Rome, 1633), pp. i-ii.

Copernican or Brunian *animists* had dared to transgress the traditional limits of astronomy to support ancient Pythagorean errors and heresies.

The present chapter is also a contribution to the neglected but necessary project of bridging the apparent gap between Bruno and Galileo. Unfortunately, most historians who write about Galileo do not discuss the various links to Bruno's works, trial, or censorship.[942] Most books about Galileo do not even mention that Bruno's statements about Earth's motion were *censured* by the Inquisition in 1597—almost two decades before some of *the same clergymen* censured similar arguments by Copernicus and Zúñiga, and silenced Galileo. Most books about Galileo do not mention that Bruno's books about the moving Earth were banned and burned long before books by Foscarini, Kepler, and Galileo were banned too. Most historians do not mention that Kepler recognized that Galileo's discoveries of 1610 seemed to confirm claims by Bruno, since Copernicus had *not* predicted mountains on the Moon, the existence of other moons and innumerably many stars, whereas Bruno had.

Since Bruno was a condemned heresiarch, Catholic writers usually were not allowed to read any of his books, and much less, write about him.[943] At the very least, it was unseemly; at worst, it was censored. Consequently, in the 1600s there is an odd silence about the prolific and notorious Bruno in the Italian literature, even in discussions that are directly relevant to his major topics of publication, such as the *anima mundi* and the existence of many worlds. For example, note that Inchofer smeared Galileo by comparing him

---

[942] Westman writes: "Most recent Galileo scholars have all but ignored Bruno," in Robert S. Westman, *The Copernican Question* (Berkeley: University of California Press, 2011), p. 367. A couple of historians who have not neglected the continuity between Bruno and Galileo are: Saverio Ricci, *La Fortuna del Pensiero di Giordano Bruno: 1600-1750* (Florence: Le Lettere, 1990), and, Laura S. Varanini, "La *Dissertatio cum Nuncio Sidereo* fra Galileo e Bruno," in *Bruniana & Campanelliana*, 9 (1), (2003), 207-15.

[943] Westman notes that Bruno's books were in a category of censorship whereby persons who printed, sold, owned, "handled in whatever manner," or discussed them could be fined, "severely punished," or tortured. Westman, *Copernican Question*, pp. 367-68. Hence, Gatti writes: "His name was studiously avoided by most throughout the seventeenth century, even where his influence, as recent studies have shown, was undoubtedly felt, at times in decisive terms." Gatti, *Essays on Giordano Bruno*, p. 194. In the archives of the Index, Leen Spruit has analyzed the "virtually complete" records of licenses granted during 1615-1640 for reading prohibited books, and he found only nine licenses granted for reading individual works by Bruno. (Interestingly, six of those nine are in the years 1633-1636.) Leen Spruit, "Roman Reading Permits for the Works of Bruno and Campanella," *Bruniana & Campanelliana*, 18 (2), (2012), 195-97.

with ancient heretics and recent *Protestants*, especially Gilbert, Kepler, and Lansberge. All of these handpicked "New-Pythagoreans" that Inchofer overtly excoriated at length were Protestant, except for Galileo. However, crafty Inchofer did not discuss the fact that certain *Catholic clergymen* too had committed similar offences and heresies like Galileo. By the time Inchofer wrote, most of these so-called New-Pythagoreans were dead — except Galileo. Doctor Gilbert had died in 1603; Kepler died in 1630; and Lansberge had died most recently, in December 1632. Thus, Inchofer portrayed Galileo as a deviant Catholic standing alone with the dead Protestant heretics. Inchofer did not discuss the Catholic New-Pythagoreans: friar Bruno the heretic, the banned-book author Father Foscarini, the censured Zúñiga, or friar Campanella the former heretic. It is impossible to imagine that Inchofer was unaware of them—he just chose not to discuss them. He quoted verbatim the Decree of 1616 against Copernicus, Zúñiga, and Foscarini, so he knew about them. Plus, Inchofer discussed Bruno's claims more than Galileo's, but without naming Bruno at all. Only tenuously or cautiously did Galileo insinuate certain questionable ideas that Bruno had boldly and repeatedly affirmed in many books.

It is noteworthy that while animism is present in the works of several Protestant Copernicans, it is missing in the printed works of these Catholics: Copernicus, Zúñiga, Foscarini, and Galileo. It leads me to wonder whether its absence was caused not merely because they did not believe in it, I don't know if they did, but perhaps because they knew that publishing some such notions was inappropriate? In this regard, Galileo's private letters to Dini and Christina seem to imply something to that effect, as Wootton has argued. It is noteworthy that by 1633 Inchofer had read and criticized Galileo's letter to Christina, the only document in which Galileo referred explicitly to the *anima mundi*.[944] During Galileo's lifetime two famous writers, originally Dominican friars, had asserted animism: Campanella and Bruno, yet both were imprisoned for years, interrogated, censured, and brutally tortured or killed. And in fact, the very same Roman Inquisitors clearly accused both of them of holding notions of the *anima mundi*, in 1594 and 1597, respectively.

---

[944] See Inchofer's report of April 1633; he mistakenly referred to Galileo's letter as being addressed to the "Archiduci Florentiae." See Inchofer, "Ragioni del Secondo Voto di Melchiorre Inchofer," in Berti, *Il processo originale di Galileo*, p. 101.

As we have seen, prominent Copernicans, including Galileo, rejected the traditional division between heavens and Earth, not merely by placing the Earth in the heavens but by positing a universal spiritual substance that "vivifies" and "nourishes" all things. In Bruno's case, this belief took a form that was particularly offensive and heretical to his Catholic Inquisitors: Bruno's modified Copernican theory reeked of old pagan heresies. The debates about the *anima mundi* reveal that at least some Catholic authorities reacted against the "Pythagorean" belief in Earth's motion because it pertained to pagan and heretical beliefs about animism, pantheism, and even polytheism. Notions that, in another time, might seem fanciful, by 1600 instead seemed disturbing in the volatile context of the Protestant Reformation. What centuries later seemed to be an essentially astronomical and physical matter, the Earth's motion, was originally deeply connected to long-lasting religious debates, not just about the literal meaning of Scriptures, but about conflicts between Christianity and heretical pagan beliefs.

Conclusion

For centuries, some Catholic theologians construed Pythagorean theories as overtly anti-Christian. Pythagoras was known for allegedly being the son of the god Apollo, allegedly the fifth incarnation of an ancient, immortal soul. Some said that this demigod had lived in Hell and remembered his sufferings there. According to Iamblichus, Pythagoras was "the most handsome and god-like of those ever recorded in history," a miracle-worker sent from Apollo's domain to enlighten humans to live properly.

Just as in Christianity the miracles of Jesus and his disciples were proof of His divinity, likewise, the pagans told stories about the miracles of Pythagoras and his disciples. Similarly to Jesus, Pythagoras predicted events, cured people, calmed storms, walked on air, instead of water; he was seen in two cities at once, and returned to life after death. Both Jesus and Pythagoras calmed bodies of water so that their disciples could cross. While the Christians broke bread, ate meat, and drank wine, some of the Pythagoreans rejected such acts as improper and impure. They said that the Earth moves because it is alive and it has a soul. Furthermore, the most famous follower of Pythagoras, Apollonius of Tyana, was reputed to perform miracles similar to those of Jesus: predicting events, healing, exorcising demons, and resurrecting the dead.

Church Fathers construed such claims as dangerous threats to people's faith in Jesus Christ. They accused Pythagoras and his disciples of faking their deaths. They denied that living men are formed from dead ones, and that souls are imprisoned in bodies. They complained that belief in transmigration had caused "profane corruptions of Christianity," adopted by magicians and fornicators.

Origen said that demons concocted lies about Pythagoras to attack people's belief in Jesus Christ. Irenaeus condemned heretics for comparing themselves to Christ and believing in lies: the transmigration of souls, the powers of numbers and monads. He said, they "were sent forth by Satan to bring dishonor upon the Church." The Christians criticized Pythagoras for using magic, for teaching that souls live in successive bodies, that the world is eternal, and that souls who philosophize travel to the stars. They denounced philosophers who claimed that many worlds exist, some with suns and moons, some inhabited.

Lactantius ridiculed claims about Pythagoras, Apollonius, and transmigration. He complained that they taught evil lies and forgeries of the miracles of Christ. Epiphanius too denounced Pythagoras for transmigration and the dissolution of bodies, contrary to the Christian promise of Resurrection, and for saying that the Sun, the Moon, stars, and planets are parts of God's body. Other theologians also criticized Pythagoras for the doctrine of transmigration, including Saint Jerome, who complained that philosophers sought knowledge from many sources, rather than having full faith in the Bible. Saint Chrysostom denounced Pythagoras and Plato as extremely evil, he denied their doctrine of transmigration as shameful and indecent. Chrysostom said that Pythagoras "practiced ten thousand kinds of sorcery," to deceive the foolish with false doctrines about the soul: "this is the snare of the Devil." Chrysostom complained that pagan philosophy was full of contradictions and was the mother of all mischief: philosophers disparaged faith because they insisted on trying to figure things out by themselves. Chrysostom praised instead the mind of Christ: "For it is not of Plato, nor of Pythagoras, but it is Christ himself, putting His own things in our mind." Hermias mocked Pythagoras for his folly about transmigration, and he denied the theory that "there are many and endless worlds." Saint Augustine criticized Pythagoras for being a necromancer who tried to divine the future by communicating with demons or the dead. Augustine repudiated Porphyry for believing in transmigration, and for being the most bitter enemy of the Christians.

Furthermore, the early Christians denounced the followers of Pythagoras. Stories said that his slave, Salmoxis, had faked his own death to later deceive men as if he had returned from death. Reportedly Empedocles was a disciple of Pythagoras who likewise taught the transmigration of souls, that he himself had lived previous lives, and that demons manage worldly matters. Arignotus the Pythagorean was supposedly an exorcist who used Egyptian spells. Apollonius was said to be a charlatan addicted to magic and the conjuration of spirits. Supposedly he was an Egyptian god; he worshipped the Sun, had lived before, and taught that the soul is attached to the bodily prison. He gained wisdom from a demon, performed false miracles, exorcisms. Following Pythagoras, Apollonius resurrected a man and a dead bride. His disciple, Alexander of Abonoteichos, was said to be a false prophet who faked miracles including the birth of a god, son of Apollo, who resurrected the dead. Alexander too taught the transmigration of souls, he pretended to embody the soul of Pythagoras, and he ordered that Christians be stoned and expelled from a temple.

Centuries later, Giordano Bruno praised Pythagoras as the first philosopher and a saintly role model. He argued that knowledge is superior to faith, and that a new science should be created on the basis of Pythagorean principles. Bruno pondered ideas that he defended as essentially philosophical, and he died for his Pythagorean convictions. Against Catholic authorities, the Copernicans dared to think that they could uphold the truths of the Bible alongside the wisdom of Pythagoras. Therefore, Kepler, Campanella, and Galileo endured various tribulations.

Aside from Cardinal Bellarmino and Melchior Inchofer, other clergymen voiced concern about the resurgence of ancient heresies. Even in Protestant countries, some clergymen agreed with some of the religious crimes listed by Catholics and the ancient Church Fathers. Decades after John Wilkins had defended the theory of many worlds in 1638, in his *Discovery of a World in the Moon*, an Anglican clergyman denounced Pythagorean heresies, namely the Reverend Father William, Lord Bishop of Coventry and Litchfield in England.

In 1699 Bishop William wrote a letter to Richard Bentley, outlining a chronology of the life of Pythagoras, along with detailed critiques against the Pythagoreans. The Bishop argued that everyone who labors to conform to God also avoids what is known to be contrary to God, and that "If we judge this way of Pythagoras, according to the Accounts they give of him, we can reason to believe, that (as the Apostle tells us of them whom the Heathens worshipped), his Gods were no better than Devils."[945]

---

[945] Father William, "A Chronological Account of the Life of Pythagoras, and of other famous Men, his Contemporaries: With an Epistle to the Rev. Dr. Bentley, about Porphyry's and Jamblichus's Lives of Pythagoras" (30 March 1699), in John Somers, ed., *A Collection of Scarce and Valuable Tracts, on the Most Interesting and Entertaining Subjects*, Vol. 3 (London: F. Cogan, 1748), 140.

The Bishop rejected such accounts as "impudent diabolical Fictions," and said that Pythagoras used "fraudulent Ways" to win admiration. He criticized especially the doctrine of the transmigration of souls, including the claim that Pythagoras spent 207 years in hell. Bishop William argued that this was not merely idle fancy, but that it plainly shows "a pernicious devilish Design" to confuse the Christian doctrine of the Resurrection of the Body. Because, if there were souls in all humans, animals, and plants, and souls reborn in them indifferently, then in the end there would be more bodies to resurrect, than souls to animate them: "What would the Devil not give to have these Things believed by all Mankind?"[946]

Bishop William denounced Porphyry and Iamblichus as "wicked philosophers," who hated Christianity. Rejecting their accounts as lies, he even decried the music of the spheres as "a lie framed by false imagination." He cited critiques by Chrysostom, Julian the Apostate, and Cyril of Alexandria. The Bishop explained that Philostratus's *Life of Apollonius* and the biographies of Pythagoras by Porphyry and Iamblichus all aimed to supersede the miracles of Jesus the Savior with false feats of heathen philosophers. About Philostratus, he commented that "Among all the Writers that I know, there was scarce a greater Liar in the World."[947] He added that "nor was there a greater impostor than Apollonius," and he likewise criticized Hierocles as "perfectly blinded by Prejudice and Malice." He conjectured that Iamblichus too tried to subvert Christian religion but could not openly attack it because he lived under Christian rule. Iamblichus had noted that Pythagoras was either the son of Apollo or at least the soul of one of Apollo's companions in heaven, but Bishop William commented: "He would have said rather, one of Pluto's companion's in hell."

He summarized Iamblichus's *On the Pythagorean Life*: "In short, as well for History, as for Doctrinal Matters, from one End to the other, it hath so much of the Devil in it, that it seems to have been wholly written by his Inspiration."[948]

[946] Ibid., 142.
[947] Ibid., 153.
[948] Ibid., 157.

Index